An Introduction to

Language

THIRD EDITION

Victoria Fromkin · Robert Rodman

Victoria Fromkin
University of California, Los Angeles

Robert Rodman
North Carolina State University, Raleigh

An Introduction to Language

THIRD EDITION

Holt, Rinehart and Winston
New York   Chicago   San Francisco   Philadelphia
Montreal   Toronto   London   Sydney   Tokyo
Mexico City   Rio de Janeiro   Madrid

To Disa, Emily, and Zachary

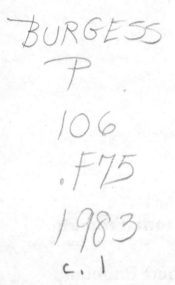

Library of Congress Cataloging in Publication Data

Fromkin, Victoria.
  An introduction to language.

  Includes bibliographies and index.
  1. Language and languages.   2. Linguistics.
I. Rodman, Robert, joint author.   II. Title.
P106.F75   1983   410   82-18719

ISBN 0-03-059779-X

CBS COLLEGE PUBLISHING
Holt, Rinehart and Winston
The Dryden Press
Saunders College Publishing

Preface

SINCE ANTIQUITY interest in linguistics—the study and science of human language—has had both practical and philosophical motivations. From a practical side, linguistics can provide a theoretical basis for a variety of practical applications. To name just a few, these applications include the treatment of language disorders such as aphasia or reading problems, the planning of "language arts" curricula in the schools, the fight against illiteracy in many nations of the world, the development of automatic, computer-generated speech production and recognition, the learning of foreign languages, and the simplification of legal language. Philosophical interests have also spurred language study, because from earliest times language has been considered a mirror of the mind.

For these reasons both the first and second editions of this text were directed toward students of many disciplines. The book is used in courses for nonlinguistics as well as linguistics students, for majors in computer science and English, in speech pathology and anthropology, in communication studies and philosophy. This third edition continues and further develops this approach. It does, however, reflect new thinking in the field as well as a reorganization of material.

We have aimed to dispel a number of myths about language and to discuss the various aspects of language from both an historical and current point of view. Part One, "The Nature of Human Language," is concerned with questions such as: What is language? What is a grammar? What is the origin of language?

What it is you know when you know English, Zulu, Twi, Cherokee, Eskimo, Spanish, Russian, and any other language is examined in Part Two, "Grammatical Aspects of Language." Chapter 2 discusses speech sounds or phonetics and includes an expanded section on machines that "talk" and "understand." Chapter 3 on phonology demonstrates how sounds form patterns. Chapter 5 shows that written forms of languge arose very late in the history of human language. Chapters 4, 6, and 7 discuss other grammatical aspects of language—how words are formed (morphology); what words, phrases, and sentences mean (semantics); and how words are put together to form sentences (syntax). These chapters have been substantially revised since the second edition. Although a formal descriptive apparatus is still included, it receives less emphasis; distinctions between phonetic and phonemic segments and phonological and morphophonemic rules are clarified; and the section on pragmatics is enlarged.

Chapters 8 and 9 of Part Three, "Social Aspects of Language," consider language in society and how languages change over time. Some of the questions raised in this section are: Why are there many languages and how are they related? How and why do languages change? Are some languages or dialects superior to others? Is there any hope for a universal language? Can languages be "obscene" or "sexist"?

Part Four, "The Biological Aspects of Language," includes Chapter 10 on child language, Chapter 11 on animal communication systems, and Chapter 12 on brain mechanisms underlying language knowledge and use. These chapters have been expanded considerably. The sign languages of the deaf, especially AMESLAN (American Sign Language), are discussed in greater detail. The newest findings on whether chimpanzees and gorillas can learn language are presented, as are the latest techniques for brain and language studies. In every chapter the universals underlying the diversity of phenomena observed in human language are highlighted.

As in the previous editions we have been primarily concerned with basic ideas rather than a detailed exposition of the grammar of English or any other language. The text assumes no previous knowledge on the part of the reader and aims at stimulating the student to further investigate language, this incredibly complex, unique human ability. Toward this goal a short list of references is given at the end of each chapter. Also included are exercises ranging in difficulty and type to enhance the student's interest in and comprehension of the textual material.

We have had enormous help from friends, colleagues, students, teaching assistants, instructors who assigned the text to their classes, and reviewers. We wish to convey our profound gratitude to all of the individuals who provided feedback, criticisms, corrections, and suggestions. We continue to be especially grateful to the thousands of students who have listened to our lectures, questioned our concepts, completed our assignments, and in these and other ways helped us to rewrite this book.

V.F.
R.R.

Contents

PART ONE

The Nature of Human Language

Just as birds have wings, man has language. The wings give the bird its peculiar aptitude for aerial locomotion. Language enables man's intelligence and passions to acquire their peculiar characters of intellect and sentiment.
G. H. Lewes, *The Study of Psychology*

Chapter 1

What Is Language?

*When we study human language, we are approaching what
some might call the "human essence," the distinctive qualities of
mind that are, so far as we know, unique to man.*

Noam Chomsky, *Language and Mind*

B.C.   **Johnny Hart**

By permission of Johnny Hart and Field Enterprises, Inc.

Whatever else people may do when they come together—whether they play, fight, make love, or make automobiles—they
talk. We live in a world of words. We talk to our friends, our associates, our
wives and husbands, our lovers, our teachers, our parents and in-laws. We
talk to busdrivers and total strangers. We talk face to face and over the telephone. And everyone responds with more talk. Television and radio further
swell this torrent of words. As a result, hardly a moment of our waking lives
is free from words, and even in our dreams we talk and are talked to. We
also talk when there is no one to answer. Some of us talk aloud in our sleep.
We talk to our pets and sometimes to ourselves. And we are the only animals
that do this—that talk.

The possession of language, more than any other attribute, distinguishes
humans from other animals. To understand our humanity one must understand the language that makes us human. According to the philosophy expressed in the myths and religions of many peoples, it is language that is the
source of human life and power. To some people of Africa, a newborn child
is a *kuntu,* a "thing," not yet a *muntu,* a "person." Only by the act of learning language does the child become a human being.[1] Thus according to this
tradition, we all become "human" because we all know at least one language. But what does it mean to "know" a language?

---

[1] Diabate, Massa-Makan. "Oral Tradition and Mali Literature," in *The Republic of Mali*
(Mali Information Center).

Linguistic Knowledge

When you know a language, you can speak and be understood by others who know that language. This means you have the capacity to produce sounds that signify certain meanings and to understand or interpret the sounds produced by others. We are referring here to normal-hearing individuals. Deaf persons produce and understand sign languages just as hearing persons produce and understand spoken languages.

Everyone knows a language. Why write an entire book on what appears to be so simple a phenomenon? After all, five-year-old children are almost as proficient at speaking and understanding as are their parents. Yet the ability to carry out the simplest conversation requires profound knowledge that speakers are unaware of. This is as true of speakers of Japanese as of English speakers, of Eskimos as of Navajos. The fact that we may know something unconsciously is not unique to language. A speaker of English can produce a sentence with two relative clauses like

My goddaughter who lives in Sweden is named Disa, which was the name of a Viking queen.

without knowing what a relative clause is. This is parallel to knowing how to walk without understanding or being able to explain the neurophysiological control mechanisms that permit one to do so.

What, then, do you know if you know English or Quechua or French or Mohawk or Arabic?

Probably without being aware of it, you know the sounds that are part of your language as well as those that are not. This knowledge is often revealed by the way speakers of one language pronounce words from another language. If you speak only English, for example, you may (and usually do) substitute an English sound for a non-English sound when pronouncing "foreign" words. How many of you pronounce the name *Bach* with a final *k* sound? This is not the German pronunciation. The sound represented by the letters *ch* in German is not an English sound. If you pronounce it as the Germans do, you are using a sound outside of the English sound system. Have you noticed that French people speaking English often pronounce words like *this* and *that* as if they were spelled *zis* and *zat?* This is because the English sound represented by the initial letters *th* is not part of the French sound system, and the French mispronunciation reveals the speakers' unconscious knowledge of this fact.

Knowledge of the sound patterns of a language also includes knowing which sounds may start a word, end a word, and follow each other. The name of a former president of Ghana was *Nkrumah*. Ghanaians pronounce this name with an initial sound identical to the sound ending the English word *sing* (for most Americans). But most speakers of English would mispronounce it (by Ghanaian standards) by inserting a short vowel before or after the *n* sound. Similarly, *Ngaio Marsh*, the Australian mystery story writer's first name, is usually mispronounced in this way. There is a good reason for these "errors." No word in English begins with the *ng* sound. Children who learn English discover this fact about our language, just as Ghanaian and Australian aboriginal children learn that words in their language may begin with the *ng* sound.

Knowing the sounds and sound patterns in one's language constitutes only one part of our linguistic knowledge. A most important part of knowing a language is knowing that certain sounds or sound sequences signify or represent different concepts or "meanings." That is, if you know English, you know that *boy* means something different from *toy* or *girl* or *pterodactyl*. Knowing a language is therefore knowing the system that relates sounds and meanings. If you don't know a language, the sounds spoken to you will be pretty much incomprehensible. This is because the relationship between speech sounds and the meanings they represent is, for the most part, an **arbitrary** one. You have to learn (when you are acquiring the language) that the sounds represented by the letters *house* (in the written form of the language)

signify the concept ⌂ ; if you know French, this same "meaning" is

represented by *maison;* if you know Twi, it is represented by *ɔdaŋ*; if you know Russian, by *dom;* if you know Spanish, by *casa.*

Similarly, the concept ✍ is represented by *hand* in English, *main* in French, *nsa* in Twi, and *ruka* in Russian.

The following are words with definite meanings in some different languages. How many of them can you understand?

a. kyinii	d. asubuhi	g. wartawan
b. doakam	e. toowq	h. inaminatu
c. odun	f. bolna	i. yawwa

If you don't know the languages from which these words are taken, you undoubtedly don't know that they mean the following:

a. a large parasol (in a Ghanaian language, Twi)
b. living creature (in an American Indian language, Papago)
c. wood (in Turkish)
d. morning (in Swahili)
e. is seeing (in a California Indian language, Luiseño)
f. to speak (in a Pakistani language, Urdu); ache (in Russian)
g. reporter (in Indonesian)
h. teacher (in a Venezuelan Indian language, Warao)
i. right on! (in a Nigerian language, Hausa)

These different words show that the sounds of words are only given meaning by the language in which they occur. The idea that something is called **X** because it looks like X or called **Y** because it sounds like Y was satirized by Mark Twain in his book *Eve's Diary:*

The minute I set eyes on an animal I know what it is. I don't have to reflect a moment; the right name comes out instantly. . . . I seem to know just by the shape of the creature and the way it acts what animal it is. When the dodo came along he [Adam] thought it was a wildcat. . . . But I saved him. . . . I just spoke up in a quite natural way . . . and said "Well, I do declare if there isn't the dodo!"

No matter what one's opinion of Eve's wisdom as compared to Adam's, it is clear that neither the shape nor other physical attributes determine the sounds or names of most creatures or objects in any language, as is so clearly shown by the Herman cartoon. A pterodactyl *could* have been called Ron.

HERMAN   **Jim Unger**

This arbitrary relationship between the form (sounds) and meaning of a word in spoken language is also true of the sign languages used by the deaf. This is easy to prove. If you watch a sign interpreter on television with the audio turned off, it is highly doubtful that you will understand the message being conveyed (unless of course you know American Sign Language— ASL—or Signed English). A nonhearing user of Chinese Sign Language would also find it difficult to understand a user of ASL. Many signs, of course, may originate as visual imitations of their referents; they may be **mimetic** (similar to miming) or **iconic** (with a nonarbitrary relationship between form and meaning) to begin with. But signs change historically as do words, and the iconicity is lost. These signs become conventional; in the same sense that knowing the sounds of words does not reveal their meaning, so knowing the shape or movement of the hands does not reveal the meaning of the gestures in sign languages.

Thus, the **conventional** and **arbitrary** nature of form–meaning relationships in languages—spoken and sign—is universal.

There is, however, some "sound symbolism" in language. That is, there are words whose pronunciation suggests the meaning. A small group of words in the vocabulary of most languages is "onomatopoeic"—the sounds of the words "imitate" the sounds of "nature." Even here, the sounds differ from one language to another, reflecting the particular sound system of the language. In English we say *cockadoodledoo* and in Russian they say *kukuriku* to represent the rooster's crow.

One also finds particular sound sequences that seem to relate to a particular concept. In English many of the words beginning with *gl* have to do with sight, such as *glare, glint, gleam, glitter, glossy, glaze, glance, glimmer, glimpse,* and *glisten.* Many rhyming word pairs begin with *h*: *hoity-toity, harum-scarum, hotsy-totsy, higgledy-piggledy.* But these are a very small part of any language, and *gl* may have nothing to do with "sight" words in another language.

When you know English you know these *gl* words, the onomatopoeic words, and all the words in the basic vocabulary of the language. You know their sounds and you know their meanings. It's extremely unlikely, of course, that there are any speakers of English who know the 450,000 words listed in *Webster's Third New International Dictionary.* But even if they did, and that was all they knew, they would not know English. Imagine trying to learn a foreign language by buying a dictionary and memorizing words. No matter how many words you learned, you would not be able to form the simplest phrases or sentences in the language or understand what was said by a native speaker. No one speaks in isolated words. (Of course you could search in your traveler's dictionary for individual words to find out how to say something like "car—gas—where?" After many tries, a native might understand this question and then point in the direction of a gas station. If she answered you in a sentence, however, it is highly probable that you would be unable to understand her or even look up what she said in your dictionary, since you would not know where one word ended and another began.)

Your knowledge of a language enables you to combine words to form phrases, and phrases to form sentences. Unfortunately, you can't buy a dictionary with all the sentences in any language, since no dictionary can list all the *possible* sentences. Knowing a language means being able to produce new sentences never spoken before and to understand sentences never heard before. The linguist Noam Chomsky refers to this ability as part of the "creative aspect" of language use. This doesn't mean that every speaker of a language can create great literature, but it does mean that you, and all persons who know a language, can and often do "create" new sentences every time you speak and are able to understand new sentences "created" by others. This is because language use is not limited to stimulus–response behavior. We are "free" from the constraints of either internal or external events or states. If someone steps on our toes we will "automatically" respond with a scream or gasp or grunt. These sounds are really not part of language; they are involuntary reactions to stimuli. After we automatically cry out, however, we can say "That was some clumsy act, you big oaf" or "Thank you very much for stepping on my toe because I was afraid I had elephantiasis and now that I can feel it hurt I know it isn't so," or any one of an infinite number of sentences, because the particular sentence we produce is not controlled by any stimulus.

Actually, even some involuntary cries are constrained by our own language system, and the filled pauses that are sprinkled through conversational speech—like *er* or *uh* or *you know* in English—often contain sounds found only in the language. French speakers, for example, fill their pauses with the vowel sound that starts their word for egg—*oeuf*—and doesn't occur in English words or cries or pauses.

Of course knowing a language also means knowing what sentences are appropriate in various situations; saying "Hamburger costs $2.00 a pound" after someone has just stepped on your toe during a discussion on the weather in Britain would hardly be an appropriate response, but it would be possible.

Consider, for example, the following sentence:

> Daniel Boone decided to become a pioneer because he dreamed of pigeon-toed giraffes and cross-eyed elephants dancing in pink skirts and green berets on the wind-swept plains of the Midwest.

You might not believe the sentence; you might question its logic; you might even understand it to mean different things; but you can understand the sentence, although it is very doubtful that you have heard or read it before now.

It is obvious, then, that when you know a language you can recognize and understand and produce new sentences. All of them do not have to be as "wild" as the Daniel Boone sentence. In fact if you go through this book counting the number of sentences you have ever seen or heard before, we predict the number would be very small. Next time you write an essay or an exam or a letter see how many of your sentences are new. It can't be that all possible sentences are stored in your brain and that when you speak you pull out a sentence which seems to fit the situation, or that when you hear a sentence you match it with some sentence already stored. How can one have in his or her memory a totally novel sentence never heard before?

In fact, it can be shown that simple memorization of all the possible sentences in a language is impossible *in principle*. If for every sentence in the language one can form a longer sentence, then there is no limit on the length of any sentence and therefore no limit on the number of sentences. We can illustrate this by a well-known example in English. When you know the language, you know you can say:

> This is the house.
>> *or*
>
> This is the house that Jack built.
>> *or*
>
> This is the malt that lay in the house that Jack built.
>> *or*
>
> This is the dog that chased the cat that killed the rat that ate the malt that lay in the house that Jack built.

And one needn't stop there. How long, then, is the longest sentence? One can also say:

The old man came.

or

The old, old, old, old, old man came.

How many "old's" are too many? Seven? Twenty-three?

We will not deny that the longer these sentences become, the less likely one would be to hear or to say them. A sentence with 276 occurrences of "old" would be highly unlikely in either speech or writing, even to describe Methuselah. But such a sentence is *theoretically* possible. That is, if you know English, you have the knowledge to add any number of adjectives as modifiers to a noun, as is illustrated in the Wizard of Id cartoon.

THE WIZARD OF ID   **Brant Parker and Johnny Hart**

By permission of Johnny Hart and Field Enterprises, Inc.

To memorize and store an infinite set of sentences would require an infinite storage capacity. But the brain is finite, and even if it were not we could not store totally novel sentences.

But when you learn a language you must learn something, and that something must be finite. The vocabulary is finite (however large it may be), and that can be stored. If sentences in a language were formed by putting one word after another in any order, then one's knowledge of a language could be described simply by a list of words. That this is not the case can be seen by examining the following strings of words:

(1) a. John kissed the little old lady who owned the shaggy dog.
    b. Who owned the shaggy dog John kissed the little old lady.
    c. John is difficult to love.
    d. It is difficult to love John.
    e. John is anxious to go.
    f. It is anxious to go John.
    g. John who was a student flunked his exams.
    h. Exams his flunked student a was who John.

If you were asked to put a star or asterisk before the examples that seemed "funny" or "no good" to you, which ones would you "star"?[2] Our "intuitive" knowledge about what "is" or "is not" a good sentence in English convinces us to "star" *b, f,* and *h*. Which ones did you "star"?

---

[2] It has become customary in presenting linguistic data to use the asterisk before any examples that speakers reject for one reason or another. We shall use this notation throughout the book.

Would you agree with our judgments about the following?

(2) a. What he did was climb a tree.
  b. *What he thought was want a sports car.
  c. Drink your beer and go home!
  d. *What are you drinking and go home?
  e. I expect them to arrive a week from next Thursday.
  f. *I expect a week from next Thursday to arrive them.
  g. Linus lost his security blanket.
  h. *Lost Linus security blanket his.

   If you "starred" the same ones we did, then it is clear that not all strings of words constitute sentences in a language, and our knowledge of the language determines which do and which do not. Therefore, in addition to knowing the words of the language you must know some "rules" to form the sentences and to make the judgments that you made about the examples in (1) and (2). These rules must be finite in length and finite in number so they can be stored in our finite brains. Yet they must permit us to form and understand an infinite set of new sentences as was discussed above. How this is possible will be discussed in Chapter 7.
   We can say then that a language consists of all the sounds, words, and possible sentences. And when you know a language you know the sounds, the words, and the rules for their combination.

What You Know and What You Do: Linguistic Knowledge and Performance

"What's one and one and one and one and one and one and one and one and one and one?"
"I don't know," said Alice. "I lost count."
"She can't do Addition," the Red Queen interrupted.
Lewis Carroll. *Through the Looking-Glass*

PEANUTS   **Charles Schulz**

© 1964 United Feature Syndicate, Inc.

   We have mentioned some aspects of speakers' linguistic knowledge such as the ability to form longer and longer sentences by joining sentences and phrases together or adding modifiers to a noun. We also pointed out that such sentences are theoretically possible, but hardly practical. Whether one limits the number of adjectives to three, five, or eighteen in speaking, it is impossible to limit the number one could add if desired. This demonstrates that there is a difference between having the necessary knowledge to produce sentences of a language and the way we use this knowledge in linguistic performance or behavior. It is a difference between what one *knows,* which some linguists refer to as one's linguistic **competence** or **capacity,** and how one *uses* this knowledge in actual behavior, which we can refer to as linguistic **performance.**

You, as a speaker, have the knowledge to understand or produce very long sentences (in fact, as noted above, no limit can be set on the length of a sentence in any language). But when you attempt to use that knowledge—when you perform linguistically—there are physiological and psychological reasons why you limit the number of adjectives, adverbs, clauses, and so on. You may run out of breath; your audience may leave; you may lose track of what has been said if the sentence is too long and overloads your short-term memory; and, of course, you don't live forever.

When we speak we have a certain message to put forth. At some stage in the act of producing speech we have our thoughts organized into strings of words. But errors occur. We all produce speech errors or "slips of the tongue" such as the one in the Wizard of Id cartoon.

WIZARD OF ID   **Brant Parker and Johnny Hart**

By permission of Johnny Hart and Field Enterprises, Inc.

Such errors also show the difference between our linguistic knowledge and the way we use that knowledge in performance.

In discussing what you know about your language it is important to repeat that much of your knowledge is not conscious. You learn the linguistic system—the sounds, structures, meanings, words, and rules for putting them all together—without anyone teaching them to you and without being aware that you are learning any rules at all. Just as we may be unconscious of the rules that allow us to stand or walk, to crawl on all fours if we choose, to jump or catch a baseball, or to ride a bicycle, our unconscious ability to speak and understand, and to make judgments about sentences reveals our knowledge of the rules of our language. This knowledge represents a complex cognitive system. The nature of this system is what this book is all about.

What Is Grammar?

We use the term "grammar" with a systematic ambiguity. On the one hand, the term refers to the explicit theory constructed by the linguist and proposed as a description of the speaker's competence. On the other hand, [it refers] to this competence itself.

N. Chomsky and M. Halle, *The Sound Pattern of English*

DESCRIPTIVE GRAMMAR

When you learn a language you learn the sounds used in that language, the basic units of meaning, such as words, and the rules to combine these to form new sentences. The elements and rules constitute the **grammar** of a language. The grammar, then, is what we *know;* it represents our linguistic competence. To understand the nature of language we must understand the nature of this internalized, unconscious set of rules which is part of every grammar of every language.

Every human being who speaks a language knows the grammar. When linguists wish to describe a language they attempt to describe the grammar of the language that exists in the minds of its speakers. There may of course be some differences between the knowledge that one speaker has and that of another. But there must be shared knowledge because it is this grammar that makes it possible for speakers to talk to and understand one another. To the extent that the linguist's description is a true model of the speakers' linguistic capacity, it will be a good or bad description of the grammar of the language, and of the language itself. Such a model is called **descriptive grammar.** It doesn't tell you how you *should* speak; it describes your basic linguistic knowledge; it explains how it is possible for you to speak and understand, and it explains what it is you know about the sounds, words, phrases, and sentences of your language.

We have used the word *grammar* in two ways: the first in reference to the grammar speakers have in their brains; the second as the model or description of this internalized grammar. Almost two thousand years ago the Greek grammarian Dionysius Thrax defined grammar as that which permits one to either speak a language or speak about a language. From now on we will not differentiate these two meanings, since the linguist's descriptive grammar is an attempt at a formal statement (or theory) of the speakers' grammar. That is, when we say in later chapters that there is a rule in the grammar such as: "every sentence has a noun phrase subject and a verb phrase predicate," this is posited as a rule in both the "mental" grammar and the model of it— the linguist's grammar. And when we say that a sentence is *grammatical* we mean that it is formed in keeping with the rules of both grammars; conversely, an *ungrammatical* (starred) sentence deviates in some way from these rules. If, however, we posit a rule for English which does not agree with your intuitions as a speaker, then there is something wrong with our grammar, or the grammar we are describing is in some way different from the grammar which represents your linguistic competence; that is, your language is not the one we are describing. If, however, there is a mistake, it must be in our descriptive grammar. Although the rules of your grammar may differ from the rules of someone else's grammar, there can't possibly be a mistake in your grammar. This is because according to linguists no language or variety of a language (called a dialect) is superior to any other in a *linguistic* sense. Every grammar is equally complex and logical and capable of producing an infinite set of sentences to express any thought one might wish to express. If something can be expressed in one language or one dialect, it can be expressed in any other language or dialect. You might use different means and different words, but it can be expressed. Because grammars are what determine the nature of the languages, no grammar is to be preferred except perhaps for nonlinguistic reasons.

PRESCRIPTIVE GRAMMARS

"I don't want to talk grammar. I want to talk like a lady."
G. B. Shaw, *Pygmalion*

The views that are expressed in the section above about descriptive grammars are not those of all grammarians now or in the past. From ancient times until the present there have been "purists" who have believed that language change is corruption and that there are certain correct forms which all "educated" people should use in speaking and writing. The Greek Alexandrians in the first century, the Arabic scholars at Basra in the eighth century, and numerous English grammarians of the eighteenth and nineteenth centuries held this view. They wished to *prescribe* the rules of grammar rather than described the rules. **Prescriptive grammars** were therefore written.

With the rise of capitalism and the emergence of a new middle class, there was a desire on the part of this new social group to have their children educated and to have them learn to speak the dialect of the "upper" classes. This led to the publication of many prescriptive grammars. In 1762 a very influential grammar, *A Short Introduction to English Grammar with Critical Notes*, was written by Bishop Robert Lowth. Lowth, influenced by Latin grammar and by personal preference, prescribed a number of new rules for English. Before the publication of his grammar, practically everyone— upper-, middle-, and lower-class speakers of English—said *I don't have none; You was wrong about that;* and *Mathilda is fatter than me.* Lowth, however, decided that "two negatives make a positive" and therefore one should say *I don't have any,* that even if *you* is singular it should be followed by the plural *were,* and that *I* not *me, he* not *him, they* not *them,* and so forth should follow *than* in comparative constructions. Because Lowth was very influential and because the rising new class wanted to speak "properly," many of these new "rules" were legislated into English grammar, at least for the "prestige" dialect. Note that grammars such as Lowth wrote are very different from the descriptive grammars we have been discussing. They are less interested in describing the rules people know than in telling them what rules they should know.

"Grammarians" who are worried about the decline of our language did not die off with the good Bishop. In 1908, an American grammarian, Thomas R. Lounsbury, wrote: "There seems to have been in every period in the past, as there is now, a distinct apprehension in the minds of very many worthy persons that the English tongue is always in the condition approaching collapse and that arduous efforts must be put forth persistently to save it from destruction."

Today, our bookstores are filled with books by language "purists" attempting to do just that. Edwin Newman, for example, in his books *Strictly Speaking* (subtitled *Will America Be the Death of English?*) and *A Civil Tongue,* rails against those who, for example, use the word *hopefully* to mean "I hope" as in "Hopefully, it will not rain tomorrow" instead of using it "properly" to mean "with hope." What Newman fails to recognize is that in the course of time language changes, and words change meaning, and the meaning of "hopefully" has been broadened for most English speakers to include both usages. Other "saviors" of the English language blame television, the schools, and even the National Council of Teachers of English for failing to preserve the standard language and they mount attacks against those college and university professors who suggest that Black English and other dialects are viable, living, complete languages. While not mentioned by name, the authors of this textbook would clearly be among those who would be criticized by these new prescriptivists.

There is even a literary organization dedicated to the proper use of the English language called the Unicorn Society of Lake Superior State College, which issues an annual "dishonor list" of words and phrases they do not approve of, including the word "medication," which they say "We can no longer afford. . . . It's too expensive. We've got to get back to the cheaper 'medicine.'"[3] At least these guardians of the English language have a sense of humor, but they as well as the other prescriptivist purists are bound to fail. Language is vigorous and dynamic. It changes. All languages and dia-

---

[3] L. A. *Times,* Jan. 2, 1978, Part 1. p. 21.

lects are expressive, complete, and logical and as much so as they were 200 or 2000 years ago. If sentences are muddled this is because language is a powerful tool for expressing one's thoughts and because some speakers' performance abilities may be lacking. Prescriptivists should be more concerned about the thoughts of the speakers than the language they use. "Hopefully" this book will convince you of this.

When we talk of the grammar of a language we are also differentiating the notion of grammar from **teaching grammars,** which are used to help speakers learn another language, or even a second dialect. In some countries where it is economically or socially advantageous to speak a "prestige" dialect, people who do not speak it natively may wish to learn it. Teaching grammars state explicitly the rules of the language, list the words and their pronunciations, and thus are aids in learning a new language or dialect.

In this book we shall not be primarily interested in either prescriptive or teaching grammars. We shall, however, discuss the question further in Chapter 8 when we discuss standard and nonstandard dialects.

Language Universals

In a grammar there are parts which pertain to all languages; these components form what is called the general grammar. . . . In addition to these general (universal) parts, there are those which belong only to one particular language; and these constitute the particular grammars of each language.
Du Marsais, c. 1750

The way we are using the word *grammar* differs in another way from its most common meaning. In our sense, the grammar includes everything speakers know about their language—the sound system, called **phonology,** the system of meanings, called **semantics,** the rules of word formation, called **morphology,** and the rules of sentence formation, called **syntax.** It also of course includes the vocabulary of words—the **dictionary** or **lexicon.** Many people think of the grammar of a language as referring solely to the syntactic rules. This latter sense is what students usually mean when they talk about their class in "English grammar."

Our aim is more in keeping with that stated in 1784 by the grammarian John Fell in "Essay Towards an English Grammar": "It is certainly the business of a grammarian to find out, and not to make, the laws of a language." This is just what the linguist attempts to do—to find out the laws of a language, and the laws that pertain to *all* languages. Those laws that pertain to all human languages, representing the universal properties of language, constitute what may be called a **universal grammar.**

Throughout the ages, philosophers and linguists have been divided on the question of whether there are universal properties that hold for all human languages and are unique to them. Most modern linguists are on the side of the "universalists," since common, universal properties are found in the grammars of all languages. Such properties may be said to constitute a "universal" grammar of human language.

About 1630, the German philosopher Alsted first used the term *general grammar* as distinct from *special grammar.* He believed that the function of a *general grammar* was to reveal those features "which relate to the method

and etiology of grammatical concepts. They are common to all languages."
Pointing out that "general grammar is the pattern 'norma' of every particular
grammar whatsoever," he implored "eminent linguists to employ their insight in this matter."[4]

Three and a half centuries before Alsted, the scholar Robert Kilwardby
held that linguists should be concerned with discovering the nature of language in general. So concerned was Kilwardby with universal grammar that
he excluded considerations of the characteristics of particular languages,
which he believed to be as "irrelevant to a science of grammar as the material of the measuring rod or the physical characteristics of objects were to
geometry."[5] In a sense, Kilwardby was too much of a universalist, for the
particular properties of individual languages are relevant to the discovery of
language universals, and are, in addition, of interest for their own sake.

The emphasis these scholars placed on the universal properties of language may lead someone attempting to study Latin, Greek, French, or Swahili as a second language to assert, in frustration, that those ancient scholars
were so hidden in their ivory towers that they confused reality with idle
speculation. Yet the more we investigate this question the longer the list of
"universals" grows. The following list is far from complete but it gives us an
idea of some universal facts about human language. Some are facts about
language in general, and others refer to specific characteristics and properties of the languages of the world.

1. Wherever humans exist, language exists.
2. There are no "primitive" languages—all language are equally complex and equally capable of expressing any idea in the universe. The
   vocabulary of any language can be expanded to include new words for
   new concepts.
3. All languages change through time.
4. The relationships between the sounds and meanings of spoken languages and between gestures (signs) and meanings of sign languages
   are for the most part arbitrary.
5. All human languages utilize a finite set of discrete sounds (or gestures)
   that are combined to form meaningful elements or words, which themselves form an infinite set of possible sentences.
6. All grammars contain rules for the formation of words and sentences
   of a similar kind.
7. Every spoken language includes discrete sound segments, like p, n,
   or a, which can all be defined by a finite set of sound properties or
   features. Every spoken language has a class of vowels and a class of
   consonants.[6]
8. Similar grammatical categories (for example, noun, verb) are found in
   all languages.
9. There are semantic universals, such as "male" or "female," "animate" or "human," found in every language in the world.
10. Every language has a way of referring to past time, the ability to ne-
    gate, the ability to form questions, issue commands, and so on.

[4] V. Salmon, review of *Cartesian Linguistics* by N. Chomsky, *Journal of Linguistics*
(1969) 5: 165–187.
[5] V. Salmon, op. cit.
[6] Sign languages of the deaf do not, of course, use sounds. They are discussed in a later
section.

11. Speakers of all languages are capable of producing and comprehending an infinite set of sentences. Syntactic universals reveal that every language has a way of forming sentences similar to the following:

> Linguistics is an interesting subject.
> I know that linguistics is an interesting subject.
> You know that I know that linguistics is an interesting subject.
> Guinevere knows that you know that I know that linguistics is an interesting subject.
> Is it a fact that Guinevere knows that you know that I know that linguistics is an interesting subject?

12. Any normal child, born anywhere in the world, of any racial, geographical, social, or economic heritage, is capable of learning any language to which he or she is exposed. The differences we find among languages cannot be due to biological reasons.

It seems that Alsted and Du Marsais (and we could add many other "universalists" from all ages) were not spinning idle thoughts. We all speak "human language."

In the Beginning: Language Origin

God created the world by a Word, instantaneously, without toil and pains.
The Talmud

Nothing, no doubt, would be more interesting than to know from historical documents the exact process by which the first man began to lisp his first words, and thus to be rid for ever of all the theories on the origin of speech.
M. Müller, 1871

The universality of language as a unique characteristic of the human animal also led to the question of how language originated. All religions and mythologies contain stories of language origin. Philosophers through the ages have argued the question. Scholarly works have been written on the subject. Prizes have been awarded for the "best answer" to this eternally perplexing problem. Theories of divine origin, evolutionary development, and language as a human invention have all been suggested.

Such widespread speculation is not surprising. Man's[7] curiosity about himself led to his curiosity about language. Many of the early theories on the origin of language resulted from man's interest in his own origins and his own nature. Because man and language are so closely related, it was believed that if one knew how, when, and where language arose, perhaps one would know how, when, and where man arose.

---

[7] In English and in many (most?) other languages, the masculine forms of nouns and pronouns are used as the general, or generic, term. We would have liked to avoid this but found ourselves constrained by common usage. Had we said "Woman's curiosity about herself led to her curiosity about language," this would have been interpreted as referring only to women. Using the word "man" in this sentence, and other sentences throughout the book, we are sure that the interpretation will be "man and woman." Wherever "man" or "mankind" or a similar generic term is used, the reader is asked to consider these general terms embracing the whole of humanity, unless of course the meaning can specifically be related to the male members of the species.

The difficulties inherent in answering these questions about language are immense. Anthropologists think that man has existed for at least one million years, and perhaps for as long as five or six million years. But the earliest deciphered written records are barely six thousand years old, dating from the writings of the Sumerians of 4000 B.C. These records appear so late in the history of the development of language that they provide no clue at all to the origin of language.

One might conclude that the quest for this knowledge is doomed to failure. The only hard evidence we have about ancient languages is written, but speech precedes writing historically by an enormous period of time, and even today there are thousands of speech communities speaking perfectly "up-to-date" languages that lack writing systems. The language or languages used by our earliest ancestors are irretrievably lost.

For these reasons, scholars in the latter part of the nineteenth century, who were only interested in "hard science," ridiculed, ignored, and even banned discussions of language origin. In 1886, the Linguistic Society of Paris passed a resolution "outlawing" any papers concerned with this subject.[8]

This ban was reconfirmed in 1911 and was further supported by the president of the Philological Society of London, Alexander Ellis, who concluded in his address to the Society that:

> . . . We shall do more by tracing the historical growth of one single work-a-day tongue, than by filling wastepaper baskets with reams of paper covered with speculations on the origin of all tongues.

That such resolutions did not put an end to the interest is clear from the fact that just a few years ago the linguist John P. Hughes felt compelled to write:

> . . . a word or two should be said in any serious linguistic work to counter the arrant nonsense on this subject which is still circulated in Sunday supplement science features. According to this pseudo-evolutionary foolishness, based on nothing but rampant imagination, language originated among our caveman ancestors when someone tried to tell the hitherto speechless tribe about the wolf he had killed, and was forced to give an imitation of the wolf . . . or when he hit his thumb with the mallet while sharpening a stone spear, so that *ouch* became the word for "pain". . . and similar fairy stories.[9]

This view sharply diverges from that put forth two hundred years earlier by Lord Monboddo, the Scottish anthropologist:

> The origin of an art so admirable and so useful as language . . . must be allowed to be a subject, not only of great curiosity, but likewise very important and interesting, if we consider, that it is necessarily connected with an inquiry into the original nature of man, and that primitive state in which he was, before language was invented. . . .[10]

---

[8] *La Société n'admet aucune communication concernant . . . l'origine du langage . . .*" ("The Society does not accept any paper concerning the origin of language . . .") La Société de Linguistique, Section 2, Statuts (1886).

[9] John P. Hughes. 1969. *The Science of Language* (Random House. New York.)

[10] James Burnett, Lord Monboddo, *Of the Origin and Progress of Language* (1774).

It is not only in Sunday supplements that one finds "pseudo-evolutionary foolishness." Some of the greatest linguists and philosophers continue to be interested in this question, and speculative theories on language origin have provided valuable insights into the nature and development of language. For these reasons, the learned scholar Otto Jespersen stated that "linguistic science cannot refrain forever from asking about the whence (and about the whither) of linguistic evolution."

In this chapter, some of the ideas about the origin of language will be examined, both because they may shed light on the nature of language and because there is continuing interest in the subject.

GOD'S GIFT TO MANKIND?

> And out of the ground the Lord God formed every beast of the field, and every fowl of the air; and brought them unto Adam to see what he would call them: and whatsoever Adam called every living creature, that was the name thereof.
> Genesis 2:19

According to Judeo-Christian beliefs, God gave Adam the power to name all things. Similar beliefs are found throughout the world. According to the Egyptians, the creator of speech was the god Thoth. According to the Babylonians, the language giver was the god Nabû. According to the Hindus, we owe our unique language ability to a female god; Brahma was the creator of the universe, but language was given to us by his wife, Sarasvati.

The belief in the divine origin of language has continued through the ages. Cotton Mather wrote his M.A. thesis at Harvard on the question, providing a detailed defense in support of this theory. Almost three hundred years later, Lester Grabbe, pointing to the existence in far-removed cultures of stories similar to the Tower of Babel, concluded:

> . . . no acceptable theory has yet been propounded which can satisfactorily answer why man even has the faculty of speech—or language—if there is no Creator. On the other hand, the Genesis account is in complete agreement with all established scientific fact.[11]

Belief in the divine origin of language is closely intertwined with the magical properties man has associated with language and the spoken word. Children in all cultures utter "magic" words like *abracadabra* to ward off evil or bring good luck. Despite the childish jingle "Sticks and stones may break my bones, but names will never hurt me," name-calling is insulting, cause for legal punishment, and feared. In some cultures, when certain words are used, one is required to counter them by "knocking on wood." Language is used to bring down the curses of the gods. Prayers are offered, and thus man converses with his gods in language. According to the Bible, only the true God would respond when called upon; the false idols did not know the "word of God." The anthropologist Bronislaw Malinowski has pointed out that in many cultures words are used to control events and become sources of power when chanted over and over: "The repetitive statement of certain words is believed to produce the reality stated."

[11] Lester Grabbe, "Origin of Languages," *The Plain Truth* (Aug.–Sept. 1970).

One finds taboo words all over the world. In western societies one is adjured not to "take the Lord's name in vain." In folk tales, forbidden names, such as *Rumpelstiltzkin,* can break spells if discovered. Personal names also carry special properties—a Jewish child is not to be named after a living person, and in some cultures it is forbidden to utter the name of someone who has died. In ancient Egypt every person was given two names, one of which was secret. If the secret name was discovered, the discoverer had power over the person. In Athens, in the fifth century B.C., a ventriloquist named Euricles pretended he had a demon in him; special powers were attributed to the ventriloquist's voice. In *The Wasps,* Aristophanes mentions the "sly prophet Euricles" who "hidden in other people's bellies produces much amusement."

The linguist David Crystal reports that someone is attempting to test the idea that the world will end when the billion names of God have been uttered by attaching a prayer wheel to an electronic speech synthesizer.[12]

The belief in the divine origin of language and its magical properties is also manifested by the fact that in many religions only special languages may be used in prayers and rituals. The Hindu priests of the fifth century B.C. believed that the original pronunciations of Vedic Sanskrit had to be used. This led to important linguistic study, since their language had already changed greatly since the hymns of the Vedas had been written. Until recently, only Latin could be used in the Catholic Mass. Among Moslems, the Koran was not to be translated and could be read only in Arabic; and Hebrew continues to be the one language used in the prayers of orthodox Jews throughout the world.

These myths and customs and superstitions do not tell us very much about language. They do tell us about the importance of language to men and the miraculous properties they attach to it. In addition, discussions of the divine origin of language, although not likely to settle the question to the satisfaction of anyone seeking "scientific proof," may provide insights into the nature of human language.

In 1756, a Prussian statistician-clergyman, Johann Peter Suessmilch, delivered a paper before the Prussian Academy in which he reasoned that man could not have invented language without thought, and that thought depends on the prior existence of language. The only escape from the paradox is to presume that God must have given language to man. Suessmilch, unlike other philosophers such as Rousseau (whose ideas will be discussed below), did not view primitive languages as "less developed" or "imperfect." He suggested just the opposite—that all languages are "perfect" and thus the reflection of God's perfection. He cites examples from the European languages, from Semitic languages, and from languages of "primitive" people to prove the perfection of all human language. To oppose the idea that there are primitive languages, he noted that the great and abstract ideas of Christianity can be discussed even by the "wretched Greenlanders."

Suessmilch made other sophisticated observations. He pointed out that any child is able to learn perfectly the language of the Hottentots although adults cannot, revealing his awareness of the difference between acquisition of first and second languages. This observation anticipated the current "critical age hypothesis," which states that beyond a certain age a human being

---

[12] David Crystal, *Linguistics* (Penguin, Middlesex, England. 1971).

is incapable of acquiring a first language. He also pointed out, as did many philosophers of antiquity, that all languages have grammars which are highly regular, for otherwise children would be unable to learn them.

The arguments presented by Suessmilch were based on observations concerning the "universality" of linguistic properties, the relation between psychological and linguistic constraints, and the interdependence of reason and language. He presented powerful arguments, but ones that had less to do with language origin than with language itself.

At the present time there is no way to "prove" or "disprove" the divine-origin theory, just as one cannot argue scientifically for or against the existence of God.

THE FIRST LANGUAGE

> *Imagine the Lord talking French! Aside from a few odd words in Hebrew, I took it completely for granted that God had never spoken anything but the most dignified English.*
> Clarence Day, *Life with Father*

Among the proponents of the divine-origin theory a great interest arose in the language used by God, Adam, and Eve. Men have not always been pessimistic about discovering an answer to this question. For millennia, "scientific" experiments have reportedly been devised to verify particular theories of language origin. In the fifth century B.C. the Greek historian Herodotus reported that the Egyptian Pharaoh Psammetichus (664–610 B.C.) sought to determine the most primitive "natural" language by experimental methods. The monarch was said to have placed two infants in an isolated mountain hut, to be cared for by a servant who was cautioned not to utter a single word in their presence on pain of death. The Pharaoh believed that without any linguistic input the children would develop their own language and would thus reveal the original tongue of man. Patiently the Egyptian waited for the children to become old enough to talk. According to the story, the first word uttered was *bekos*. Scholars were consulted, and it was discovered that *bekos* was the word for "bread" in Phrygian, the language spoken in the province of Phrygia (the northwest corner of modern Turkey). This ancient language, which has long since died out, was thought, on the basis of this "experiment," to be the original language.

Whether James IV of Scotland (1473–1513) had read the works of Herodotus is not known. According to reports he attempted a replication of Psammetichus's experiment, but his attempt yielded different results. The Scottish children matured and "spak very guid Ebrew," providing "scientific evidence" that Hebrew was the language used in the Garden of Eden.

Two hundred years before James's "experiment," the Holy Roman Emperor Frederick II of Hohenstaufen was said to have carried out a similar test, but without any results; the children died before they uttered a single word.

The legend of Psammetichus shows that the Pharaoh was willing to accept "evidence" even if it was contrary to national interests. A German scholar, J. G. Becanus (1518–1572), demonstrated real chauvinistic zeal. He argued that German must have been the primeval language, since the language given by God must have been a perfect language, and since, according to him, German was the most superior language in the world, it had to be the language used by God and by Adam. Becanus carried his arguments further: German persisted as the perfect language because the early Cimbrians (who were Germans) did not contribute to the building of the Tower of Babel. Later, according to this theory, God caused the Old Testament to be translated from German into Hebrew.

Other proposals were put forth. In 1830 the lexicographer Noah Webster asserted that the "proto-language" must have been Chaldee (Aramaic), the language spoken in Jerusalem during the time of Jesus. In 1887, Joseph Elkins maintained in *The Evolution of the Chinese Language* that "there is no other language which can be more reasonably assumed to be the speech first used in the world's gray morning than can Chinese. . . . Hence, Chinese is regarded . . . as the . . . primeval language."

The belief that all languages originated from a single source is found in Genesis: ". . . the whole earth was of one language, and of one speech." The Tower of Babel story attempts to account for the diversity of languages. In this, and in similar accounts, the "confusion" of languages *preceded* the dispersement of peoples. (According to some Biblical scholars, *Babel* derives from the Hebrew *bilbel*, meaning "confusion"; others say it derives from the name Babylon.) Genesis continues: "Therefore is the name of it called Babel; because the Lord did there confound the language of all the earth: and from thence did the Lord scatter them abroad upon the face of all the earth."

A legend of the Toltecs, given by the native Mexican historian Ixtlilxochitl, also explains the diversity of languages by a similar account: ". . . after men had multiplied, their languages were confused, and not being able to understand each other, they went to different parts of the earth."

A study of the history of languages does indeed show that many languages develop from a single one, as will be discussed in later chapters. But in these attested cases the "confusion" comes *after* the separation of peoples. Any view that maintains a single origin of language must provide some explanation for the number of language *families* that exist. The Bible explains this as an act of God, Who at Babel created from one language many, all of which would eventually become individual multilanguage families. The monogenetic theory of languages—the single-origin theory—is related to a belief in the monogenetic origin of man. Many scientists today believe, instead, that man arose in many different places on earth. If this is the case, there were many proto-languages, from which the modern language families developed.

It is clear that we are no further along today in discovering the original language (or languages) than was Psammetichus when he attempted to use "experimental methods" to answer this question. Any such experiment is bound to fail. For obvious reasons, linguists would not attempt to duplicate such tests—while we may applaud the Pharaoh's motivation we must condemn his lack of humanity. But the misfortunes of life can be as cruel as a Pharaoh. There have been a number of cases of children reared in environments of extreme social isolation. Such reported cases go back at least to the eighteenth century. In 1758, Carl Linnaeus first included *Homo ferus* (wild or feral man) as a subdivision of *Homo sapiens*. According to Linnaeus, a defining characteristic of *Homo ferus* was his lack of speech or observable language of any kind. All the cases in the literature support his view.

The most dramatic cases of children raised in isolation are those described as "wild" or "feral" children, who have reportedly been reared with wild animals or have lived alone in the wilderness. In 1920 two feral children, Amala and Kamala, were found in India, supposedly having been reared with wolves. The most celebrated case, documented in François Truffaut's film *The Wild Child,* is that of Victor, "the wild boy of Aveyron," who was found in 1798. It was ascertained that he had been left in the woods when a very young child and had somehow survived. He was in his early teens when he was discovered. In addition, there are cases of children whose isolation resulted from deliberate efforts to keep them from normal social intercourse. As recently as 1970 a child, called Genie in the scientific reports, was discovered who had been confined to a small room under conditions of physical restraint, and who had received only minimal human contact from the age of eighteen months until almost fourteen years. None of these children, regardless of the cause of isolation, was able to speak or knew any language at the time of reintroduction to society. Genie, however, did begin to acquire language afterwards.

It appears from these case histories that the human ability to acquire language requires adequate linguistic stimulation. A child totally devoid of human company will not learn language, not even Phrygian, or "very guid Ebrew."

HUMAN INVENTION OR THE CRIES OF NATURE?

> *Language was born in the courting days of mankind; the first utterances of speech I fancy to myself like something between the nightly love lyrics of puss upon the tiles and the melodious love songs of the nightingale.*
> Otto Jespersen, *Language, Its Nature, Development and Origin*

The Greeks speculated about everything in the universe. It is therefore not surprising that the earliest surviving linguistic treatise which deals with the origin and nature of language should be Plato's *Cratylus* dialogue. A commonly held view among the classical Greeks was that at some ancient time there was a "legislator" who gave the correct, natural name to everything. Plato, in this dialogue, has Socrates express this idea:

. . . not every man is able to give a name, but only a maker of names; and this is the legislator, who of all skilled artisans in the world is the rarest . . . only he who looks to the name which each thing by nature has, and is, will be able to express the ideal forms of things in letters [sounds] and syllables.

It was not one of their many gods who named all things, but this wise "legislator." The question of language origin was closely tied to the debate among the Greeks as to whether there is a truth or correctness in "names" regardless of the language, as opposed to the view that words or names for things result merely from an agreement—a convention—between speakers. This debate between the **naturalists** and the **conventionalists** was one of the first major linguistic arguments. In the *Cratylus* dialogue, Socrates analyzes and develops etymologies for the names of Homeric heroes, the Greek gods, mythological figures, the stars, the elements, and even abstract qualities— the proper and common nouns of language. In his attempt to justify the "trueness" or "naturalness" of these names, it is clear that he, at least in part, recognizes the humor in such an approach, for he says that "the heads of the givers of names were going round and round and therefore they imagined the world was going round and round."

In fact, it is clear from a reading of this delightful dialogue that Plato recognized the "arbitrariness" of certain words, and believed that both natural and conventional elements exist in language.

The naturalists argued that there is a natural connection between the forms of language and the essence of things. They pointed to onomatopoeic words—words whose sounds are imitative of the meaning represented—and suggested that these form the basis of language, or at least the core of the basic vocabulary.

The idea that the earliest form of language was imitative, or "echoic," was reiterated by many scholars up to recent times. According to this view, a dog, which emits a noise that (supposedly) sounds like "bow-wow," would be designated by the word *bow-wow*. To refute this position one need merely point to the small number of such words in any language and, in addition, to the fact that words alone do not constitute language.

A parallel view states that language at first consisted of emotional ejaculations of pain, fear, surprise, pleasure, anger, and so on. This theory—that the earliest manifestations of language were "cries of nature" that man shared with animals—was the view proposed by Jean Jacques Rousseau in the middle of the eighteenth century. Rousseau, a founder of the Romantic movement, became concerned with the nature and origin of language while seeking to understand the nature of the "noble savage." Two of his treatises deal with the origin of language.[13] According to him, both emotive cries and gestures were used by man, but gestures proved to be too inefficient for communicating, and so man invented language. It was out of the natural cries that man "constructed" words.

Rousseau's position was essentially that of the **empiricists,** who held that all knowledge results from the perception of observable data. Thus, the first words were names of individual things and the first sentences were one-word sentences. General and abstract names were invented only later, as were the "different parts of speech," and more complex sentences. Rousseau expressed this in the following way: The more limited the knowledge, the more extensive the dictionary. . . . General ideas can come into the mind only with the aid of words, and the understanding grasps them only through propositions.[14]

It is difficult to understand his reasoning. How was man able to acquire the ability for abstract thought through his use of concrete words if he was not, from the very beginning, equipped with special mental abilities? But, according to Rousseau, it is not man's ability to reason that distinguished him from animals (the view held by the earlier French philosopher Descartes); rather, it is his "will to be free." According to Rousseau, it is this freedom that led to the invention of languages. He did not explain how this freedom permitted speakers to associate certain sounds with certain meanings and to construct a complex system of rules that permitted them to con-

[13] Jean Jacques Rousseau, "Discourse on the Origin and Foundations of Inequality Among Men" (1755) and "Essay on the Origin of Languages" (published posthumously, 1822).

[14] Rousseau, "Essay on the Origin of Languages," in P. H. Salus, ed. 1969. *On Language: Plato to Von Humboldt* (Holt, Rinehart and Winston. New York.)

struct new sentences. Rousseau based some of his ideas on the assumption that the first languages used by humans were crude and primitive languages "approximately like those which the various savage nations still have today." It is interesting that this man, who spent his life fighting inequality, should espouse such a position. Just one year after Rousseau's treatise, Suessmilch, arguing against Rousseau and in favor of the divine-origin theory, maintained the equality and perfection of all languages.

Almost two hundred years after Rousseau suggested that both the "cries of nature" and gestures formed the basis for language development, Sir Richard Paget argued for an "oral gesture theory":

> Human speech arose out of a generalized unconscious pantomimic gesture language—made by the limbs and features as a whole (including the tongue and lips) —which became specialized in gestures of the organs of articulation, owing to the human hands (and eyes) becoming continuously occupied with the use of tools. The gestures of the organs of articulation were recognized by the hearer because the hearer unconsciously reproduced in his mind the actual gesture which had produced this sound.[15]

It is difficult to know exactly how the tongue and lips and other vocal organs were used as "pantomimic gestures." But it is of interest that there are a number of scholars today who accept a "motor theory of speech perception," which is a sophisticated version of Paget's last statement.

The view that human language developed out of an earlier gestural communication system is found in the publications of Gordon Hewes.[16] He does not claim, however, that this was the only system utilized, but points to the cases where gestures are used where speech cannot be used (as for the deaf) or where speech is not feasible (under noisy conditions or where unknown languages are being spoken).

Another hypothesis concerning the development of human language suggests that language arose out of the rhythmical grunts of men working together. The Soviet aphasiologist A. R. Luria accepted this view in 1970:

> There is every reason to believe that speech originated in productive activity and arose first in the form of abbreviated motions which represented certain work activities and pointing gestures by which men communicated with one another. . . . Only considerably later, as shown by speech paleontology, did verbal speech develop. Only in the course of a very long historical period was the disassociation of sound and gesture accomplished.[17]

One of the more charming views on language origin was suggested by Otto Jespersen. He proposed a theory stating that language derived from song as an expressive rather than a communicative need, with love being the greatest stimulus for language development.

Just as with the theories of divine origin of language, many of these proposals in support of the idea that man invented language, or that it arose in the course of man's development—whether out of the cries of nature, the vocal mimicry of gestures, the songs of love, or the grunts of labor—are inconclusive. The debate is unsettled and it continues.

---

[15] Richard Paget. 1930. *Human Speech* (Harcourt, Brace. New York.)

[16] Gordon Hewes, "The Current Status of the Gestural Theory of Language," *Annals N. Y. Acad. Science* 280 (1976): 482–504.

[17] A. R. Luria. 1970. *Traumatic Aphasia* (Humanities Press. New York.), p. 80.

HUMAN ORIGIN IS LANGUAGE ORIGIN

> *But language just happened. It happened because language is*
> *the most natural outcome in a world of people where babies*
> *babble, and mothers babble back—and where the baby also has*
> *the potential for metaphor.*
> Louis Carini

In 1769, thirteen years after Suessmilch's famous defense of the divine origin of language in opposition to the "invention" theory, the Prussian Academy reopened the discussion. They offered a prize for the best paper on the very same question. Johann Herder, the German philosopher and poet, won the prize with an essay that opposed both views. Herder argued against Rousseau's theory that language developed out of the "cries of nature" which man shared with animals by citing the fundamental differences between human language and the instinctive cries of animals. Herder felt that language and thought are inseparable, and that man must be born with a capacity for both. He agreed with Suessmilch that without reason, language could not have been invented by man, but he went further in stating that without reason, Adam could not have been taught language, not even by the Divine Father:

> Parents never teach their children language, without the latter at the same time inventing it themselves. The former only direct their children's attention to the difference between things, by certain verbal signs, and thus do not supply these, but by means of language only facilitate and accelerate for the children the use of reason.[18]

These very insightful remarks foreshadowed the view held by some present-day linguists that no one teaches children the rules of grammar—children discover them.

Herder's main point was that language ability is innate. One cannot talk of man existing before language. Language is part of our essential human nature and was therefore neither invented nor handed down as a gift. Herder drew on the universality, or uniformity, of all human languages as an argument to justify a monogenetic theory of origin. According to him, we have all descended from the same parents, and all languages therefore descended from one language. He put forth this theory to explain why languages, despite their diversity, have universal common properties. Even though the monogenetic theory is not widely accepted today, the universality of human language is accepted, and can be plausibly explained by Herder's argument that man, by nature, is everywhere the same. Herder accepted the Cartesian **rationalist** position that human languages and animal cries are as different from each other as human thought and animal instinct: "It is not the organization of the mouth which creates language for if a man were dumb all the days of his life, if he reflected, language must lie within his soul."[19]

Language and Evolution

Despite the earlier "bans" on speculation regarding the origin of human language, the interest in this question has been rekindled. Two scholarly societies, the American Anthropological Association and the

---

[18] J. G. Herder, "Essay on the Origin of Language," in Salus, op. cit.
[19] Herder, op. cit.

New York Academy of Sciences, held forums to review recent research on the topic (in 1974 and 1976). Research being conducted in various disciplines is providing data which were unavailable earlier and which are directly related to the development of language in the human species.

Scholars are now concerned with how the development of language is related to the evolutionary development of the human species. There are those who view language ability as a difference in degree between humans and other primates, and those who see the onset of language ability as a qualitative leap. The linguists who, in their evolutionary approach, take a "discontinuity" view believe that language is species-specific, and among these linguists there are those who further believe that the brain mechanisms which underlie this language ability are specific to language, rather than being a mere offshoot of more highly developed cognitive abilities. This latter view holds that all humans are innately or genetically equipped with a unique language learning ability or with genetically determined, specifically linguistic, neurological mechanisms. Such linguists agree with the earlier views of Herder.

In trying to understand the development of language, scholars past and present have debated the role played by the vocal tract and the ear. The linguist Philip Lieberman suggests that "nonhuman primates lack the physical apparatus that is necessary to produce the range of human speech."[20] He links the development of language with the evolutionary development of the speech production and perception apparatus. This, of course, would be accompanied by changes in the brain and the nervous system toward greater complexity. Lieberman's view implies that the languages of our human ancestors of millions of years ago may have been syntactically and phonologically simpler than any language known to us today. This still begs the question, however, because the notion "simpler" is left undefined. One suggestion is that this primeval language had a smaller phonetic inventory.

Certainly one evolutionary step must have resulted in the development of a vocal tract capable of producing the wide variety of sounds utilized by human language, as well as the mechanism for perceiving and distinguishing them. That this step is insufficient to explain the origin of language is evidenced by the existence of mynah birds and parrots, which have this ability. Their imitations, however, are merely patterned repetitions. (See Chapter 11 on animal languages.)

Human language utilizes a fairly small number of sounds, which are combined in linear sequence to form words. Each sound is reused many times, as is each word. Suessmilch pointed to this fact as evidence of the "efficiency" and "perfection" of a language. Indeed, the discreteness of these basic linguistic elements—these sounds—was noted in the earliest views of language.

Children learn very early in life that the continuous sounds of words like *bad* and *dad* can be "broken up" into discrete segments. In fact, children that know these two words may on their own produce the word *dab*, though they have never heard it before. Mynah birds can learn to produce the sounds *bad* and *dad,* but no bird could ever produce the sound *dab* without actually hearing it.

On the other hand we also know that the ability to hear speech sounds is

---

[20] Philip Lieberman, "Primate Vocalizations and Human Linguistic Ability," *J. Acoustical Soc. Am.* (1976) 44:1574–1584.

not a necessary condition for the acquisition and use of language. Humans who are born deaf learn the sign languages that are used around them, and these are as "creative" and complex as spoken languages. And deaf children acquire these languages in the same way as hearing children do—without being taught—by mere exposure.

Perhaps, then, the major evolutionary step in the development of language relates to evolutionary changes in the brain.

Although we are still far from knowing how language arose, and it is doubtful that we will ever know for certain, we have in our search for its origins made much progress in understanding the nature of human language.

SUMMARY

We are all intimately familiar with at least one language. Yet few of us ever stop to consider what we know when we know a language. There is no book that contains the English or Russian or Zulu language. One can list the words of a language in a dictionary, but not all the possible sentences, and a language consists of these sentences as well as words. Though we can't list all sentences, we can list the rules a speaker uses to produce and understand an infinite set of "possible" sentences.

These rules comprise the **syntax** of a language. You learn these rules when you learn the language and you also learn the sound system of the language (the **phonology**) and the ways in which sounds and meanings are related (the **semantics**). The sounds and meanings of words are related in an **arbitrary** fashion. That is, if you had never heard the word *syntax* you would not, by its very sounds, know what it meant. Language, then, is a system that relates sounds with meanings, and when you know a language you know this system.

This *knowledge* (your linguistic **competence**) is different from your behavior (your linguistic **performance**). Even if you woke up one morning and decided to stop talking (as the Trappist monks did after they took a "vow of silence"), you would still have knowledge of your language. This ability or competence underlies linguistic behavior. If you didn't know the language, you couldn't speak, but if you know the language, you may choose not to speak.

The **grammar** of a language represents the linguistic knowledge or capacity of its speakers. It includes the basic sounds, words, and rules for the formation, pronunciation, and interpretation of sentences. Linguistic knowledge represented in the grammar is not conscious knowledge. An explicit description of one's linguistic knowledge is called a **descriptive grammar.** Such a grammar is a model of the "mental" grammar known by every speaker of the language. It doesn't teach the rules of the language; it describes the rules that are already known.

A grammar that attempts to legislate what your grammar should be is called a **prescriptive grammar.** It prescribes; it doesn't describe, except incidentally. Teaching grammars are also written to help people learn a foreign language or a dialect of their language that differs from their own.

The more linguists investigate the thousands of languages of the world and describe the ways in which they differ from each other, the more they discover that these differences are limited. There are **universals** of language that pertain to all parts of linguistic grammars. The difference between *universal* or *general* grammar and specific or *special* grammars has been the concern of grammarians and philosophers throughout history.

Our curiosity about ourselves and our most unique possession, language, has also led to numerous theories about language origin. There is no way at present to "prove" or "disprove" these hypotheses, but they are of interest for the light they shed on the nature of human language.

The idea that language was God's gift to mankind is found in religions throughout the world. The continuing belief in the miraculous powers of language is tied to this notion. The assumption of the divine origin of language stimulated interest in discovering the first primeval language. There are legendary "experiments" in which children were isolated in the belief that their first words would reveal the original language. Children will learn the language spoken to them; if they hear no language they will speak none. Actual cases of socially isolated children show that language develops only when there is sufficient linguistic input.

Opposing theories suggest that language is a human invention. The Greeks believed that an ancient "legislator" gave the true names to all things. Others have suggested that language developed from "cries of nature," or "early gestures," or onomatopoeic words, or even from songs to express love.

There is at present a renewed interest among biologists and linguists in the question of language origin. Various evolutionary theories that are now proposed oppose both the divine-origin and the invention theory. Rather, it is suggested that in the course of evolution both the human species and language developed. Some scholars suggest that this occurred simultaneously, and that from the start the human animal was innately equipped to learn language. In fact there are those who believe that it is language which makes human nature human. Studies of the evolutionary development of the brain provide some evidence for physiological, anatomic, and "mental" preconditions for language development.

EXERCISES

1. Part of your knowledge of English includes knowing what sound sequences occur in the language. When new products are put on the market the manufacturers have to think up new names for them, and these names must conform to the allowable sound patterns. Suppose you were hired by a manufacturer of soap products and your job was to name five new products. What names might you come up with? List them.

   We are not interested in the *spelling* of the words but in how they are pronounced. Therefore, describe in any way you can how the words you list should be pronounced. Suppose, for example, you named one soap powder *Blick*. You can describe the sounds in any of the following ways:

   a. *bl* as in "blood," *i* as in "pit," *ck* as in "stick"
   b. *bli* as in "bliss," *ck* as in "tick"
   c. *b* as in "boy," *lick* as in "lick" and so on.

2. Consider the following sentences. Put a star (*) after those that do not seem to conform to the rules of *your* grammar, that are ungrammatical for you. If you can, state why you think the sentence is ungrammatical.

a. Robin forced the Sheriff go.
b. Napoleon forced Josephine to go.
c. The Devil made Faust go.
d. He passed by a large sum of money.
e. He came by a large sum of money.
f. He came a large sum of money by.
g. Did in a corner little Jack Horner sit?
h. Elizabeth is resembled by Charles.

i. Nancy is eager to please.
j. It is easy to frighten Emily.
k. It is eager to love a kitten.
l. That birds can fly amazes.
m. The fact that you are late to class is surprising.
n. Has the nurse slept the baby yet?
o. A glass tipped over which was full of water.
p. I was surprised for you to get married.
q. I wonder who and Mary went swimming.
r. Myself bit John.

3. It was pointed out in this chapter that a small set of words in languages may be onomatopoeic, that is, there may be words whose sounds "imitate" what they refer to: *ding-dong, tick-tock, bang, zing, swish, plop* are such words in English. Make up a list of ten such words. Test them on at least five friends to see if they are truly "nonarbitrary" as to sound and meaning.

4. Although sounds and meanings of most words in all languages are arbitrarily related, this is not necessarily true in all systems of communication. There are some systems in which the "signs" unambiguously reveal their "meaning."

   A. Describe (or draw) five different signs that directly show what they mean. Example: a road sign indicating an S curve.
   B. Describe any other communication system that, like language, consists of arbitrary symbols. Example: traffic signals where *red* means *stop* and *green* means *go.*

5. Consider these two statements:

   a. I learned a new word today.
   b. I learned a new sentence today.

   Do you think the two statements are equally probable, and if not, why not?

6. State some "rule of grammar" that you have been taught in school or that someone has stated to be the "correct" way to say something but that you do not generally use in speaking. For example, you may have been taught (or corrected in a composition class) that *It's me* is incorrect and that the correct form is *It's I.* Yet you always use *me* in such sentences, your friends do also, and, in fact, *It's I* sounds funny to you.

   A. How might you argue against someone who tells you you are wrong?
   B. How does this demonstrate the difference between descriptive and prescriptive grammars?

7. Which of the following do you think are *not* universals of language and why?
   a. writing systems;
   b. arbitrarily related forms and meanings;
   c. articles (words like "a" and "the");
   d. syntactic rules that determine which sentences are well formed;
   e. methods to enlarge the vocabulary;
   f. words for "sidewalk," "adultery," "desert," "mountain";
   g. words for kinship terms that refer to parents, siblings, in-laws, and so on;
   h. prefixes;
   i. ways to combine sentences or phrases or words into complex units;
   j. pronouns.

8. Compare the ideas of Rousseau, Herder, and Suessmilch on the origin of language. Note the similarities and the differences. Argue in favor of one of these theories or argue for another point of view refuting all three positions.

9. Invent your own theory of language origin. For example, you might suggest that language arose because extraterrestrial creatures who already had a language possessed the bodies of cavewomen.

REFERENCES

Chomsky, Noam. 1975. *Reflections on Language.* Pantheon Books. New York.
Chomsky, Noam. 1972. *Language and Mind,* enlarged ed. Harcourt Brace Jovanovich. New York.
Curtiss, S. 1977. *Genie: A Psycholinguistic Study of a Modern-Day "Wild Child."* Academic Press. New York.
Dingwall, W. O. 1977. "The Evolution of Human Communication Systems" in H. Whitaker and H. A. Whitaker, eds., *Studies in Neurolinguistics,* vol. 4. Academic Press. New York.
Fromkin, V. A., S. Krashen, S. Curtiss, D. Rigler, and M. Rigler. "Language Development Beyond the Critical Age," *Brain and Language,* vol. 1., no. 1 (1974).
Jesperson, O. Reprinted 1964. *Language,* Ch. XXI. W. W. Norton. New York.
Lane, Harlan. 1976. *The Wild Boy of Aveyron.* Harvard University Press. Cambridge, Mass.
Lieber, Justin. 1975. *Noam Chomsky: A Philosophic Overview.* St. Martin's Press. New York.
Lieberman, Philip. 1975. *On the Origins of Language.* Macmillan. New York.
Lyons, John. 1970. *Noam Chomsky.* Viking. New York.
Plato. 1967. *Cratylus.* Loeb Classical Library. Harvard University Press. Cambridge, Mass.
Rousseau, J. J., and J. G. Herder. 1966. *On the Origin of Language,* trans. by J. H. Moran and A. Gode. Frederick Ungar. New York.
Stam, J. 1976. *Inquiries in the Origin of Language: The Fate of a Question.* Harper & Row. New York.

PART TWO

Grammatical Aspects of Language

We may think of a grammar, represented somehow in the mind, as a system that specifies the phonetic, syntactic, and semantic properties of an infinite class of potential sentences. The child knows the language so determined by the grammar he has acquired. This grammar is a representation of his "intrinsic competence."
N. Chomsky, *"On Cognitive Structures and Their Development: A Reply to Piaget"*

Chapter 2

Phonetics: The Sounds of Language

The voice is articulated by the lips and the tongue. . . . Man speaks by means of the air which he inhales into his entire body and particularly into the body cavities. When the air is expelled through the empty space it produces a sound, because of the resonances in the skull. The tongue articulates by its strokes; it gathers the air in the throat and pushes it against the palate and the teeth, thereby giving the sound a definite shape. If the tongue would not articulate each time, by means of its strokes, man would not speak clearly and would only be able to produce a few simple sounds.

Hippocrates, *De Carnibus*, VIII (ca. 400 B.C.)

When we hear a language we do not know, it sounds like gibberish. We don't know where one word ends and another begins. And even if we did we wouldn't understand the meaning.

In using language to speak or understand, the sounds produced or heard are related by the language system to certain meanings. Anyone who knows a language knows what sounds are in the language and how they are "strung" together and what these different sound sequences mean. Although the sounds of French or Xhosa or Quechua are uninterpretable to someone who does not speak those languages, and although there may be some sounds in one language that are not in another, all the languages of the world together comprise a limited set of sounds.

The study of these speech sounds, utilized by all human languages to represent meanings, is called **phonetics**. To describe speech sounds one has to decide what an "individual sound" is and how one sound differs from another.

This is not as easy as it may seem. You "know" there are three sounds in the word *cat,* one represented by *c*, one by *a*, and one by *t*. Yet, physically the word is just one continuous sound. You can *segment* the one sound into parts because you know the language. If you heard someone clearing his throat you would be unable to segment the sounds into a sequence of discrete units. When you speak you do not produce one sound, and then another, and then another. If you want to say *cat* you don't utter each sound separately; you move your organs of speech continuously, and you produce a continuous sound.

Despite the fact that the sounds we produce and the sounds we hear and comprehend are continuous signals, everyone who has ever attempted to analyze language has accepted the notion that speech utterances can be segmented into individual pieces. According to an ancient Hindu myth, the god Indra, in response to an appeal made by the other gods, attempted for the first time to break speech up into its separate elements. After he accomplished this feat, according to the myth, the sounds could be regarded as language. Indra thus was the first phonetician.

The early Greeks recognized the continual, ever-changing nature of the speech signal. Perhaps this is why they considered Hermes, the messenger of the gods who was always on the move, to be the god of speech. But the fleeting nature of the continually changing sound did not prevent the Greeks from attempting linguistic analysis. Hermogenes, one of the characters in Plato's *Cratylus* dialogue, asks if language can be analyzed by taking it to pieces, and Socrates answers that there is no better way to proceed.

In this sense music is similar to speech. A person who has not studied music cannot write the sequence of individual notes combined by a violinist into one changing continuous sound. A trained musician, however, finds it a simple task. Every human speaker, without special training, can segment a speech signal; when we learn the language we learn to segment an utterance into its basic discrete elements of sound.

To analyze speech into pieces one cannot start with merely the acoustic physical signal, or even with the movements of the vocal organs used to produce speech. Where would the breaks come? The difficulties in such an attempt would be further complicated because no two speakers ever say the "same thing" identically. In fact, the same speaker never says the "same thing" twice in exactly the same way. Yet speakers understand each other because they know the same language. One's knowledge of a language determines when physically different sounds are judged to be the same, because we know which aspects or properties of the signal are important and which are not. The phonetic properties that distinguish one sound, say *b*, in English from *d* remain fairly invariant or constant across all speakers and times.

We have already asserted that language and speech are not identical. Our linguistic knowledge, our mental grammar, imposes a system on the sounds produced and heard.

We are capable of making many sounds that we know intuitively (because we know the language) are not speech sounds in our language. An English speaker can and often does make a clicking sound which writers sometimes represent as *tsk tsk tsk*. But these sounds are not part of the English sound system. They never occur as part of the words of the sentences we produce. In fact, it is very difficult for many English speakers to combine this clicking sound with other sounds as Xhosa speakers do. But a click is a speech sound in Xhosa, Zulu, Sotho, and Hottentot, just like the *k* or *t* or *b* in English.

What is or is not an individual speech sound therefore depends on the particular language. *Tsk* is a speech sound in Xhosa but not in English; *th* is a sound in English but not in French. But the sound we produce with our mouth closed when we have a tickle in our throats is not a speech sound in *any* language, nor is the sound we produce when we sneeze.

The science of phonetics attempts to describe all the sounds used in language—the sounds that constitute a small but extremely important fraction of the totality of sounds that human beings are capable of producing.

The process by which we use our linguistic knowledge to produce a meaningful utterance is a very complicated one. It can be viewed as a chain of events starting with an "idea" or message in the brain of the speaker and ending with a similar message in the brain of the hearer. The message is put into a form that is dictated by the language we are speaking. It must then be transmitted by nerve signals to the organs of speech articulation, which produce the different physical sounds heard by the listener.

Speech sounds can be described at any stage in this chain of events. The study of the physical properties of the sounds themselves is called **acoustic phonetics.** The study of the way listeners perceive these sounds is called **auditory phonetics. Articulatory phonetics** is the study of how the vocal tract produces the sounds of language, which we will be primarily concerned with.

Articulatory Phonetics

HIGGINS: *Tired of listening to sounds?*
PICKERING: *Yes. It's a fearful strain. I rather fancied myself because I can pronounce twenty-four distinct vowel sounds, but your hundred and thirty beat me. I can't hear a bit of difference between most of them.*
HIGGINS: *Oh, that comes with practice. You hear no difference at first; but you keep on listening, and presently you find they're all as different as A from B.*
G. B. Shaw, *Pygmalion*

Because all normal languages involve sounds produced by the upper respiratory tract, to understand the nature of language it is necessary to understand the nature of these sounds and how they are produced. Articulatory phonetics attempts to provide a framework to do so.

AIRSTREAM MECHANISMS

The production of any speech sound (or any sound at all) involves the movement of an airstream. Most speech sounds are produced by pushing lung air out of the body through the mouth and sometimes also through the nose. Since lung air is used, these sounds are called **pulmonic** sounds; since the air is pushed *out,* they are called **egressive.** The majority of sounds used in languages of the world are thus produced by a **pulmonic egressive** airstream mechanism. All the sounds in English are produced in this manner.

Other airstream mechanisms are used in other languages to produce sounds called **ejectives, implosives,** and **clicks.** Instead of lung air, the body of air in the mouth may be moved. When this air is sucked in instead of flowing out, **ingressive** sounds, like implosives and clicks, are produced. When the air in the mouth is pushed out, ejectives are produced; they are thus also **egressive** sounds. Implosives and ejectives are produced by a **glottalic airstream mechanism,** while clicks are produced by a **velaric airstream mechanism.** Ejectives are found in many American Indian languages as well as African and Caucasian languages. Implosives also occur in the languages of the American Indians and throughout Africa, India, and Pakistan. Clicks occur in the Southern Bantu languages such as Xhosa and Zulu, and in the languages spoken by the Bushmen and Hottentots. A detailed description of these different airstream mechanisms goes beyond the requirements of an introductory text such as this. They are mentioned to show that sounds can be classified according to the airstream mechanism used to produce them. In the rest of this chapter we will be discussing only sounds produced by a pulmonic egressive airstream mechanism.

VOICED AND VOICELESS SOUNDS

The airstream from the lungs moves up through the trachea, or windpipe, and through the opening between the vocal cords, which is called the **glottis** (see Figure 2-1).

If the vocal cords are apart, the airstream is not obstructed at the glottis

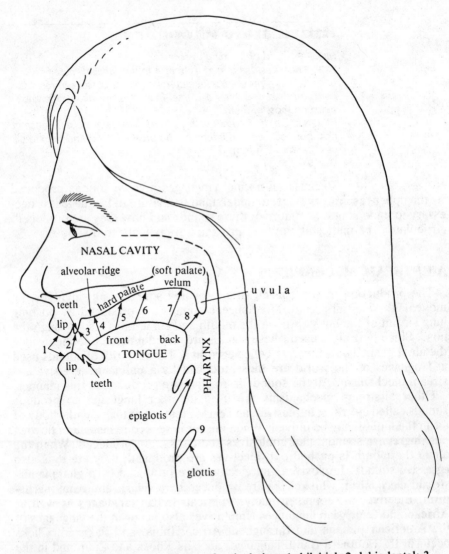

Figure 2-1 The vocal tract. Places of articulation: 1, bilabial; 2, labiodental; 3, dental or interdental; 4, alveolar; 5, palatoalveolar; 6, palatal; 7, velar; 8, uvular; 9, glottal.

and it passes freely into the **supraglottal** cavities (the parts of the vocal tract above the glottis). The sounds produced in this way are called **voiceless** sounds. The sounds represented by *p, t, k,* and *s* in the English words *pit, tip, kit, sip,* and *kiss* are voiceless sounds.

If the vocal cords are together, the airstream forces its way through and causes them to *vibrate.* Such sounds are called **voiced** sounds and are illustrated by the sounds spelled *b, d, g,* and *z* in the words *bad, god, dog, zebra,* and *buzz.* If you put a finger in each ear and say "z-z-z-z-z" you can feel the vibrations of the sound as it goes through the vibrating vocal cords. If you now say "s-s-s-s-s" you will not feel these vibrations (although you might hear a hissing sound in your mouth). When you whisper, you are making all the speech sounds voiceless.

The voiced/voiceless distinction is a very important one in English. It is this phonetic feature or property that distinguishes between word pairs like *pig/big, fine/vine, tin/din, seal/zeal.* The first word of each pair starts with a voiceless sound and the second word with a voiced sound. All other aspects of the sounds of these words are identical; the position of the lips and tongue is the same in each of the paired words.

The state of the vocal cords during speech permits us to classify speech sounds into two large classes, then: **voiced** and **voiceless.** We can specify each voiced sound as [+ voiced] and each voiceless sound as [− voiced], because [− voiced] is a descriptive term that is equivalent to voiceless.

Words may also be distinguished if the *final* sounds differ as to vocal cord position, as in *nap* and *nab, writ* and *rid, rack* and *rag, wreath* and *wreathe, rich* and *ridge.* You will notice that the English spelling system does not represent these differences perfectly; for example, the *ck* which ends *rack* represents a simple [− voiced] *k* sound. We will discuss sounds and spelling in a later section. In these pairs of words the first word ends in a voiceless (or [− voiced]) sound and the second word ends in a voiced ([+ voiced]) sound.

Sounds must differ from each other in ways other than voicing. That is, *p, t, k* are all voiceless, and *b, d, g* are all voiced, but these sounds are distinct from one another. What other phonetic properties distinguish sounds?

NASAL VS. ORAL SOUNDS

If you say *pad, bad,* and *mad* you will notice that the initial sounds are very similar. The *p, b,* and *m* are all produced by closing the lips. *p* differs from *b* because in producing the voiceless *p* the vocal cords are apart, the glottis is open. *b* is voiced because the vocal cords are together and vibrating. If you put your hands over your ears and keep your lips together for the *b* you will feel the hum of the vibrations. If you do the same and say "m-m-m-m" or *mad* you will see that *m* is also a voiced sound. What, then, distinguishes the *m* from the *b*?

m is a **nasal** sound. When you produce *m,* air escapes not only through the mouth (when you open your lips) but also through the nose.

In Figure 2-1 notice that the roof of the mouth is divided into the **hard palate** and the **soft palate,** or **velum.** The hard palate is the bony structure at the front of the mouth. You can feel this hard palate with your finger. As you move your finger back you can feel the section of the palate where the flesh becomes soft and is movable. This soft, movable part is called the **velum.** Hanging down from the end of the soft palate, or velum, is the **uvula,** which

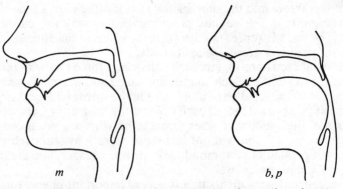

m   *b, p*

Figure 2-2 Position of lips and velum for *m* (lips together, velum down) and *b, p* (lips together, velum up).

you can see in a mirror if you open your mouth wide and say "aaah." When the velum is raised all the way to touch the back of the throat, the passage through the nose is cut off. When the nasal passage is blocked in this way, the air can escape only through the mouth. Sounds produced this way are called **oral** sounds. *p* and *b* are oral sounds. When the velum is lowered, air escapes through the nose as well as the mouth. Sounds produced this way are called **nasal** sounds. *m*, *n*, and *ng* are the nasal consonants of English. The diagrams in Figure 2-2 show the position of the lips and the velum when *m* and *p* or *b* are articulated.

The difference between *bad* and *mad*, *dot* and *not*, is due only to the position of the velum in the first sounds of the words. In *bad* and *dot* the velum is raised, preventing air from entering the nasal cavity. *b* and *d* are therefore *oral* sounds. In *mad* and *not* the velum is lowered and air travels through the nose as well as the mouth. *m* and *n* are therefore *nasal* sounds. Note that *b*, *d*, *m*, and *n* are all voiced.

Words with final consonants, alike in all other respects, may differ with respect to the oral–nasal distinction. The final sounds of *rib* and *rim*, *mad* and *man*, *dig* and *ding* (the *ng* represents one sound[1]) are identical except the first of each pair is oral, the second is nasal.

These **phonetic features,** or properties, enable us to classify all speech sounds into four classes: voiced, voiceless, nasal, oral. One sound may belong to more than one class, as shown in Table 2-1. We can also classify these sounds by specifying them as + or − for each phonetic property we have discussed:

	p	t	k	b	d	g	m	n	ng (ŋ)[1]
Voiced	−	−	−	+	+	+	+	+	+
Nasal	−	−	−	−	−	−	+	+	+

It is easy, by this method, to determine the different classes of speech sounds. All sounds marked [+ voiced] are in the class of voiced sounds, all sounds marked [− voiced] are in the class of voiceless sounds, all sounds

---

[1] The single sound usually represented by *ng* in the English spelling system can also be symbolized by ŋ. Phonetic symbols for all the sounds will be discussed below.

Table 2-1 Classes of Speech Sounds

	Oral (− nasal)	Nasal (+ nasal)
Voiced (+ voiced)	b d g	m n ng (ŋ)
Voiceless (− voiced)	p t k	All nasal consonants in English are voiced

marked [+ nasal] are in the class of nasal sounds, and those marked [− nasal] are in the class of oral sounds.

Below we will discuss many other phonetic features. Each feature will determine a class of speech sounds. These classes will be most easily specified by using pluses and minuses, much as we did in the previous paragraph.

PLACES OF ARTICULATION

If *b*, *d*, and *g* are all voiced nonnasal (oral) sounds, what distinguishes them? We know they are distinct because we recognize *brew*, *drew*, and *grew*, and *bash*, *dash*, and *gash* as different words, with different meanings. There must be other phonetic features that distinguish them besides those already discussed.

Labials By moving the tongue and lips we are able to change the shape of the oral cavity and in this way produce different sounds. When we produce a *b*, *p*, or *m* we **articulate** by bringing both lips together. These sounds are therefore called **bilabials.**

We also use our lips to form *f* and *v*, as in *fine* and *vine*. In this case we articulate by touching the bottom lip to the upper teeth. Hence these sounds are called **labiodental.** The five sounds that comprise the three bilabials *b*, *p*, and *m* and the two labiodentals *f* and *v* form the class of **labial** sounds.

Alveolars When we articulate a *d*, *n*, *t*, *s*, or *z*, we raise the tip of the tongue to the hard palate right at the point of the bony tooth ridge, called the **alveolar ridge** (see Figure 2-1). Sounds produced by raising the tongue tip to the alveolar ridge are called **alveolar** sounds. If you say *do, new, two, Sue, zoo* you will notice that the first sounds in all these words are produced by raising your tongue tip toward the alveolar ridge. The *t* and *s* are voiceless alveolar sounds, and the *d*, *z*, and *n* are voiced. Only *n* is nasal.

Velars Another group of sounds is produced by raising the back of the tongue to the soft palate or velum. The sounds ending the words *back, bag,* and *bang* are produced this way and are called **velar** sounds.

Interdentals To produce the sounds represented by *th* beginning the words *thin* and *then* you insert the tip of the tongue between the upper and lower teeth. These are **interdental** sounds. The *th* in *thin* and *ether* is a voiceless interdental, and the *th* in *then* and *either* is a voiced interdental.

Palatals (or Alveopalatals) If you raise the front part of your tongue to a point on the hard palate just behind the alveolar ridge, you can produce the sounds in the middle of the words "me*sh*er" and "mea*s*ure." The sound in the first word (spelled *sh*) is voiceless and the sound in the second word (spelled *s*) is voiced. They are both **palatal** (sometimes called **alveo-palatal** or **postalveolar**) sounds. In English the voiced palatal never begins words (except in words borrowed from the French like *genre* and *gendarme*, which some English speakers produce with a French pronunciation). The voiceless palatal sound begins the words *shoe, shut, sure,* and *sugar,* and ends the words *rush, push,* and *lush.*

MANNERS OF ARTICULATION

Stops We already have a number of distinct phonetic properties to describe many overlapping classes of speech sounds. Both *t* and *s*, for example, are in the class of voiceless oral alveolar sounds. But what distinguishes the *t* from the *s* sound?

Once the airstream enters the oral cavity it may be stopped, it may be partially obstructed, or it may flow freely out of the mouth. Sounds that are stopped **completely** in the oral cavity for a brief period are, not surprisingly, called **stops.** All other sounds are called **continuants** because the stream of air continues without interruption through the mouth opening. *p, b, m, t, d, n, k, g,* and *ng* sounds in words like ta*p*, ta*b*, ta*m*, ta*t*, ta*d*, ta*n*, tac*k*, ta*g*, and ta*ng* are stops that occur in English.

In the production of nasal stops *n, m,* and *ng,* as in the words above, the air does continue through the nose, but there is a blockage of the airflow in the mouth. When you produce these sounds the air is completely blocked either at the lips or where the tongue touches the alveolar ridge or velum.

The nonnasal stops are also called **plosives** because the air that is blocked in the mouth "explodes" when the closure is released. This does not occur with nasal stops because the air has an "escape route" through the nose.

b, p, and *m* are bilabial stops, with the airstream stopped at the mouth by the complete closure of the lips.

d, t, and *n* are alveolar stops. The airstream is stopped by the tongue making a complete closure at the alveolar ridge.

g, k, and *ng* are velar stops with the complete closure at the velum.

In Quechua, a major language spoken in Bolivia and Peru, one finds *uvular* stops as well. These are produced when the back of the tongue is raised and moved backward to form a complete closure with the uvula. The letter *q* in words in this language, as in the language name, usually represents a uvular stop, which may occur voiced or voiceless.

We can classify all sounds into two classes (which of course intersect with other classes). Stops belong to the class specified as [−continuant] and non-stops belong to the class of [+continuant] sounds.

Aspirated vs. Unaspirated Sounds During the production of voiceless sounds the glottis is open and the air passes freely through the opening between the vocal cords. When a voiceless sound is followed by a voiced sound, as it often is, the vocal cords must close.

Voiceless sounds may differ among themselves, depending on the "timing" of the vocal cord closure. In English when we pronounce the word *pit* there is a brief period of voicelessness immediately after the *p* sound is released. That is, after the lips come apart the vocal cords remain open for a very short time. Such sounds are called **aspirated** because an extra puff of air is produced. When we pronounce the *p* in *spit*, however, the vocal cords start vibrating as soon as the lips are opened. Such sounds are called **unaspirated.** Similarly, the *t* in *tick* and the *k* in *kin* are aspirated voiceless stops, while the *t* in *stick* and the *k* in *skin* are unaspirated. If you hold a strip of paper before your lips and say *pit*, the "aspiration" will be shown by the fact that the paper is pushed by the puff of air. The paper will not move when you say *spit*.

Figure 2-3 shows in diagrammatic form the timing of the articulators (in this case the lips) in relation to the state of the vocal cords. Notice that in the production of the voiced *b* the vocal cords are vibrating throughout the closure of the lips and continue to vibrate for the vowel production after the lips are opened. In the unaspirated *p* in *spin* the vocal cords are open during the lip closure and come together and start vibrating as soon as the lips open. In the production of the aspirated *p* in *pin* the vocal cords remain apart for a brief period after the lip closure is released.

Although you might not have noticed that the *p*'s in *pin* and *spin* or *pit* and *spit* were actually different sounds, this is an important difference in the phonetic description of the sounds which we will discuss in greater detail in Chapter 3.

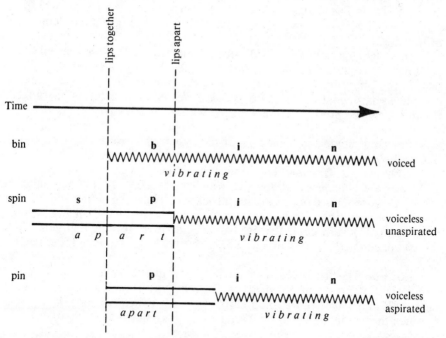

Figure 2-3 Timing of articulators and vocal cord vibration for voiced, voiceless unaspirated, and voiceless aspirated stops.

Fricatives In the production of some sounds, the airstream is not completely stopped but is obstructed from flowing freely. If you put your hand in front of your mouth and produce an *s*, *z*, *f*, *v*, *th*, or *sh* sound you will feel the air coming out of your mouth. The passage in the mouth through which the air must pass, however, is very narrow, and this causes turbulence. The air particles are pushed against one another, producing *noise* because of the *friction*. Such sounds are called **fricatives.** (You may also hear them referred to as **spirants,** from the Latin word spirare, "to blow.")

In the production of the labiodental fricatives *f* and *v*, the friction is created at the lips, where a narrow passage permits the air to escape.

In the production of the fricatives *s* and *z* the friction is created at the alveolar ridge.

In the production of the alveopalatal or palatal fricatives, in *mesher* and *measure*, the friction or noise is created as the air passes through the narrow opening behind the alveolar ridge.

In the production of the *th* sounds in *thin* and *then*, the friction occurs at the opening between the tongue and teeth.

Most dialects of modern English do not include velar fricatives, although they occurred in an earlier stage of English in such words as *right*, *knight*, *enough*, and *through*, where the *gh* occurs in the spelling. If you raise the back of the tongue as if you were about to produce a *g* or *k*, but stop just short of touching the velum, you will produce a velar fricative. The *ch* ending in the German pronunciation of the composer's name, *Bach*, is a velar fricative. Some speakers of modern English substitute a voiceless velar fricative in words like *bucket* and a voiced velar fricative in such words as *wagon*. Both voiced and voiceless velar fricatives occur in many languages of the world.

In some languages of the world—for example, Arabic—**pharyngeal** fricatives occur, which are produced by pulling the tongue root towards the back wall of the pharynx. It is difficult to pull the tongue far enough to make a complete pharyngeal stop closure, but both voiced and voiceless pharyngeal fricatives can be produced and contrast with velar fricatives.

Affricates Some sounds are produced by a stop closure followed immediately by a slow release of the closure characteristic of a fricative. These sounds are called **affricates.** The sounds that begin and end the words *church* and *judge* are voiceless and voiced affricates, respectively. Phonetically, an affricate is a sequence of a stop plus a fricative. Thus, the *ch* in *church* is the same as the sound combination *t* + *sh*, as you can see by prolonging the pronunciation of the affricate. This is also revealed by observing that very often in fast speech *white shoes* and *why choose* may be pronounced identically.

Sibilants The fricatives that are italicized in the words "*s*ip," "*z*ip," "*sh*oe," "lei*s*ure," and "mea*s*ure" and the affricates in the words "*ch*urch" and "*j*ug" represent a class of sounds called **sibilants.** When you produce these sounds the friction causes a "hissing" noise.

Obstruents The nonnasal stops, the fricatives, and the affricates form a class of sounds that can be distinguished from all other sounds. Since the airstream cannot escape through the nose, it is totally obstructed in its passage through the vocal tract. These sounds are called **obstruents;** all other sounds are called **sonorants.** Nasal stops are sonorants because although the air is blocked in the mouth it continues to "resonate" and move through the nose.

Fricatives are continuant obstruents because despite the obstruction that causes the friction, the air is not completely stopped in its passage through the oral cavity. Nonnasal stops and affricates are noncontinuant obstruents because there is complete blockage of the air during the production of these sounds. The closure of a stop is released abruptly, as opposed to the closure of an affricate, which is released gradually, causing friction. In addition, all the affricates in English are sibilants.

Using these phonetic properties, we can form additional classes as shown in Table 2-2.

Table 2-2 Four Classes of Speech Sounds Specified by Three Features

Features	Oral Stops	Affricates	Fricatives	Nasal Stops
Sonorant	−	−	−	+
Continuant	−	−	+	−
Sibilant	−	+	+ or −	−

Liquids The sounds *l* and *r* are also sonorants. There is some obstruction of the airstream in the mouth, but not enough to cause friction. These sounds are called **liquids.**

l is a **lateral** sound. The front of the tongue makes contact with the alveolar ridge, but the sides of the tongue are down, permitting the air to escape laterally over the sides of the tongue.

The sound *r* is usually formed in English by curling the tip of the tongue back behind the alveolar ridge. Such sounds are called **retroflex** sounds. In some languages the "r" may be a **trill,** which is produced by the tip of the tongue vibrating against the roof of the mouth. It is possible that in an earlier stage of English the "r" was a trill. A trilled "r" occurs in many contemporary languages, such as Spanish.

In addition to the alveolar trill, uvular trills also occur, as in French. A uvular trill is produced by vibrating the uvula. In other languages the "r" is produced by a single **tap** instead of a series of vibrating taps. In Spanish both the alveolar trill and the alveolar tap occur. If you substitute one for the other in certain contexts you will produce a different word. One may also produce an "r" by making the tongue **flap** against the alveolar ridge. Some speakers of British English pronounce the "r" in the word *very* with a flap. It sounds like a "very fast" *d*. Most American speakers produce a flap instead of a *t* or *d* in words like *writer* and *rider,* and *latter* and *ladder.* For many speakers these pairs are pronounced identically in normal conversational style.

In English, *l* and *r* are regularly voiced. When they follow voiceless sounds, as in *please* or *price,* they may be automatically "de-voiced" at least partially. Many languages of the world have a voiceless *l*. Welsh is such a language; the name *Lloyd* in Welsh starts with a voiceless *l*.

Some languages may lack liquids entirely, or have only a single one. The Cantonese dialect of Chinese has the single liquid *l*. Japanese, on the other hand, lacks an *l* but has an *r*. These differences make some English words difficult for Cantonese or Japanese speakers to pronounce. Other differences, needless to say, make these languages difficult for English speakers to pronounce.

Acoustically (that is, as physical sounds) *l* and *r* are very similar, which is why they are grouped together in the class of liquids and why they function as a single class of sounds in certain circumstances. For example, the only two consonants permitted after an initial *k*, *g*, *p*, or *b* sound in English are the liquids *l* and *r*. Thus we have *plate, prate, bland, brand* but no word starting with *ps, bt, pk,* etc. (Notice that in words like *psychology* or *pterodactyl* the *p* is not pronounced).

Glides The sounds *y* and *w* are produced with little or no obstruction of the airstream in the mouth. When occurring in a word, they must always be either preceded or followed directly by a vowel. In articulating *y* or *w* the tongue moves rapidly in gliding fashion either toward or away from a neighboring vowel, hence the term **glide.** Glides are transition sounds, being partly like consonants and partly like vowels, and they are sometimes called **semivowels.**

In producing the glide *y*, the blade of the tongue is raised toward the hard palate, so it is called a **palatal** glide. The tongue is in a position almost identical to that assumed in producing the vowel sound as in the word *beat*. In pronouncing *you* the tongue moves rapidly over the *y* to the *ou* vowel.

The glide *w* is produced by both raising the back of the tongue toward the velum and simultaneously rounding the lips. It is thus a **labiovelar** glide. In the dialect of English where speakers have different pronunciations for *which* and *witch*, the labiovelar glide in the first word is voiceless, and in the second word it is voiced. The position of the tongue and the lips when one produces a *w* is very similar to the positions for the production of the vowel sound in *lute*, but the *w* is a glide because the tongue moves quickly to the vowel that follows.

To produce the *h* that starts words such as *house, who,* and *hair,* the glottis is open as in the production of voiceless sounds. No other modification of the airstream mechanism occurs in the mouth. In fact, the tongue and lips are usually in the position for the production of the following vowel as the airstream passes through the open glottis. The air or noise produced at the glottis is heard as *h* and for this reason *h* is often classified as a **voiceless glottal fricative.** The *h* is also classified as a glide by some linguists, since it differs from "true" consonants in that there is no obstruction in the oral cavity and it also differs from vowels. When it is both preceded and followed by a vowel it is often voiced, as in *ahead* or *cohabit*.

If the air is stopped completely at the glottis by tightly closed vocal cords, the sound produced is a **glottal stop.** This is the sound often used instead of a *t* in words like *button* and *Latin*. It also may occur in colloquial speech at the end of words like *don't, won't,* or *can't*. In one New York dialect it regularly replaces the *tt* sound in words like *bottle*. If you say "ah-ah-ah-ah" with one "ah" right after another, but do not sustain the vowel sound, you will be producing glottal stops between the vowels. Like the *h*, it differs from both consonants and vowels (which we have not yet discussed) and is classified as a glide by some linguists. Because the air is completely blocked at the glottis, other linguists classify it as a stop.

VOWELS

In every language of the world, speech sounds can be divided into two major classes—**consonants** and **vowels.** In the production of consonants the flow of air is obstructed as it travels through the mouth. Vowels are produced with no oral obstruction whatsoever. Speakers usually know "intuitively" which sounds are vowels and which are consonants. Vowels usually constitute the "main core," or the **nucleus,** of syllables.

FRANK AND ERNEST   **Bob Thaves**

Reprinted by permission. © 1980 NEA, Inc.

Some sounds do not fall easily into one of these two classes. Glides, for example, are like vowels in that there is little oral obstruction, but they are also like consonants in that their duration is very short; they always occur either before or after a vowel.

Liquids are like consonants in some ways and vowels in others. Because they are produced with obstructions in the oral cavity they are like consonants. But acoustically they have "resonances" like vowels.

To show the way all the sounds we have discussed group themselves into overlapping classes, we can use the two features—**vocalic** and **consonantal** —and mark each segment as being either plus or minus for each feature, as in Table 2-3.

Table 2-3 Vocalic and Consonantal Groupings

Features	Classes			
	Consonants	Vowels	Glides	Liquids
Consonantal	+	−	−	+
Vocalic	−	+	−	+

Different linguists use different features or different names for the same features. Thus, for example, another book or article about phonetics might refer to the feature we have called *vocalic* by the term *syllabic*. Liquids can be syllabic, that is, form a separate syllable, as in the words "med*al*" or "fev*er*," or nonsyllabic, as in the words "*l*ead" or "*r*ead" or "dea*l*" or "dea*r*".

The syllabicity of liquids may also be shown by describing the words in which they function as syllables as having short vowels before the liquids.

By the system we have provided in Table 2-3, consonants and vowels are distinct classes; they do not share any feature. Glides, however, are like consonants in that they are in the class of [− vocalic] segments, but they are like vowels in that they are in the class of [− consonantal] segments. Similarly, liquids are in the [+ consonantal] class with consonants and the [+ vocalic] class with vowels. In studying languages of the world we find this to be a helpful classification because glides can function as consonants and liquids can function as vowels in certain contexts.

The quality of vowels is determined by the particular configuration of the vocal tract. Different parts of the tongue may be raised or lowered. The lips may be spread or pursed. The passage through which the air travels, however, is never so narrow as to obstruct free flow of the airstream.

Vowel sounds carry pitch and loudness; you can sing vowels. They may be long or short. Vowels can "stand alone"—they can be produced without any consonants before or after them. One can say the vowels of *beat*, *bit*, or *boot*, for example, without the initial *b* or the final *t*. It is much more difficult to produce a *b* or a *t* without some kind of vowel attached.

There have been many different schemes for describing vowel sounds. They may be described by articulatory features, as we have classified consonants. Many beginning students of phonetics find this method more difficult to apply to vowel articulations than to consonant articulations. When you make a *t* you feel your tongue touch the alveolar ridge. When you make a *p* you can feel your two lips come together or you can watch the lips move in a mirror. Since vowels are produced without any articulators touching or even coming very close together, it is often difficult to figure out just what is going on. One of the authors of this book almost gave up as a linguist and phonetician at the beginning of her graduate work because she couldn't understand what was meant by "front," "back," "high," and "low" vowels.

But these terms do have meaning. If you watched an x-ray movie of someone talking you would understand why vowels have traditionally been classified according to three questions:

1. How high is the tongue?
2. What part of the tongue is involved; that is, what part is raised? What part is lowered?
3. What is the position of the lips?

There are other distinguishing features, such as length, nasalization, and tenseness, which we will discuss below.

Tongue Position The three diagrams in Figure 2-4 show that the vowel in the word *heat* and the word *hoot* is very high in the mouth. But in *heat* it is the front part of the tongue which is raised and in *hoot* it is the back part of the tongue. (Prolong the vowels of these words and you may be able to feel your tongue rise.) To produce the vowel sound of *hot* or *bar* or *ah* the back of the tongue is lowered. (The reason a doctor asks you to say "ah" in examining your throat is that the tongue is low and he can thus see over it.)

The vowel in *bit* or *hit* is similar to that in *beat* or *heat* but the tongue is a little lower in the mouth.

Lip Rounding Vowels also differ as to whether the lips are rounded. Thus, the vowels in *boot*, *put*, *boat*, *bought* (or *bore*) are produced with the back of the tongue at decreasing heights just as the front vowels in *beet*, *bit*, *bait*, *bet*, and *bat*. But these back vowels are all pronounced with the lips pursed or **rounded**, which is not the case with the English front vowels. The low vowel in *hot* or *bar* is, as we noted above, also a back vowel but it is produced without any lip rounding. Similarly, the vowels in *butt*, the initial and final vowels in *America*, and the final vowel in *Rosa* are unrounded but are not produced with the front part of the tongue.

Using these phonetic properties or dimensions of the tongue—front to back, high to low, lip rounding vs. nonrounding—we can classify some of the vowels that occur in English as in Table 2-4.

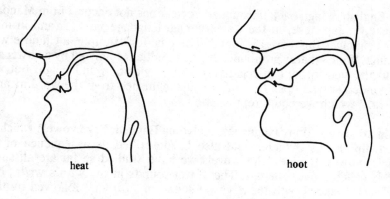

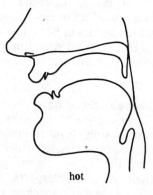

Figure 2-4 Position of the tongue in producing the vowels in *heat, hoot,* and *hot* (or *ha*).

You will notice in Table 2-4 that there are no words with front-rounded vowels. This is because we included only English vowel sounds and front vowels are never rounded in English. This is not true of all languages. French and Swedish, for example, have both front- and back-rounded vowels.

Table 2-4 A Classification Scheme for Some American English Vowels

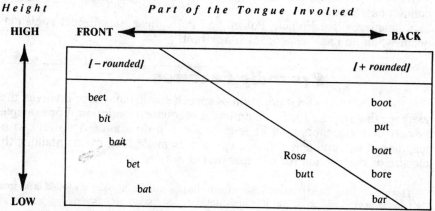

Tongue Height		Part of the Tongue Involved	
HIGH	**FRONT** ◄─────────────►	**BACK**	
	[− rounded]	*[+ rounded]*	
	beet		boot
	b*i*t		p*u*t
	ba*it*		boat
	bet	Rosa	bore
	bat	b*utt*	
LOW			bar

In English, a high back unrounded vowel does not occur, but in Mandarin Chinese, in Japanese, in the Cameroonian language Fe?Fe?, and in many other languages this vowel is found. There is, for example, a Chinese word meaning "four" that is pronounced with an initial *s* followed by a vowel similar to the one in b*oo*t in regards to tongue position and height but with nonrounded spread lips. This word is distinguished from the word meaning "speed," which we could represent by *soo*.

Diphthongs Many languages, including English, have vowels which are called **diphthongs**, which could also be described as a sequence of two sounds, vowel + glide. The vowels we have studied so far are all simple vowels called **monophthongs**. The vowel sounds in the words wr*i*te, b*i*te, m*i*te are produced with the *a* vowel sound of "f*a*ther" followed by the *y* glide. The vowels in b*ou*t, br*ow*n, h*ou*r are produced by some speakers of English with a similar *a* sound followed by the glide *w*, and by others with the low front vowel which occurs in *bat* followed by *w*. The third diphthong that occurs in English is the vowel sound in b*oy* and s*oi*l and that may be described as the vowel that occurs in *bore* (without the *r*) followed by the *y* glide.

Tense and Lax Vowels Some linguists use the terms **tense** and **lax** to distinguish the vowels in the following pairs: *beet/bit, bait/bet, boot/put, boat/bought*. The tongue position is fairly similar for the vowels in each pair, with the vowel of the first word being *tense* and of the second word, *lax*. It is also true, however, that the lax vowels are produced with tongue heights slightly lower than their tense counterparts. Tense vowels are sometimes also slightly diphthongized for some speakers of English. For such speakers the tense front vowels are followed by a short *y* glide, and the back tense rounded vowels by a short *w* glide.

Nasal (Nasalized) Vowels Vowels, like consonants, can be produced with a raised velum that prevents the air from escaping through the nose, or with a lowered velum that permits air to pass through the nasal passage. When the nasal passage is blocked, **oral** vowels are produced; when the velum is lowered, **nasal** or **nasalized** vowels are produced. In English nasal vowels occur only before nasal consonants, and oral vowels occur only before oral consonants. The words *bean, bin, bane, Ben, ban, boon, bun, bone; beam, bam, boom;* and *bing, bang, bong* are examples of words that contain nasalized vowels.

In languages like French, Polish, and Portuguese, nasalized vowels may occur when no nasal consonant is adjacent.

Prosodic Features

The production of speech sounds may also involve other methods that require special features for adequate description. For example, vowels or consonants may be long or short in duration.[2] A vowel can be lengthened by prolonging it. A consonant is made long by maintaining the closure or obstruction for a longer period of time.

[2] This use of "long" and "short" is *not* used by linguists to distinguish the *i* sound in *bit* from the *i* sound in *bite*, and so on, as it is in dictionaries and "grammar" books.

When we speak we also change the **pitch** of our voice. The pitch produced depends upon how fast the vocal cords vibrate; the faster they vibrate, the higher the pitch. In physical or acoustic terms, pitch is referred to as the **fundamental frequency** of the sound signal.

We are also able to change the loudness of the sounds and sound sequences.

In many languages, some syllables or vowels are produced with a change in pitch (usually higher), more loudly, and longer than other vowels in the word or sentence. They are referred to as **stressed.**

In Chapter 3, we will discuss the ways in which *length, pitch*, and the complex feature *stress* are **prosodic** features used to distinguish words and the meanings of sentences in different ways in different languages.

You should keep in mind that the phonetic properties and features we have discussed are broad terms covering many even finer distinctions. In this chapter we are merely attempting to present a general view as to how such phonetic properties differentiate the sounds found in human languages, and how they are produced.

The Phonetic Alphabet

B.C.   **Johnny Hart**

By permission of Johnny Hart and Field Enterprises, Inc.

> *Once a Frenchman who'd promptly said "Oui"*
> *To some ladies who'd asked him if houi*
> > *Cared to drink, threw a fit*
> > *Upon finding that it*
> *Was a tipple no stronger than toui.*
> Anonymous

> *The one-l lama,*
> *He's a priest.*
> *The two-l llama,*
> *He's a beast.*

> *And I will bet*
> *A silk pajama*
> *There isn't any*
> *Three-l lllama.*
> Ogden Nash[3]

---

[3] "The Lama." From *Verses from 1929 On* by Ogden Nash. Reprinted by permission of Curtis Brown Ltd., London, on behalf of the Estate of Ogden Nash.

In our discussion of the phonetic properties or features that are used to distinguish and define speech sounds, we were faced with certain problems. We noted, for example, that in English the letter *p* was used to represent both the aspirated voiceless stop in *pit* and the unaspirated voiceless stop in *spit*.

Alphabetic spelling represents the pronunciations of words. But it is often the case that the sounds of the words in a language are rather unsystematically represented by **orthography**—that is, by spelling.

Suppose all Earthlings were destroyed by some horrible catastrophe, and years later Martian astronauts exploring Earth discovered some fragments of English writing that included the following sentence:

Did h*e* beli*e*ve that C*ae*sar could s*ee* the p*eo*ple s*ei*ze the s*ea*s?

How would a Martian linguist decide that *e*, *ie*, *ae*, *ee*, *eo*, *ei*, and *ea* all represented the same sound? To add to her confusion, she might later stumble across this sentence:

The sill*y* am*oe*ba stole the k*e*y to the mach*i*ne.

English speakers know the pronunciation of these words and know that *y*, *oe*, *ey*, and *i* also represent the same sound as the italicized letters in the first sentence. But how could a Martian know this?

This inconsistent spelling system prompted Ambrose Bierce to define *orthography* as "the science of spelling by the eye instead of the ear." When Mark Twain wrote: "They spell it Vinci and pronounce it Vinchy; foreigners always spell better than they pronounce,"[4] he was fully aware that it is not only "foreigners" whose spelling differs from pronunciation.

The discrepancy between spelling and sounds gave rise to a movement of English "spelling reformers." They wanted to revise the alphabet so that one letter would correspond to one sound, and one sound to one letter, thus simplifying spelling. This is a **phonetic alphabet.**

George Bernard Shaw followed in the footsteps of three centuries of spelling reformers in England. In typical Shavian manner he pointed out that we could use the English spelling system to spell *fish* as *ghoti*—the *gh* like the sound in *enough*, the *o* like the sound in *women*, and the *ti* like the sound in *nation*. Shaw was so concerned about English spelling that he included in his will a provision for a new "Proposed British Alphabet" to be administered by a "Public Trustee" who would have the duty of seeking and publishing a more efficient alphabet. This alphabet was to have at least forty letters to enable "the said language to be written without indicating single sounds by groups of letters or by diacritical marks." After Shaw's death in 1950, 450 designs for such an alphabet were submitted from all parts of the globe. Four alphabets were judged to be equally good, and the £500 prize was divided among their designers. An "expert" collaborated with these four to produce the alphabet designated in Shaw's will. Shaw also stipulated in his will that his play *Androcles and the Lion* be published in the new alphabet, with "the original Doctor Johnson's lettering opposite the transliteration page by page and a glossary of the two alphabets." This version of the play was published in 1962.

---

[4] Ambrose Bierce, *The Devil's Dictionary;* Mark Twain, *The Innocents Abroad.*

This new alphabet was not the first phonetic alphabet. In 1617, Robert Robinson produced an alphabet that attempted to provide a relationship between "articulation" and the shapes of the letters. In 1657, Cave Beck produced *A Universal Character,* a publication described on its title page as "The Universal Character by which all the Nations in the World may understand one another's Conceptions, Reading out of one Common Writing their own Mother Tongues." In 1668, Bishop John Wilkins proposed a similar universal alphabet; and in 1686, Francis Lodwick published "An Essay Towards an Universal Alphabet," which he had worked out and circulated many years before. Lodwick's aim was to provide an alphabet "which should contain an Enumeration of all such Single Sounds or Letters as are used in any Language. . . . All single sounds ought to have single and distinct characters" and no one character shall "have more than one Sound, nor any one Sound be expressed by more than one Character." Lodwick, like Cave Beck before him and others who followed him, did not use Roman letters. He designed his own "letters" in such a way that similar sounds were represented by similar symbols. Even in Shaw's lifetime, the phonetician Henry Sweet, the prototype for Shaw's own Henry Higgins, produced a phonetic alphabet.

If we look at English spelling, it is easy to understand why there has been so much concern about spelling systems. Different letters may represent a single sound, as shown in the following:

to   too   two   through   threw   clue   shoe

A single letter may represent different sounds:

	*da*me	*da*d	*fa*ther	*ca*ll	vill*a*ge	m*a*ny
or:	*p*in/s*p*in		*k*in/s*k*in		*t*ick/s*t*ick	

A combination of letters may represent a single sound:

*sh*oot	*ch*aracter	*Th*omas	*ph*ysics
ei*th*er	dea*l*	rou*gh*	na*ti*on
c*oa*t	gla*ci*al	*th*eater	pl*ai*n

Some letters have no sound at all in certain words in which they occur:

*m*nemonic	*w*hole	resig*n*	*gh*ost
*p*terodactyl	*w*rite	hol*e*	cor*p*s
*p*sychology	s*w*ord	deb*t*	*g*naw
bou*gh*	lam*b*	is*l*and	*k*nife

Some sounds are not represented in the spelling. In many words the letter *u* represents a *y* sound followed by a *u* sound:

c*u*te	(compare: l*oo*t)
f*u*tile	(compare: f*oo*l)
*u*tility	(compare: *oo*ze)

One letter may represent two sounds; the final *x* in *Xerox* represents a *k* followed by an *s*.

All these discrepancies between spelling and sounds seem to argue in favor of the spelling reformers. One may wonder why they didn't win their struggle. One may also wonder how such a chaotic spelling system arose.

The inventor of printing is a major culprit. When scribes used to write manuscripts they would often write words more or less as they pronounced them. But after the invention of printing, the spelling of words became relatively fixed. The present English spelling system is very much like that used in Shakespeare's time, although pronunciation has changed considerably. Pronunciation changes much more rapidly than spelling. What would we do with all the millions of books printed in English if we attempted to change all the spelling to conform to present pronunciation? Even if these books were reprinted and a law passed requiring all new books to conform to some new system of spelling, it would not be too long before the same problem would occur again.

To illustrate how spelling represents an older pronunciation, consider the words *knight* and *night*. They are pronounced identically today. At one time, the *k* was pronounced in the first word and the *gh* in both. At some point in the history of the English language we stopped pronouncing a *k* when it occurred at the beginning of a word and was followed by *n*. As for the sound spelled *gh* in words like *right*, it was once pronounced like the last sound in the German word *Bach*. This sound disappeared completely in many dialects of English, including most American English dialects.

If the spelling reformers could legislate an end to language change, then maybe their plan would be feasible. But this is impossible. Language is continually changing, and this change, apart from making spelling systems obsolete, also creates different dialects of the same language. An additional problem for the reformers is to determine which dialect the spelling should reflect. Should the same word of British and American English be spelled differently if pronounced differently? If not, how should a word like *schedule* be spelled? The British pronounce it as if it were spelled *shedyule* and the Americans pronounce it as if it were spelled *skedjule* or *skejual*. Such pronunciations lend some credence to Shaw's remark: "England and America are two countries separated by the same language." Even if the spelling reformers decided to spell British and American English differently, what would they do with the American dialects? Should *Cuba* be spelled *Cuber* with a final *r*, as Bostonians pronounce it, or without the *r*? What about the words *cot* and *caught* or *horse* and *hoarse* or *pin* and *pen*? Some Americans pronounce these pairs identically, and others pronounce them differently.

There are further arguments against the spelling reformers, some of which will be discussed in later chapters. In any case, although English spelling does create some difficulties for children learning to read and write (as well as for many adult "poor spellers"), the system is not quite as chaotic as it appears to be.

But whether or not one wishes to take sides for or against spelling reform in English, it is clear that to describe the sounds of English, or any other language, one cannot depend on the spelling of words. In 1888 the International Phonetic Association (IPA) developed a phonetic alphabet that could be used to symbolize the sounds found in all languages. Since many languages use a Roman alphabet like that used in the English writing system, the IPA phonetic symbols are based on the Roman letters. These phonetic symbols have a consistent value, unlike ordinary letters, which may or may not represent the same sounds in the same or different languages.

It is of course impossible to construct any set of symbols that will specify all the minute differences between sounds. Even Shaw recognized this when in his will he directed his Trustee

to bear in mind that the proposed British Alphabet does not pretend to be exhaustive as it contains only sixteen vowels whereas by infinitesimal movements of the tongue countless different vowels can be produced all of them in use among speakers of English who utter the same vowels no oftener than they make the same fingerprints.

Even if we could specify all the details of different pronunciations, we would not want to. A basic fact about speech is that no two utterances are ever physically the same. That is, if a speaker says "Good morning" on Monday and Tuesday there will be some slight differences in the sounds he produces on the two days. In fact if he says "Good morning" twice in succession on the same day, the two utterances will not be physically identical. If another speaker says "Good morning" the physical sounds (that is, the acoustic signal) produced will differ widely from that produced by the first speaker. Yet all the "Good mornings" are considered to be repetitions of the same utterance.

This is an interesting fact about language. Some differences in the sounds of an utterance are important, and other differences can be ignored. Even though we never produce or hear exactly the same utterance twice, speakers know when two utterances are the same or different. Some properties of the sounds must be more important linguistically than others.

A phonetic alphabet should include enough symbols to represent the "crucial" differences. At the same time it should not, and cannot, include all noncrucial differences, since such differences are infinitely varied.

A list of phonetic symbols which can be used to represent all the basic speech sounds of English is given on pages 56–57. The symbols omit many details about the sounds and how they are produced in different words, and in different places in words. These symbols are meant to be used by persons knowing English.

To differentiate between the spelling of a word and the pronunciation we will sometimes enclose the phonetic symbols in brackets [ ]. Thus the word spelled *boat* would be **transcribed phonetically** as [bot].

The list of phonetic symbols for consonants, vowels, and diphthongs includes a number of examples of English words given in English spelling. In all cases the different spellings represent the same sound in the American dialect being described. Some of these pronunciations may differ from yours, and in a number of cases where this is so the examples may be confusing. For example, some speakers of American English pronounce the words *cot* and *caught* identically. In the dialect described here, *cot* and *caught* are pronounced differently, so *cot* is given as an example for the symbol [a] and *caught* for the symbol [ɔ]. Many speakers who pronounce *cot* and *caught* identically pronounce *car* and *core* differently. If you use the vowel of *car* to say *cot* and the vowel of *core* to say *caught* you will be approximating the dialect that distinguishes the two words. There are a number of English dialects in which an *r* sound is not pronounced unless it occurs before a vowel. Speakers of this dialect would pronounce the word *bird* with a vowel not symbolized in the chart; that is [ɜ]. The phonetic transcription of *bird* for these speakers would thus be [bɜd]. The selection of the dialect described below is rather arbitrary; it is in fact a mixture of a number of dialects in the attempt to provide at least the major symbols that can be used to describe dialects of American English.

In the chart the first symbols given are those most widely used by American linguists and phoneticians; where these symbols differ from those of the International Phonetic Alphabet (IPA), the IPA symbols are given in parentheses. Although we believe that all phoneticians should adopt the IPA symbols, we will use the American symbols in this book because so many students will encounter these symbols in other American publications.

Consonants

Symbol	Examples
p	s*p*it s*p*ot s*p*eak ti*p* a*pp*le am*p*le hiccou*gh*
p^h	*p*it *p*ot *p*eak *p*rick *p*laque a*pp*ear
b	*b*at ta*b* am*b*le *b*rick *b*lack *b*u*bb*le *b*ur*b*le
m	*m*at ta*m* a*m*ble s*m*ack a*m*nesia E*mm*y ca*m*p co*mb*
t	s*t*ick s*t*uff pi*t* po*t* kiss*ed* kick*ed* stuff*ed* wri*t*e
t^h	*t*ick *t*ough *t*op in*t*end *p*terodactyl a*tt*ack
d	*d*ip ca*d* *d*rip guar*d* sen*d*ing men*d* love*d* cur*ed* ri*d*e
D (ɾ)	wri*t*er ri*d*er la*tt*er la*dd*er
n	*n*ap ca*n* s*n*ow k*n*ow m*n*emonic a*n*y desig*n* *g*nostic *p*neumatic
k	s*k*in sti*ck* criti*que* o*ch*er e*x*ceed as*k*ing criti*c*
k^h	*k*in *c*at *ch*arisma *c*ritique *c*ritic me*ch*anic *c*lose
g	*g*irl *g*uard bur*g* *g*ab ba*g* o*g*re a*g*nostic lon*g*er Pitts-bur*gh*
ŋ	si*ng* lo*ng* thi*nk* fi*ng*er si*ng*er a*n*kle
f	*f*at *f*ish philoso*ph*y *f*racture *f*lat *ph*logiston co*ff*ee ree*f* cou*gh* com*f*ort
v	*v*at *v*eal do*v*e gra*v*el ri*v*al an*v*il ra*v*age *v*alue
s	*s*ap *s*kip *s*nip *ps*ychology pa*ss* pat*s* pack*s* democra*cy* *sc*issors fa*s*ten de*c*eive de*sc*ent *s*clerosis *ps*eudo pea*ce*
z	*z*ip jaz*z* ra*z*or pad*s* kisse*s* *X*erox *x*ylophone de*s*ign la*z*y *s*cissors mai*z*e lie*s* phy*s*ics pea*s* magne*s*ium
θ	*th*igh *th*rough wra*th* *th*istle e*th*er wrea*th* *th*ink mo*th* ari*th*metic Me*th*uselah tee*th* Ma*tth*ew
ð	*th*e *th*eir *th*en wrea*the* la*the* mo*th*er ei*th*er ra*th*er tee*the*
š (ʃ)	*sh*oe *sh*y mu*sh* mar*sh* mi*ss*ion na*t*ion fi*sh* gla*c*ial *s*ure deduc*t*ion Ru*ss*ian logi*c*ian
ž (ʒ)	mea*s*ure vi*s*ion a*z*ure rou*g*e (for those who do not pronounce this word with the same ending sound as in ju*dg*e) ca*s*ualty deci*s*ion Carte*s*ian
č, tš (tʃ)	*ch*oke *ch*urch ma*tch* fea*t*ure ri*ch* lun*ch* righ*te*ous consti*t*uent
ǰ, dž (dʒ)	ju*dg*e mi*dg*et *G*eorge ma*g*istrate *j*ello *g*elatine re*g*ion re*s*idual
l	*l*eaf fee*l* *l*ock cal*l* pa*l*ace sing*le* mi*l*d p*l*ant pu*l*p app*l*aud

r	reef fear rock car Paris singer prune carp furl cruel
y (j)[5]	you yes bay playing feud use
w	witch swim mowing queen
ʍ	which where what whale (for those dialects that do not pronounce witch and which the same)
h	who hat rehash hole whole
ʔ	bottle button glottal (only for the dialect whose speakers substitute for the tt sound the sound which occurs between the vowels as in uh-uh)

Vowels

Symbols	Examples
i	beet beat we see sea receive key believe amoeba people Caesar vaseline serene fiend money lily
ɪ (ι)	bit consist injury malignant bin been
e	bate bait ray profane great eight gauge rain reign they
ε	bet serenity reception says guest dead said
æ	pan act laugh anger laboratory (American English) comrade rally
u	boot who sewer duty through poor to too two move Lou
U	put foot butcher could
ʌ	but tough among oven does cover flood bird herd word fur
o	boat go beau grow though toe own over melodious
ɔ	bought caught wrong stalk core saw ball author awe
a	pot father palm car sergeant honor hospital melodic
ə	sofa alone principal science telegraph symphony roses difficult suppose melody melodious wanted kisses the father America

Diphthongs

Symbols	Examples
ay	bite sight by die dye Stein aisle choir liar island height sign
aw, æw	about brown doubt coward
ɔy	boy doily

The symbol ə is called a schwa. It will be used in this book only to represent unstressed vowels, such as those in the examples after it on the chart. It is very similar phonetically to the wedge symbol ʌ, which will be used only in stressed syllables. There is great variation in the way different speakers of English pronounce vowels. We apologize if the symbols used and the words that illustrate them deviate from your dialect.

[5] American linguists use [y] for the glide; in IPA it is used for the high front rounded vowel that occurs in the French tu.

Using these symbols, we can now unambiguously represent the pronunciations of words. For example, words spelled with *ou* may have different pronunciations. To distinguish between the symbols representing sounds and the alphabet letters, we put the phonetic symbols between brackets, as discussed above and as is illustrated by the following:

SPELLING	PRONUNCIATION
though	[ðo]
thought	[θɔt]
rough	[rʌf]
bough	[baw]
through	[θru]
would	[wʊd]

Notice that only in *rough* do the letters *gh* represent any sound; that is, the sound [f]. Notice also that *ou* represents six different sounds, and *th* two different sounds. The *l* in *would*, like the *gh* in all but one of the words above, is not pronounced at all.

Obviously the symbols given in the list are not sufficient to represent the pronunciation of words in all languages. We would need other symbols for the voiceless velar fricative in the German word *Bach* (which is symbolized phonetically as [x]) or for the French uvular trill, [R], or for the French rounded high front vowel in *tu* "you" (singular), which can be symbolized as [y] or [ü]. We mentioned above that the American use of [y] as the symbol for the palatal glide instead of [j] can create difficulties if we wish to represent the sounds of other languages. The French rounded vowels can be symbolized as follows:

[y] [ü] as in *tu* [ty] [tü] "you" (singular)	The tongue position is as for [i], but the lips are rounded
[ø] as in *bleu* [blø] "blue"	The tongue position is as in [e], but the lips are rounded
[œ] as in *heure* [œ] "hour"	The tongue position is as in [ɛ], but the lips are rounded

We noted above that vowels may be oral or nasal. To designate nasality the **diacritic** mark [˜] is placed over the vowel, as in the English words:

bomb [bãm] *boon* [būn] *bean* [bĩn]

The French nasalized vowels that may occur when there is no nasal consonant adjacent may also be symbolized in this way. Note that in the French spelling system an *n* (which is silent in the words below) is included to indicate that the preceding vowel is nasalized.

[ɛ̃] as in *vin* [vɛ̃] "wine"
[ã] as in *an* [ã] "year"
[õ] as in *son* [sõ] "sound"
[œ̃] as in *brun* [brœ̃] "brown"

Other diacritics help distinguish long from short phonetic segments. A long segment may be indicated by a [:] placed after a symbol or by doubling the symbol. Long vowels or consonants are sometimes called **geminates.** In

Italian, for example, both long or geminate and short consonants occur: [papa] means "Pope" and [pap:a] or [pappa] means "porridge." In Korean, [kul] means "oyster" and [ku:l] or [kuul] means "tunnel." To differentiate a voiceless lateral liquid like the *ll* in the Welsh name *Lloyd* the symbol [̥] is placed under the segment; thus *Lloyd* in Welsh would be phonetically transcribed as [l̥ɔyd], whereas in English it would be [lɔyd].

Phonetic Features

Now that we have a phonetic alphabet—a set of symbols which can be used to differentiate all the phonetic sound segments in a one symbol-one sound fashion—we can classify the nonvowel sounds of American English in an articulatory fashion as shown in Table 2-5.

Table 2-5   Classification of Nonvowel Sounds

If there are more than one symbol in the cell, the rightmost is voiced, the others are voiceless. The nasals, liquids, and [y] are voiced; [h] is voiceless.

	Bilabial	Labiodental	Interdental	Alveolar	Postalveolar Palatal/ Alveopalatal	Velar	Labiovelar	Glottal
Nasal Stop	m			n		ŋ		
Oral Stop	p pʰ b			t tʰ d		k kʰ g		ʔ
Fricative		f v	θ ð	s z	š ž			
Glide					y		ʍ w	h
Liquid				l r				
Affricate					č ǰ			

Table 2-5 is a helpful chart in that it classifies the sounds. These are classes that will be discussed further in Chapter 3, where it will be shown how these groups of sounds pattern in languages and are used in the phonological rules of languages.

We can also use the plus (+) and minus (−) system of classification, in which case it is not necessary to include both the features "voiced" and "voiceless" or "oral" and "nasal" since any segment that is marked [−nasal] must be [+oral], and any segment that is marked [−voiced] must be [+voiceless]. Other features can be used to group these consonants into larger, more inclusive classes needed in phonological rules. For example, the labial and alveolar sounds are all articulated at the front of the mouth, while the palatal, velar, and glottal sounds are produced at the back. One can thus use the feature "back" or "front" to divide these sounds into two classes. The features [+anterior] for "front" sounds, and [−anterior] for "back" sounds are generally used by linguists. Similarly, the alveolar, postalveolar, or palatal sounds are all produced by raising the blade of the tongue. These sounds are designated as **coronal**. Velars and labials would thus be [−coronal] while palatals and alveolars would be [+coronal].

Table 2-6 Phonetic Feature Specifications of American English Consonants

Phonetic Features	p	pʰ	b	m	t	tʰ	d	n	k	kʰ	g	ŋ	f	v	θ
Sonorant	−	−	−	+	−	−	−	+	−	−	−	+	−	−	−
Consonantal	+	+	+	+	+	+	+	+	+	+	+	+	+	+	+
Continuant	−	−	−	−	−	−	−	−	−	−	−	−	+	+	+
Voiced	−	−	+	+	−	−	+	+	−	−	+	+	−	+	−
Aspirated	−	+	−	−	−	+	−	−	−	+	−	−	−	−	−
Nasal	−	−	−	+	−	−	−	+	−	−	−	+	−	−	−
Anterior	+	+	+	+	+	+	+	+	−	−	−	−	+	+	+
Coronal	−	−	−	−	+	+	+	+	−	−	−	−	−	−	+

Phonetic Features	ð	s	z	š	ž	č	ǰ	l	r	y	ʍ	w	h	ʔ
Sonorant	−	−	−	−	−	−	−	+	+	+	+	+	−	−
Consonantal	+	+	+	+	+	+	+	+	+	−	−	−	−	−
Continuant	+	+	+	+	+	−	−	+	+	+	+	+	+	
Voiced	+	−	+	−	+	−	+	+	+	+	−	+	−	−
Aspirated	−	−	−	−	−	−	−	−	−	−	−	−	−	−
Nasal	−	−	−	−	−	−	−	−	−	−	−	−	−	−
Anterior	+	+	+	−	−	−	−	+	+	+	−	−	−	−
Coronal	−	+	+	+	+	+	+	+	+	+	−	−	−	−

Using a feature specification of this kind, all the sounds can be grouped into all the classes of which they are members. In Table 2-6 all sounds marked + for a certain feature belong in one class (for example, [+ continuant]s) and all those marked − for a feature belong in another class (for example, [−continuant]s, which includes stops and affricates). It is not necessary to include some of the features we used to describe the sounds in the earlier sections. In English, for example, the feature "liquid" is unnecessary since [l] and [r], the only liquids, are already distinguished as being the only sounds which are both [+ sonorant] and [+consonantal].

Vowels can also be classified by the use of pluses and minuses. Again we see that it is not necessary to include all the features that were used in the previous description of the vowels, since [−back] vowels are equivalent to "front" vowels and mid vowels can be specified as being both [− high] and [−low]. All of this and more is presented in Table 2-7.

We will refer to these classes of sounds in Chapter 3.

Table 2-7 Phonetic Feature Specifications of Stressed American English Vowels

Phonetic Features	Phonetic Segments										
	i	ɪ	e	ɛ	æ	ʌ	u	ʊ	o	ɔ	a
High	+	+	−	−	−	−	+	+	−	−	−
Low	−	−	−	−	+	+	−	−	−	−	+
Back	−	−	−	−	−	+	+	+	+	+	+
Round	−	−	−	−	−	−	+	+	+	+	−
Tense	+	−	+	−	−	−	+	−	+	−	+

Acoustic Phonetics: The Physical Properties of Speech Sounds

Throughout this chapter we have been describing speech sounds according to the ways in which they are produced. We have been describing their articulatory features, or properties—the position of the tongue, the lips, the velum, the state of the vocal cords, the airstream mechanisms, whether the articulators obstruct the free flow of air, and so on. All of these articulatory characteristics are reflected in the physical characteristics of the sounds produced.

Speech sounds can also be described in physical or **acoustic** terms. Physically, a sound is produced whenever there is a disturbance in the position of air molecules. The question asked by ancient philosophers as to whether a sound is produced if a tree falls in the middle of the forest with no one there to "hear" it has been answered by the science of acoustics. Objectively, a sound is produced; subjectively, there is no sound. In fact, there are sounds we can't hear because our ears are not sensitive to all changes in air pressure (which result from the movement of air molecules). Acoustic phonetics is concerned only with speech sounds, all of which can be heard by the human ear.

When we push air out of the lungs, small pulses of air are pushed through the vibrating glottis, and these in turn push the mouth air. This creates small variations in the air pressure, due to the wavelike motion of the air molecules.

The sounds we produce can be described in terms of how fast the variations of the air pressure occur. This determines the **fundamental frequency** of the sounds, which for the hearer determines the **pitch.** We can also describe the extent of the variations; the larger the size of the variations in air pressure, the greater the **intensity,** which determines the **loudness** of the sound. The particular **quality** of the sound is determined by the shape of the vibrations, or wave; this in turn is determined by the shape of the vocal tract when the air is flowing through it.

An important tool in acoustic research was provided by the invention of a machine called a **sound spectrograph.** When you speak into a microphone connected to this machine (or when a tape recording is plugged in), a "picture" is made of the speech signal. The patterns produced are called **spectrograms** or, more vividly, "visible speech." In the last few years these pictures have been referred to as **voiceprints.** A spectrogram of the words *heed, head, had,* and *who'd* is shown in Figure 2-5. Time in milliseconds moves horizontally from left to right; vertically, the "graph" represents pitch (or, more technically, frequency). Notice that for each vowel there are a number of very dark bands which differ in their placement according to their pitch. These represent the **overtones** produced by the shape of the vocal tract and are called the **formants** of the vowels. Because the tongue is in a different position for each vowel, the formant frequencies, or overtone pitches, differ for each vowel. It is the different frequencies of these formants that account for the different vowel qualities you hear. The pitch of the entire utterance (intonation contour) is shown by the "voicing bar" marked *P* on the spectrogram. When the striations are far apart the vocal cords are vibrating slowly and the pitch is low; when the striations are close together the vocal cords are vibrating rapidly and the pitch is high.

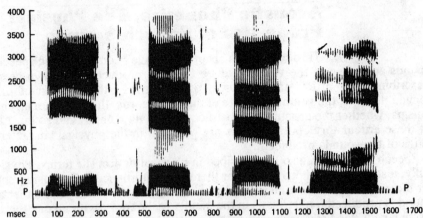

Figure 2-5 A spectrogram of the words *heed, head, had,* and *who'd,* as spoken in a British accent (speaker: Peter Ladefoged, February 16, 1973).

By studying spectrograms of all speech sounds and many different utterances, acoustic phoneticians have learned a great deal about the basic components that are used to synthesize speech.

A new interest in voiceprints has arisen. Spectrograms are being used in law courts as "evidence" to identify speakers. Spectrograms have been made from taped phone conversations, for example, and compared with spectrograms of the speech of individuals accused of making these phone calls. The claim that voiceprints are as conclusive as fingerprints has been challenged. A person cannot change his fingerprints, but a speaker may pronounce a word or a sentence very differently on two occasions, and, in addition, his speech may be very similar to another speaker's. Because of such factors the opinion on the reliability of voiceprint identification is far from unanimous. In fact, a large section of the scientific community involved in speech research is concerned that popular opinion will accept voiceprints as infallible (influenced by Dick Tracy comic strips and various TV "who-done-it" programs). In March 1976 a meeting of the Speech Communication Committee of the Acoustical Society of America unanimously passed the following resolution: "The Technical Committee on Speech Communication is concerned that 'voiceprints' have been admitted as legal evidence on the basis of claims which have not yet been evaluated scientifically."

There have been attempts to make more definite judgments on the reliability of voiceprint identification, but scientific opinion remains divided, with the majority opinion still skeptical. Further research, improvement of methods, and more careful training of the "analysts" may in time make spectrograms a valuable aid in legal cases.

Talking Machines

Machines which, with more or less success, imitate human speech, are the most difficult to construct, so many are the agencies engaged in uttering even a single word—so many are the inflections and variations of tone and articulation, that the mechanician finds his ingenuity taxed to the utmost to imitate them.

Scientific American (January 14, 1871)

In 1950, the English mathematician Alan M. Turing published a paper entitled "Computing Machinery and Intelligence." Turing began his paper: "I propose to consider the question, 'Can machines think?'" To answer this question one must decide the criteria to be considered. Turing decided that a machine can think if it can pass itself off as a human being to a real human being, not counting physical characteristics such as appearance, voice, mobility, and so on. Turing assumed that his thinking machine would understand and produce language.

The difficulties in automatic speech recognition and production are immense. Yet there are hundreds of computer scientists, engineers, phoneticians, linguists, psychologists, and philosophers who are now working in this research area.

Early efforts toward building "talking machines" were more concerned with machines that could produce sounds that imitated human speech than with machines that could "think" of what to say. In 1779, Christian Gottlieb Kratzenstein won a prize for building such a machine ("an instrument constructed like the *vox humana* pipes of an organ which . . . accurately express the sounds of the vowels") and for answering a question posed by the Imperial Academy of St. Petersburg: "What is the nature and character of the sounds of the vowels *a*, *e*, *i*, *o*, *u* [which make them] different from one another?" Kratzenstein constructed a set of "acoustic resonators" similar to the shapes of the mouth when these vowels are articulated and set them resonating by a vibrating reed that produced puffs of air similar to those coming from the lungs through the vibrating vocal cords.

Twelve years later, Wolfgang von Kempelen of Vienna constructed a more elaborate machine with bellows to produce a stream of air, such as is produced by the lungs, and with other mechanical devices to "simulate" the different parts of the vocal tract. Von Kempelen's machine so impressed the young Alexander Graham Bell, who saw a replica of the machine in Edinburgh in 1850, that he, together with his brother Melville, attempted to construct a "talking head," making a cast from a human skull. They used various materials to form the velum, palate, teeth, lips, tongue, and so on, and constructed cheeks out of rubber and a metal larynx. The vocal cords were made by stretching a slotted piece of rubber over a structure. They used a keyboard control system to manipulate all the parts with an intricate set of levers. This ingenious machine produced vowel sounds and some nasal sounds and even a few short combinations of sounds.

With the advances in the acoustic theory of speech production and the technological developments in electronics, machine production of speech sounds has made great progress. We no longer have to build actual physical models of the speech-producing mechanism; we can now imitate the process by producing the physical signals electronically.

Research on speech has shown that all speech sounds can be reduced to a small number of acoustic components. One way to produce artificial or **synthetic** speech is to mix these important parts together in the proper proportions depending on the speech sounds one wishes to imitate. It is rather like following a recipe for making soup, which might read: "Take two quarts of water, add one onion, three carrots, a potato, a teaspoon of salt, a pinch of pepper, and stir it all together."

This method of producing synthetic speech would include a recipe which might read: "Start with a buzzing noise corresponding to the puffs of air like those coming through the vibrating vocal cords, add different ingredients that correspond to the different vowel qualities or formants (these being the 'overtones' resulting from the different vocal tract shapes), add the 'hissing' noise produced when fricatives occur, add nasal 'resonances' for any nasal sounds, cut off the 'buzz' to produce 'stops,''' and so on. This is highly oversimplified but a more exact description would require technical knowledge of acoustic phonetics.

Although the acoustic theory of speech production is very advanced, some of the speech that is synthesized still has a "machine quality," though it is highly intelligible despite this, and in a few cases hard to distinguish from human speech. A "talking" machine, however, only "talks" when we tell it *what* to say and *how* to say it and so is only imitating human speech on a phonetic level. This does, nevertheless, require a high level of knowledge about the important acoustic cues to which listeners pay attention in their "decoding" of spoken speech.

MACHINES FOR UNDERSTANDING SPEECH

Much of the research aimed at achieving automatic speech recognition depends on our understanding of the acoustics of speech. To produce machines that can comprehend speech (or to program a computer to "understand" spoken language) is much more difficult than to produce machines that can synthesize speech. By now you should have some idea of why it is so difficult. It is even difficult for humans to "read" a spectrogram if they don't know the language, the speaker, and even what was said. Language is filled with redundancies that enable a human to "decode" a very noisy or distorted utterance. We can understand what is said to us because of our linguistic knowledge. The difficulty of programing a computer to have and to use linguistic knowledge in comprehending speech is enormous.

The speech signal is not physically divided into discrete sounds. Our ability to "segment" the signal arises from our knowledge of the grammar, knowing what to consider important, what to ignore, how to pair certain sounds with certain meanings, what sounds or words may be "deleted" or "pushed together," when two different speech signals are linguistically "the same" and when two similar signals are linguistically "different." The difficulty may be illustrated by recalling how hard it is for a nonspeaker of French even to divide an incoming French speech signal into separate words, let alone separate phonemic segments.

Yet, despite these problems, research on both automatic speech recognition and speech synthesis proceeds for practical and for "pure research" motives. We use synthetic speech in many "controlled" perception experiments to find out what features of the speech signal are important for perception. This knowledge then helps us to write "recognition" programs. A machine can only be programed to do what we tell it and can only "know" what we know. Thus we are pushed to learn more, to fill in all gaps in our knowledge of the communication process. As we gain more knowledge, recognition programs will be improved.

As of this writing (late 1982) there are a number of systems that can recognize words spoken in "isolation," with nearly 100 percent accuracy under ideal conditions, but with vocabularies limited to about one hundred words. Most of these systems can only respond to speakers who "register" their voices in advance with the computer by pronouncing, often repeatedly, each word in the vocabulary.

Several companies are marketing automatic speech-recognition systems that recognize sequences of words provided that the speaker puts pauses of about one-tenth of a second between each word. These systems have nearly 100 percent accuracy under ideal conditions of low noise and perfect speaker performance.

Recognition of continuous speech—that is, speech with no pauses between words—has also been accomplished. For good performance, the speaker must pause every third or fourth word. As the number of words spoken continuously without pause increases beyond four, system accuracy decreases rapidly.

Most automatic speech-recognition systems operate by "remembering" key features of the speech signal at the time the speaker registers the vocabulary. The system then attempts to match those features later when called upon to recognize an actual utterance. As the vocabulary grows this method becomes slower because there are more patterns to compare and less reliable because there are more chances for a mismatch. The problem of recognizing continuous speech is immense, since two words spoken in isolation have different acoustical properties than the same two words spoken together (for example, "did you" [dɪdyu] may sound like "dija" [dɪǰə] spoken in continuous sequence).

The difficulties encountered in trying to develop systems of speech recognition are a dramatic indication of how complex and vast the human capacity for language must be.

SUMMARY

The science of speech sounds is called **phonetics.** It aims to provide the set of **features,** or properties, that can describe all the sounds used in human language.

When we speak, the physical sounds we produce are continuous stretches of sound, which are the physical representations of strings of **discrete linguistic segments.**

All human speech sounds fall into classes according to their phonetic properties or features; that is, according to how they are produced. Sounds may be either **voiced** or **voiceless; oral** or **nasal; labial, alveolar, palatal, velar, uvular,** or **glottal.** They may also be **fricatives** or **stops** and either **consonants, vowels, glides,** or **liquids.** In addition, vowels are distinguished according to the position of the tongue and lips: **high, mid,** or **low** tongue; **front** or **back** tongue; **rounded** or **unrounded** lips. There are general and regular processes (rules) in languages that utilize these classes of sounds.

To describe these speech sounds we cannot depend on the way words are spelled. Conventional spellings represent only partially the pronunciation of words. For this reason, a **phonetic alphabet** is used, in which each phonetic symbol stands for one and only one sound. The phonetic symbols that can be used to represent the sounds of English are presented in this chapter.

In addition to phonetic symbols, each phonetic segment may be specified by a binary system of classification listing all its phonetic features. Thus, a sound marked + for a certain feature (for example, [+ voiced]) belongs to the class containing all voiced segments; a sound marked [− voiced] belongs to the class of voiceless segments.

Diacritics to specify such properties as nasalization, length, or voicelessness may also be combined with the phonetic symbols for more detailed phonetic transcription.

By means of these phonetic features one can describe all speech sounds.

Speech sounds may be described by their physical properties. The study of the physical characteristics of speech sounds is called **acoustic phonetics.** Some of the major physical, or acoustic, features are **fundamental frequency** (or **pitch**), **intensity** (or **loudness**), and **formants** (overtone pitches for vowels).

As a step toward Turing's goal of constructing a "thinking machine," linguists and engineers are attempting to "teach" computers to speak and to understand spoken language. Attempts to produce **synthetic speech** by mechanical means go back at least 200 years. The advances in electronic technology and in the understanding of the acoustics of speech production have brought us close to our goal of synthesizing speech sounds. Our knowledge of the important acoustic properties of speech was aided greatly by the development of an instrument called a **sound spectrograph,** which produces a visual display of the physical acoustic signal called a **spectrogram.** Acoustic analysis of speech sounds can also be performed by computers.

Automatic **speech recognition** (or "understanding") is a much more difficult task. Humans use their linguistic knowledge to comprehend a spoken message. The physical signal alone is not enough to account for our ability to understand speech. At present, no machine can be programed to contain even a fraction of the knowledge that every speaker has about his or her language. There is, however, serious ongoing research in this field, which should also help to contribute to our understanding of speech production and perception.

EXERCISES

1. A. Write the phonetic symbol for the *first* sound in each of the following words, according to the way you pronounce it. Example: *ooze* [u], *psycho* [s].

   a. though
   b. easy
   c. contact
   d. pneumonia
   e. thought
   f. judge
   g. Thomas
   h. physics
   i. civic
   j. usury

   B. Write the phonetic symbol for the *last* sound in each of the following:

   a. fleece
   b. neigh
   c. long
   d. health
   e. watch
   f. cow
   g. rough
   h. cheese
   i. bleached
   j. rags

   C. Write the phonetic symbol for the vowel sound in each of the following:

   a. coat
   b. steel
   c. play
   d. fight
   e. cool
   f. hot
   g. cut
   h. put
   i. pat
   j. tease

2. Below is a phonetic transcription of one of the verses in the poem *The Walrus and the Carpenter* by Lewis Carroll. The speaker who transcribed it may not have exactly the same pronunciation as you; there are many alternate correct versions. But there is *one* major error in each line that is an impossible pronunciation for any American speaker. Write the word in which the error occurs; give the correct phonetic transcription of the word. There may be an extra symbol, or a symbol missing, or a wrong symbol in the word.

a. ðə tʰãym hæz cʌ̃m

b. ðə wɔlrʌs sed

c. tʰu tʰɔlk əv mẽni θĩŋz

d. əv šuz ãnd šɪps

e. ænd silĩŋ wæx

f. əv kʰæbəgəz ænd kʰĩŋz

g. ænd way ðə si ɪs bɔylĩŋ hat

h. ænd wɛθər pʰɪgz hæv wĩŋz.

3. Write the symbol that corresponds to each of the following phonetic descriptions; then give an English word that contains this sound. Example: voiced alveolar stop—[d], *d*og.

a. voiced bilabial stop
b. low front vowel
c. lateral liquid
d. lax high back rounded vowel
e. velar nasal consonant
f. voiceless alveolar fricative
g. voiced affricate
h. palatal glide
i. tense front mid vowel
j. voiced interdental fricative
k. voiceless labiodental fricative

4. Each of the following consists of members of a class of sounds all sharing one or more common properties plus one sound that is not a member of that class. For example [p] [pʰ] [b] [m] [k] is the class of bilabial consonants except for [k], which does not belong to that class. Identify the sound that does not belong to the class and name the feature or features that define the class.

a. [g], [p], [b], [d]
b. [f], [p], [m], [θ], [v], [b]
c. [æ], [u], [i], [e], [ɛ], [a]
d. [z], [v], [s], [ž], [g]

e. [t], [z], [d], [n], [f], [s], [š], [ž]
f. [m], [n], [b], [ŋ]
g. [g], [k], [b], [d], [p], [v], [t]
h. [a], [u], [e], [w], [i], [o]

5. In each of the following pairs of words the italicized sounds differ by one or more phonetic properties (features). State the differences and, in addition, state what properties they have in common. Example: ph*o*ne—ph*o*nic. The *o* in *phone* is mid, tense, round. The *o* in *phonic* is low, unround. Both are back vowels.

a. ba*th*—ba*th*e
b. redu*c*e—redu*c*tion
c. *c*ool—*c*old
d. wi*f*e—wi*v*es
e. fa*c*e—fa*c*ial

f. h*ea*l—h*ea*lth
g. cat*s*—dog*s*
h. *im*polite—*in*decent
i. democra*t*—democra*c*y
j. m*ou*se—mice

6. A phonetic symbol is actually a "cover term" for a composite of distinct phonetic properties or features. Define each of the symbols below by marking a + or a − for each given feature depending on whether the property is present or absent.

A.	m	l	θ	z	ǰ	t	v	pʰ
Sonorant								
Consonantal								
Continuant								
Voiced								
Aspirated								
Nasal								
Anterior								
Coronal								

B.	a	o	ɪ	u	i	ʌ	æ	ɛ
High								
Low								
Back								
Tense								
Round								

7. Write the following in regular English spelling:
   a. nõm čãmski ɪz ə lĩŋgwɪst hu tʰičəz æt ēm ay tʰi
   b. fõnɛtɪks ɪz ðə stʌdi ʌv spič sãw̃ndz
   c. ɔl læ̃ŋgwɪǰəz yuz sãw̃ndz pʰrodust bay ðə ʌpər rɛspərətɔri sɪstəm
   d. ĩn wʌ̃n dayələkt kʰat ðə nãw̃n ænd kʰɔt ðə vʌrb ar pʰrõnãw̃nst ðə sēm
   e. sʌ̃m pʰipəl θĩŋk fõnɛtɪks ɪz vɛri ĩntərɛstĩŋ

8. Which of the following are *not* English words:

   a. [θrot]   b. [skrič]   c. [blaft]   d. [know]
   e. [pʰrɪl]   f. [bæč]   g. [fruit]   h. [may]
   i. [flit]   j. [flat]   k. [gnostɪk]   l. [yūnəkʰɔrn]

   Which do you think could become English words (be added to the vocabulary) and which could not. State your reasons.
   For the words above that you believe to be in the English language, spell them according to our regular spelling system.

9. Can you think of any practical uses for automatic speech recognition and synthesis? For example, one possible use would be in the postal service. Imagine a machine that would sort packages for individual states by being given verbal instructions. The mail clerk could put a package on a conveyer belt and say "10028," "94619," and so on, and the computer would automatically route the package to the correct bin. A prototype of such a system is actually in service. Think up as many such uses as you can. (*Hint:* Consider libraries, business offices, aircraft cockpits, and so on.)

10. The use of "voiceprints" for speaker identification is based on the fact that no two speakers ever talk *exactly* alike. List some of the differences you have noticed in the speech of different individuals. Can you think of any possible reasons why such differences exist?

11. Match the sounds under column A with *one or more features* from column B.

A.	B.
a. [ð]	1. [+ voiced]
b. [ũ]	2. [− anterior]
c. [t]	3. [+ nasal]
d. [z]	4. [+ back]
e. [ŋ]	5. [+ sonorant]
f. [ʍ]	6. [+ coronal]
g. [b]	7. [− continuant]
h. [v]	8. [+ continuant]
i. [θ]	

REFERENCES

Abercrombie, David. 1967. *Elements of General Phonetics*. Aldine. Chicago.

Chomsky, N., and M. Halle. 1968. *The Sound Pattern of English*, ch. 8. Harper & Row. New York.

Denes, P. B., and E. N. Pinson. 1973. *The Speech Chain*. Anchor Books. New York.

Flanagan, J. L. "The Synthesis of Speech," *Scientific American*, vol. 226, no. 2 (Feb. 1972), pp. 48–58.

International Phonetic Association. 1949. *Principles of the International Phonetic Association*, rev. ed. IPA. London.

Jakobson, R., and M. Halle. 1956. "Fundamentals of Language," *Janua Linguarum* 1. Mouton. The Hague.

Jones, Daniel. 1956. *An Outline of English Phonetics*, 8th ed. Heffer, Cambridge, England.

Ladefoged, Peter. 1981. *Elements of Acoustic Phonetics*, 2nd ed. University of Chicago Press. Chicago.

Ladefoged, Peter. 1975. *A Course in Phonetics*. Harcourt Brace Jovanovich. New York.

Chapter 3

Phonology: The Sound Patterns of Language

Phonology is the study of telephone etiquette.

A high school student[1]

I believe that phonology is superior to music. It is more variable and its pecuniary possibilities are far greater.

Erik Satie (from the cover of a record album)

Phonology is not the study of telephone etiquette nor is it the study of telephones. Rather, phonology is the study of the sound patterns found in human language; it is also the term used to refer to the kind of knowledge that speakers have about the sound patterns of their particular language. Because everyone who knows a language knows (unconsciously of course) its phonology, it may indeed be superior to music, as there are many people who neither know nor care about music. But, unlike Satie, we see no reason to compare the two in value. And we would certainly not encourage anyone to become a phonologist for the reasons given by Satie. We are not sure what "pecuniary possibilities" he had in mind (not knowing any rich phonologists), and the sound systems of the world's languages are less varied than they are similar. It is true that speech sounds as physical entities may be infinitely varied, but when they function as elements in a language, as phonological units, they are highly constrained. This is, in fact, one of the reasons why the study of the sound systems of language is a fascinating one, for it reveals how human linguistic ability enables one to extract regularities from the constantly varying physical sounds. Despite the infinite variations which occur when we speak, all speakers of a language agree that certain utterances are the "same" and others are "different." Phonology tells us why this is the case.

Linguists are interested in how sound systems may vary, and also in the phonetic and phonological universals found in all languages. We find that the same relatively small set of phonetic properties characterizes all human speech sounds, that the same classes of these sounds are utilized in lan-

[1] As reported in Amsel Greene. 1969. *Pullet Surprises*. (Scott, Foresman & Co. Glenview, Ill.)

70

guages spoken from the Arctic Circle to the Cape of Good Hope, and that the same kinds of regular patterns of speech sounds occur all over the world. When you learn a language you learn which speech sounds occur in your language and how they pattern according to regular rules.

Phonology is concerned with this kind of linguistic knowledge. Phonetics, as discussed in the previous chapter, provides the means for describing speech sounds; phonology studies the ways in which speech sounds form systems and patterns in human language. The phonology of a language is then the system and pattern of the speech sounds. We see that the word *phonology* is thus used in two ways, either as the *study* of sound patterns in language or as *the* sound pattern of a language.

Phonological knowledge permits a speaker to produce sounds which form meaningful utterances, to recognize a foreign "accent," to make up new words, to add the appropriate phonetic segments to form plurals and past tenses, to produce "aspirated" and "unaspirated" voiceless stops in the appropriate context, to know what is or is not a sound in one's language, and to know that different phonetic strings may represent the same "meaningful unit." Since the grammar of the language represents the totality of one's linguistic knowledge, knowledge of the sound patterns—the *phonology*—must be part of this grammar. In this chapter we shall discuss the kinds of things that speakers know about the sound system of their language—their phonological knowledge.

Phonemes: The Phonological Units of Language

In the physical world the naive speaker and hearer actualize and are sensitive to sounds, but what they feel themselves to be pronouncing and hearing are "phonemes."
Edward Sapir, 1933

For native speakers, phonological knowledge goes beyond the ability to produce all the phonetically different sounds of their language. It includes this, of course. A speaker of English can produce the sound [θ] and knows that this sound occurs in English, in words like *thin* [θɪn] or *ether* [iθər] or *bath* [bæθ]. English speakers may or may not be able to produce a "click" or a velar fricative, but even if they can, they know that such sounds are not part of the phonetic inventory of English. Many speakers are unable to produce such "foreign" sounds. French speakers similarly know that the [θ] is not part of the phonetic inventory of French and often find it difficult to pronounce a word like *thin* [θɪn], pronouncing it as [sɪn].

An English speaker also knows that [ð], the voiced counterpart of [θ], is a sound of English, occurring in words like *either* [iðər], *then* [ðɛ̃n], and *bathe* [beð].

Knowing the sounds (the phonetic units) of a language is only a small part of one's phonological knowledge.

In Chapter 1 we discussed the fact that knowing a language implies knowing the set of words which comprise the vocabulary, or lexicon, of that language. You might know fewer or more words than your next-door neighbor, but each word you have learned is stored in your brain or mind, in memory, as part of the grammar of the language. When you know a word, you know both its **form** (the sounds that represent it) and its **meaning.** We have already seen that the relationship between the form and the meaning of a word is arbitrary; one must learn *both;* knowing the meaning does not tell you its pronunciation, and knowing the sounds of a word does not tell you what it means (if you didn't know this already).

Consider the forms and meanings of the following words in English:

sink   fine   chunk
zink   vine   junk

Each word differs from the other words in both form and meaning. The difference in meaning between *sink* and *zink* is "signaled" by the fact that the initial sound of the first word is *s* [s] and the initial sound of the second word is *z* [z]. The forms of the two words—that is, their sounds—are identical except for the initial consonants. [s] and [z] are therefore able to distinguish or **contrast** words. These are thus said to be **distinctive** sounds in English. Such distinctive sounds are called **phonemes.**

We see from *fine* and *vine* and from the contrast between *chunk* and *junk* that [f], [v], [č] and [ǰ] must also be phonemes in English for the same reasons, because if you substitute a [v] for [f] or a [ǰ] for [č] the meaning of the word changes.

Even if we did not know what phonetic property or features distinguish these sounds we would know that these sound segments represent phonemes in the English phonological system. Phonetics provides the means to describe the sounds, to show how they differ; phonology tells us that they function as phonemes, are able to contrast meanings of words.

MINIMAL PAIRS

B.C.   **Johnny Hart**

By permission of Johnny Hart and Field Enterprises, Inc.

A first rule of thumb one can use to determine the phonemes of any language is to see if substituting one sound for another results in a change of meaning. If it does, the two sounds represent different phonemes. When two different forms are identical in every way except for one sound segment that occurs in the same place in the string, the two words are called **minimal pairs.** *Sink* and *zink* are minimal pairs, as are *fine* and *vine,* and *chunk* and *junk.* Note that *seed* [sid] and *soup* [sup] are not minimal pairs because they differ in two sounds, the vowels and the final consonants. Similarly, *bar* [bar] and *rod* [rad] are not minimal pairs because although only one sound differs in the two words, the [b] occurs initially and the [d] occurs finally. Of course we can find a minimal pair which shows that [b] and [d] are phonemes in English: *bean* and *dean, bark* and *dark, Bill* and *dill, rib* and *rid.* Substituting a [d] for a [b] changes the meaning.

[b] and [d] also contrast with [g] as is shown by the following:

bill/dill/gill   rib/rid/rig

Thus, [b], [d] and [g] are all phonemes in English and constitute a **minimal set.** We have many minimal sets in English which make it relatively "easy" for us to know what the English phonemes are. All the following words are identical except for the vowels; therefore each vowel represents a phoneme.

beat	[bit]	[i]	boot	[but]	[u]
bit	[bɪt]	[ɪ]	but	[bʌt]	[ʌ]
bait	[bet]	[e]	boat	[bot]	[o]
bet	[bɛt]	[ɛ]	bought	[bɔt]	[ɔ]
bat	[bæt]	[æ]	bout	[bawt]	[aw]
bite	[bayt]	[ay]	bot	[bat]	[a]

You may not know what a *bot* is and neither did we when we wrote the first two editions of this book. We did not include [a] in this minimal set in those editions, but one of our more erudite readers informed us that a *bot* is the larva of a *botfly.* However we can show that [a] is a phoneme of English as well as [ʊ] and [ɔy]—which are not part of the minimal set listed above— by means of other minimal pairs in which these vowels contrast meanings.

seed	[sid]	sod	[sad]	[i] / [a]
hit	[hɪt]	hot	[hat]	[ɪ] / [a]
feet	[fit]	foot	[fʊt]	[i] / [ʊ]
fail	[fel]	full	[fʊl]	[e] / [ʊ]
sigh	[say]	soy	[sɔy]	[ay] / [ɔy]
bough	[baw]	boy	[bɔy]	[aw] / [ɔy]

As the B.C. cartoon shows, the contrasts between

crick [ɪ]   *creek* [i]   *crook* [ʊ]   *croak* [o]

illustrate that there are other minimal sets in English. *Crack* [æ], *crock* [a], and *crake* [e] (a short-billed bird) are also members of this contrasting set.

Although [bat], for some of us, and [bʊt] are not actual words in English, they are sequences or strings of sounds all of which represent phonemes, and the sequences of these phonemes are permissible in English. (We will discuss permissible sequences below.) One might then say that they are nonsense words (permissible forms with no meanings) or *possible* words. Similarly, *creck* [krɛk], *cruke* [kruk], *crawk,* [krɔk], *cruk* [krʌk] and *crike* [krayk] are nonexistent, nonoccurring, but possible words in English. Note that at one time [bɪk] (spelled *Bic*) was not an English word. Before its introduction and before TV commercials talked about a "flick of the Bic" it must have been a possible word, for it is now a real one. One would hardly expect a new product to come on the market with the name [ɣik], since [ɣ] (the voiced velar fricative) does not represent an English phoneme. Possible but nonoccurring words, as *Bic* once was, are **accidental gaps** in the vocabulary. An accidental gap is a form which "obeys" all the phonological rules of the language—that is, it includes native phonemes in a permitted order—but which has no meaning. An actual, occurring word is a combination of both a permitted form and a meaning.

Further examples of minimal pairs in English provide evidence for other phonemes. Change in the phonetic form produces a change in the meaning. When such a change in meaning is the result of the substitution of just one sound segment for another, the two different segments must represent distinctive phonemes. There is no other way to account for these particular meaning contrasts.

*s*in	*th*in	[s]	[θ]	me*s*her	mea*s*ure	[š]	[ž]	*ch*in	*g*in	[č]	[ǰ]
*d*o	*z*oo	[d]	[z]	*r*ink	*l*ink	[r]	[l]	*f*ine	*v*ine	[f]	[v]
*w*oo	*y*ou	[w]	[y]	e*th*er	ei*th*er	[θ]	[ð]	si*n*	si*ng*	[n]	[ŋ]
*m*ote	*n*ote	[m]	[n]	*h*igh	*w*hy	[h]	[w]	*d*en	*th*en	[d]	[ð]

FORM AND MEANING

We have said above that when the substitution of one sound segment for another results in a difference in meaning this is *sufficient* evidence that the two sounds represent two different phonemes. But note that *two different forms* may be *identical in meaning,* as shown by the fact that some speakers pronounce the word *economics* as [ikɔ̃nãmɪks] and others as [ɛkɔ̃nãmɪks]. These two forms are not minimal pairs, since the substitution of [i] for [ɛ] or vice versa does not change the meaning. Similarly, some speakers pronounce *ration* as [rešɔ̃n] and others as [ræšɔ̃n]. Such pairs do not tell us whether [i] and [ɛ] or [e] and [æ] represent phonemes in the language. We know, however, that these are contrastive sounds from such pairs as *beat/bet* [i]/[ɛ] and *bait/bat* [e]/[æ]. The different pronunciations of *economics* or *ration* are **free variations;** one meaning (of each word) is represented by two different phonemic forms.

Homonyms or homophones also show that two words of different meanings may have identical forms; that is, may be pronounced exactly alike. Thus [sol] can mean "sole," or "soul," and the sentence "Greta Garbo ate her cottage cheese with *relish* [rɛləš]" could mean she ate with "gusto" or with a particular kind of sauce.

Thus the determining fact is whether there is *both* a change in form (pronunciation) and a change in meaning. When this occurs we know that the substituted sound segments represent different phonemes.

DISTINCTIVE FEATURES

In order for two phonetic forms to differ and to contrast meanings there must be some phonetic difference between the substituted sounds. The minimal pairs *seal* and *zeal* show us that [s] and [z] represent two contrasting phonemes in English. From the discussion of phonetics in Chapter 2 we know that the only difference between [s] and [z] is a voicing difference; [s] is voiceless or [− voiced] and [z] is voiced or [+ voiced]. It is this phonetic feature that distinguishes the two words. Voicing thus plays a special role in English (and in many other languages). It also distinguishes *feel* and *veal* [f] / [v] and *ether* and *either* [θ] / [ð]. It distinguishes one phoneme from another and in English is therefore a **distinctive feature** (or a **phonemic feature**).

When two words are exactly alike phonetically except for one feature, the phonetic difference is distinctive, since this difference alone accounts for the meaning contrast. Note that a single feature has two values, + and −; for example, [± nasal], or [± voicing], or [± consonantal], and so forth. When we say that a phonetic feature is distinctive we are saying that the + value of that feature found in certain words contrasts with the − value of that feature in other words.

The minimal pairs given below illustrate some of the distinctive features in the phonological system of English.

bat   [bæt]   mat   [mæt]   The difference in meaning between *bat* and *mat* is due only to the difference in nasality between [b] and [m]. [b] and [m] are identical in all features except for the fact that [b] is oral ([− nasal]) and [m] is nasal ([+ nasal]). Thus, nasality ([± nasal]) is a distinctive feature of English consonants.

rack   [ræk]   rock   [rak]   The two words are distinguished only because [æ] is a front vowel and [a] is a back vowel. They are both low, unrounded vowels. [± back] is therefore a distinctive feature of English vowels.

see   [si]   zee   [zi]   The difference in meaning is due only to the voicelessness of the [s] in contrast to the voicing of the [z]. The two words are phonetically identical in all other respects. Therefore voicing ([± voiced]) is a distinctive feature of English consonants.

SOUNDS THAT ARE NOT PHONEMES: FEATURES THAT DO NOT CONTRAST

The method of substituting one sound for another to determine whether the new form creates a new meaning may also be used to show that all sounds which occur phonetically in a language may not represent separate phonemes. Again, this is a "tool" which may be helpful in analysis, but one must remember that it is the presence of contrast, not the lack of contrast, that shows the phonemic distinctions.

In Chapter 2 we pointed out that *phonetically* both oral and nasalized vowels occur in English. The following examples show this.

bean   [bĩn]   bead   [bid]
roam   [rõm]   robe   [rob]

Nasalized vowels only occur in English before nasal consonants. If one substituted an oral vowel for the nasal vowels in *bean* and *roam* the meanings of the two words would not be changed. Try to say these words keeping your velum up until your tongue makes the stop closure of the [n] or your lips come together for the [m]. It will not be easy for you because in English we automatically lower the velum when producing vowels before nasals.

Or try to produce a nasal vowel (lower your velum immediately after you articulate the consonant) in the words *by*, *see*, or *go* to produce [bãy], [sĩ], and [gõ]. If you spoke like this people would probably say you have a "nasal twang" but they would understand you to be saying *by*, *see*, and *go*. Changing the forms of the words by substituting nasalized vowels does not change the meanings.

We have seen above that a substitution of [i] for [ɛ] in *economics* does not change the meaning of the word. Thus, the fact that in one or more words the substitution of one sound for another may not change the meaning shows that this is not sufficient evidence for deciding whether two sounds represent two phonemes. But there is a difference between the substitution of [i] and [ɛ] in *economics* and the substitutions we have observed between oral and nasalized vowels. [i] and [ɛ] were shown by a number of examples to represent different phonemes. We can find no such cases to demonstrate that [i] and [ĩ], for example, represent different phonemes. That is, there are no two words, different in meaning, in which the *only* difference phonetically is that in one word a vowel is oral and in the other the vowel—identical in all other respects—is nasal.

A further, more important difference between [i] and [ɛ] and [i] and [ĩ] (or [u] and [ũ], [o] and [õ], [a] and [ã], and so on) is that there are no general principles in the phonology of English which tell us when [i] occurs and when [ɛ] occurs. One must learn, when learning the words, that [i] occurs in *beat* and [ɛ] occurs in *bet*.

There is, however, a general principle, or a *rule*, that tells us, or *predicts*, when a vowel will be oral and when the same vowel phoneme will be nasalized. Consider the following sets of words and nonwords:

WORDS						**NONWORDS**		
bee	[bi]	*bead*	[bid]	*bean*	[bĩn]	*[bĩ]	*[bĩd]	*[bin]
lay	[le]	*lace*	[les]	*lame*	[lẽm]	*[lẽ]	*[lẽs]	*[lem]
baa	[bæ]	*bad*	[bæd]	*bang*	[bæ̃ŋ]	*[bæ̃]	*[bæ̃d]	*[bæŋ]

The words show us where oral and nasal vowels can occur in English: oral vowels in final position and before nonnasal consonants; nasalized vowels only before nasal consonants. The "nonwords" show us where oral and nasalized vowels *cannot* occur: where oral vowels can occur, nasalized vowels cannot occur, and vice versa. Thus the oral vowels and their nasalized counterparts never contrast. Nasalization of vowels in English is predictable by a rule, which can be stated as:

(1) Nasalize a vowel or diphthong (vowel + glide) when it occurs before a nasal.

The value of the feature [± nasal] can always be predicted for the class of vowel segments in English. When a feature is always predictable by a general principle or rule it is not a distinctive, or phonemic, feature for that class of segments. Thus, the feature [± nasal] is not a distinctive feature for English vowels, although it is distinctive for English consonants.

Yet we have seen that nasalized vowels do occur phonetically. We can conclude then that there is no one-to-one correspondence between phonetic segments and phonemes in a language. In fact, from the examples given above we see that one phoneme may be realized phonetically, or pronounced, as more than one phonetic segment. Each vowel phoneme in English is realized as either an oral vowel or a nasal vowel depending on its context.

PHONEMES, PHONES, AND ALLOPHONES

Some new terminology may help to clarify things a bit. A phonetic unit or segment is called a **phone**. A **phoneme** is a more abstract unit. One must know the phonological rules of the language to know how to pronounce it, since in one context it may be realized as one phone (for example, [i]) and in another context as a different phone (for example, [ĩ]). To distinguish between phonemes and phones we will use slashes / / to enclose phonemic segments or phonemic transcriptions of words and will continue to use the square brackets [ ] for phonetic segments or phonetic transcriptions. Thus, we will represent the vowel phoneme in *bead* and *bean* as /i/ in both words. This phoneme is pronounced (or realized) as [i] in *bead* [bid] and [ĩ] in *bean* [bĩn].

We have seen that a single phoneme may be phonetically realized or pronounced as two or more phones. The different phones that "represent" or are *derived* from one phoneme are called the **allophones** of that phoneme. An **allophone** is therefore a predictable phonetic variant of a phoneme. In English, each vowel phoneme has both an oral and a nasalized allophone. The choice of the allophone is not random or haphazard in most cases; it is *rule-governed*. This was illustrated above by demonstrating that there is a general principle determining the occurrence of oral and nasalized vowels in English. No one explicitly teaches you these rules. You "construct" them yourself; language acquisition is to a great extent rule construction. You probably do not even know that you know these rules; yet you produce the nasalized allophones of the vowel phonemes automatically whenever they occur before nasal consonants.

When two or more sounds never occur in the same phonemic context or environment they are said to be in **complementary distribution.** The examples of the words and nonwords given on page 76 illustrate the way that oral and nasalized allophones of each vowel phoneme are in complementary distribution, as shown in Table 3-1.

Table 3-1   Distribution of Oral and Nasal Vowels in English

	At the End of a Word	*Before Nasal Consonants*	*Before Oral Consonants*
Oral vowels	Yes	No	Yes
Nasal vowels	No	Yes	No

When oral vowels occur, nasal vowels do not occur, and vice versa. It is in this sense that the phones are said to *complement* each other or to be in *complementary distribution.*

PREDICTABILITY OF REDUNDANT FEATURES

Nasality is a predictable or **redundant** feature for vowels in English (but not consonants). Whether a vowel is [+ nasal] or [− nasal] is said to be redundant because it depends on other aspects of the word. If the vowel occurs before a nasal consonant, you know that the vowel is [+ nasal]; the value of this feature is therefore redundant. It is not specific to any particular word but determined by a general rule.

The nasality feature, however, is not redundant for consonants in English; whether or not a consonant is [+ nasal] cannot be predicted by a general rule but must be specified for each word. There is no rule which can predict that the word *bean* will have a final *n* rather than a *d*; in learning the word we must learn that the final consonant is the nasal consonant /n/ and not /d/, or /s/, or /g/, and so on. Similarly, the fact that *meat* begins with a bilabial nasal is an arbitrary fact about this particular word. The first consonant must therefore be specified as [+ nasal] to distinguish it from the [− nasal] specification of the first consonant in the word *beat*.

But, the fact that the vowel in *bean* is nasalized is not a fact about only this word but about all the words in which the vowel is followed by a nasal consonant. If you didn't learn the rule you would not pronounce the words according to the normal English pronunciation.

The rule stated above is one found in many languages of the world. This is not surprising; it is a very plausible or "natural" rule, since it is more difficult to prevent nasalizing a vowel before a nasal consonant than it is to nasalize it in this context; to prevent nasalization, one's timing of the velic closure must be very precise.

This does not mean, however, that nasality cannot be distinctive for vowels in other languages. We have already seen some examples of nasalized vowels in French in Chapter 2. In the Ghanaian language, Akan (or Twi), nasalized and oral vowels occur both phonetically and phonemically, as the following examples illustrate; nasalization is a distinctive feature for vowels in Akan.

[ka]	"bite"	[kã]	"speak"
[fi]	"come from"	[fĩ]	"dirty"
[tu]	"pull"	[tũ]	"hole/den"
[nsa]	"hand"	[nsã]	"liquor"
[či]	"hate"	[čĩ]	"squeeze"
[pam]	"sew"	[pãm]	"confederate"

These examples show that vowel nasalization is not predictable in Akan. There is no rule which says that all vowels are nasalized before nasal consonants as shown by the last minimal pair. Furthermore, after identical consonants one finds word-final oral vowels contrasting with word-final nasalized vowels; here we see that the change of form (that is, the substitution of nasalized for oral vowels, or vice versa) does change the meaning. Both oral and nasal vowel phonemes must therefore exist in Akan.

Notice that two languages may have the same phonetic segments (phones) but have two different phonemic systems. Both oral and nasalized vowels exist in English and Akan phonetically; English has no nasalized vowel phonemes but Akan does. The same phonetic segments function differently in the two languages. Nasalization of vowels in English is *redundant* and *nondistinctive;* nasalization of vowels in Akan is *nonredundant* and *distinctive*.

We can further illustrate the fact that two languages can have the same set of phonetic segments with different phonemic systems by examining the voiceless stops. In the previous chapter we pointed out that in English both aspirated and unaspirated voiceless stops occur. The voiceless aspirated stops [pʰ] [tʰ] [kʰ] and the voiceless unaspirated stops [p] [t] [k] are in complementary distribution in English, as is shown by stating the environments or contexts in which they occur:

WORD (OR SYLLABLE) INITIALLY BEFORE A STRESSED VOWEL			AFTER A WORD (OR SYLLABLE) INITIAL /S/		
[pʰ]	[tʰ]	[kʰ]	[p]	[t]	[k]
pill	till	kill	spill	still	skill
[pʰɪl]	[tʰɪl]	[kʰɪl]	[spɪl]	[stɪl]	[skɪl]
par	tar	car	spar	star	scar
[pʰar]	[tʰar]	[kʰar]	[spar]	[star]	[skar]

Despite the phonetic difference between the unaspirated and aspirated phones, speakers of English (if they are not analyzing the sounds as linguists or phoneticians) usually consider the *p* in *pill* and *spill* to be the "same" sound, just as they consider the [i] and [ĩ] that represent the phoneme /i/ in *bead* and *bean* to be the "same." Again, this is because the difference between them, in this case the feature "aspiration," is *predictable, redundant, nondistinctive, nonphonemic* (these are all equivalent terms). The aspirated and the nonaspirated phones are in complementary distribution. Voiceless stops are always aspirated when they occur at the beginning of a word before stressed vowels, and voiceless stops are always unaspirated after an initial /s/. This is a fact about English phonology. There are two *p* sounds (or phones) in English, but only one *p* phoneme. (This is also true of *t* and *k*.) Remember that a phoneme is an abstract unit. We do not utter phonemes; we produce phones. /p/ is a phoneme in English that is realized phonetically (pronounced) as either [p] or [pʰ]. [p] and [pʰ] are allophones of the phoneme /p/. Another way of stating this same fact is to say that the [p] and [pʰ] are *derived* from /p/ by a rule which can be stated as:

(2) Aspirate a voiceless stop, /p/, /t/, or /k/, when it occurs word initially or syllable initially before a stressed vowel.

In the discussion on oral and nasalized vowels above, we saw that the same phones (phonetic segments) can occur in two languages but may pattern differently because the phonemic system is different. Aspiration of voiceless stops further illustrates this. Both aspirated and unaspirated voiceless stops occur in English and Thai, but they function differently in the two languages. In English aspiration is not a phonemic or distinctive feature since it is predictable. In Thai, however, it is not predictable as is shown by the following examples.

VOICELESS UNASPIRATED		VOICELESS ASPIRATED	
[paa]	"forest"	[pʰaa]	"to split"
[tam]	"to pound"	[tʰam]	"to do"
[kat]	"to bite"	[kʰat]	"to interrupt"

The voiceless unaspirated and the voiceless aspirated stops in Thai are not in complementary distribution as they occur in the same positions in the minimal pairs above; they contrast and are therefore phonemes in Thai. Thus both English and Thai have the phones [p] [pʰ] [t] [tʰ] [k] and [kʰ]. In

English they represent three phonemes /p/ /t/ /k/; in Thai each phone represents a separate phoneme—/p/ /pʰ/ /t/ /tʰ/ /k/ /kʰ/. [± aspiration] is a distinctive feature in Thai; it is a nondistinctive but phonetic feature in English.

The minimal pairs *seal/zeal, fine/vine, sink/zinc, mesher/measure,* and *chin/gin* show that voicing is a distinctive feature in English. The initial sounds of the first words of the pair are all [− voiced] and in the second words are [+ voiced]. They differ in no other way. *Pill/bill, till/dill,* and *kill/gill* also contrast in that the initial sounds of the first words of the pairs are voiceless and of the second words are voiced. But the voiceless stops are also aspirated. They differ by two phonetic features. Is it the aspiration or the voicing difference that signals the phonemic difference in these pairs? As we have already seen that voicing must be a distinctive feature from the minimal pairs in which it is the *only* difference, and as we cannot predict when voicing will occur but can predict when aspiration will occur as stated in Rule (2), we can conclude that what distinguishes the *pill/bill* pairs phonemically is voicing rather than aspiration.

VOICELESS UNASPIRATED			VOICELESS ASPIRATED			VOICED		
/spɪl/	[spɪl]	"spill"	/pɪl/	[pʰɪl]	"pill"	/bɪl/	[bɪl]	"bill"
/stɪl/	[stɪl]	"still"	/tɪl/	[tʰɪl]	"till"	/dɪl/	[dɪl]	"dill"
/skɪl/	[skɪl]	"skill"	/kɪl/	[kʰɪl]	"kill"	/gɪl/	[gɪl]	"gill"

In Thai, voiced stops also occur. Thus, just as in English, voiceless unaspirated, voiceless aspirated, and voiced phones occur. But in Thai these phones represent phonemes. [± voicing] and [± aspiration] are *both* distinctive or phonemic features in Thai, as is shown by the three-way minimal contrastive sets in Thai:

VOICELESS UNASPIRATED			VOICELESS ASPIRATED			VOICED		
/paa/	[paa]	"forest"	/pʰaa/	[pʰaa]	"to split"	/baa/	[baa]	"shoulder"
/tam/	[tãm]	"to pound"	/tʰam/	[tʰãm]	"to do"	/dam/	[dãm]	"black"

The phonetic feature matrices for the labial stops in the three Thai words would be identical to the phonetic specifications of the labials in *spit, pit,* and *bit* in English. But the Thai phonemic specifications would differ in that the /p/ in "forest" would have to be marked [− aspirated] and the /pʰ/ in "to split" would have to be marked [+ aspirated], as aspiration is contrastive.

Once more we see that the same phonetic segments can form different phonemic patterns in different languages.

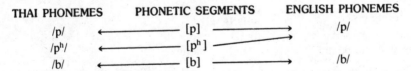

THAI PHONEMES	PHONETIC SEGMENTS	ENGLISH PHONEMES
/p/	[p]	/p/
/pʰ/	[pʰ]	
/b/	[b]	/b/

The phonetic facts alone do not tell us what is distinctive or phonemic. The phonetic representation of utterances shows what speakers know about the *pronunciation* of utterances; the phonemic representation of utterances shows what the speakers know about the abstract underlying phonology.

That *pot* /pat/ and *spot* /spat/ both include a /p/ reveals the fact that English speakers consider the [pʰ] in *pot* [pʰat] and the [p] in *spot* [spat] to be phonetic manifestations of the same phoneme /p/.

In learning a language a child learns which features are distinctive in that language and which are not. One phonetic feature may be distinctive for one class of sounds but predictable or nondistinctive for another class of sounds, as, for example, the feature *nasality* in English. [+ nasal] is a distinctive feature for English consonants but a nondistinctive, predictable phonetic feature for English vowels. In French, it is distinctive for both consonants and vowels.

Aspiration in English is totally predictable. It is nondistinctive for any class of sounds.

The values of some features are predictable because of the segments which precede or follow; that is, context determines the value of the feature. Aspiration cannot be predicted in isolation but only when a voiceless stop occurs in a word, since the presence or absence of the feature depends on *where* the voiceless stop occurs and what precedes or follows it. It is determined by its phonemic environment. Similarly, the oral or nasal quality of a vowel depends on its environment. If it is followed by a nasal consonant it is predictably [+ nasal].

Some features, however, may be predictable or redundant due to the specification of the other features of that segment. That is, given the presence of certain features one can predict the value of other features without any reference to the surrounding segments.

In English, as pointed out in the preceding chapter, all front vowels are predictably nonround. Unlike French, there are no rounded front vowels in English. We can thus say that if a vowel in English is specified as [− back] it is also redundantly, predictably [− round].

In French all voiceless stops are unaspirated, in all environments. Thus, any segment specified as $\begin{bmatrix} -\text{continuant} \\ -\text{voiced} \end{bmatrix}$ is predictably [− aspirated] both phonetically and phonemically.

For certain classes of sounds, the values of some features are universally implied for all languages. Thus, all stops, that is, [−continuant] segments, are universally [− vocalic].

FREE VARIATION

We noted that in some words two phonemes may occur interchangeably without changing the meaning of the words, as in the initial vowel of *economics,* which some people pronounce with an /i/ and others pronounce with an /ɛ/. We said that these two phonemes were in *free variation* in that particular word. Obviously, these phonemes are not optionally substitutable in all words, since *beat* and *bet* mean different things.

The phonology of a language includes rules that relate the phonemic representations of words to their phonetic representations. The phonemic representation need only include the *nonpredictable distinctive* features of the string of phonemes that represent the words. The phonetic representation includes all the *linguistically relevant phonetic* aspects of the sounds.

The phonetic representation does not include *all* the physical properties of the sounds of an utterance, since the physical signal may vary in many ways that have little to do with the phonological system. The absolute pitch of the sounds, or whether the utterance is spoken slowly or fast, or whether the speaker shouts or whispers is not linguistically significant. The phonetic transcription is thus also an abstraction from the physical signal; it includes the nonvariant phonetic aspects of the utterances, those features that remain relatively the same from speaker to speaker and from one time to another.

Minimal pairs and complementary distribution of phonetic units are helpful clues in the attempt to discover the inventory of phonemes in a language. By themselves, however, they do not determine the phonemic representation of utterances, as will be shown below in the discussion on phonological rules.

The grammar of a language includes the kind of information we have been discussing: what the distinctive phonemic units of the language are; which phonetic features are phonemic or distinctive; and which are nonphonemic or predictable. Thus, a grammar of French would not include a /θ/ as part of the phonemic representation of any word, just as a grammar of English would not include a /x/. English would have one voiceless labial stop phoneme, /p/, but Thai would have two, /p/ and /pʰ/. Both would include /b/. These examples show that two languages may have the same phonetic segments but a different set of phonemes. The grammar must account for both the phonemes in the language and the way they are pronounced.

Sequences of Phonemes

If you were to receive the following telegram, you would have no difficulty in correcting the "obvious" mistakes:
BEST WISHES FOR VERY HAPPP BIRTFDAY
because sequences such as BIRTFDAY do not occur in the language.
Colin Cherry, *On Human Communication*

We demonstrated above that one's knowledge of the phonological system includes more than knowing the phonetic inventory of sounds in the language. It even goes beyond knowing the phonemes of the language.

Speakers also know that the phonemes of their language cannot be strung together in any random order to form words. The phonological system determines which phonemes can begin a word, end a word, and follow each other.

That speakers have knowledge of such sequential rules is not too difficult to demonstrate. Suppose you were given four cards, each of which had a different phoneme of English printed on it:

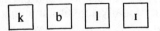

If you were asked to arrange these cards to form all the "possible" words which these four phonemes could form, you might order them as:

b	l	ɪ	k
k	l	ɪ	b
b	ɪ	l	k
k	ɪ	l	b

These are the only arrangements of these phonemes permissible in English. */lbkɪ/, */ɪlbk/, */bkɪl/, */ɪlkb/, and so on are not possible words in the language. Although /blɪk/ and /klɪb/ are not *existing* words (you will not find them in a dictionary), if you heard someone say:

"I just bought a beautiful new *blick*."

you might ask: "What's a 'blick'?" But if you heard someone say:

"I just bought a beautiful new *bkli*."

you would probably just say "What?"

Your knowledge of English "tells" you that certain strings of phonemes are permissible and others are not. After a consonant like /b/, /g/, /k/, or /p/ another similar consonant is not permitted by the rules of the grammar. If a word begins with an /l/ or an /r/, every speaker "knows" that the next segment must be a vowel. That is why */lbɪk/ does not sound like an English word. It violates the restrictions on the sequencing of phonemes.

Other such constraints exist in English. If the initial sound of *church* begins a word, the next sound must be a vowel. [čat] or [čon] or [čækari] are possible words in English, but *[člit] and *[čpæt] are not.

Another *sequential constraint* in English pertains to *clusters* (one or more consonants) of nasal consonants followed by nonnasal (oral) stops within words. For the most part, only the labial /m/ occurs before the labials /p/ and /b/, only the alveolar /n/ occurs before the alveolars /t/ and /d/, and only the velar /ŋ/ occurs before the velars /k/ and /g/, as is illustrated by the following:[2]

ample	-mp-	*but no*	*-mt-	*-mk-
amble	-mb-	*but no*	*-md-	*-mg-
antler	-nt-	*but no*	*-np-	*-nk-
handle	-nd-	*but no*	*-nb-	*-ng-
ankle	-ŋk-	*but no*	*-ŋp-	*-ŋt-
angle	-ŋg-	*but no*	*-ŋb-	*-ŋd-

This constraint (which occurs in many languages of the world) states that only **homorganic** nasal + nonnasal consonant clusters may occur. *Homorganic* consonants are those which are articulated at the same place of articulation, that is, labial, alveolar, palatal, velar.

All languages have constraints on the permitted sequences of phonemes, though different languages have different constraints. Children learn these rules when they learn the language, just as they learn what the phonemes are and how they are related to phonetic segments. In Asante Twi, a word may end only in a vowel or a nasal consonant. /pik/ is not a possible Twi word, because it breaks the sequential rules of the language, and /ŋŋu/ is not a possible word in English for similar reasons, although it is an actual word in Twi.

---

[2] There are exceptions to this rule, and we have oversimplified it at this point. Actually, the constraint applies primarily to "simple" words rather than to complex words that include, for example, prefixes like *un-* meaning "not." In words such as *unbound* or *uncap* an /n/ is followed by /b/ and /k/ respectively. We shall see in Chapter 4, however, that there are prefixes ending with nasals which do obey this constraint.

Speakers of all languages have the same kinds of knowledge. They know what sounds are part of the language, what the phonemes are, and what phonemic and phonetic sequences may occur. The specific sounds and sound sequences may differ, but the phonological systems include similar *kinds* of rules.

Natural Classes

The rules in English phonology which determine the conditions under which vowels are nasalized, voiceless stops are aspirated, or which state that only homorganic nasal clusters may occur within a word are general rules. They apply to classes of sounds. They also apply to all the words in the vocabulary of the language, and they even apply to nonsense words that are not in the language but could enter the language (like *sint* or *peeg* or *sparg,* which would be /sɪnt/ and /pig/ and /sparg/ phonemically and [sĩnt] and [pʰig] and [sparg] phonetically.

There are of course less general rules found in all languages and there may also be exceptions to these general rules. But what is of greater interest is that the more we examine the phonologies of the many thousands of languages of the world, the more we find that phonological rules apply to the same broad general classes of sounds, like the ones we have mentioned— nasals, voiceless stops, alveolars, labials, and so on. This is understandable and really not surprising since such rules often have phonetic explanations and these classes of sounds are defined by phonetic features. For this reason such classes are called **natural classes** of speech sounds.

A **natural class** is one in which the number of features which must be specified to define that class is smaller than the number of features required to distinguish any member of that class.

The class of voiceless stops—/p, t, k/—can be specified by two features: $\begin{bmatrix} -\text{continuant} \\ -\text{voiced} \end{bmatrix}$. But /p/ alone would require four features to distinguish it from all other consonants:

$$\begin{bmatrix} -\text{continuant} \\ -\text{voiced} \\ +\text{anterior} \\ -\text{coronal} \end{bmatrix}$$

When we discussed the aspiration of voiceless stops above we pointed out that *all* the members of this class became aspirated in the given environments. Thus aspiration refers to a natural class of sounds, which, as stated above, can be defined by two features. If, instead, only /p/ and /t/ were aspirated then we would have to refer to the class of sounds that were

$$\begin{bmatrix} -\text{continuant} \\ -\text{voiced} \\ +\text{anterior} \end{bmatrix}$$

And if only /p/ and /k/ were aspirated the number of features that defined these two sounds as distinct from all other phonemes would be even greater. The more features that have to be mentioned, the less general the process. Thus, the class of sounds that includes /p/, /t/, and /k/ is "more natural" than the class of sounds that includes only /p/ and /t/.

If the English vowel nasalization rule applied only before /m/ and not before /n/ or /ŋ/, and this rule was stated using pluses and minuses to define the class before which vowels were nasalized, it would be stated:

Nasalize vowels when they occur before a segment that is $\begin{bmatrix} +\text{nasal} \\ -\text{coronal} \\ +\text{anterior} \end{bmatrix}$

rather than by the more general rule:

Nasalize vowels when they occur before a segment that is [+ nasal]

Children should find it easier to learn a rule that applies to a natural class of sounds since they would have to extract from the speech input fewer features than they would if the rule applied to a less natural class. It should also be easier to remember such a rule.

This fact about phonological rules illustrates why individual phonemic segments are better regarded as combinations or complexes of features than as indissoluble whole segments. If such segments are not specified as feature-matrices, the similarities among /p/, /t/, and /k/ or /m/, /n/, and /ŋ/ would not be revealed. It would appear that it should be just as easy for a child to learn a rule such as

(a) Nasalize vowels before /p/, /i/, or /z/

as to learn a rule such as

(b) Nasalize vowels before /m/, /n/, or /ŋ/

Rule (a) has no phonetic explanation whereas rule (b) does. It is easier to raise the velum to produce a nasalized vowel in anticipation of a following nasal consonant than to prevent the velum from raising before the consonant closure.

The use of feature notation therefore reveals what is going on in the languages of the world and provides explanations for why certain rules are in some sense "more natural" or "simpler" to learn than others. The phonetic features that were presented in Chapter 2 therefore define the various phonetic and phonological natural classes that function in the world's languages.

The Rules of Phonology

No rule is so general, which admits not some exception.
Robert Burton, *The Anatomy of Melancholy*

But that to come
Shall all be done by the rule.
Shakespeare, *Antony and Cleopatra*

As discussed above, all who know a language know the basic vocabulary of that language. This means they know that an object like "pot" is represented by a given sequence of phonemes, /pat/. In other words, they know both the sounds and the meanings of these linguistic units. This knowledge must be part of the way they "store" these words in their mental dictionary, because when they want to refer to the concept "pot" they don't produce the sounds [tʰap]. But they needn't represent the sounds of this word by including all the phonetic features of these sounds, as we saw in the discussion on phonemes, as long as the relationship between the phonemic representation they have stored and the phonetic pronunciation is "rule-governed." The rules that relate the minimally specified phonemic representation to the phonetic representation form part of a speaker's knowledge of the language. They are part of the grammar.

Rules (1) and (2) given above are rules of English grammar. They make certain predictions about English pronunciation. We repeat them, with some slight changes, for easy reference.

(1) Nasalize vowels and diphthongs before nasals.
(2) Aspirate voiceless stops at the beginning of a word or syllable before stressed vowels (and optionally at the end of a word).

Both rules specify the *class of sounds* affected by the rules (in (1) vowels and diphthongs and in (2) voiceless stops); both rules specify the context or phonemic environment of the relevant sounds ("before nasals" and "at the beginning of a word or syllable before stressed vowels . . ."); and both rules state what phonetic changes are to occur ("nasalize" and "aspirate"). All three kinds of information must be included in the statement of a phonological rule or it would not explicitly reveal the regularities that we know. As stated in Chapter 1, the rules of grammar written by linguists or posited as being in the grammar should duplicate the actual rules known unconsciously by speakers.

ASSIMILATION RULES

The vowel nasalization rule is an **assimilation** rule; it *assimilates* one segment to another by "copying" a feature of a sequential phoneme, thus making the two phones more similar. Assimilation rules are, for the most part, caused by articulatory or physiological processes. There is a tendency when we speak to increase the *ease of articulation*. Assimilation rules in languages reflect what phoneticians often call **coarticulation**—the spreading of phonetic features either in anticipation of sounds or the perseveration of articulatory processes. This "sloppiness" tendency may become regularized as rules of the language.

The following examples illustrate how the English vowel nasalization rule applies to the phonemic representation of words and shows the assimilatory nature of the rule, that is, the [−nasal] feature value of the vowel in the phonemic representation is changed to a [+nasal] is the phonetic representation:

	"Bob"	"bomb"	"beep"	"beam"
Phonemic representation	/b a b/	/b a m/	/b i p/	/b i m/
Nasality: feature value	− −	− +	− −	− +
Apply nasal rule (1)	NA[a]	↓	NA	↓
Nasality: feature value	− −	+ +	− −	+ +
Phonetic representation	[b a b]	[b ã m]	[b i p]	[b ĩ m]

[a] NA means "not applicable."

There are many other examples of assimilation rules in English and other languages. There is an **optional** ("free variation") rule in English that, particularly in fast speech, devoices the nasals and liquids in words like *snow* [sn̥o], *slow* [sl̥o], *smart* [sm̥art], *probe* [pr̥ob], and so on. The feature [− voiced] of the *s* carries over onto the following segment.

Vowels may also become devoiced or voiceless in a voiceless environment. In Japanese, high vowels are devoiced when preceded and followed by voiceless obstruents as in words like *sukiyaki;* the /u/ becomes [ʉ]. This is also an assimilation rule.

The English vowel nasalization and devoicing rules and the Japanese devoicing rule *change feature specifications*. That is, in English the [− nasal] value of phonemic vowels is changed to [+ nasal] phonetically when they occur before nasals. Vowels in Japanese are phonemically voiced and the rule changes certain vowels into phonetically voiceless segments.

Although the rules we have discussed are phonetically plausible, as are other assimilation rules, and can be explained by natural phonetic processes, this does not mean that all these rules occur in all languages. For example, there is a nasal assimilation rule in Akan that nasalizes voiced stops when they follow nasal consonants, as shown in the following example:

/ɔ ba/ [ɔba] "he comes"   /ɔm ba/ [ɔmma] "he doesn't come"

The /b/ of the verb "come" becomes an [m] when it follows the negative prefix [m].

This rule has a phonetic explanation; the velum is lowered to produce the nasal consonant and remains down during the following stop. While it is a phonetically "natural" assimilation rule, it does not occur in the grammar of English; the word *amber,* for example, shows an [m] followed by a [b]. A child learning Akan must learn this rule, just as a child learning English learns to nasalize all vowels before nasal consonants, a rule that does not occur in the grammar of Akan.

Assimilation rules, such as the ones we have discussed in English, Japanese, and Akan, often have the function of changing the value of phonemic features. They are *feature-changing rules*. Although nasality is nondistinctive for vowels in English, it is a distinctive feature for consonants, and rule (1) therefore changes a feature value.

FEATURE ADDITION RULES

All phonological rules are not assimilation rules. Rule (2), which aspirates voiceless stops in certain contexts in English, simply adds a nondistinctive feature. Aspiration is neither present nor absent in the phonemic feature matrices in English. This was pointed out above when we discussed why /p/ and /b/, for example, were distinguished by the feature [± voiced] rather than the feature [± aspiration]. But /p/ and /b/ (and all phonetic symbols) are simply cover symbols that do not reveal the phonemic distinctions. In the phonemic and phonetic feature matrices, these differences are made explicit, as shown in the following phonemic *matrix*.

	/p/	/b/
Consonantal	+	+
Vocalic	−	−
Continuant	−	−
Labial	+	+
Voiced	−	+	← distinctive difference

The nondistinctive feature "aspiration" is not included in these phonemic representations because aspiration is predictable. The phonemic and phonetic differences between the bilabial stops in *pit*, *spit*, and *bit* illustrate this:

	pit	/pɪt/	[pʰɪt]	*spit*	/spɪt/	[spɪt]	*bit*	/bɪt/	[bɪt]
Distinctive features									
Consonantal		+	+		+	+		+	+
Vocalic		−	−		−	−		−	−
Labial		+	+		+	+		+	+
Continuant		−	−		−	−		−	−
Voiced		−	−		−	−		+	+
Apply rule		↓			NA[a]			NA	
Nondistinctive									
Aspirated		+							

[a] NA means "not applicable."

In the phonemic representations of all three words there is no feature value specified for the nondistinctive feature [± aspirated]. Phonemically, /p/ and /b/ are neither "aspirated" nor "unaspirated." The specification of this feature depends on the context of the /p/—where it occurs in a word. Rule (2) given above would apply only to the voiceless stops: /p/, /t/, and /k/. It would add the [+ aspirated] designation to the voiceless stops in words like *pin*, *tin*, *kin*, *peal*, *teal*, and *keel*, but would do nothing to *spin*, *steal*, *skin*, and so on, or to any of the voiced stops.

SEGMENT-DELETION AND ADDITION RULES

In addition to assimilation (feature-changing) and feature-addition rules, phonological rules can delete or add entire phonemic segments. In French, for example, as demonstrated by Sanford Schane,[3] word-final consonants are deleted when the following word begins with a consonant or a liquid, but are retained when the following word begins with a vowel or a glide:

Before a consonant:	petit tableau	[pəti tablo]	"small picture"
	nos tableaux	[no tablo]	"our pictures"
Before a liquid:	petit livre	[pəti livr]	"small book"
	nos livres	[no livr]	"our books"

[3] Sanford Schane. 1968. *French Phonology and Morphology.* M.I.T. Press. Cambridge, Mass. In Schane's complete analysis, many words that are pronounced with a final consonant actually have a vowel as their word-final segment in phonemic representation. The vowel prevents the rule of word-final consonant deletion from applying. The vowel itself is deleted by another, later rule.

Before a vowel:	petit ami	[pətit ami]	"small friend"
	nos amis	[noz ami]	"our friends"
Before a glide:	petit oiseau	[pətit wazo]	"small bird"
	nos oiseaux	[noz wazo]	"our birds"

This is a general rule in French applying to all word-final consonants. In the chapter on phonetics we distinguished these four classes of sounds by the following features:

	CONSONANTS	LIQUIDS	VOWELS	GLIDES
Consonantal	+	+	−	−
Vocalic	−	+	+	−

Using these classes, we can state the French rule very simply:

Delete a word-final consonant when it occurs before the class of [+ consonantal] segments (that is, consonants and liquids).

In the grammar of French, *petit* would be phonemically /pətit/. It need not be additionally represented as /pəti/, since the rule determines the phonetic shape of the word.

"Deletion rules" also show up as **optional** rules in fast speech or more casual speech in English. They result, for example, in the common contractions changing *he is* [hi ɪz] to *he's* [hiz] or *I will* [ay wɪl] to *I'll* [ayl]. In ordinary everyday speech most of us also "delete" the unstressed vowels that are italicized in words like the following:

myst*e*ry gen*e*ral mem*o*ry fun*e*ral pers*o*nal vig*o*rous Barb*a*ra

Phonological rules that can delete whole segments can thus be either optional or obligatory.

Phonological rules may also add whole segments. In Greenlandic there is a rule that inserts a vowel between two consonants when these come at the end of a word or when followed by a suffix that begins with a consonant.

In English, another *optional* rule inserts a voiceless stop after a nasal followed by a voiceless consonant. Thus, many speakers pronounce *mince*, which is phonemically /mɪns/, as [mɪnts] identically with *mints* /mɪnt + s/, or *sense* and *cents* identically as [sɛnts], although the first word phonemically has no /t/. One of the authors of this book regularly receives letters addressed to "Professor Frompkin," which reflect the writers' pronunciation of her name, which she pronounces as [frãmkɪn] but which others pronounce as [frãmpkɪn]. The voiceless stop that is inserted is always *homorganic*—produced at the same place of articulation—as the nasal. That is, it is labial [p] after the labial [m], the alveolar [t] after the alveolar [n], or the velar [k] after the velar [ŋ].

MOVEMENT (METATHESIS) RULES

Phonological rules may also move phonemes from one place in the string to another. Such rules are called **metathesis rules**. They are less common, but they do exist. In some dialects of English, for example, the word *ask* is pronounced [æks] but the word *asking* is pronounced [æskĩŋ]. In these dialects a metathesis rule "switches" the /s/ and /k/ in certain contexts. It is interesting that at an earlier stage of English the Old English verb was *aksian* with the /k/ preceding the /s/. An historical metathesis rule switched these two consonants, producing *ask* in most dialects of English. Children's speech shows many cases of metathesis (which are then later corrected as the child approaches the adult grammar): *aminal* for *animal* and *pusketti* for *spaghetti* are common children's pronunciations.

In Hebrew there is a metathesis rule that reverses a pronoun-final consonant with the first consonant of the following verb if the verb starts with a sibilant. These are in "reflexive" verb forms, as shown in the following examples:

NONSIBILANT INITIAL VERBS		SIBILANT INITIAL VERBS	
kabel	lehit-kabel	tsadek	lehits-tadek
"to accept"	"to be accepted"	"to justify"	"to apologize"
			(not *lehit-tsadek)
pater	lehit-pater	sames	lehis-tames
"to fire"	"to resign"	"to use for"	"to use"
			(not *lehit-sames)
bayes	lehit-bayes	sader	lehis-tader
"to shame"	"to be ashamed"	"to arrange"	"to arrange oneself"
			(not *lehit-sader)

We see then that phonological rules may do the following:

1. Change feature values (e.g., vowel nasalization rule in English);
2. Add new features (e.g., aspiration in English);
3. Delete segments (e.g., final consonant deletion in French);
4. Add segments (e.g., vowel insertion in Greenlandic);
5. Reorder segments (e.g., metathesis rule in Hebrew).

These rules, when applied to the phonemic representations of words and phrases, result in phonetic forms that differ (or may differ) substantially from the phonemic forms. If such differences were unpredictable one would find it difficult to explain how we as speakers can understand what we hear or how we produce utterances that represent the meanings we wish to convey. The more we look at languages, however, the more we see that many aspects of the phonetic forms of utterances which appear at first to be irregular and unpredictable are actually rule-governed. We learn, or construct, these rules when we are learning the language as children. The rules represent "patterns," or general principles.

FROM ONE TO MANY AND FROM MANY TO ONE

In the discussion on how phonemic representations of utterances are realized phonetically, it might have been concluded that each phoneme is represented by a set of allophones which "belong" only to that phoneme. That is, phoneme A is represented by the phonetic segments [a] and [a'], phoneme B by [b] and [b'], phoneme C by [c] and [c'], and so on, and phoneme A can never be realized as [b] or [c]. This would be a neat and tidy mapping of phonemic representations onto phonetic representations. But the mind is capable of greater complexities, which show up in the phonological rules of grammars. Consider the italicized vowels in the following pairs of words:

	A			B	
/i/	comp*e*te	[i]	comp*e*tition	[ə]
/ɪ/	med*i*cinal	[ɪ]	med*i*cine	[ə]
/e/	maint*ai*n	[e]	maint*e*nance	[ə]
/ɛ/	t*e*legraph	[ɛ]	t*e*legraphy	[ə]
/æ/	an*a*lysis	[æ]	an*a*lytic	[ə]
/a/	s*o*lid	[a]	s*o*lidify	[ə]
/o/	ph*o*ne	[o]	ph*o*nology	[ə]
/u/	Talm*u*dic	[u]	Talm*u*d	[ə]

In column A all the italicized vowels are stressed vowels and show a variety of different vowel phones; in column B all the italicized unstressed vowels are pronounced [ə]. Yet the "reduced" vowels of column B must be derived from different underlying phonemes, since when they are stressed they show up as different vowels in column A. If the italicized vowel of *compete* were not phonemically /i/, there would be no way to account for the particular quality of the stressed vowel. Thus, one might say that [ə] is an allophone of all English vowel phonemes. The rule to derive the schwa can be stated simply as:

(3) Change a vowel into a [ə] when it is unstressed.

This rule is oversimplified because when an unstressed vowel occurs as the final segment of a word it retains its full vowel quality, as shown in words like *confetti, cocoa,* or *democracy.* Try to state this rule in its more correct form.

The rule that "reduces" unstressed vowels to schwas is another example of a rule that changes feature values.

In a phonological description of a language we do not know, we can't always tell from the phonetic transcription what the phonemic representation is. But given the phonemic representation and the phonological rules, one can always derive the correct phonetic transcription. Of course in our internal, mental grammars this is no problem, since the words are listed phonemically and we know the rules of the language.

Another example may help to illustrate this aspect of phonology.

In English, /t/ and /d/ are both phonemes, as is illustrated by the minimal pairs *tie/die* and *bat/bad*. When /t/ or /d/ occurs between a stressed and an unstressed vowel they both become a flap [D]. For many speakers of English, *writer* and *rider* are pronounced identically as [rayDər]. Yet speakers know that *writer* has a *phonemic* /t/ because of *write* /rayt/, and that *rider* has a *phonemic* /d/ because of *ride* /rayd/. The "flap rule" may be stated as:

(4) An alveolar stop becomes a voiced flap when preceded by a stressed vowel and followed by an unstressed vowel.

The application of this rule is illustrated as follows:

PHONEMIC REPRESENTATION	write /rayt/	writer /rayt + ər/ ↓	ride /rayd/	rider /rayd + ər/ ↓
"flap rule"	NA	D	NA	D
PHONETIC REPRESENTATION	[rayt]	[rayDər]	[rayd]	[rayDər]

We are omitting other phonetic details which are also determined by phonological rules, such as the fact that in *ride* the vowel is slightly longer than in *write* because it is followed by a voiced [d]. We are using the example only to illustrate the fact that two distinct phonemes may be realized phonetically as the same sound.

Such cases show that one cannot arrive at a phonological analysis by simply inspecting the phonetic representation of utterances. If we just looked for minimal pairs as the only evidence for phonology, we would have to conclude that [D] was a phoneme in English because it contrasts phonetically with other phonetic units: *riper* [raypər], *rhymer* [raymər], *riser* [rayzər], and so forth. Grammars are much more complex than this. The fact that *write* and *ride* change their phonetic forms when suffixes are added shows that there is an intricate mapping between phonemic representations of words and phonetic pronunciation.

Note that in the case of the "schwa rule" and the case of the "flap rule" the allophones derived from the different phonemes by rule are different in features from all other phonemes in the language. That is, there is no /D/ phoneme, but there is a [D] phone.

Similar rules showing there is no one-to-one relation between phonemes and phones are found in other languages. In both Russian and German, when voiced obstruents occur at the end of a word (or syllable) they become voiceless. Both voiced and voiceless obstruents do occur in German as phonemes, as is shown by the following minimal pair:

Tier [ti:r] "animal" *dir* [di:r] "to you"

At the end of a word, however, only [t] occurs; the words meaning "league," *Bund*, and "colorful" (singular), *bunt*, are phonetically identical and pronounced [būnt]. Should they then be phonemically identical; that is, /būnt/?

If *Bund* and *bunt* were represented phonemically as /bunt/, identically with the phonetic pronunciation, there would be no way of deriving the [d] in the plural of *Bunde* [bŭndə]. If, however, the singular and plural stems are represented phonemically as /bund/ and /bunt/ and there is a rule in the grammar of German which says "devoice obstruents at the end of a word," we would get the following derivations:

PHONEMIC REPRESENTATION	/bund/	/bundə/	/bunt/	/buntə/
devoicing rule	t	NA	NA	NA
PHONETIC REPRESENTATION	[būnt]	[bŭndə]	[būnt]	[būntə]

This is another example to show that the phonetic realization of two distinct phonemes may be identical in certain environments. The rule is one that, like the vowel reduction rule in English and the homorganic nasal rule, changes the specifications of features. In the case of German, the phonemic representation of the final stop in *Bund* is /d/, specified as [+ voiced]; this is changed by the rule above to [− voiced] to derive the phonetic [t] in word-final position.

This rule in German further illustrates that one cannot decide what the phonemic representation of a word is, given only the phonetic form, since [būnt] can be derived from either /bund/ or /bunt/. But given the phonemic representations and the rules of the language, the phonetic forms are automatically determined.

Tone and Intonation

In Chapter 2 we mentioned that speakers of all languages vary the pitch of their voices when they talk, and that the pitch produced depends upon how fast the vocal cords vibrate; the faster they vibrate, the higher the pitch.

The way pitch is used linguistically differs from language to language. In English, it doesn't much matter whether you say *cat* with a high pitch or a low pitch. It will still mean "cat." But if you say *ba* with a high pitch in Nupe (a language spoken in Nigeria), it will mean "to be sour," whereas if you say *ba* with a low pitch, it will mean "to count." The pitch "contour" *is* important in English; *John is going* as a statement is said with a falling pitch, but as a question the pitch rises at the end. Languages that use the pitch of *individual syllables* to contrast meanings are called **tone** languages. Languages that use pitch syntactically (for example, to change a sentence from a statement to a question) or in which the changing pitch of a *whole sentence* is otherwise important to the meaning are called **intonation** languages.

TONE

It is probably safe to say that most of the languages in the world are tone languages. There are more than 1000 tone languages in Africa alone; many languages of Asia, such as Chinese, Thai, and Burmese, are tone languages, as are many American Indian languages.

Thai is a language that has contrasting pitches, or tones. The same string of "segmental" sounds represented by [naa] will mean different things if one says the sounds with a low pitch, a mid pitch, a high pitch, a falling pitch from high to low, or a rising pitch from low to high. Thai therefore has five linguistic tones:

nàa	[__]	low tone	"a nickname"
naa	[—]	mid tone	"rice paddy"
náa	[⎺]	high tone	"younger maternal uncle or aunt"
nâa	[⟍]	falling tone	"face"
nǎa	[⟋]	rising tone	"thick"

In Nupe, there are three tones:

bá	[⎺]	high tone	"to be sour"
bā	[—]	mid tone	"to cut"
bà	[＿]	low tone	"to count"

In Twi we find contrasts between high and low pitch (tone):

dùà	[＿]	low + low	"tail"
dùá	[＿⎺]	low + high	"tree"
dòtó	[＿⎺]	low + high	"go buy"
kótò	[⎺＿]	high + low	"crab"

In some tone languages the pitch of each tone is "level"; in others, the direction of the pitch (whether it glides from high to low, or from low to high) is important. Tones that "glide" are called **contour** tones; tones that don't are called **level,** or **register,** tones. In a tone language it is not the absolute pitch of the syllables that is important but the relations between the pitch of different syllables. This would have to be so, since some individual speakers have high-pitched voices, others low-pitched, and others medium-pitched. In fact, in many tone languages one finds a falling-off of the pitch, or a "downdrifting."

In the following sentence in Twi, it is the *relative* rather than the *absolute* pitch that is important:

Kòfí hwèhwé áduàné kàkrà mà n'àdàmfò bá.
"Kofi searches for a little food for his friend's child."

The tones can be specified as follows:

low high low high high low low high low high low low high low high

The actual pitches of these syllables would be rather different from each other, shown as follows (the higher the number, the higher the pitch):

8.	fí							
7.		hwé á						
6.	kò			né				
5.		hwè			krá			
4.			dùà			dám		
3.				kà			bá	
2.					mà nà			
1.						fò		

The lowering of the pitch is called **downdrift.** In languages with downdrift —and many tone languages in Africa are downdrift languages—a high tone that occurs after a low tone, or a low tone after a high tone, is lower in pitch than the preceding similarly marked tone. Note that the first high tone in the sentence is given the pitch value 8. The next high tone (which occurs after an intervening low tone) is 7; that is, it is lower in pitch than the first high tone.

This example shows that in analyzing tones, just as in analyzing segments, all the physical properties need not be considered; only essential features are important in language—in this case, whether the tone is "high" or "low" in relation to the other pitches, but not the specific pitch of that tone.

INTONATION

In languages that are not tone languages, such as English, pitch still plays an important role. The way we use pitch can be illustrated by a sign occasionally seen in men's lavatories:

We aim to please. You aim too, please.

Two sentences can be exactly the same phonetically except for the overall pitch contour of the utterance. The pitch contour, which is called the **intonation** of the sentence, can be used to distinguish between two different meanings. Note sentences a and b:

a. What did you put in my drink, Jane?

b. What did you put in my drink, Jane?

In sentence a the questioner is asking what Jane put in the drink. In sentence b the questioner is asking if someone put Jane in the drink. In sentence a the pitch rises sharply on the word *drink* and then falls off. In sentence b the sharp rise is on *Jane* and it continues to rise without any decrease.

Sentence c illustrates that a written sentence may be ambiguous (may have two meanings):

c. Tristram left directions for Isolde to follow.

When spoken it can be disambiguated by changing the intonation. If it means that Tristram wanted Isolde to follow him, it is pronounced with the rise in pitch on the first syllable of *follow,* followed by a fall in pitch, as in d:

d. Tristram left directions for Isolde to follow.

The sentence can also mean that Tristram left a set of directions he wanted Isolde to use. If this is the intention, the highest pitch comes on the second syllable of *directions,* as in e:

e. Tristram left directions for Isolde to follow.

The way we have indicated pitch is of course highly oversimplified. Before the big rise in pitch the voice does not remain on the same monotone low pitch. These pitch diagrams indicate merely when there is a special change in pitch.

Thus pitch plays an important role in both tone languages and intonation languages but functions in different ways.

Stress

By permission of Johnny Hart and Field Enterprises, Inc.

WORD STRESS

In English and many other languages, one or more of the syllables in each content word (words other than the little words like *to*, *the*, *a*, *of*, and so on) **is stressed.** The stressed syllable is marked by ´ in the following examples:

súbject   noun, as in "The subject of the story . . ."
subjéct   verb, as in "He'll subject us to his boring stories."
pérvert   noun, as in "My neighbor is a pervert."
pervért   verb, as in "Don't pervert the idea."[4]

In some words, more than one vowel may be stressed, but if so, one of these stressed vowels receives greater stress than the others. The most highly stressed vowel is indicated by a ´ over the vowel (this is the vowel receiving the **accent,** or **primary** stress, or **main** stress); the other stressed vowels are indicated by marking a ` over the vowels (these vowels receive **secondary** stress).

rèsignátion   phònétic   sỳstemátic
fùndaméntal   ìntrodúctory   rèvolútion

Generally, speakers of a language know which syllable receives primary stress or accent, which receives secondary stress, and which are not stressed at all; it is part of their knowledge of the language. The stress pattern of a word may differ from dialect to dialect. For example, in most varieties of American English the word *láboratòry* has two stressed syllables; in one dialect of British English it receives only one stress [ləbɔ́rətri]. Because the vowel qualities in English are closely related to whether they are stressed or not, the British vowels differ from the American vowels in this word; in fact, in the British version one vowel "drops out" completely because it is not stressed.

One can then specify each vowel as either [+ stress] or [− stress]. Vowels

---

[4] These minimal pairs show that stress in English is contrastive.

specified as [+ stress] may be [+ accent] or [− accent]. If there is only one stressed vowel in the word it will also be [+ accent]. One can also designate stress by numbers. The primary stressed or accented vowel can be designated by placing a "1" over the vowel; secondary stress can be designated by a "2"; unstressed vowels are left unmarked.

2 1   2   1
resignation   systematic

To stress a syllable, one may change the *pitch* (usually by raising it), make the syllable *louder,* or make it *longer.* We often use all three of these phonetic features to stress a syllable.

SENTENCE AND PHRASE STRESS

When words are combined into phrases and sentences, one of the syllables receives greater stress than all others. That is, just as there is only one primary stress in a word spoken in isolation (for example, in a list), only one of the vowels in a phrase (or sentence) receives primary stress or accent; all the other stressed vowels are "reduced" to secondary stress. A syllable that may have received the main stress when the word was not in a phrase may have only secondary stress in a phrase, as is illustrated by these examples:

hót + dóg	→ hótdòg	("frankfurter")
hót + dóg	→ hòt dóg	("an overheated dog")
réd + cóat	→ Rédcòat	("a British soldier")
réd + cóat	→ rèd cóat	("a coat that is red")
white + hóuse	→ Whíte Hòuse	("the president's house")
white + hóuse	→ whìte hóuse	("a house painted white")

These minimal pairs show that stress may be predictable if phonological rules include nonphonological information; that is, the phonology is not totally independent of the rest of the grammar. In English we place primary stress on an adjective followed by a noun when the two words are combined in a compound noun, but we place the stress on the noun when the words are combined in a noun phrase in which the noun is modified by the adjective. The differences between the pairs above are therefore predictable:

NOUN COMPOUNDS	ADJECTIVE + NOUN PHRASE
Whíte House	white hóuse
Rédcoat	red cóat
hótdog	hot dóg
bláckboard	black bóard
blúebird	blue bírd

The stress differences between the noun and verb pairs discussed in the previous section are also predictable from the word category.

In the English sentences used above to illustrate intonation contours, one may also describe the differences by referring to the word on which the main stress is placed. For example, in *We àim to pléase* the primary stress is on the word *please*, and in *Yòu àim tóo, plèase* the primary stress is on *too*.

Vowel and Consonant Length

In English if you pronounce a word by sustaining the vowel—that is, by making it *longer*—the meaning of the word doesn't change. Vowel length is noncontrastive in English. Long and short vowels do occur in English, however, but they do not contrast. All the English vowels occur slightly longer before voiced consonants than before voiceless ones, and also at the end of words, as shown in the following examples:

"beat"   /bit/   [bit]
"bead"   /bid/   [bi:d]
"bee"   /bi/   [bi:]
"bit"   /bɪt/   [bɪt]
"bid"   /bɪd/   [bɪ:d]
"loot"   /lut/   [lut]
"lewd"   /lud/   [lu:d]
"Lou"   /lu/   [lu:]

Because the vowels with longer duration are predictable, vowel length in English is nonphonemic.

In other languages, however, vowel length is nonpredictable and whether a vowel is long or short in duration can distinguish meanings. Consider the following minimal pairs in Japanese.

biru   "building"   tsuji   "proper name"
bi:ru "beer"   tsu:ji "moving the bowels"

When teaching at a university in Japan, one of the authors of this book inadvertantly pronounced Ms. Tsuji's name as Tsu:ji-san. The effect of this error quickly taught him to respect vowel length in Japanese.

Consonant length also is contrastive in Japanese. A consonant may be lengthened by prolonging the closure: a long *t* [tt] can be produced by holding the tongue against the alveolar ridge twice as long as for a short *t* [t]. The following minimal pairs illustrate the fact that consonant length is also phonemic in Japanese.

shite   "doing"   saki   "ahead"
shitte "knowing"   sakki "before"

Function of Phonological Rules

The function of the phonological rules in a grammer is to provide the phonetic information necessary for the pronunciation of utterances. One may illustrate this in the following way:

input   PHONEMIC (DICTIONARY) REPRESENTATION OF WORDS
IN A SENTENCE
↓
Phonological rules (P-rules)
↓
output PHONETIC REPRESENTATION OF WORDS IN A SENTENCE

That is, the input to the P-rules is the **phonemic representation;** the P-rules apply or operate on the phonemic strings and produce as output the **phonetic representation.**

This should not be interpreted as meaning that when we speak we necessarily apply one rule after another. Speaking is part of linguistic performance; phonological rules represent part of one's grammar, which in turn is equivalent to one's knowledge of the language. The rules reveal the more abstract relationship between phonemic and phonetic representations. The grammar does not describe how we use this grammar in speech production or comprehension.

Thus, to state that there is a phonological rule which nasalizes vowels before nasal consonants in English is to state an abstract rule or principle or formula. This doesn't mean that you necessarily start with a nonnasal vowel and then apply the rule when you are speaking. It means that your knowledge of English and the distribution of oral and nasal vowels is represented by this statement.

The rules however may indeed be applied in performance. "Slips of the tongue," in which we deviate in some way from the intended utterance, show that such rules are applied or are "real."

For example, someone who intended to say *gone to seed* [gãn tə sid] said instead *god to seen* [gad tə sĩn]. The final consonants of the first and third words were reversed. But notice that the reversal of the consonants also changed the nasality of the vowels. The first vowel /a/ was a nasalized [ã] in the intended utterance; in the actual utterance the nasalization was "lost," since it no longer occurred before a nasal consonant. But the vowel in the third word which was the nonnasal [i] in the intended utterance became [ĩ] in the error, since it was followed by *n*. The nasalization rule applied.

Another speech error shows the application of the aspiration rule. For the intended *stick in the mud* [stɪk ĩn ðə mʌd], the speaker said *smuck in the tid* [smʌk ĩn·ðə tʰɪd]. When the /t/ occurred incorrectly as the initial consonant of the last word it was pronounced as an aspirated [tʰ], although in the intended utterance after the /s/ it would have been pronounced as a [t].

An examination of the phonologies of different languages shows rules that add features, change features, add segments, delete segments, and transpose or switch segments. This must mean that human linguistic ability permits us to form such rules. Just as all possible sounds are not found in languages, so all conceivable rules are not. No language has ever been found which includes a rule specifying that all the phonemes in a word should be reversed or that every third phoneme should be deleted or that one should add an /l/ before a word just in case the word has thirteen phonemes. These rules are logically but not phonologically possible. We see then that the forms of grammars, and their phonological parts, are not as variable as Satie seemed to think. There are universal constraints on the phonological systems that humans can learn.

The Formalization of Phonological Rules

Form follows function.
Slogan of the Bauhaus school of architecture

In this chapter all the examples of phonological rules we have considered have been stated in words. That is, we have not used any special "formal devices" or "formal notations." We could, however, have stated the rules using special symbols that would make the rules look more like "mathematical" formulas.

A number of such notational devices are used as part of the theory of phonology. They do more than merely save paper or abbreviate long statements. They provide a way to express the generalizations of the language that may be obscured otherwise.

For example, if we used our + and − feature value notation in the rule that nasalizes vowels before nasal consonants, it could be stated as:

(5) $\begin{bmatrix} +\text{vocalic} \\ -\text{consonantal} \end{bmatrix}$ becomes [+nasal] before a [+nasal].

This clearly shows that just one feature is changed and that it is an assimilatory rule.

When we discussed *natural classes of speech sounds* we referred to the explanatory power of the feature notation. We were showing that certain kinds of formalization are important in any theory. We can illustrate this point by assuming a rule that nasalizes a vowel before, and only before, a /p/. By stating this without features, we could say: Nasalize a vowel before a /p/. This seems to be as simple and general a rule as the nasalization rule. Yet it is a strange and highly unlikely rule. To state this rule with features, we would have to write:

(6) $\begin{bmatrix} +\text{vocalic} \\ -\text{consonantal} \end{bmatrix}$ becomes [+nasal] before a $\begin{bmatrix} +\text{consonantal} \\ -\text{vocalic} \\ +\text{labial} \\ -\text{voiced} \\ -\text{continuant} \end{bmatrix}$.

We can see at a glance that Rule (6) is more complex (you have to mention more features) than Rule (5), and that the features mentioned have nothing in common. Rule (5) seems like a "natural" rule and Rule (6) does not. But that is exactly what we want to reveal. Without the use of features the difference between the two rules is hidden. The use of such feature notation to represent phonemes is, then, part of the theory of phonology. The formal notation is not used merely because it is somehow more "elegant" but because it better represents what we know about phonological rules.

Instead of writing "becomes" or "occurs" we can use an arrow, →, to show that the segment on the left of the arrow is or becomes whatever is on the right of the arrow:

(7) $\begin{bmatrix} +\text{vocalic} \\ -\text{consonantal} \end{bmatrix}$ → [+nasal] before a [+nasal].

The phonological environment, or context, is also important to specify in a rule. In many languages vowels are nasalized before but not after a nasal. We can formalize the notions of "environment" or "in the environment" and the notions of "before" and "after" by the following notations:

a slash, /, to mean "in the environment of"
a dash, –, placed before or after the segment(s) that determine the change

Using these notations we can write the above rule:

(8) $\begin{bmatrix} +\text{vocalic} \\ -\text{consonantal} \end{bmatrix} \rightarrow [+\text{nasal}] \, / - [+\text{nasal}].$

This rule reads: "A vowel (that is, a segment which is specified as vocalic and nonconsonantal) becomes ($\rightarrow$) nasalized in the environment (/) before (–) a nasal segment.
If we write the rule as

(9) $\begin{bmatrix} +\text{vocalic} \\ -\text{consonantal} \end{bmatrix} \rightarrow [+\text{nasal}] \, / \, [+\text{nasal}] - .$

it reads: "A vowel becomes nasalized in the environment *after* a nasal." The fact that the dash follows the [+ nasal] shows that a vowel which comes *after* it is changed.
Some of the rules discussed above state that the segment to be changed by the rule occurs at the beginning or end of a word. We can use a double cross, #, to signify a word boundary.
See if you can read the following rule:

(10) $\begin{bmatrix} -\text{continuant} \\ -\text{voiced} \end{bmatrix} \rightarrow [+\text{aspirated}] \, / \, \# - \begin{bmatrix} -\text{consonantal} \\ +\text{vocalic} \\ +\text{stressed} \end{bmatrix} .$

If the formal devices and notational system we have been discussing haven't completely confused you, you should be able to see that this is our old friend the "aspiration rule" and should be read: "A voiceless stop (a segment that is [– continuant] and [– voiced]) becomes ($\rightarrow$) aspirated in the environment (/) after a word boundary (#–) (that is, at the beginning of a word) before a stressed vowel (a segment that is [– consonantal] and [+ vocalic] and [+ stressed])." Note that the environment dash occurs between the # and the vowel segment.
The aspiration rule as stated in Rule (10) does not specify that voiceless stops are aspirated when they occur in the middle of a word at the beginning of a syllable before a stressed vowel. Yet the following examples show that the rule as stated is incorrect since it only applies at the beginning of a word.

repeat /ripít/ [rəpʰít]   versus   *compass* /kʌ́mpəs/ [kʰʌ́mpəs]

Because every word-initial segment is also syllable-initial, we can fix up

Rule (10) by using a different symbol for syllable boundary, say, $. By substituting $ for # the rule will apply to all the proper phonemes. Note that we do not have to write two rules, one for word-initial voiceless stops and one for syllable-initial voiceless stops before stressed vowels. Where one rule will suffice, to state the process in two rules would obscure the generalization.

Sometimes the ability to state once what appears to be two rules is not so obvious. Consider the two environments in which we pointed out that vowel phonemes are lengthened (become [+long]): before voiced obstruents and at the end of words. We can, of course, formalize these two environments in two rules:

(11) a. [−consonantal] → [+long] / − $\begin{bmatrix} +\text{consonantal} \\ -\text{vocalic} \\ +\text{voiced} \end{bmatrix}$.
      (vowels and glides)

   b. [− consonantal] → [+ long] / − **#**.

By writing two rules, we seem to be missing a generalization, since both Rule (11a) and Rule (11b) apply to vowels and glides and add the feature [+ long]. To **collapse** or combine two or more rules that have *identical parts* we can use another device, braces { }, and can collapse Rules (11a) and (11b) into (11c).

(11) c. [−consonantal] → [+long] / − $\left\{ \begin{matrix} \begin{bmatrix} +\text{consonantal} \\ -\text{vocalic} \\ +\text{voiced} \end{bmatrix} \\ \text{\#} \end{matrix} \right\}$.

The braces signify that the rule applies *either* before voiced consonants *or* before a word boundary. Thus the brace notation permits us to express a general rule in a general fashion.

In the discussion on the English "flap rule" which specifies that a /t/ and /d/ becomes [D] after a stressed vowel and before an unstressed vowel we noted that there may be a phonetic difference in vowel length between *write* and *ride*. This is, of course, due to Rule (11c), which would apply to *ride* /rayd/ to produce [ray:d] but would not apply to *write* /rayt/ which phonetically is [rayt].

Though *write* and *ride* are pronounced by most speakers with phonetically different vowel diphthongs, some speakers pronounce *writer* and *rider* with different vowel lengths, and others pronounce these words with the same length, usually the longer variety.

How can this be accounted for when in *writer* and *rider* the phonetic vowels both occur before the *voiced* flap [D]?

This difference reveals another interesting aspect of phonological rules. In many cases the ordering of the rules is important. Speakers who apply the "flap rule" first will have no phonetic contrast; *writer* and *rider* will be identical phonetically—[ray:Dər]. But speakers who apply the vowel lengthening rule *before* the flap rule will only have a longer vowel in *rider*, as can be seen by the following **derivations:**

PHONEMIC	"writer"	"rider"		"writer"	"rider"
REPRESENTATION	/rayt + ər/	/rayd + ər/		/rayt + ər/	/rayd + ər/
1. Flap rule	Ď	Ď	1. Vowel length	NA	ay:
2. Vowel length	ay:	ay:	2. Flap rule	Ď	Ď
PHONETIC					
REPRESENTATION	[ray:Dər]	[ray:Dər]		[rayDər	ray:Dər]

The ordering of the rules, permitted by the theory, is a formal way of showing how a speaker's grammar specifies the pronunciation of words and sentences. We do not necessarily apply rules in sequence when we pronounce these words in speech performance. Just as phonemes are abstractions, explicit rule ordering is also an abstraction. There is, however, some evidence from speech errors that ordering of this kind may actually occur in performance. The specified order of rules is part of the formal apparatus of the theory of phonology.

We mention only one other "notational device" that helps reveal generalizations in phonology. Suppose there was a rule in some language to shorten a vowel when the vowel occurs before two consonants or one consonant. We could write this rule using the brace notation:

$$\textbf{(12)} \quad \begin{bmatrix} +\text{vocalic} \\ -\text{consonantal} \end{bmatrix} \rightarrow [-\text{long}] \, / - \left\{ \begin{matrix} \begin{bmatrix} -\text{vocalic} \\ +\text{consonantal} \end{bmatrix} \begin{bmatrix} -\text{vocalic} \\ +\text{consonantal} \end{bmatrix} \\ \begin{bmatrix} -\text{vocalic} \\ +\text{consonantal} \end{bmatrix} \end{matrix} \right\}$$

If we use V for vowels and C for consonants, this can be written as:

$$\textbf{(13)} \quad V \rightarrow [-\text{long}] \, / - \left\{ \begin{matrix} CC \\ C \end{matrix} \right\}.$$

This rule gives us the result we want; by using the braces we have collapsed two rules, both of which apply to vowels and both of which shorten the vowels. But there are identical parts in the two rules that are repeated. This seems to miss a generalization we would want to capture. That is, we should have some notational device which clearly and simply shows that the rule applies before two consonants or one consonant. To collapse rules like this, we use parentheses, ( ), around an "optional" segment or segments. That is, the rule really states that a vowel is always shortened before one consonant and there may or may not be a second consonant. The presence of the second consonant does not affect the rule. Using parentheses, we can state the rule as:

$$\textbf{(14)} \quad V \rightarrow [-\text{long}] \, / - C \, (C)$$

This rule then reads: "A vowel is shortened in the environment before two consonants (with the C in parentheses included) or before one consonant."

The importance of formal devices such as feature notations, arrows, slashes, dashes, braces, and parentheses is that they enable us to express linguistic generalizations. Since the grammar that linguists write for any particular language aims to express in the most general fashion a speaker's linguistic competence, the notations that permit them to do this are part of the theory of phonology.

We have not discussed all the formalisms used in phonology to capture linguistic generalizations. Actually, our main purpose here is to help you understand the *kinds* of phonological processes (rules) found in the languages of the world. Thus, this discussion of formal notations as such is brief, since it is intended mainly for those who wish to read further in phonology and who may come across rules written in this way.

SUMMARY

Part of one's knowledge of a language is knowledge of the sound system—the **phonology** of that language. The phonology of the language includes the inventory of **phones,** the phonetic segments that occur in the language, and the ways in which they pattern. It is this patterning that determines the inventory of the more abstract phonological units, the **phonemes** of the language. Phonemes are the segments used to differentiate between the meanings of words. These are distinguished by **distinctive features.** When phones occur in **complementary distribution,** they are **allophones**—predictable phonetic variants—of phonemes.

The phonology of a language also includes constraints on the *sequences* of phonemes in the language, as exemplified by the fact that in English two stop consonants may not occur together at the beginning of a word.

The relationship between the **phonemic representation** of words and sentences and the **phonetic representation** (the pronunciation of these words and sentences) is determined by general **phonological rules.**

Phonological rules in a grammar apply to phonemic strings and may alter them in various ways to reveal how they are pronounced:

1. They may be **assimilation** rules that change feature values of segments, thus spreading phonetic processes. The rule that nasalizes vowels in English before nasal consonants is such a rule.

2. They may add nondistinctive features that are predictable from the context. The rule that aspirates voiceless stops at the beginning of words and syllables in English is such a rule, since aspiration is a nonphonemic, nondistinctive **redundant** feature.

3. They may add segments that are not present in the phonemic string. The rule in Greenlandic that inserts a vowel between two consonants is an example of an addition rule.

4. They may delete phonemic segments in certain contexts. The many contraction rules are deletion rules in English.

5. They may transpose or move segments in a string. These **metathesis** rules occur in many languages like Hebrew. The rule in certain American dialects that changes an /sk/ to [ks] in final position is also a metathesis rule.

Phonological rules often refer to entire classes of sounds rather than to individual sounds. These are **natural classes,** dependent on the phonetic properties or features that pertain to all the members of each class, such as voiceless sounds, voiced sounds, stops, fricatives, consonants, vowels, or, using +'s and −'s, the class specified as [−voiced] or [+consonantal] or [−continuant] or [+nasal].

Words in some languages may also be phonemically distinguished by the pitch of the syllables or vowels. Such languages are called **tone** languages. Other **intonation** languages use pitch variations over phrases and sentences but not phonemically to distinguish individual words. Thai is a tone language, while English is an intonation language.

Stress, vowel **length,** and consonant length may also be used phonemically. Examples were provided from English and Japanese to show how words and phrases may be distinguished by different stress or length patterns.

A tool a linguist (or a student of linguistics) can use to discover the phonemes in a language is to look for **minimal pairs,** which are distinguished by one sound occurring in the same position in these words. Some pairs, such as *beat* and *meat,* contrast by means of a single distinctive feature, in this case, [±nasal], where /b/ is [−nasal] and /m/ is [+nasal]. Other minimal pairs may show sounds contrasting in more than one feature, for example, *rip* vs. *rim,* where /p/ is $\begin{bmatrix} -\text{voiced} \\ -\text{nasal} \end{bmatrix}$ and /m/ is $\begin{bmatrix} +\text{voiced} \\ +\text{nasal} \end{bmatrix}$. The /b/ − /m/ contrast shows that [±nasal] is a *distinctive feature* in English. Other pairs, like *sink* /s/ − *zink* /z/ show that [±voiced] is also a distinctive feature used to contrast phonemes in English.

The phonological rules in a language refer to the distinctive features of phonemes. Such rules show that the phonemic shape of words or phrases is not identical with their phonetic form. Although the rules may be very complex, they are never too complex to be learned, since these rules represent what speakers of a language know. We all learn the basic phonological units of our language—the phonemic segments—and the phonemic representation of words. The phonemes are not the actual phonetic sounds, but are abstract mental constructs that are realized as sounds by the operation of rules such as those described above. No one teaches us these rules. And yet all speakers of a language know the phonology of their language better than any linguist who tries to describe it. The linguist's job is to make explicit what we know unconsciously about the sound pattern of our language.

In the writing of rules, linguists use certain formal devices to permit better generalizations of the phonological processes. Features are used rather than whole segments, and other devices such as braces and parentheses collapse rules when the rules contain similar parts. Such devices are used only if they are able truly to represent what speakers know about the sound patterns of their language.

EXERCISES

1. Consider the distribution of [e] and [ɛ] in the following Spanish words

p[e]sa	"weight"	p[ɛ]ska	"fishing"
v[e]na	"vein"	v[ɛ]nga	"come"
p[e]ra	"pear"	p[ɛ]rla	"pearl"
pap[é]	"he swallowed"	pap[ɛ]l	"paper"
com[é]	"he is eating"	com[ɛ]n	"they are eating"

(*Exercise 1 continued on p. 106*)

(*Exercise 1 continued from p. 105*)

Are [e] and [ɛ] allophones of one phoneme or do they represent two phonemes? State your reasons.

If you believe they are allophones of one phoneme, state the rule (informally if you wish) that specifies when each vowel occurs phonetically.

2. The indefinite singular article in English is either *a* or *an*, as shown in the following phrases:

    a hotel, a boy, a use, a wagon, a big man, a yellow rug, a white house,
    an apple, an honor, an orange curtain, an old lady

    State the rule that determines when *a* is used and when *an* is used. If possible do not list individual sound segments but make the rule as general as possible, referring to *features* or *classes* of segments.

3. Consider the distribution of [r] and [l] in Korean in the following words:

rupi	"ruby"	mul	"water"
kiri	"road"	pal	"big"
saram	"person"	soul	"Seoul"
iruɯmi	"name"	ilkop	"seven"
ratio	"radio"	əlmana	"how much"
		ipalsa	"barber"

    ([ɯ] is a high back unrounded vowel. It does not affect your analysis in this problem.)

    Are [r] and [l] allophones of one or two phonemes? State your reasons and state the rule by which they can be derived if you conclude that they are allophones of a single phoneme.

4. In some dialects of English the following words have different vowels, as is shown by the phonetic transcriptions.

A		**B**		**C**	
bite	[bʌyt]	bide	[bayd]	tie	[tay]
rice	[rʌys]	rise	[rayz]	by	[bay]
type	[tʌyp]	bribe	[brayb]	sigh	[say]
wife	[wʌyf]	wives	[wayvz]	die	[day]
tyke	[tʌyk]	time	[taym]		
		nine	[nayn]		
		tile	[tayl]		
		tire	[tayr]		
		writhe	[rayð]		

    A. How may the classes of sounds that end the words in columns A and B be characterized? That is, what feature specifies all the final segments in A and all the final segments in B?
    B. How do the words in column C differ from those in columns A and B?
    C. Are [ʌy] and [ay] in complementary distribution? Give your reasons.
    D. If [ʌy] and [ay] are allophones of one phoneme, should they be derived from /ʌy/ or /ay/? Why?
    E. What is the *phonetic* representation of *life* and *lives*?
    F. What would the *phonetic* representations of the following words be?

        a. trial   b. bike   c. lice   d. fly   e. mine

    G. State the rule that will relate the phonemic representations to the phonetic representations of the words given above.

5. The following sets of *minimal pairs* show that English /p/ and /b/ contrast in initial, medial, and final positions.

INITIAL   MEDIAL   FINAL

pit/bit   rapid/rabid   cap/cab

Find similar sets of minimal pairs for each pair of consonants given:

a. /k/–/g/   d. /m/–/n/   g. /l/–/r/
b. /b/–/v/   e. /b/–/m/   h. /p/–/f/
c. /s/–/š/   f. /č/–/ǰ/   i. /s/–/z/

6. Pairs like *top* and *chop, dunk* and *junk, so* and *show* reveal that /t/ and /č/, /d/ and /ǰ/, and /s/ and /š/ are distinct phonemes in English. Although it is difficult to find a minimal pair to distinguish /z/ and /ž/ they both occur in similar, if not identical, environments such as *razor* and *azure*. Consider these same pairs of nonpalatalized and palatalized consonants in the following data. (The palatal forms are optional and often occur in casual speech.)

NONPALATALIZED   PALATALIZED

[hɪt mi]   "hit me"   [hɪč yu]   "hit you"
[lid hīm] "lead him"   [liǰ yu]   "lead you"
[pæs ʌs]   "pass us"   [pæš yu]   "pass you"
[luz ðɛ̃m] "lose them"   [luž yu]   "lose you"

State the rule that specifies when the /t/ /d/ /s/ /z/ may become palatalized (that is, pronounced as [č], [ǰ], [š], and [ž]). See if you can use feature notations to reveal generalizations.

7. Here are some words in Japanese. (The spelling *ch* is [č] and *ts* [ts] is an alveolar affricate.)

tatami	"mat"	tomodachi	"friend"	uchi	"house"
tegami	"letter"	totemo	"very"	otoko	"male"
chichi	"father"	tsukue	"desk"	tetsudau	"help"
shita	"under"	ato	"later"		
matsu	"wait"	deguchi	"exit"		
natsu	"summer"	tsutsumu	"wrap"		
chizu	"map"	kata	"person"		
koto	"fact"	tatemono	"building"		
		te	"hand"		

In addition, Japanese words (except for certain loan words) never contain the phonetic sequences *[ti] or *[tu]. Consider *ch* ([č]) and *ts* [ts] to be single phones.

A. Based on these data, are [t], [č], and [ts] in complementary distribution?
B. State the distribution, first in words, then using features.
C. Give a phonemic analysis of these data insofar as [t], [č], and [ts] are concerned. That is, identify the phoneme or phonemes, and the allophones.
D. Give the phonemic representation of the Japanese words given above.

8. a. The English verbs in column A have stress on the next-to-last syllable (called the **penultimate**), while the verbs in column B have their last syllable stressed. State a rule that can predict where stress occurs in these verbs.

   b. In the verbs in column C, stress also occurs on the final syllable. What do you have to add to your rule that will account for this? In the forms in columns A and B the final consonants had to be considered; in the forms in column C consider the vowels.

A	B	C
astónish	collápse	expláin
éxit	exíst	eráse
imágine	tormént	surpríse
cáncel	revólt	combíne
elícit	adópt	caréen
práctice	insíst	atóne
solícit	contórt	equáte

9. Below are listed fifteen "words." Some of them could be English "words" and others are definitely "foreign." For each "word" state whether it could or could not be an English word. For those which you mark as "foreign" give all the reasons you can think of for making this decision.

   a. [klǽnp]   f. [fɔlərayt]   k. [žoli]
   b. [tligɪt]   g. [splad]   l. [šɛktər]
   c. [prɪsk]   h. [vuzapm]   m. [θeməret]
   d. [trigãn]   i. [ŋar]   n. [ǰrudki]
   e. [æləposg]   j. [skwɪz]   o. [mlop]

10. Consider these *phonetic* forms of the following Hebrew words:

[v] − [b]		[f] − [p]	
bika	"lamented"	litef	"stroked"
mugbal	"limited"	sefer	"book"
šavar	"broke" (masc.)	šataf	"washed"
šavra	"broke" (fem.)	para	"cow"
ʔikev	"delayed"	mitpaxat	"handkerchief"
bara	"created"	haʔalpim	"the Alps"

(In answering the questions below, you should consider these words and the phonetic sequences as representative of what may occur in Hebrew. In your answers consider classes of sounds rather than just individual sounds.)

   A. Are [b] and [v] allophones of one phoneme, and therefore in complementary distribution?

   B. Does the same rule, or lack of a rule, which describes the distribution of [b] and [v] apply to the distribution of [p] and [f]?

   C. Here is a word with one phone missing. A blank appears in place of the missing sound: hid __ ik. Which *one* of the following statements is correct? (Only one is correct.)

   a. [b] but not [v] could occur in the empty slot.
   b. [v] but not [b] could occur in the empty slot.
   c. Either [b] or [v] could occur in the empty slot.
   d. Neither [b] nor [v] could occur in the empty slot.

D. Which one of the following statements is correct about the incomplete word ____ana?

a. [f] but not [p] could occur in the empty slot.
b. [p] but not [f] could occur in the empty slot.
c. Either [p] or [f] could fill the blank.
d. Neither [p] nor [f] could fill the blank.

E. Now consider the following possible words (in *phonetic* transcription):

laval   surva   labal   palar   falu   razif

If these words actually occur in Hebrew, would they:

a. Force you to revise your conclusions about the distribution of labial stops and fricatives you reached on the basis of the first group of words given above?
b. Support your original conclusions?
c. Neither support nor disprove your original conclusions?

11. State the following rules using the "formal devices" discussed at the end of the chapter.

Example: Aspirate a voiceless stop consonant at the end of a word.

$$\begin{bmatrix} -\text{continuant} \\ -\text{voice} \end{bmatrix} \rightarrow [+\text{aspirated}] \ / - \#$$

A. A vowel is stressed in the environment after a word boundary (at the beginning of a word).
B. A voiced consonant becomes nasal before a nasal.
C. A voiceless segment becomes voiced between two vowels.
D. A voiced consonant becomes voiceless either before a voiceless consonant or at the end of a word.
E. A vowel is lengthened before one or two voiced consonants.

REFERENCES

Anderson, Stephen R. 1974. *The Organization of Phonology*. Academic Press. New York.

Chomsky, N., and M. Halle. 1968. *The Sound Pattern of English*. Harper & Row. New York.

Hyman, Larry M. 1975. *Phonology: Theory and Analysis*. Holt, Rinehart and Winston. New York.

Schane, S. A. 1973. *Generative Phonology*. Prentice-Hall. Englewood Cliffs, N.J.

Chapter 4

Morphology: The Words of Language

B.C.   **Johnny Hart**

By permission of Johnny Hart and Field Enterprises, Inc.

A word is dead
When it is said,
Some say.
I say it just
Begins to live
That day.

Emily Dickinson, "A Word"

Every speaker of a language knows thousands, even tens of thousands, of words. Knowing a word means knowing both its sound and its meaning. Someone who doesn't know English would not know where one word begins or ends in hearing an utterance like [ðəkʰætètðərǽt]. It isn't even possible to tell how many words have been said. If you are a speaker of English, however, you will have no difficulty in segmenting the sounds into the individual words *the cat ate the rat*. Similarly, someone who doesn't know Potawatomi would not know whether [kwapmuknanuk] (which means "They see us.") was one, two, or more words. It is, in fact, only one word, as any speaker of Potawatomi could tell you.

The sounds (pronunciation) and the meaning of a word are inseparable. This was pointed out by the nineteenth-century Swiss linguist Ferdinand de Saussure, who discussed the *arbitrary* union between the sounds (form) and meaning (concept) of the **linguistic sign.** In this sense every word is a linguistic sign.

We have already seen that speakers of a language know by virtue of their phonological knowledge whether a string of sounds *could* be a word in their language. If they did not know the meaning of *plarm,* they would conclude either that it was a word they didn't know or that it wasn't a word in English. They would know, however, that it was a possible English word. If someone told them that a *plarm* was a particular kind of water rat, *plarm* would become a sound-meaning unit, a linguistic sign, a word.

Just as a particular string of sounds must be united with a meaning for it to be a word, so a concept or meaning must be united with specific sounds. Before 1955 the word *googol* [gugəl] did not exist as an English word. Now, at least among mathematicians and scientists, it is a word. The word was "coined" by the 9-year-old nephew of Dr. Edward Kasner, an American mathematician, to mean "the number 1 followed by 100 zeros," a number equal to 10^{100}. The number existed before the word was invented, but no word represented this particular numerical concept. When the concept and sounds were united, a word came into being. In fact, from this word another word, *googolplex,* was formed to mean "1 followed by a googol of zeros."

The words we know form part of our linguistic knowledge, part of our internalized grammars. Since each word is a sound-meaning unit, each word stored in our mental dictionaries must be stored with its unique phonological representation, which determines its pronunciation (when the phonological rules are applied), and with its meaning.

Each word must include other information as well. The dictionary representation of a word must include whether it is a noun, a verb, an adjective, an adverb, a preposition, a conjunction. That is, it must specify what **grammatical category,** or **syntactic class,** it is in. Some words, like *love,* may be either a noun or a verb, as shown by the sentences *I love you* and *You are the love of my life.* The classes of words, the syntactic categories—such as nouns, verbs, adjectives, and so on—will be discussed in more detail in Chapter 7. The semantic properties of words, which represent their meanings, will be discussed in Chapter 6.

Open and Closed Classes of Words

In English, nouns, verbs, adjectives, and adverbs make up the largest part of the vocabulary. They are "open" classes, because we can and regularly do add new words to these classes. *Googol,* for example, was added to the class of nouns. A new verb, *stonewall,* meaning "to be obstructive," entered American English during the political scandals of the 1970's. New adverbs like *weatherwise* and *saleswise* have been added, as well as adjectives like *biodestructible.*

The other syntactic categories are, for the most part, "closed" sets. It is not easy to think of new conjunctions or prepositions or pronouns that have entered the language recently. There is a small set of personal pronouns such as *I, me, mine, he, she,* and so on. With the growth of the feminist movement some proposals have been made for adding a new neutral singular pronoun, which would be neither masculine nor feminine, and which could be used as the general, or **generic,** form. If such a pronoun existed it might have prevented the department chairperson in a large university from making the incongruous statement: "We will hire the best person for the job regardless of his sex." The UCLA psychologist Donald MacKay has suggested that we use "e" [i] for this pronoun with various alternative forms; others point out that *they* is already being used as a neutral third-person singular, as in the sentence "Anyone can do it if they try hard enough." Because of the "closed" nature of the set of pronouns, we would predict that *they* has a better chance to serve this need than a completely new pronoun.

The separation between "open" and "closed" classes of words has psychological and neurological validity. Certain groups of brain-damaged patients have greater difficulty in using or understanding or reading closed-class words than they do open-class words. Some even interpret a word like *in* to mean *inn,* or a word like *which* to mean *witch* when they are asked to read and use such words in sentences. Other patients do just the opposite. Such effects of brain damage on language will be further discussed in Chapter 12. We mention this fact here merely to show that linguistic analysis of words is attested to by researchers in other areas of science.

WORD SETS

Another interesting thing about the words we know is that some words seem to be related to each other in a special way. The short story writer O. Henry once said: "Most wonderful of all are words, and how they make friends one with another. . . ." Perhaps he was thinking of words like the following:

phone	phonic
phonetic	phoneme
phonetician	phonemic
phonetics	allophone
phonology	telephone
phonologist	telephonic
phonological	euphonious

All the above words are related in both sound and meaning. They all include the same phonological form with a meaning identical to that of the first word, *phone. Phone* seems to be a minimal form in that it can't be divided into more elemental structures. *ph* doesn't mean anything, and *pho* [fo] has no relation in meaning to the identical sounds in the word *foe,* and *-one* /on/ is not related to the sound unit /on/, meaning "own." But all the other words on the list contain this same word as part of their structure. The phonological rules of English "tell us" that in *phonetic, phonetics, phonology, phonologist, phonemic* the pronunciation is [fən] instead of [fōn], but the same element *phone* /fon/ is present, with its identical meaning, "pertaining to sound," in all these words.

Notice further that in the following pairs of words the meanings of all the words in column B consist of the meanings of the words in column A plus the meaning "not":

A	B
desirable	undesirable
likely	unlikely
inspired	uninspired
happy	unhappy
developed	undeveloped
sophisticated	unsophisticated

Webster's Third New International Dictionary lists about 2700 adjectives beginning with *un-,* the meaning of which speakers of English would know if they knew the word without the *un-.*

The Broom Hilda Cartoon reflects the knowledge that speakers have about the meaning of *un-.*

BROOM HILDA   **Russell Myers**

Reprinted by permission of Tribune Company Syndicate, Inc.

If the most elemental units of meaning, the basic linguistic signs, are assumed to be the words of a language, it would be a coincidence that *un* has the same meaning in all the column B words above, or that *phone* has the same meaning in all the words in the preceding list. But this is obviously no coincidence. The words *undesirable, unlikely, uninspired, unhappy,* and the others in column B consist of at least two meaningful units: *un + desirable, un + likely,* and so on.

It is also a fact about English words that their internal structure is subject to rules. Thus *uneaten, unadmired, ungrammatical* are words in English, but **eatenun, *admiredun, *grammaticalun* (to mean "not eaten," "not admired," "not grammatical") are not, because we do not form a negative meaning of a word by suffixing *un* (that is, by adding it to the end of the word), but by prefixing it (that is, by adding it to the beginning).

The study of the internal structure of words, and of the rules by which words are formed, is called **morphology.** Just as knowledge of a language implies knowledge of the phonology, so it also implies knowledge of the morphology.

In this chapter we will be discussing how words are formed in English and other languages and what it is speakers of a language know about word formation, about the morphology of their language.

Morphemes: The Minimal Units of Meaning

"They gave it me," Humpty Dumpty continued . . . , "for an un-birthday present."

"I beg your pardon?" Alice said with a puzzled air.

"I'm not offended," said Humpty Dumpty.

"I mean, what is an un-birthday present?"

"A present given when it isn't your birthday, of course."

Lewis Carroll, *Through the Looking-Glass*

LUTHER   **Brumsic Brandon, Jr.**

When Samuel Goldwyn, the pioneer moviemaker, announced: "In two words: *im-possible*" he was reflecting the common view that words are the basic meaningful elements in a language. We have already seen that this cannot be so, since some words are formed by combining a number of distinct units of meaning. The traditional term for the most elemental unit of grammatical form is **morpheme.** The word is derived from the Greek word *morphē,* meaning "form." Linguistically speaking, then, Goldwyn should have said: "In two morphemes: *im-possible.*"

A single word may be composed of one or more morphemes:

one morpheme	boy, desire
two morphemes	boy + ish, desire + able
three morphemes	boy + ish + ness, desire + able + ity
four morphemes	gentle + man + li + ness, un + desire + able + ity
more than four morphemes	un + gentle + man + li + ness
	anti + dis + establish + ment + ari + an + ism[1]

A morpheme may be defined as the **minimal linguistic sign,** a grammatical unit in which there is an arbitrary union of a sound and a meaning and that cannot be further analyzed. As we shall see below, this may be too simple a definition, but it will serve our purposes for now. Every word in every language is composed of one or more morphemes.

BOUND AND FREE MORPHEMES

If we look at the examples given above we can see that some morphemes like *boy, desire, gentle,* and *man* can constitute words by themselves. Other morphemes like *-ish, -able, un-, -ness,* and *-li* are never words but always parts of words. Thus, *un-* is like *pre- (prefix, predetermine, prejudge, prearrange),* and *dis- (disallow, disobey, disapprove, dislike),* and *bi- (bipolar, bisexual, bivalved)* and occurs only before other morphemes. Such morphemes are called **prefixes.** Other morphemes occur only as **suffixes,** after other morphemes. English examples of such morphemes are *-er (singer, performer, reader, beautifier), -ist (typist, copyist, pianist, novelist, collaborationist, Marxist),* and *-ly (manly, bastardly, sickly, orderly, friendly),* to mention only a few.

These prefix and suffix morphemes have traditionally been called **bound morphemes,** because they cannot occur "unattached," as distinct from **free morphemes** like *man, bastard, sick, prove, allow, judge,* and so on. Of

---

[1] Some speakers of English would have even more morphemes than this.

course in speaking we seldom use even free morphemes alone. We combine all morphemes into larger units—phrases and sentences.

In all languages morphemes are the minimal linguistic signs. In Turkish, if you add -*ak* to a verb, you derive a noun, as in:

dur, "to stop"   *dur* + *ak*, "stopping place"
bat, "to sink"   *bat* + *ak*, "sinking place" or "marsh/swamp"

In English, in order to express reciprocal action we use the phrase *each other* as in *understand each other, love each other*. In Turkish, one simply adds a morpheme to the verb: *anla* "understand," *anla* + *š* "understand each other," *sev* "love," *sev* + *iš* "love each other."

In Piro, an Arawakan language spoken in Peru, a single morpheme, *kaka*, can be added to a verb to express the meaning "cause to": *cokoruha* "to harpoon," *cokoruha* + *kaka* "to cause to harpoon"; *salwa* "to visit," *salwa* + *kaka* "to cause to visit."

In Karok, an American Indian language spoken in the Pacific northwest, if you add -*ak* to a noun, it forms a locative adverbial meaning "in, on, or at": *ikrivra:m* "house," *ikrivra:mak* "in a house"; *ʔa:s* "water," *ʔa:sak* "in water." Note that it is accidental that both Turkish and Karok have a suffix -*ak*. Despite the similarity in form, the two meanings are different.

Also in Karok, the suffix -*ara* has the same meaning as our suffix -*y*, that is, "characterized by," as in *ʔa:x* "blood," *ʔax* + *ara* "bloody"; *apti:k* "branch," *aptikara* "branchy."

The examples illustrate "free" morphemes like *boy* in English, *dur* in Turkish, *salwa* in Piro, and *ʔa:s* in Karok. Prefix and suffix morphemes were also illustrated. Some languages also have **infixes,** morphemes that are conjoined to other morphemes by inserting them into a morpheme. Bontoc, a language spoken in the Philippines, is such a language, as is illustrated by the following:

NOUNS/ ADJECTIVES		VERBS	
fikas	"strong"	*fum*ikas	"to be strong"
kilad	"red"	*kum*ilad	"to be red"
fusul	"enemy"	*fum*usul	"to be an enemy"

In this language the infix -*um*- is inserted after the first consonant of the noun or adjective. Knowing that *pusi* means "poor," what do you think would be the most likely meaning of *pumusi*? And if *ŋumitad* means "to be dark," what would the Bontoc word for the adjective "dark" be?

Crans and Huckles and Other Such Morphemes

We have already defined a morpheme as the basic element of meaning, as a phonological form that is arbitrarily united with a particular meaning and that cannot be analyzed into simpler elements. This definition has presented problems for linguistic analysis for many years, although it holds for most of the morphemes in a language. Consider words like *cranberry, huckleberry*, and *boysenberry*. The *berry* part is no problem, but *huckle* and *boysen* occur only with *berry*, as did *cran* until the drink *cranapple* juice came on the market.

To account for forms like *huckle, boysen,* and *cran,* we have to redefine the notion "morpheme". Some morphemes are not meaningful in isolation but acquire meaning by virtue of their connection with other morphemes in words. Thus the morpheme *huckle* when joined with *berry* has the meaning of a special kind of berry which is small, round, purplish-blue, and so on.

Just as there seem to be some morphemes which occur only in a single word (that is, combined with another morpheme), there are other morphemes which occur in many words, combining with different morphemes, but for which it is very difficult to find a constant meaning. How would you define the *-ceive* in *receive, perceive, conceive,* or the *mit* in *remit, permit, commit, submit?* There are also words that seem to be composed of prefix + stem morpheme in which the stem morphemes, like the *cran* above, never occur alone. Thus we find *inept* but no **ept, inane* but no **ane, incest* but no **cest, inert* but no **ert, disgusted* but no **gusted, lukewarm* but no **luke.*

To complicate things a little further, there are words like *strawberry* where the *straw* has no relationship to any other kind of *straw, gooseberry,* which is unrelated to *goose,* and *blackberries,* which may be blue or red.

We do not expect to solve this problem here. Different linguists have provided different solutions over the years. We will treat these "funny" forms as morphemes, recognizing that some morphemes acquire their meaning only by connection to the morphemes in the words in which they occur.

Even though linguists have not been able to agree on a solution to the problem, speakers are not troubled by it. The difficulty is that our linguistic knowledge is unconscious knowledge and that as language learners and users we have greater ability to formulate grammars (without knowing that we do) than linguists have to discover what these grammars are.

Morphological Rules of Word Formation

© 1974 United Feature Syndicate, Inc.

When the Mock Turtle listed the different branches of Arithmetic for Alice as "Ambition, Distraction, Uglification, and Derision,"

Alice was very confused:

"I never heard of 'Uglification,'" Alice ventured to say. "What is it?"

The Gryphon lifted up both its paws in surprise. "Never heard of uglifying!" it exclaimed. "You know what to beautify is, I suppose?"

"Yes," said Alice doubtfully: "it means—to make—anything—prettier."

"Well, then," the Gryphon went on, "if you don't know what to uglify is, you *are* a simpleton."

Alice wasn't really such a simpleton, since *uglification* was not a common word in English until Lewis Carroll used it. We have already noted that there are gaps in the lexicon, words which do not but could exist. Some of the gaps are due to the fact that a permissible sound sequence has no meaning attached to it (like *blick* or *slarm* or *krobe*). Other gaps are due to the fact that possible combinations of morphemes have not been made (like *ugly* + *ify* or possibly *linguistic* + *ism*). The reason morphemes can be combined in this way is that there exist, in every language, rules which relate to the formation of words, **morphological rules,** which determine how morphemes combine to form new words.

The Mock Turtle added *-ify* to the adjective *ugly* and formed a verb. Many verbs in English have been formed in this way: *purify, amplify, simplify, falsify. -ify* conjoined with nouns also forms verbs: *objectify, glorify, personify.* Notice that the Mock Turtle went even further; he added the suffix *-cation* to *uglify* and formed a noun, *uglification,* as in *glorification, simplification, falsification, purification.*

DERIVATIONAL MORPHEMES

There are other morphemes in English that change the category, or grammatical class, of words. These are sometimes called **derivational morphemes** because when they are conjoined to other morphemes (or words) a new word is **derived,** or formed. And, as noted, the derived word may be in a different grammatical class than the underived word. Thus, when a verb is conjoined with the suffix *-able,* the result is an adjective, as in *desire* + *able* or *adore* + *able.* A few other examples are:

NOUN TO ADJECTIVE	VERB TO NOUN	ADJECTIVE TO ADVERB
boy + ish	acquitt + al	exact + ly
virtu + ous	clear + ance	quiet + ly
Elizabeth + an	accus + ation	
pictur + esque	confer + ence	**NOUN TO VERB**
affection + ate	sing + er	moral + ize
health + ful	conform + ist	vaccin + ate
alcohol + ic	predict + ion	brand + ish
life + like	free + dom	

Other derivational morphemes do not cause a change in grammatical class. Many prefixes fall into this category:

a + moral	mono + theism
auto + biography	re + print
ex + wife	semi + annual
super + human	sub + minimal

There are also suffixes of this type:

vicar + age	Trotsky + ite
long + er	Commun + ist
short + est	music + ian
Americ + an	pun + ster

New words may enter the dictionary in this fashion, created by the application of morphological rules. It is often the case that when such a word as, for example, *Commun + ist* enters the language, other possible complex forms will not, such as *Commun + ite* (as in *Trotsky + ite*) or *Commun + ian* (as in *grammar + ian*). There may however exist alternative forms: *Marxian/Marxist*. The redundancy of such alternative forms, all of which conform to the regular rules of word formation, may explain some of the accidental gaps in the lexicon. This further shows that the actual words in the language constitute only a subset of the possible words.

Some of the morphological rules are very **productive** in that they can be used quite freely to form new words from the list of free and bound morphemes. The suffix *-able* appears to be a morpheme that can be freely conjoined with verbs to derive an adjective with the meaning of the verb and the meaning of *-able*, which is something like "able to be" as in *accept + able*, *blam(e) + able, pass + able, change + able, breath + able, adapt + able*, and so on. The meaning of *-able* has also been given as "fit for doing" or "fit for being done."

Such a rule might be stated as:

(1) VERB + able = "able to be VERB-ed"
accept + able = "able to be accepted"

The productivity of this rule is illustrated by the fact that we find *-able* in such morphologically complex words as *un + speakabl(e) + y* and *un + come + at + able*.

We have already noted that there is a morpheme in English meaning "not" which has the form *un-* and which when combined with adjectives like *afraid, fit, free, smooth, American,* and *British* forms the antonyms, or negatives, of these adjectives; for example, *unafraid, unfit, unfree, unsmooth, unAmerican, unBritish*.

We can also add the prefix *un-* to derived words that have been formed by morphological rules:

un + believe + able
un + accept + able
un + talk + about + able
un + keep + off + able
un + speak + able

The rule that forms these words may be stated as:

(2) un + ADJECTIVE = "not–ADJECTIVE"

This seems to account for all the examples cited. Yet we find *happy* and *unhappy, cowardly* and *uncowardly,* but not *sad* and **unsad* or *brave* and **unbrave*.

These starred forms may of course be merely accidental gaps in the lexicon. Certainly if someone refers to a person as being *unsad we would know that the person referred to was "not sad," and an *unbrave person would not be brave. But as the linguist Sandra Thompson[2] points out, it may be the case that the "un- Rule" is not as productive for adjectives composed of just one morpheme as for adjectives that are themselves derived from verbs. The rule seems to be freely applicable to an adjectival form derived from a verb, as in *unenlightened, unsimplified, uncharacterized, unauthorized, undistinguished*, and so on.

It is true, however, that one cannot always know the meaning of the words derived from free and derivational morphemes from the morphemes themselves. Thompson has also pointed out that the *un-* forms of the following have unpredictable meanings:

unloosen   "loosen, let loose"
unrip   "rip, undo by ripping"
undo   "reverse doing"
untread   "go back through in the same steps"
unearth   "dig up"
unfrock   "deprive (a cleric) of ecclesiastic rank"
unnerve   "fluster"

Thus, although the words in a language are not the most elemental sound-meaning units, they (plus the morphemes) must be listed in our dictionaries. The morphological rules also are in the grammar, revealing the relation between words and providing the means for forming new words.

Morphological rules may be more productive (can usually be used to form new words) or less productive. The rule that adds an *-er* to verbs in English to produce a noun meaning "one who performs an action (once or habitually)" appears to be a very productive morphological rule; most English verbs accept this suffix: *lover, hunter, predictor* (note that *-or* and *-er* have the same pronunciation), *examiner, examtaker, analyzer,* and so forth.

Now consider the following:

sincerity   from   *sincere*
warmth   from   *warm*
moisten   from   *moist*

The suffix *-ity* is found in many other words in English, like *chastity, scarcity, curiosity.* And *-th* occurs in *health, wealth, depth, width, growth.* We find *-en* in *sadden, ripen, redden, weaken, deepen.*

Yet the phrase *The fiercity of the lion* sounds somewhat strange, as does the sentence *I'm going to thinnen the sauce.* Someone may use the word *coolth,* but, as Thompson points out, when such words as *fiercity, thinnen, fullen,* or *coolth* are used, usually it is either a speech error or the speaker is attempting humor.

It is possible that this is because a morphological rule that was once productive (as shown by the existence of related pairs like *scarce/scarcity*) is no longer. Our knowledge of the related pairs, however, may permit us to use

[2] S. A. Thompson, "On the Issue of Productivity in the Lexikon," *Kritikon Litterarum* 4 (1975): 332–349.

these examples in forming new words, on **analogy** with the existing lexical items.

"PULLET SURPRISES"

That speakers of a language know the morphemes of that language and the rules for word formation is shown as much by the "errors" made as by the nondeviant forms produced. Morphemes combine to form words. These words form our internal dictionaries. No speaker of a language knows all the words. Given our knowledge of the morphemes of the language and the morphological rules, we can often guess the meaning of a word we do not know. Sometimes, of course, we guess wrong. Amsel Greene collected errors made by her students in vocabulary-building classes and published these in a delightful book called *Pullet Surprises*.[3] The title is taken from a sentence written by one of her high-school students: "In 1957 Eugene O'Neill won a Pullet Surprise." What is most interesting about these errors is how much they reveal about the students' knowledge of English morphology. Consider the creativity of these students in the following examples.

WORD	STUDENT'S DEFINITION
deciduous	"able to make up one's mind"
longevity	"being very tall"
fortuitous	"well protected"
gubernatorial	"to do with peanuts"
bibliography	"holy geography"
adamant	"pertaining to original sin"
diatribe	"food for the whole clan"
polyglot	"more than one glot"
gullible	"to do with sea birds"
homogeneous	"devoted to home life"

The student who used the word *indefatigable* in the sentence *She tried many reducing diets, but remained indefatigable* clearly shows morphological knowledge: *in*, meaning "not" as in *ineffective; de*, meaning "off" as in *decapitate; fat*, as in "fat"; *able*, as in *able;* and combined meaning, "not able to take the fat off."

Word Coinage

As we have seen above, new words may be added to the vocabulary or lexicon of a language by derivational processes. New words may also enter a language in a variety of other ways. Some are created outright to fit some purpose. Madison Avenue has added many new words to English, such as *Kodak, nylon, Orlon,* and *Dacron.* Specific brand names such as *Xerox, Kleenex, Jell-o, Frigidaire, Brillo,* and *Vaseline* are now sometimes used as the general name for different brands of these same types of products. Notice that some of these words were created from existing words: *Kleenex* from the word *clean* and *Jell-o* from *gel,* for example.

[3] Amsel Green. 1969. *Pullet Surprises.* Scott, Foresman & Co. Glenview, Ill.

COMPOUNDS

. . . the Houyhnhnms have no Word in their Language to express any thing that is evil, except what they borrow from the Deformities or ill Qualities of the Yahoos. Thus they denote the Folly of a Servant, an Omission of a Child, a Stone that cuts their Feet, a Continuance of foul or unseasonable Weather, and the like, by adding to each the Epithet of Yahoo. For instance, Hhnm Yahoo, Whnaholm Yahoo, Ynlhmnawihlma Yahoo, and an ill contrived House, Ynholmhnmrohlnw Yahoo.
Jonathan Swift, *Gulliver's Travels*

*She played upon her music-box a fancy air by chance,
And straightway all her polka-dots began a lively dance.*

*"A milkweed and a buttercup, and cowslip," said sweet Mary,
"Are growing in my garden-plot, and this I call my dairy."*
Peter Newell, *Pictures and Rhymes*

© 1972 United Feature Syndicate, Inc.

New words may be formed by stringing together other words to create **compound** words. There is almost no limit on the kinds of combinations that occur in English, as can be seen by the examples in the following list of compounds:

	-ADJECTIVE	-NOUN	-VERB
ADJECTIVE-	bittersweet	poorhouse	highborn
NOUN-	headstrong	rainbow	spoonfeed
VERB-	carryall	pickpocket	sleepwalk

Note that *Frigidaire* is a compound formed by combining the adjective *frigid* with the noun *air*.

When the two words are in the same grammatical category, the compound will be in this category: noun + noun—*girlfriend, fighter-bomber, paper clip, elevator-operator, landlord, mailman;* adjective + adjective—*icy-cold, red-hot, worldly-wise.* In many cases, when the two words fall into different categories the class of the second or final word will be the grammatical category of the compound: noun + adjective—*headstrong, watertight, life-long;* verb + noun—*pickpocket, pinchpenny, daredevil, sawbones.* This is not always true; compounds formed with a preposition are in the category of the nonprepositional part of the compound: *overtake, hanger-on, undertake, backdown, afterbirth, downfall, uplift.*

Though two-word compounds are the most common in English, it would be difficult to state an upper limit: *three-time loser, four-dimensional space time, sergeant-at-arms, mother-of-pearl, man about town, master of ceremonies, daughter-in-law.*

Spelling does not tell us what sequence of words constitutes a compound, since some compounds are spelled with a space between the two words, others with a hyphen, and others with no separation at all, as shown for example in *blackbird, gold-tail, smoke screen.*

It is very often the case that compounds have different stress patterns from noncompounded word sequences, as we saw in Chapter 3. Thus *Réd-coat, gréenhouse, líghthouse keeper* have the primary stress on the first part of the compound, whereas *red cóat, green hóuse, light hóusekeeper* do not. There are exceptions to this: *Fífth Street* vs. *Fifth Ávenue, máilmán* vs. *póstman,* among others. Even in complex compounds like *síx-cornered hen house annex door* we find the compound stress pattern.

One of the interesting things about a compound is that you can't always tell by the words it contains what the compound means. The meaning of a compound is *not* always the sum of the meanings of its parts.

Everyone who wears a red coat is not a Redcoat. There is quite a difference between the sentences *She has a red coat in her closet* and *She has a Redcoat in her closet.* It is true, as noted above, that the two sentences sound different. But in *bedchamber, bedclothes, bedside,* and *bedtime, bed* is stressed in all of the compounds; yet a *bedchamber* is a room where there is a bed, *bedclothes* are linens and blankets for a bed, *bedside* does not refer to the physical side of a bed but the place next to it, and *bedtime* is the time one goes to bed.

Other similarly constructed compounds show that underlying the juxtaposition of words, different grammatical relations are expressed. A *houseboat* is a boat that is a house, but a *housecat* is not a cat that is a house. A *boathouse* is a house for boats, but a *cathouse* is not a house for cats, though by coincidence some cats live in cathouses. A *jumping bean* is a bean that jumps, a *falling star* is a "star" that falls, and a *magnifying glass* is a glass that magnifies. But a *looking glass* isn't a glass that looks, nor is an *eating apple* an apple that eats, nor does *laughing gas* laugh.

In all the examples given, the meaning of each compound includes at least to some extent the meanings of the individual parts. But there are other compounds that don't seem to relate to the meanings of the individual parts at all. A *jack-in-a-box* is a tropical tree, and a *turncoat* is a traitor. A *highbrow* doesn't necessarily have a high brow, nor does a *bigwig* have a big wig, nor does an *egghead* have an egg-shaped head.

As we pointed out above in the discussion of the prefix *un-,* the meaning of many compounds must be learned as if they were individual simple words. Some of the meanings may be figured out, but not all. Thus, if one had never heard the word *hunchback*, it might be possible to infer the meaning. But if you had never heard the word *flatfoot* it is doubtful you would know it was a word meaning "detective" or "policeman," even though the origin of the word, once you know the meaning, can be figured out.

Thus, although the words in a language are not the most elemental sound-meaning units, they (plus the morphemes) must be listed in our dictionaries. The morphological rules also are in the grammar, revealing the relations between words and providing the means for forming new words.

The fact that such rules exist makes it possible for us to coin new words, such as *teach-in* and *space-walk*. Dr. Seuss uses the rules of compounding when he explains that ". . . when tweetle beetles battle with paddles in a puddle, they call it a *tweetle beetle puddle paddle battle*."[4]

Not only English has rules for conjoining words to form compounds: French *cure-dent*, "toothpick"; German *Panzerkraftwagen*, "armored car"; Russian *četyrexetažnyi*, "four storied"; Spanish *tocadiscos*, "record-player." In the American Indian language Papago the word meaning "thing" is *haʔichu*, and when combined with *doakam*, "living creatures," the compound *haʔichu doakam* means "animal life."

In Twi if one combines the word meaning "son" or "child," ɔba, with the word meaning "chief," ɔhene, one derives the compound ɔheneba, meaning "prince." Or if you add the word for "house," ofi, to ɔhene, you have a word meaning "palace," ahemfi. The other changes that occur in the Twi compounds are due to phonological and morphological rules in the language.

In Thai the word for "cat" is *mɛɛw*, the word for "watch" (in the sense of "to watch over") is *fâw*, and the word for "house" is *bâan*. The word for "watch cat" (like a watch dog) is the compound *mɛɛwfâwbâan*—literally, "catwatchhouse."

Compounding is thus a very common and frequent process for enlarging the vocabulary of all languages.

ACRONYMS

Drawing by D. Fradon; © 1974 The New Yorker Magazine, Inc.

[4] T. S. Geisel. 1965. *Fox in Sox*. Random House. New York. p. 51.

Acronyms are words derived from the initials of several words. Such words are pronounced as the spelling indicates: NASA as [næsə], UNESCO as [yunɛsko], and CARE as [kʰer]. *Radar,* from "radio detecting and ranging," *laser,* from "light amplification by stimulated emission of radiation," and *scuba* from "self-contained underwater breathing apparatus," show the creative efforts of word coiners, as does *snafu,* which is rendered in polite circles as "situation normal, all fouled up."

BLENDS

THE WIZARD OF ID   **Brant Parker and Johnny Hart**

By permission of Johnny Hart and Field Enterprises, Inc.

Blends are compounds that are "less than" compounds. *Smog,* from *smoke + fog; motel,* from *motor + hotel; urinalysis,* from *urine + analysis* are examples of blends that have attained full lexical status in English. The word *cranapple* may actually be a blend of *cranberry* and *apple. Broasted,* from *broiled + roasted,* is a blend that has limited acceptance in the language, as does Lewis Carroll's *chortle,* from *chuckle + snort.* Carroll is famous for both the coining and the blending of words. In *Through the Looking-Glass* he described the "meanings" of the made-up words he used in "Jabberwocky" as follows:

> . . . "Brillig" means four o'clock in the afternoon—the time when you begin *broiling* things for dinner. . . . "Slithy" means "lithe and slimy." . . . You see it's like a portmanteau—there are two meanings packed up into one word. . . . "Toves" are something like badgers—they're something like lizards—and they're something like corkscrews . . . also they make their nests under sun-dials—also they live on cheese. . . . To "gyre" is to go round and round like a gyroscope. To "gimble" is to make holes like a gimlet. And "the wabe" is the grass-plot round a sun-dial. . . . It's called "wabe" . . . because it goes a long way before it and a long way behind it. . . . "Mimsy" is "flimsy and miserable" (there's another portmanteau for you).

Carroll's "portmanteaus" are what we have called blends, and such words can become part of the regular lexicon.

BACK-FORMATIONS

New words may be formed from already existing words by "subtracting" an affix thought to be part of the old word. Thus *peddle* was derived from *peddler* on the mistaken assumption that the *er* was the "agentive" suffix. Such words are called **back-formations.** The verbs *hawk, stoke, swindle,* and *edit* all came into the language as back-formations—of *hawker, stoker, swin-*

dler, and *editor. Pea* was derived from a singular word, *pease,* by speakers regarding *pease* as a plural. Language purists sometimes rail against back-formations and cite *enthuse* (from *enthusiasm*) and *ept* (from *inept*) as examples of language corruption. Nonetheless, many accepted words have entered the language this way.

EXTENDING WORD FORMATION RULES

New words may also be formed from already existing words which appear to be analyzable—that is, composed of more than one morpheme.

The word *bikini,* for example, is from the Bikini atoll of the Marshall Islands. Since the first syllable *bi-* in other cases, like *bi-polar,* means "two," some clever person called a topless bathing suit a *monokini.* Historically, a number of new words entered the English lexicon in this way. Based on analogy with such pairs as *act/action, exempt/exemption, revise/revision,* new words *resurrect, preempt, televise* were formed from the older words *resurrection, preemption,* and *television.*

ABBREVIATIONS

Abbreviations of longer words or phrases also may become "lexicalized": *nark* for *narcotics agent; tec* (or *dick*) for *detective; telly,* the British word for *television; prof* for *professor; teach* for *teacher;* and *doc* for *doctor* are only a few examples of such "short forms" that are now used as whole words. Some other examples are *ad, bike, math, gas, gym, phone, bus, van.* This process is sometimes called **clipping.**

WORDS FROM NAMES

The creativity of language word coinage (or vocabulary addition) is delightfully revealed by the number of words in the English vocabulary that derive from proper names of individuals or places. Willard R. Espy[5] has compiled a book of 1,500 such words and they include some old favorites like:

sandwich: named for the fourth Earl of Sandwich, who put his food between two slices of bread so that he could eat while he gambled;

robot: after the mechanical creatures in the Czech writer Karel Capek's play R.U.R., the initials standing for "Rossum's Universal Robots";

gargantuan: named for the creature with a huge appetite created by Rabelais;

jumbo: named after an elephant brought to the U.S. by P. T. Barnum. ("Jumbo olives" need not be as big as an elephant, however.)

Espy admits to ignorance of the Susan, an unknown servant, from whom we derived the compound *lazy susan,* or the Betty or Charlotte or Chuck from whom we got *Brown Betty, Charlotte Russe,* or *Chuck Wagon.* He does, however, point out that *denim* was named for the material used for

---

[5] W. R. Espy. 1978. *O Thou Improper, Thou Uncommon Noun: An Etymology of Words That Once Were Names.* Clarkson N. Potter, Inc. New York.

overalls and carpeting which originally was imported "de Nimes" ("from Nimes") in France and *argyle* from the kind of socks worn by the heads of Argyll of the Campbell clan in Scotland.

Morphology and Syntax: Inflectional Morphology

". . . and even . . . the patriotic archbishop of Canterbury found it advisable—"

"Found what?" said the Duck.

"Found it," the Mouse replied rather crossly: "of course you know what 'it' means."

"I know what 'it' means well enough, when I find a thing," said the Duck: "it's generally a frog or a worm. The question is, what did the archbishop find?"

Lewis Carroll, *Alice's Adventures in Wonderland*

"My boy, Grand-père is not the one to ask about such things. I have lived eighty-seven peaceful and happy years in Montoire-sur-le-Loir without the past anterior verb form."

Drawing by Opie; © 1973 The New Yorker Magazine, Inc.

Linguists traditionally have made a distinction between *morphology*, the combining of morphemes into words, and *syntax*, the combining of words into sentences. In the discussion of derivational morphology and compounding, we saw that certain aspects of morphology have syntactic implications in that nouns can be derived from verbs, verbs from adjectives, adjectives from nouns, and so on. There are other ways in which morphology is dependent on syntax, as we shall see in the discussion of *inflection*.

We also saw above that the definition of a morpheme as a minimal unit of meaning was too simple, since some morphemes have constant form but become meaningful only when combined with other morphemes. That is, the morpheme *-ceive* or *-mit* cannot be assigned an intrinsic meaning, yet, as speakers of English, we recognize it as a separate grammatical unit. When we combine words to form sentences, these sentences are combinations of morphemes. It is not always possible to assign a meaning to some of these morphemes, however. For example, what is the meaning of *it* in the sentence *It's hot in July* or in *The Archbishop found it advisable*? What is the meaning of *to* in *He wanted her to go*? *To* has a grammatical "meaning" as an infinitive marker, and *it* is also a morpheme required by the syntactic, sentence-formation rules of the language.

Similarly, there are "bound" morphemes that, like *to*, are for the most part purely grammatical markers, representing such concepts as "tense," "number," "gender," "case," and so forth.

Such "bound" grammatical morphemes are called **inflectional** morphemes: they never change the syntactic category of the words or morphemes to which they are attached. They are always attached to complete words. Consider the forms of the verb in the following sentences:

a. I sail the ocean blue.
b. He sail*s* the ocean blue.
c. John sail*ed* the ocean blue.
d. John has sail*ed* the ocean blue.
e. John is sail*ing* the ocean blue.

In sentence *b* the *s* at the end of the verb is an "agreement" marker; it signifies that the subject of the verb is "third-person," is "singular," and that the verb is in the "present tense." It doesn't add any "lexical meaning." The *-ed* and *-ing* endings are morphemes required by the syntactic rules of the language to signal "tense" or "aspect."

English is no longer a highly inflected language. But we do have other inflectional endings. The plurality of a count noun,[6] for example, is usually marked by a plural suffix attached to the singular noun, as in *boy/boys, cat/cats,* and so on.

An interesting thing about inflectional morphemes in English is that they usually "surround" derivational morphemes. Thus, to the derivationally complex word *un + like + ly + hood,* one can add a plural ending to form *un + like + ly + hood + s* but not **unlikeslyhood.*

Some grammatical relations can be expressed either inflectionally (morphologically) or syntactically. We can see this in the following sentences:

The boy'*s* book is blue.	The book *of* the boy is blue.
He love*s* books.	He is a lov*er* of books.
The planes *which* fly are red.	The *flying* planes are red.
He is hungri*er* than she.	He is *more* hungry than she.

Perhaps some of you form the comparative of *beastly* only by adding *-er*. *Beastlier* is often used interchangeably with *more beastly*. There are speakers who say either. We know the rule that determines when either form of the comparative can be used or when just one can be used. So does Alice: " 'Curiouser and curiouser!' cried Alice (she was so much surprised, that for the moment she quite forgot how to speak good English)."

---

[6] "Count" nouns can be counted: *one boy, two boys,* and so forth. Noncount nouns cannot be counted: **one rice, *two rices,* and so on.

Some languages are highly inflective. The noun in Finnish,[7] for example, has many different inflectional endings, as shown in the following example (don't be concerned if you don't know what all the specific case endings mean):

mantere	nominative singular (sg.)
mantereen	genitive (possessive) sg.
manteretta	partitive sg.
mantereena	essive sg.
mantereeseen	illative sg.
mantereita	partitive plural (pl.)
mantereisiin	illative pl.
mantereiden	genitive pl.

These forms of the noun meaning "continent" are just some of the inflected forms of this noun.

In discussing derivational and compounding morphology, we noted that knowing the meaning of the distinct morphemes may not always reveal the meaning of the morphologically complex word. Such words, in addition to the morphemes, must be listed in our dictionaries with their meanings. This is not true of the words formed by the rules of inflectional morphology. If one knows the meaning of *linguist,* one also knows the meaning of *linguists;* if one knows the meaning of *analyze,* one knows the meaning of *analyzed* and *analyzes* and *analyzing.* One might then suggest that the difference between inflectional morphology and derivational morphology is that the inflected words are determined by the syntax of the language, and the derived words are part of the lexicon or dictionary.

The Pronunciation of Morphemes

In Chapter 3, we presented a number of examples showing that one morpheme may have different pronunciations, that is, different phonetic forms, in different contexts. Thus *write* /rayt/ is pronounced [rayt] but is pronounced [ráyDər] or [ráy:Dər] when the suffix *-er* is added.

Similarly, different pronunciations of vowels occur in English depending on whether they are stressed or unstressed. The particular phonetic forms of some morphemes are determined by regular phonological rules that refer only to the phonemic context as is true of the alternate vowel forms of the following sets:

m[ɛ́]l[ə]dy	m[ə]l[ó]dious	m[ə]l[á]dic
h[á]rm[ə]ny	h[à]rm[ó]nious	h[à]rm[á]nic
s[í]mph[ə]ny	s[ì]mph[ó]nious	s[ì]mph[á]nic

The vowel rules that determine these pronunciations are rather complicated and beyond the scope of this text. The examples are presented simply to show that the morphemes in "*melody,*" "*harmony,*" and "*symphony*" vary phonetically in these words.

[7] Examples from L. Campbell, "Generative Phonology vs. Finnish Phonology: Retrospect and Prospect," *Texas Linguistic Forum* 5 (1977): 21–58.

Another example of a morpheme in English with different phonetic forms is the plural morpheme. Consider the following nouns.

I	II	III	IV
cab	cap	buss	child
cad	cat	bush	ox
bag	back	buzz	mouse
love	cuff	garage	sheep
lathe	faith	match	criterion
cam		badge	
can			
bang			
call			
bar			
spa			
boy			

All the nouns in Column I end in voiced nonsibilant sounds and to form the plural you add the voiced [z]. All the words in II end in voiceless nonsibilant sounds and you add a voiceless [s]. The words in III end in both voiced and voiceless sibilants, which form their plurals with the insertion of a schwa followed by [z].

Children do not have to learn the plural rule by memorizing the individual sounds that require the [z] or [s] or [əz] plural ending, since these sounds form natural classes, as discussed in Chapter 3. A grammar that included lists of these sounds would not reveal the regularities in the language and would fail to reveal what a speaker knows about the regular plural formation rule.

The regular plural rule does not work for a word like *child,* which in the plural is *children,* or for *ox,* which becomes *oxen,* or for *sheep,* which is unchanged phonologically in the plural. *Child, ox,* and *sheep* are **exceptions** to the regular rule. One learns these exceptional plurals when learning the language. If the grammar represented each unexceptional or regular word in both its singular and plural forms—for example, *cat* /kaet/, *cats* /kæts/; *cap* /kæp/, *caps* /kæps/; and so on—it would imply that the plurals of *cat* and *cap* were as irregular as the plurals of *child* and *ox.* But this is not the case. If a new toy appeared on the market called a *glick* /glɪk/, a young child who wanted two of them would ask for two *glicks* /glɪks/ and not two *glicken,* even if the child had never heard anyone use that plural form. This is because the child would know the regular rule to form plurals. A grammar that describes such knowledge (the internalized mental grammar) must then include the general rule.

Notice that this rule which determines the phonetic representation or pronunciation of the plural morpheme is somewhat different from some of the other phonological rules we have discussed. The "aspiration rule" in English applies to a word whenever the phonological description is met; it is not the case, for example, that a /t/ is aspirated only if it is part of a particular morpheme. The "flap rule," which changes the phonetic forms of the morphemes *write* and *ride* when a suffix is added, is also completely automatic, depending solely on the phonological environment. But the plural rule applies only to the inflectional plural morpheme. To see that it is not "purely" phonological in nature, consider the following words:

race	[res]	ray	[re]	ray + pl. [rez]	*[res]
souse	[saws]	sow	[saw]	sow + pl. [sawz]	*[saws]
rice	[rays]	rye	[ray]	rye + pl. [rayz]	*[rays]

The examples show the [z] in the plural is not determined by the phonological context since in an identical context an [s] occurs.

MORPHOPHONEMICS

FRANK AND ERNEST   **Bob Thaves**

Reprinted by permission. © 1981 NEA, Inc.

The rule that determines the phonetic form of the plural morpheme has traditionally been called a **morphophonemic rule,** in that its application is determined by both the morphology and the phonology. When a morpheme has alternate phonetic forms, these forms are called **allomorphs** by some linguists. Thus [z], [s], and [əz] would be allomorphs of the regular plural morpheme, and determined by rule.

Suppose, for example, that the regular, productive, plural morpheme has the phonological form /z/ with the meaning "plural." The regular "plural rule" can be stated in a simple way:

(3) a. Insert an [ə] before the plural ending when a regular noun ends in a sibilant (/s/, /z/, /š/, /ž/, /č/, or /ǰ/).

b. Change the voiced /z/ to voiceless [s] when it is preceded by a voiceless sound.

If neither (3a) nor (3b) applies, then /z/ will be realized as [z]; no segments will be added and no features will be changed.

The "plural rule" will derive the phonetic forms of plurals for all regular nouns (remember, this is the *plural* /z/):

PHONEMIC REPRESENTATION	*bus + pl.* /bʌs + z/	*bat + pl.* /bæt + z/	*bag + pl.* /bæg + z/
rule (3a)	↓ ə	NA[a]	↓ NA
rule (3b)	NA	↓ s	NA
PHONETIC REPRESENTATION	[bʌsəz]	[bæts]	[bægz]

[a] NA means "not applicable."

As we have formulated these rules, (3a) must be applied before (3b). If we applied the two parts of the rule in reverse order, we would derive incorrect phonetic forms:

PHONEMIC REPRESENTATION	/bʌs + z/
rule (3b)	s
rule (3a)	ə
PHONETIC REPRESENTATION	*[bʌsəs]

The plural-formation rule illustrates once again that phonological rules can insert *entire segments* into the phonemic string: an [ə] is added by the first rule. It also illustrates the importance of *ordered* rules in phonology.

An examination of the rule for the formation of the past tense of verbs in English shows some interesting parallels with the plural formation of nouns.

I	II	III	IV
grab	reap	state	is
hug	peak	cloud	run
seethe	unearth		sing
love	huff		have
buzz	kiss		go
rouge	wish		hit
judge	pitch		
fan			
ram			
long			
kill			
care			
tie			
bow			
hoe			

The productive regular past tense morpheme in English is /d/, *phonemically,* but [d] (Column I), [t] (Column II), or [əd] (Column III) *phonetically,* again depending on the final phoneme of the verb to which it is attached.

The past-tense rule in English, like the plural-formation rule, must include morphological information. Note that after a vowel or diphthong the form of the past tense is always [d], even though it is possible to follow a vowel or diphthong with a [t] as in *tight, bout, rote.* When the word is a verb, and when the final alveolar represents the past tense morpheme, however, it must be a voiced [d] and not a voiceless [t].

There is a plausible explanation for why a [ə] is inserted in the past tense of regular verbs ending with alveolar stops (and in nouns ending with sibilants). Since in English we do not contrast long and short consonants, it is difficult to perceive a difference in consonantal length. If we added a [z] to *squeeze* we would get [skwizz] which would be hard for English speakers to distinguish from [skwiz]; similarly if we added [d] to *load* it would be [lodd] phonetically in the past and [lod] in the present, which would also be difficult to perceive.

Just as there were no regular rules to determine the plural forms of exceptional nouns like *child/children, man/men, sheep/sheep, criterion/criteria,* so also there are no regular rules to specify the past tense of the verbs in Column IV.

When, as children, we are acquiring (or constructing) the grammar, we have to learn specifically that the plural of *man* is *men* and that the past of *go* is *went*. This is the reason why we often hear children say *mans* and *goed;* they first learn the regular rules, and before they learn the exceptions to these rules they apply the rules generally to all the nouns and verbs. These children's errors, in fact, support our position that the regular rules exist.

The irregular forms then must be listed separately in our mental dictionaries, as **suppletive** forms. It is interesting to note that when a new word enters the language it is the regular inflectional rules which apply. The plural of *Bic* is thus *Bics*, not **Bicken*.

The past tense of the verb *hit*, as in the sentence *Yesterday, John hit the roof*, and the plural of the noun *sheep*, as in *The sheep are in the meadow*, show that some morphemes seem to have no phonological shape at all. We know that *hit* in the above sentence is *hit* + past because of the time adverb *yesterday*, and we know that *sheep* is the phonetic form of *sheep* + plural because of the plural verb form *are*. Thousands of years ago the Hindu grammarians suggested that some morphemes have a zero-form; that is, they may not have any phonological representation. In our view, however, since we would like to hold to the definition of a morpheme as a sound-meaning constant form, we will suggest that the morpheme *hit* is marked as both present and past in the dictionary, and the morpheme *sheep* is marked as both singular and plural. Other linguists would analyze these words differently.

Some of the sequential constraints on phonemes that were discussed in Chapter 3 may show up as phonological and morphophonemic rules. The English homorganic nasal constraint applies between some morphemes as well as within a morpheme. The negative prefix *in-*, which, like *un-*, means "not," in words such as *inexcusable, inattentive,* and *inorganic,* has three allomorphs: [ĭn] before vowels such as in the words listed and also before alveolars in words like *intolerant, indefinable, insurmountable;* [ĭm] before labials in such words as *impossible* or *imbalance;* and [ĭŋ] before velars in words such as *incomplete* and *inglorious.* The pronunciation of this morpheme is often revealed by the spelling, as *im-* when it is prefixed to morphemes beginning with /p/ or /b/. Since we have no letter "ŋ" in our alphabet (although it exists in alphabets used in other languages) the velar [ŋ] is written as *n* in words like *incomplete.* You may not realize that you pronounce the *n* in *incomplete, inglorious, incongruous* and other such words as [ŋ] because your homorganic nasal rule is as unconscious as other rules in your grammar. It is the job of linguists and phoneticians to bring such rules to consciousness or to reveal them as part of the grammar. If you say these words in normal tempo without pausing after the *in-* you should feel the back of your tongue rise to touch the velum.

It is interesting that in Akan the negative morpheme also has three nasal allomorphs: [m] before /p/, [n] before /t/, and [ŋ] before /k/, as is shown in the following:

mɪ pɛ	"I like"	mɪ mpɛ	"I don't like"
mɪ tɪ	"I speak"	mɪ ntɪ	"I don't speak"
mɪ kɔ	"I go"	mɪ ŋkɔ	"I don't go"

We see then that one morpheme may have different phonetic forms or allomorphs. We have also seen that more than one morpheme may occur in the language which has the same meaning but different forms—like *in-*, *un-*, and *not* (all meaning "not"). It is not possible to predict which of these will occur so they are separate synonymous morphemes. It is only when the phonetic form is predictable by general rule that we find different phonetic forms of a single morpheme.

The plural and past-tense formation rules both changed feature values of segments (for example, the voiced /z/ and /d/ to voiceless [s] and [t] after voiceless sounds) and also inserted a [ə] in given environments. The nasal homorganic rule is also a feature-changing rule. Since the allomorph [ĩn] occurs before vowels where there is no consonant following by which we can determine the place of articulation features, the phonemic representation of this morpheme is /ɪn/ and the rule will assimilate the /n/ to a following consonant by changing feature values of the /n/.

In some cases different phonetic forms of the same morpheme may be derived by segment-deletion rules as in the following examples:

A		B	
sign	[sáỹn]	signature	[sígnəčər]
design	[dəzáỹn]	designate	[dézəgnèt]
paradigm	[pʰǽrədàỹm]	paradigmatic	[pʰǽrədìgmǽDək]

In none of the words in column A is there a phonetic [g], but in each corresponding word in column B a [g] occurs. Our knowledge of English phonology accounts for these phonetic differences. The "[g]–no [g]" alternation is regular and applies to words that one might never have heard before. Suppose someone said:

He was a *salignant* [səlɪgnə̄nt] man.

Even if you didn't know what the word meant, you might ask (perhaps to hide your ignorance):

Why, did he *salign* [səlẵỹn] somebody?

It is highly doubtful that you would pronounce the verb form with the *-ant* dropped as [səlɪgn]. Your knowledge of the phonological rules of English would "delete" the /g/ when it occurred in this context. The rule can be stated as:

(4) Delete a /g/ when it occurs before a final nasal consonant.[8]

Given this rule, the phonemic representation of the stems in *sign/signature*, *design/designation, resign/resignation, repugn/repugnant, phlegm/phlegmatic, paradigm/paradigmatic, diaphragm/diaphragmatic* will include a *phonemic* /g/ which will be deleted by the regular rule if a suffix is not added. By stating the *class* of sounds which follow the /g/ (nasal consonants) rather

[8] The /g/ may be deleted under other circumstances as well, as indicated by its absence in *signing* and *signer*.

than specifying any specific nasal consonant, the rule deletes the /g/ before both /m/ and /n/.

The phonological rules that delete whole segments, as well as adding segments and features and changing features, also predict the phonetic forms of morphemes. This can be further illustrated by the following words:

A			B		
bomb	/bamb/	[bãm]	bombardier	/bambadir/	[bãmbədir]
iamb	/ayæmb/	[ayæm]	iambic	/ayæmbɪk/	[ayæmbɪk]
crumb	/krʌmb/	[krʌ̃m]	crumble	/krʌmbəl/	[krʌ̃mbəl]

A speaker of English knows when to pronounce a final /b/ and when not to. The relationship between the pronunciation of the A words and their B counterparts is regular and can be accounted for by Rule (5):

(5) Delete a word-final /b/ when it occurs after an /m/.

Notice that the underlying phonemic representation of the A and B stems is the same.

PHONEMIC REPRESENTATION	/bamb/	/bamb + adir/	/bʌlb/
/b/ deletion rule	ø	NA	NA
unstressed vowel schwa rule	NA	ə	NA
PHONETIC REPRESENTATION	[bãm]	[bãmbədir]	[bʌlb]

These rules that delete the segments discussed above are general phonological rules but their application to phonemic representations results in deriving different phonetic forms of the same morpheme. We also find different morphemes with the same phonological form but different meanings. This follows from the concept of the morpheme as a sound-meaning unit. The morpheme *-er* means "one who does" in words like *singer, painter, lover, worker.* The same sounds represent the "comparative" morpheme, meaning "more," in *nicer, prettier, taller.* But notice that in *butcher* the sounds *-er* do not represent any morpheme, since a *butcher* is not one who **butches.* (In an earlier form of English the word *butcher* was *bucker,* "one who dresses bucks." The *-er* in this word was then a separate morpheme.) Similarly, in *water* the *-er* is not a distinct morpheme ending; *butcher* and *water* are single morphemes, or monomorphemic words.

We can therefore summarize what we have been discussing regarding the morpheme as a sound-meaning unit:

1. A morpheme may be represented by a single sound, such as the "without" morpheme *a-* in *amoral* or *asexual.*
2. A morpheme may be represented by a syllable, such as *child* and *-ish* in *child + ish.*
3. A morpheme may be represented by more than one syllable: by two syllables, as in *aardvark, lady, water;* or by three syllables, as in *Hackensack* or *crocodile;* or by four or more syllables, as in *salamander.*
4. Two different morphemes may have the same phonological representation: *-er* as in *singer* and *-er* as in *skinnier.*
5. A morpheme may have alternate phonetic forms; the regular plural /z/, which is either [z], [s], or [əz]; *sign* in *sign* [sayn] and *signature* [sɪgn];

or the different pronunciations of the morphemes *harmony, melody, symphony* in *harmonic/harmonious, symphonic/symphonious, melodic/melodious.*

6. For most of the lexicon, the different pronunciations can be predicted from the regular phonological rules of the language.

The grammar of the language that is internalized by the language learner includes the morphemes and the derived words of the language. The morphological rules of the grammar permit you to use and understand the morphemes and words in forming and understanding sentences, and in forming and understanding new words.

SUMMARY

Knowing a language means knowing the words of that language. When you know a word you know both its sound and its meaning; these are inseparable parts of the **linguistic sign.** Each word is stored in our mental dictionaries with its phonological representation, its meaning (semantic properties), and its syntactic class, or category, specification.

Words are not the most elemental sound-meaning units; some words are structurally complex. The most elemental grammatical units in a language are **morphemes.** Thus, *moralizers* is an English word composed of four morphemes: *moral + ize + er + s.*

The study of word formation and the internal structure of words is called **morphology.** Part of one's linguistic competence includes knowledge of the morphemes, words, their pronunciation, their meanings, and how they are combined. Morphemes combine according to the morphological rules of the language.

Some morphemes are **bound,** in that they must be joined to other morphemes, are always parts of words and never words by themselves. Other morphemes are **free,** in that they need not be attached to other morphemes. *Free, king, serf, bore* are free morphemes; *-dom,* as in *freedom, kingdom, serfdom,* and *boredom,* is a bound morpheme. Bound morphemes may be **prefixes, suffixes,** or **infixes.**

Some morphemes, like *huckle* in *huckleberry* and *-ceive* in *perceive* or *receive,* have constant phonological form but meanings determined only by the words in which they occur.

Morphemes may also be classified as **derivational** or **inflectional. Derivational morphological rules** are **lexical rules** of word formation. **Inflectional morphemes** are closely related to the rules of syntax. Unlike derivational morphemes, they are added only to complete words; they never change the syntactic category of the word. A **"closed class"** grammatical morpheme may also be inserted by syntactic rule and often functions similarly to an inflectional morpheme, for example, *of* in *the hat of the boy,* which has the same function as the inflectional morpheme *'s* in *the boy's hat.*

Grammars also include other ways of increasing the vocabulary, of adding new words to the lexicon. Words can be coined outright so that former nonsense words or possible but nonoccurring words can become words. Morphological **compounding** rules combine two or more morphemes or words to form complex *compounds,* like *lamb chop, deep-sea diver, ne'er-do-well.*

Frequently the meaning of compounds cannot be predicted from the meanings of their individual morphemes. **Acronyms** are words derived from the initial of several words like UCLA, sometimes pronounced [yuklə] or [yusiɛle]. **Blends** are similar to compounds but usually combine shortened forms of two or more morphemes or words. *Carpeteria* is a store selling carpets and the name derives from *carpet* plus the end of *cafeteria*. **Back formations, abbreviations,** and words formed from proper nouns also add to our given stock of words.

A morpheme may have different phonetic representations; these are determined by the **morphophonemic** and phonological rules of the language. Thus the regular plural morpheme is phonetically [z] and [s] or [əz], depending on the final phoneme of the noun to which it is attached. In some cases the alternate forms are not predictable by regular or general rules; such forms are called **suppletive** forms, as for example, *man/men, datum/data,* or *go/went, bring/brought.* These constitute a small set of the lexical items in a language; most of the morphemes are subject to regular rules.

While the particular morphemes and the particular morphological rules are language-dependent, the same general processes occur in all languages.

EXERCISES

1. Divide these words into their separate morphemes by placing a + between each morpheme and the next:

   a. retroactive   e. psychology   i. tourists
   b. befriended   f. unpalatable   j. holiday
   c. televise   g. grandmother   k. Massachusetts
   d. endearment   h. morphemic   l. basically

2. Consider the following data from Ewe, a West African language. (Ewe is a tone language, but the tones are unmarked in these examples, since tone is not relevant to the problem.)

EWE	ENGLISH
uwa ye xa amu	"The chief looked at a child,"
uwa ye xa ufi	"The chief looked at a tree."
uwa xa ina ye	"A chief looked at the picture."
amu xa ina	"A child looked at a picture."
amu ye vo ele ye	"The child wanted the chair."
amu xa ele ye	"A child looked at the chair."
ika vo ina ye	"A woman wanted the picture."

   A. The morpheme meaning "the" is _____.
   B. The morpheme meaning "a" is: (Choose one)

      a. xa   b. amu   c. ye   d. none of these

   C. List all the other morphemes occurring in the Ewe sentences above. (Give the Ewe morpheme and the English "gloss.")
   D. How would you say in Ewe "The woman looked at the tree"?
   E. If *oge de abo* means "A man drank wine," what would the Ewe sentence meaning "A man wanted the wine" be?

3. Below are some data from Samoan:

manao	"he wishes"	mananao	"they wish"
matua	"he is old"	matutua	"they are old"
malosi	"he is strong"	malolosi	"they are strong"
punou	"he bends"	punonou	"they bend"
atamaki	"he is wise"	atamamaki	"they are wise"
savali	"he travels"	pepese	"they sing"
laga	"he weaves"		

A. What is the Samoan for:

    a. they weave _____

    b. they travel _____

    c. he sings _____

B. Formulate a general statement (a morphological rule) that states how to form the plural verb form from the singular verb form.

4. Below are listed some words followed by the incorrect definitions provided by high-school students. (All these errors are taken from Amsel Greene's *Pullet Surprises*.)

WORD	STUDENT DEFINITION
stalemate	"husband or wife no longer interesting"
effusive	"able to be merged"
tenet	"a group of ten singers"
dermatology	"study of derms"
ingenious	"not very smart"
finesse	"a female fish"

For each of these incorrect definitions provide the possible reasons why the students made the guesses they did. Where you can exemplify by reference to other words or morphemes, giving their meanings, do so.

5. In the African language Maninka, the suffix -*li* has more than one pronunciation (like the -*ed* past tense ending on English verbs as in *reaped*, *robbed*, and *raided*). This suffix is similar to the derivational suffix -*ing*, which when added to the verb *cook* makes it a noun as in "Her cooking was great," or the suffix -*ion*, which also derives a verb from a noun as in *create* + *ion*, permitting "The creation of the world."

Consider these data from Maninka:

bugo	"hit"	bugoli	"the hitting"
dila	"repair"	dilali	"the repairing"
don	"come in"	donni	"the coming in"
dumu	"eat"	dumuni	"the eating"
gwen	"chase"	gwenni	"the chasing"

What are the two forms of the morpheme meaning "the _____ing"? Can you predict which phonetic form will occur? If so, state the rule. What are the "-ing" forms for the following verbs?

da	"lie down"
famu	"understand"
men	"hear"
sunogo	"sleep"

6. Below are some sentences in Swahili:

mtoto	amefika	"The child has arrived."
mtoto	anafika	"The child is arriving."
mtoto	atafika	"The child will arrive."
watoto	wamefika	"The children have arrived."
watoto	wanafika	"The children are arriving."
watoto	watafika	"The children will arrive."
mtu	amelala	"The man has slept."
mtu	analala	"The man is sleeping."
mtu	atalala	"The man will sleep."
watu	wamelala	"The men have slept."
watu	wanalala	"The men are sleeping."
watu	watalala	"The men will sleep."
kisu	kimeanguka	"The knife has fallen."
kisu	kinaanguka	"The knife is falling."
kisu	kitaanguka	"The knife will fall."
visu	vimeanguka	"The knives have fallen."
visu	vinaanguka	"The knives are falling."
visu	vitaanguka	"The knives will fall."
kikapu	kimeanguka	"The basket has fallen."
kikapu	kinaanguka	"The basket is falling."
kikapu	kitaanguka	"The basket will fall."
vikapu	vimeanguka	"The baskets have fallen."
vikapu	vinaanguka	"The baskets are falling."
vikapu	vitaanguka	"The baskets will fall."

One of the characteristic features of Swahili (and Bantu languages in general) is the existence of noun classes. There are specific singular and plural prefixes that occur with the nouns in each class. These prefixes are also used for purposes of agreement between the subject-noun and the verb. In the sentences given, two of these classes are included (there are many more in the language).

A. Identify all the morphemes you can detect (and give their meanings).
Example:
-toto "child"
m-   noun prefix attached to singular nouns of Class I
a-   prefix attached to verbs when the subject is a singular noun of Class I.
Be sure to look for the other noun and verb markers, including tense markers.

B. How is the "verb" constructed? That is, what kinds of morphemes are strung together and in what order?

C. How would you say in Swahili:
a. The child is falling. _____
b. The baskets have arrived. _____
c. The man will fall. _____

7. Consider the following *phonetic* data from the Bantu language Luganda. (The data have been somewhat altered to make the problem easier.) In each line, the same root or stem morpheme occurs in both columns A and B, but it has one prefix in column A meaning "a" or "an" and another prefix meaning "little" in the phonetic forms in column B.

A		B	
[ẽnato]	"a canoe"	[akaato]	"little canoe"
[ẽnapo]	"a house"	[akaapo]	"little house"
[ẽnoobi]	"an animal"	[akaoobi]	"little animal"
[ẽmpipi]	"a kidney"	[akapipi]	"little kidney"
[ẽŋkoosa]	"a feather"	[akakoosa]	"little feather"
[ẽmmããmmo]	"a peg"	[akabããmmo]	"little peg"
[ẽŋŋõõmme]	"a horn"	[akagõõmme]	"little horn"
[ẽnnĩmiro]	"a garden"	[akadĩmiro]	"little garden"
[ẽnugẽni]	"a stranger"	[akatabi]	"little branch"

(Hint: The phonemic representation of the morpheme meaning "little" is /aka/.)

In answering the following questions, base your answers on only these forms. That is, you should assume that all the words in the language follow the regularities shown here.

A. Are nasal vowels in Luganda phonemic, or are they predictable?
B. Is the phonemic representation of the morpheme meaning "garden" /dimiro/?
C. What is the phonemic representation of the morpheme meaning "canoe"? _____
D. Are [p] and [b] allophones of one phoneme?
E. If /am/ represents a bound prefix morpheme in Luganda, can you conclude that [ãmdãno] is a possible phonetic form for a word in this language starting with this prefix?
F. Is there a phonological homorganic nasal rule in Luganda?
G. If the *phonetic* representation of the word meaning "little boy" is [akapoobe], what is the *phonetic* represention for the word meaning "a boy"? What is the *phonemic* representation for "a boy"?
H. Which of the following is the *phonemic* representation for the prefix meaning "a" or "an"?

   a. /en/   b. /ẽn/   c. /ẽm/   d. /em/   e. /eŋ/

I. What is the *phonetic* representation of the word meaning "a branch"?
J. What is the *phonemic* representation of the word meaning "little stranger"?
K. State in as general terms as you can any phonological rules the Luganda data reveal.

8. Think of five morpheme suffixes. Give their meaning, what types of stems they may be suffixed to, and at least two examples of each.

   Example: -er   meaning: "doer of"; makes an agentive noun
                stem type: added to verbs
                examples: *rider,* "one who rides"
                             teacher, "one who teaches"

9. Think of five morpheme prefixes. Give their meaning, what types of stems they may be prefixed to, and at least two examples of each.

Example: *a-*   meaning: "lacking the quality"
         stem type: added to adjectives
         examples: *amoral*, "lacking morals"
                  asymmetric, "lacking symmetry"

10. Here are some Japanese verb forms that you may consider to be phonetic transcriptions. They represent two different styles (informal and formal) of present tense verbs.

INFORMAL (present tense)		FORMAL (present tense)
"call"	yobu	yobimasu
"write"	kaku	kakimasu
"eat"	taberu	tabemasu
"see"	miru	mimasu
"lend"	kasu	kashimasu
"wait"	matsu	machimasu
"leave"	deru	demasu
"go out"	dekakeru	dekakemasu
"read"	yomu	yomimasu
"die"	shinu	shinimasu
"close"	shimeru	shimemasu
"wear"	kiru	kimasu

A. List the underlying or basic verb stems for each of these Japanese verbs.
B. State the rule for deriving the present-tense *informal* verb forms from the underlying verb stems.
C. State the rule for deriving the present-tense *formal* verb forms from the underlying verb stems.
D. Can you state a rule that would allow you to derive the formal forms from the informal forms? (This would be useful if you were learning Japanese and had already learned the informal forms.)

REFERENCES

Aronoff, Mark. 1976. *Word Formation in Generative Grammar*. Linguistic Inquiry, Monograph 1. M.I.T. Press. Cambridge, Mass.

Greene, Amsel. 1969. *Pullet Surprises*. Scott, Foresman & Co. Glenview, Ill.

Marchand, Hans. 1969. *The Categories and Types of Present-Day English Word-Formation*, 2nd ed. C. H. Beck'sche Verlagsbuchhandlung. Munich.

Matthews, P. H. 1976. *Morphology: An Introduction to the Theory of Word Structure*. Cambridge University Press. Cambridge, England.

Chapter 5

Writing: The ABC's of Language

The Moving Finger writes; and, having writ,
Moves on: nor all thy Piety nor Wit
  Shall lure it back to cancel half a Line,
Nor all thy Tears wash out a Word of it.

Omar Khayyam, Rubaiyat

The palest ink is better than the sharpest memory.

Chinese proverb

In the previous chapters we have discussed language in its spoken form, and presented a phonetic alphabet for describing the sounds of human language in a written form. Of course most people who learn a written form of their language do not learn the phonetic alphabet, although many formerly unwritten languages use some phonetic symbols such as ŋ. They use the writing system indigenous to their language. In this chapter we shall examine the history, nature, and use of writing systems.

The development of writing was one of the great human inventions. It is difficult for many people to imagine language without writing; the spoken word seems intricately tied to the written word. But children speak before they learn to write. And millions of people in the world speak languages with no written form. Among these people oral literature abounds, and crucial knowledge is memorized and passed between generations. But human memory is short-lived, and the brain's storage capacity is finite. Writing overcame such problems and allowed communication across the miles and through the years and centuries. Writing permits a society to permanently record its poetry, its history, and its technology.

It might be argued that today we have electronic means of recording sound and cameras to produce films and television, and thus writing is becoming obsolete. If writing became extinct, there would be no knowledge of electronics for TV technicians to study; there would be, in fact, little technology in years to come. There would be no film or TV scripts, no literature, no books, no mail, no newspapers, no science. There would be some advantages: no bad novels, junk mail, poison-pen letters, or "unreadable" income-tax forms, but the losses would far outweigh the gains.

The History of Writing

One picture is worth a thousand words.

Chinese proverb

B.C.   **Johnny Hart**

There are almost as many legends and stories on the invention of writing as there are on the origin of language. Legend has it that Cadmus, Prince of Phoenicia and founder of the city of Thebes, invented the alphabet and brought it with him to Greece. (He later was banished to Illyria and changed into a snake.) In one Chinese fable the four-eyed dragon-god T'sang Chien invented writing, but in another, writing first appeared to humans in the form of markings on a turtle shell. In an Icelandic saga, Odin was the inventor of the runic script. In other myths, the Babylonian god Nebo and the Egyptian god Thoth gave humans writing as well as speech. The Talmudic scholar Rabbi Akiba believed that the alphabet existed before humans were created, and according to Islamic teaching, the alphabet was created by Allah himself, who presented it to man but not to the angels.

While these are delightful stories, it is evident that before a single word was ever written, uncountable billions were spoken; it is highly unlikely that a particularly gifted ancestor awoke one morning and decided "today I'll invent a writing system." Momentous inventions are rarely conceived in a moment.

PICTOGRAMS AND IDEOGRAMS

It is widely believed that the early drawings made by ancient humans were the seeds out of which writing developed. Cave drawings such as those found in the Altamira cave in northern Spain, drawn by humans living over 20,000 years ago, can be "read" today. They are literal portrayals of aspects of life at that time. We have no way of knowing why they were produced; they may well be esthetic expressions rather than communications. Later drawings, however, are clearly "picture writing," or **pictograms.** Unlike modern writing systems, each picture or pictogram is a direct image of the object it represents. There is a **nonarbitrary** relationship between the form and meaning of the symbol. Comic strips, minus captions, are pictographic —literal representations of the ideas to be communicated. This early form of "writing" did not have any direct relation to the language spoken, since the pictures represented objects in the world, rather than the linguistic names given to these objects; they did not represent the sounds of spoken language. Pictographic "writing" has been found among people throughout the world, ancient and modern; among African tribes, American Indians, Alaskan Eskimos, the Incas of Peru, the Yukagirians of Siberia, the people of Oceania. Pictograms are used today, in international road-signs and signs on public toilets showing which are for men and which for women. The advantage of such symbols is that, because they do not depend on the sounds of any language, they can be understood by anyone. The signs used by the National Park Service exemplify this. One does not need to know any English to understand them. Some of the concepts conveyed in these signs are relatively complicated, in fact; see, for example, the symbol for "environmental study area" in Figure 5-1.

In the course of time the pictogram's meaning was extended, in that the picture represented not only the original object but attributes of that object, or concepts associated with it. Thus, a picture of the sun could represent "warmth," "heat," "light," "daytime," and so on. It is easy to understand how this came about. Try to imagine a drawing to represent "heat" or "daytime." Pictograms thus began to represent *ideas* rather than objects, and such pictograms are called **ideograms** ("idea pictures" or "idea writing").

Figure 5-1 Six of seventy-seven symbols developed by the National Park Service for use as signs to indicate activities and facilities in parks and recreation areas. These are: environmental study area; grocery store; men's restroom; women's restroom; fishing; amphitheater. Certain symbols are available with a "prohibiting slash"—a diagonal red bar across the symbol that means the activity is forbidden. (National Park Service, U.S. Department of the Interior)

Later, the pictograms or ideograms became stylized, probably because of the ambiguities that could result from "poor artists" or "abstractionists" of the time. The simplifying conventions which developed so distorted the literal representations that it was no longer easy to interpret these new symbols without learning the system.

By this period in time, the form and the meaning of a pictogram were fixed in an *arbitrary* relationship. The pictograms were now *linguistic* symbols; because their forms departed drastically from the objects they represented, they became instead symbols for the *sounds* of these objects—that is, for the words of the language. This stage represents a revolutionary step in the development of writing systems.

A **word-writing system** of this kind relates the symbol to the sounds of a word, but the symbol can also stand for the concept and may still resemble it, however abstractly. Such symbols could be used to represent the words in any language, no matter how they were pronounced. The possible advantages of such a "universal" writing system motivated a Dutch journalist, Karel Johnson, and a German professor, André Eckardt, soon after World War II, to develop a pictographic system called Picto. In Picto, the phrase *I have a house in town* (or *Ich habe ein Haus in der Stadt* or *J'ai une maison en ville*) would look like this:

I	have	house	in	town
I	have	house	in	town
Ich	haben	Haus	in	Stadt
je	avoir	maison	en	ville

Unfortunately, such a system is only effective when concrete ideas are communicated. Suppose one tried to translate into Picto the following sentence from Kierkegaard's *Fear and Trembling:*

If there were no eternal consciousness in a man, if at the foundation of all there lay only a wildly seething power which writhing with obscure passions produced everything that is great and everything that is insignificant, if a bottomless void never satiated lay hidden beneath all—what then would life be but despair?

The difficulty is apparent.

Had pictographic writing been adequate to the task, there would have been no reason for it to have developed into the modern writing systems.

CUNEIFORM WRITING

Much of our information on the development described above stems from the records left by the Sumerians, an ancient people of unknown origin who built a civilization in southern Mesopotamia over five thousand years ago. Their writing system is the oldest one known. They were a commercially oriented people, and as their business deals became increasingly complex the need for permanent records arose. An elaborate pictography was developed along with a system of "tallies." Some examples are shown here:

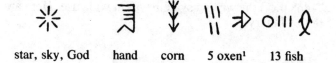

star, sky, God   hand   corn   5 oxen[1]   13 fish

Over the centuries their pictography was simplified and conventionalized. The characters or symbols were produced by using a wedge-shaped stylus that was pressed into soft clay tablets, made from the clay found on the land between the Tigris and Euphrates rivers. This form of writing is called **cuneiform**—literally "wedge-shaped" (from Latin *cuneus*). Here is an illustration of how Sumerian pictograms evolved to cuneiform:

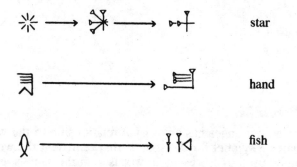

star

hand

fish

Notice that the cuneiform "words" do little to remind one of the meaning represented. As cuneiform evolved, its users began to think of the symbols more in terms of the *name* of the thing represented than of the actual thing itself. Ultimately cuneiform script came to represent words of the language, and the Sumerians were in possession of a true word-writing system.

The cuneiform writing system was borrowed by a number of peoples, most notably by the Assyrians (or Babylonians) when they conquered the Sumerians, and later by the Persians. In adopting cuneiform to their own languages, the borrowers used them to represent the *sounds* of the *syllables* in their words. In this way cuneiform evolved into a **syllabic writing system.**

In a syllabic writing system each syllable in the language is represented by its own symbol. Words are written by juxtaposing the symbols of their individual syllables. Cuneiform writing was never purely syllabic; that is, there was always a large residue of symbols which stood for whole words. The Assyrians retained a large number of word symbols, even though every word in their language could be written out syllabically if it were desired.

[1] The pictograph for "ox" evolved, much later, into our letter *A*.

Thus one could write  mātu "country" as:

ma	+	a	+	tu

The Persians (ca. 600–400 B.C.) devised a greatly simplified syllabic alphabet for their language. They had little recourse to word symbols. By the reign of Darius I (522–468 B.C.) the writing system was in wide use. Here are a few characters of the syllabary:

THE REBUS PRINCIPLE

When a graphic sign no longer has any visual relationship to the word it represents, it becomes a symbol for the sounds that represent the word. A single sign can then be used to represent all words with the same sounds—the homophones of the language. If, for example, the symbol ☉ stood for *sun* in English, it could then be used in a sentence like *My ☉ is a doctor.* Using symbols that originally represented single words to represent individual syllables in many-syllable words is writing words according to the **rebus principle.**

A rebus is a representation of words or syllables by pictures of objects whose names *sound like* the intended syllables. Thus ◉ might represent *eye* or the pronoun *I*. The sounds of the two monosyllabic words are identical, even though the meanings are not. In the same way, 🐝🍃 could represent *belief* (*be* + *lief* = *bee* + *leaf* = /bi/ + /lif/), and 🐝🍃🍃 could be the verb form, *believes.*

Similarly, 2 👄 —/tu/ + /lip/—could represent *tulip.* Proper names can also be "written" in such a way. If the symbol | stood for *rod* and the symbol ⚲ represented *man,* then, | ⚲ could be used to represent *Rodman,* although the name is unrelated to either rods or men, at least at this point in history. Often such combinations will become stylized or shortened so as to be more easily written. *Rodman*. for example, might be "written" in such a system as | 大 or even 乂.

This is not a very efficient system, because the words of many languages do not lend themselves to subdivision into sequences of sounds that represent independent meaning. It would be difficult, for example, to represent the word *English* (/ɪŋ/ + /glɪš/) in English according to the rebus principle. *Eng* by itself does not "mean" anything, nor does *glish*. In the "right" kind of language, however, a rebus system of writing can lead to a syllabic writing system, which has many advantages over word-writing. The semitic languages spoken many thousands of years ago in what is now the Middle East were, in fact, of the "right" kind.

FROM HIEROGLYPHS TO THE ALPHABET

At the time that Sumerian pictography was flourishing (around 4000 B.C.), a similar system was being used by the Egyptians, later called by the Greeks **hieroglyphics** (*hiero* "sacred," *glyphikos* "carvings"). That the early "sacred carvings" were originally pictography is shown by the following hieroglyphics:

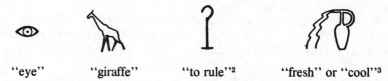

| "eye" | "giraffe" | "to rule"[2] | "fresh" or "cool"[3] |

Like the Sumerian pictograms, the hieroglyphs began to represent the sounds of the words they symbolized. This **phonetization** of the pictography made hieroglyphics a word-writing system, which paralleled the Sumerian cuneiform development. Possibly influenced by the Sumerians, the Egyptian system also became in part a syllabic writing system.

In this advanced "syllabic" stage, hieroglyphics were borrowed by many people, including the Phoenicians, a Semitic people who lived on the eastern shores of the Mediterranean. By 1500 B.C. a system involving twenty-two syllables, the West Semitic Syllabary, was in use. In this system a single symbol represents both a consonant and a following vowel (CV).

This was the system first borrowed by the Greeks in the tenth century B.C. The syllabic system proved to be very inefficient, especially for a language like Greek with a complex syllable structure. In the Semitic languages there are many monosyllabic words, and in polysyllabic words the syllables are simple and regular.

Even in a language with a "simple" and regular syllable structure the number of syllables that would have to be used is enormous. Suppose, for example, a language sound system includes twenty consonants and five vowels. Suppose further that the typical syllable was composed of a consonant plus a vowel plus a consonant: C + V + C. This would permit 2000 separate syllables: 20C × 5V × 20C.

Consider now a language like English. While there are constraints on

[2] The symbol is the Pharaoh's staff.
[3] Water trickling out of a vase.

which consonants can cluster, we still get syllables like:

I	[ay]	V	*an*	[æn]	VC
see	[si]	CV	*ant*	[ænt]	VCC
ski	[ski]	CCV	*ants*	[ænts]	VCCC
spree	[spri]	CCCV	*rant*	[rænt]	CVCC
seek	[sik]	CVC	*rants*	[rænts]	CVCCC
speak	[spik]	CCVC	*splints*	[splīnts]	CCCVCCC
scram	[skræm]	CCCVC	*stamp*	[stæmp]	CCVCC
striped	[straypt]	CCCVCC			

When you think of all the vowels and all the consonants that can occur in syllable structures of this kind it is evident that the number of syllables needed would be enormous. This kind of problem motivated the Greeks to use the symbols of the Phoenician writing system to represent the individual sounds—consonants and vowels. The Phoenicians had taken the first step by letting certain symbols stand for consonants alone. The language spoken by the Phoenicians, however, had more consonants than Greek, so when the Greeks borrowed the system they had symbols left over. These they allowed to represent vowel sounds, and thus they had developed an **alphabetic writing system.** (The word *alphabet* is derived from *alpha* and *beta,* the first two letters of the Greek alphabet.)

Alphabetic systems are those in which each symbol represents one phoneme. It is clear that such systems are primarily *phonemic* rather than *phonetic,* as is illustrated by the fact that the *p* in both *pit* and *spit* in the English alphabet system is represented by one rather than two "letters" even though the sounds are phonetically distinct.

There are arguments as to whether this event—the development of an alphabetic writing system—occurred more than once in history. Most scholars believe that all alphabetic systems in use today derive from the Greek system. This alphabet became known to the pre-Latin people of Italy, the Etruscans, who in turn passed it on to the Romans. The Roman Empire spread it throughout the world. Later, Christian missionaries used alphabetic systems to develop writing systems for many preliterate people. (Parts of the Bible have been translated into more than 1600 languages.)

It is a surprising fact that the alphabet, as we know it, did not have many beginnings. According to one linguist, the alphabet was not invented, it was *discovered.*[4] If language did not include discrete individual sounds, one could not have invented alphabetic letters to represent such sounds. When humans started to use one symbol for one phoneme they had merely brought their intuitive knowledge of the language sound system to consciousness; they discovered what they already "knew." Furthermore, children (and adults) can learn an alphabetic system only if each separate sound has some psychological reality. Since this is true of all languages, however, it is strange that this "discovery" was not made by many people in many parts of the world.

---

[4] Dr. Sven Ohman, Professor of Phonetics, University of Uppsala, Sweden; paper presented at the International Speech Symposium, Kyoto, Japan, 1969.

Modern Types of Writing Systems

. . . but their manner of writing is very peculiar, being neither from the left to the right, like the Europeans; nor from the right to the left, like the Arabians; nor from up to down, like the Chinese; nor from down to up, like the Cascagians, but aslant from one corner of the paper to the other, like ladies in England.
Jonathan Swift, *Gulliver's Travels*

We have already mentioned the three types of writing systems used in the world: *word-writing, syllable-writing,* and *alphabetic writing.*

WORD WRITING

POLONIUS: What do you read, my lord?
HAMLET: Words, words, words.
Shakespeare, *Hamlet,* II, ii

PEANUTS   **Charles Schulz**

© 1964 United Feature Syndicate

In a word-writing system the written symbol represents a whole word. The awkwardness of such a system is obvious. For example, the editors of *Webster's Third New International Dictionary* claim more than 450,000 entries. When we consider that all these are written using only twenty-six alphabetic symbols, a dot, a hyphen, an apostrophe, and a space, it is understandable why, historically, word-writing has given way to alphabetic systems in most places in the world.

The major exceptions are the writing systems used in China and Japan. The Chinese system has an uninterrupted history that reaches back more than 3500 years. For the most part it is a word-writing system, each character representing an individual word or morpheme. Longer words may be formed by combining two words or morphemes, as shown by the word meaning "business," *măimai,* which is formed by combining the words meaning "buy" and "sell."

Chinese writing utilizes a system of **characters,** each of which represents the "meaning" of a word, rather than its sounds. Chinese dictionaries and rhyme books contain tens of thousands of these characters, but to read a newspaper one need know "only" about five thousand. It is not easy to become a scholar in China! In 1956, the difficulties prompted the government of the People's Republic of China to simplify the characters. They also adopted a spelling system using the Roman alphabet, to be used along with the regular ancient system. It is doubtful whether it will replace the traditional writing, which is an integral part of Chinese culture. In China, writing is an art—calligraphy—and thousands of years of poetry and literature and history are preserved in the old system.

There is an additional reason for keeping the traditional system. Chinese is composed of a number of dialects and languages that are all mutually unintelligible in spoken form. But each dialect uses the one writing system; through writing all the Chinese can communicate. A common sight in a city like Hong Kong is for two Chinese to be talking and at the same time furiously drawing characters in the air with a forefinger to overcome their linguistic differences.

The use of written Chinese characters in this way is parallel to the use of Arabic numerals, which mean the same in all European countries. Though the word for "eight" is very different in English, Greek, and Finnish, by writing *8* you can be understood. Similarly, the word for "rice" is different in many Chinese dialects, but the written character is the same. If the writing system in China were ever to become alphabetic, each language would be as different in writing as in speaking, and communication would break down completely between the various groups.

Every writing system has some traces of word-writing. In addition to numerals in which a single symbol represents a whole word, other symbols, such as $, %, &, ¢, +, −, =, are used.

SYLLABLE WRITING

Syllabic writing systems are more efficient than word-writing systems. They are certainly less taxing on our memory. But as discussed above, they still present serious difficulties for recording the sentences of a language.

Japanese is the only major language that uses a syllabic writing system. All words in the Japanese language can be phonologically represented by about 100 different syllables, mostly of the Consonant-Vowel (CV) type. To write these syllables the Japanese have two **syllabaries,** each containing about 45 "syllable letters" and several diacritical markers. (Diacritical markers are small symbols added to a letter that alter its pronunciation, such as the two dots over the *ü* in German writing that shows it is to be pronounced as a high *front* rounded vowel [ü] or in IPA symbols [y], rather than as the high *back* rounded vowel [u], symbolized in the writing system as *u* without the dots.) One syllabary, *katakana,* is used for loan words and for special effects similar to italics in European writing. The other syllabary, *hiragana,* is used for native words alone and in combination with word signs borrowed from Chinese.

The Japanese borrowed the Chinese writing system and most of the symbols in the syllabaries. All the word symbols or characters in the Japanese word-writing system, which total more than two thousand, have a Chinese origin. The Japanese language is very different from Chinese and when writing was introduced in Japan it was found that a word-writing system alone was not suitable to Japanese. It is a highly inflected language; verbs may occur in thirty or more different forms. Thus, in Japanese writing, Chinese characters will commonly be used for the verb roots, and hiragana symbols for the inflectional markings. For example, 行 is the character meaning "go" and is pronounced [i]. The word for "went" in formal speech is pronounced [ikimashita] and is written in Japanese as 行きました、

where the hiragana symbols き ま し た stand for the syllables [ki], [ma], [shi], [ta]. Nouns, on the other hand, are not inflected in Japanese and they can generally be written using Chinese characters only.

In theory all of Japanese could be written in hiragana. There are many homophones in Japanese, however, and the use of word characters disambiguates a word that would be ambiguous if written syllabically. This seems to be a factor in the retention of the dual word/syllabic system.

In 1821, Sequoyah, often called the "Cherokee Cadmus," invented a syllabic writing system for his native language. Sequoyah's script proved very useful to the Cherokee people for a number of years, and was justifiably a point of great pride for them. The syllabary contains eighty-five symbols, many of them derived from Latin characters, and efficiently transcribes spoken Cherokee. A few symbols are shown here;

J	gu
ſ	hu
ℓℓ	we
W	ta
H	mi

English occasionally uses syllabic symbols. In words such as *OK* and *bar-b-q*, the single letters represent syllables (*b* for [bə], *q* for [kyu]).

ALPHABETIC WRITING

Alphabetic writing systems are one of the major achievements of civilization. They are easy to learn and convenient to use and are maximally efficient for transcribing any human language.

The term **sound-writing** is sometimes used in place of alphabetic writing, but this does not truly represent the principle involved in the use of alphabets. One-sound-one-letter would be inefficient, since we do not need to represent the [pʰ] in *pit* and the [p] in *spit* by two different letters. It would also be confusing, because the nonphonemic differences between sounds are seldom perceptible to speakers. Except for the phonetic alphabets whose function is to record the sounds of all languages for descriptive purposes, most, if not all, alphabets have been devised on the **phonemic principle.**

In the twelfth century, an Icelandic scholar developed an orthography derived from the Latin alphabet for the writing of the Icelandic language of his day. Other scholars in this period were also interested in orthographic reform, including the German, Notker, and the Englishman, Orm. But the Icelander, who came to be known as "The First Grammarian" (because his anonymous paper was the first entry in a collection of grammatical essays), was the only one of the time who left a record of his principles. The orthography he developed was clearly based on the phonemic principle. He used minimal pairs to show the distinctive contrasts; he did not suggest different symbols for voiced and unvoiced [θ] and [ð], nor for [f] or [v], nor for velar [k] and palatal [č], because these pairs, according to him, represented allophones of the phonemes /θ/, /f/, and /k/, respectively. He, of course, did not use these modern technical terms, but the letters of his alphabet represent the distinctive phonemes of Icelandic of that century.

King Seijong of Korea (1417–1450) realized that the same principles held true for Korean when he designed a phonemic alphabet. The king was an avid reader (so avid that his eyes suffered greatly), and he realized that the more than 30,000 Chinese characters that were being used to write the Korean language discouraged literacy among the people.

The alphabet was not reinvented by Seijong. Indian scholars had visited Korea, and the erudite monarch undoubtedly knew of the Hindu grammarians. Still, his alphabet, called *hankul,* was conceived with remarkable insight. Originally hankul had eleven vowels and seventeen consonants (it is down to fourteen consonants and ten vowels at present). The characters representing consonants were drawn according to the place and manner of articulation. For example, 人 is meant to represent the teeth, and it is a part of each consonant character in which the tongue is placed behind the teeth (that is, alveolar or alveopalatal sounds). Thus 人 alone stands for /s/ ([s] or [š]). Cross it to get 人 and you have the character for [ts] (the initial sound of German *Zeit*) and [tš] (=[č]). A bar above the character means aspiration, so 人 stands for [tsʰ] and [tšʰ] (=[čʰ]). Hundreds of years later, Francis Lodwick, Cave Beck, and Henry Sweet used a similar principle to design their phonetic alphabets.

King Seijong constructed each of eleven vowel characters by using one or more of three "atomic" characters: · | and —; for example, | was /i/, — was /u/ and | · was /a/.

Although Korean has the sounds [l] and [r], only a single "letter" was used by Seiijong because these sounds are allophonic variants of the same phoneme.[5] The same is true for the sounds [s] and [š]. Seijong knew that a narrow phonetic alphabet would be confusing to a Korean speaker.

Seijong's contribution to the Korean people has been recorded in a delightful legend. It is said that after he designed the alphabet he was afraid it would not be accepted, and so he concocted a scheme to convince the people that it was a gift from heaven. To do this he wrote each one of his new letters in honey on individual leaves that had fallen from a tree in the palace garden. When the king walked with his soothsayer in the garden the next day, the insects had eaten the honey and the leaf fiber underneath, just as he had hoped, and the leaves were etched with the alphabetic letters. The soothsayer and the Korean people were convinced that these represented a message from the gods. It is essentially this alphabet that is used in Korea today.

Many languages have their own alphabet, and each has developed certain conventions for converting strings of alphabetic characters into sequences of sound (that is, reading), and converting sequences of sounds into strings of alphabetic characters (that is, writing). As we have illustrated with English,

---

[5] See Exercise 3 of Chapter 3.

Icelandic, and Korean, the rules governing the sound system of the language play an important role in the relation between sound and character.

Most European alphabets make use of Latin (Roman) characters, minor adjustments being made to accommodate individual characteristics of a particular language. For instance, Spanish uses /ñ/ (an /n/ with a "tilde") to represent the palatilized nasal of *señor,* and German has added an "umlaut" for certain of its vowel sounds that didn't exist in Latin (for example, *über*). Such "extra" marks are called **diacritics.** Often languages resort to using two letters together to represent a single sound for which there is no corresponding single letter. English includes **digraphs** such as *sh* [š], *ch* [č], *ng* [ŋ], and so on.

Some languages that have more recently acquired a writing system use some of the IPA phonetic symbols in their alphabet. Twi, for example uses ŋ, ɔ, and ɛ.

Besides the European languages, such languages as Turkish, Indonesian, Swahili, and Vietnamese have adopted the Latin alphabet.

The **Cyrillic** alphabet, named for St. Cyril, who brought Christianity to the Slavs, is used by many Slavic languages, including Russian. It is derived directly from the Greek alphabet without Latin mediation.

The contemporary Semitic alphabets, and those used for Persian and Urdu writing, are derived from the West Semitic Syllabary.

Figure 5-2 shows a greatly abbreviated "family tree" of alphabetic writing systems.

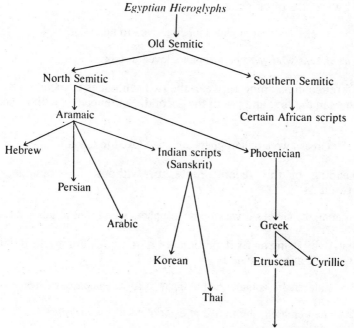

Figure 5-2 Family tree of alphabetic writing systems. (Adapted from Ernst Doblhofer. 1961. *Voices in Stone.* Viking. New York.)

Writing and Speech

. . . Ther is so great diversite
In English, and in wryting of oure tonge,
So prey I god that non myswrite thee . . .
Geoffrey Chaucer

The development of writing freed us from the limitations of time and geography, but spoken language has primacy, as is revealed in the short history of writing in the preceding pages. To understand language one cannot depend solely on its written form except as an approximation to the spoken language. Of course, linguists are interested in writing systems for their own sake, as the presence of this chapter affirms.

The written language reflects, to a certain extent, the elements and rules that together constitute the grammar of the language. The system of phonemes is represented by the letters of the alphabet, although not necessarily in a direct way. Were there no discrete sound units in language, there could be no alphabetic writing. The independence of words in a language is revealed by the spaces in the written string. But in languages where words are composed of more than one morpheme, the writing does not show the individual morphemes, even though speakers know what these are. The sentences of a language are indicated in the written form by capitals and periods. Other punctuation, such as question marks, italics, commas, exclamation marks, is used to reveal syntactic structure.

The possible ambiguity in the meanings of some sentences can be prevented by the use of commas:

(1) The Greeks, who were philosophers, loved to talk a lot.

(2) The Greeks who were philosophers loved to talk a lot.

The difference in meaning between the two sentences is specified by the use of commas in the first and not in the second. Sentence (1), with the commas, means:

(1′) The Greeks were philosophers and they loved to talk a lot.

The meaning of the second sentence, without the commas, can be paraphrased as:

(2′) Among the Greeks it was the philosophers who loved to talk a lot.

Similarly, by using an exclamation point or a question mark, the intention of the writer can be revealed.

(3) The children are going to bed at eight o'clock. (*simple statement*)

(4) The children are going to bed at eight o'clock! (*an order*)

(5) The children are going to bed at eight o'clock? (*a query*)

These punctuation marks reflect the pauses and the intonations that would be used in the spoken language.

In sentence (6) the *he* can refer to either John or someone else, but in sentence (7) the pronoun must refer to someone other than John:

(6) John said he's going.

(7) John said, "He's going."

The apostrophe used in contractions and possessives also provides syntactic information not always available in the spoken utterance.

(8) My cousin's friends   (*one cousin*)

(9) My cousins' friends   (*two or more cousins*)

Writing, then, somewhat reflects the spoken language, but occasionally punctuation marks may be unable to distinguish between two possible meanings:

(10) John whispered the message to Bill and then he whispered it to Mary.

In the normal written version of (10), *he* can refer to either John or Bill. In the spoken sentence, if *he* receives extra stress (called **contrastive stress**), it must refer to Bill; if *he* receives normal stress, it refers to John. In speaking one can usually emphasize any word in a sentence by using contrastive stress. One sometimes attempts to show this in writing by using all capital letters or underlining the emphasized word:

(11) <u>John</u> kissed Bill's wife.   (Bill didn't)

(12) John <u>kissed</u> Bill's wife.   (rather than hitting her)

(13) John kissed <u>Bill's</u> wife.   (not Dick's or his own)

(14) John kissed Bill's <u>wife</u>.   (not Bill's mother)

While such "visual" devices can help in English, it is not clear that this can be done in a language such as Chinese. In Japanese, however, this kind of emphasis can be achieved by writing a word in katakana instead of in the usual way.

The written language is also more conservative than the spoken language. When we write something—particularly in formal writing—we are more apt to obey the "prescriptive rules" taught in school, or use a more formal style, than we are to use the rules of our "everyday" grammar. "Dangling participles" (for example, *While studying in the library, the fire alarm rang*) and "sentences ending with a preposition" (for example, *I know what to end a sentence with*) abound in spoken language, but may be "corrected" by copy editors, diligent English teachers, and careful writers. A linguist wishing to describe the language that people regularly use therefore cannot depend on written records alone.

Spelling

"Do you spell it with a 'v' or a 'w'?" inquired the judge.
"That depends upon the taste and fancy of the speller, my Lord," replied Sam.

Charles Dickens, *The Pickwick Papers*

If writing represented the spoken language perfectly, spelling reformers would never have arisen. In Chapter 2 we discussed some of the problems in the English orthographic (spelling) system. These problems prompted George Bernard Shaw to write:

. . . it was as a reading and writing animal that Man achieved his human eminence above those who are called beasts. Well, it is I and my like who have to do the writing. I have done it professionally for the last sixty years as well as it can be done with a hopelessly inadequate alphabet devised centuries before the English language existed to record another and very different language. Even this alphabet is reduced to absurdity by a foolish orthography based on the notion that the business of spelling is to represent the origin and history of a word instead of its sound and meaning. Thus an intelligent child who is bidden to spell debt, and very properly spells it d-e-t, is caned for not spelling it with a b because Julius Caesar spelt the Latin word for it with a b.[6]

The irregularities between **graphemes** (letters) and phonemes have been cited as one reason "why Johnny can't read." Different spellings for the same sound, the same spellings for different sounds, "silent letters," and "missing letters"—all provide fuel for the flames of spelling-reform movements. This was illustrated earlier, but merits further examples:

SAME SOUND, DIFFERENT SPELLING	DIFFERENT SOUND, SAME SPELLING		SILENT LETTERS	MISSING LETTERS
/ay/	thought	$-\theta-$	listen	use /yuz/
	though	$-\eth-$	debt	fuse /fyuz/
aye	Thomas	$-t-$	gnosis	
buy			know	
by	ate	$-e-$	psychology	
die	at	$-æ-$	right	
hi	father	$-a-$	mnemonic	
Thai	many	$-\varepsilon-$	arctic	
height			balm	
guide			honest	
			sword	
			bomb	
			clue	
			Wednesday	

Chapters 2 and 9 discuss some of the reasons for the nonphonemic aspects of our spelling system. "Spelling is the written trace of a word. Pronunciation is its linguistic form."[7] The spelling of most of the words in English

---

[6] George Bernard Shaw, Preface to R. A. Wilson. 1948. *The Miraculous Birth of Language* (Philosophical Library. New York.)

[7] D. Bolinger. 1968. *Aspects of Language* (Harcourt Brace Jovanovich. New York.)

today is based on the Late Middle English pronunciation (that used by Chaucer) and on the early forms of Modern English (used by Shakespeare). The many changes that have occurred in the sound system of English, like the Great Vowel Shift, as discussed in Chapter 9, were not always reflected in changes in the spelling of the words that were affected.

When the printing press was introduced in the fifteenth century, not only were archaic pronunciations "frozen" but the spelling did not always represent even those pronunciations, since many of the early printers were Dutch and were unsure of English pronunciation.

During the Renaissance, in the fifteenth and sixteenth centuries, many scholars who revered Classical Greek and Latin became "spelling reformers." Unlike the later reformers who wished to change the spelling to conform to pronunciation, these scholars changed the spelling of English words to conform to their etymologies—the "original" Latin, or Greek, or French spellings. Where Latin had a *b,* they added a *b* even if it was not pronounced; and where the original spelling had a *c* or *p* or *h,* these letters were added, as is shown by these few examples:

MIDDLE ENGLISH SPELLING		"REFORMED" SPELLING
indite	→	indict
dette	→	debt
receit	→	receipt
oure	→	hour

These, then, are the reasons why modern English orthography does not represent, in all cases, what we know about the phonology of the language. In at least one respect this is a good thing. It allows us to read and understand what people wrote hundreds of years ago without the need for translations. If there were a one-to-one correspondence between our spelling and the sounds of our language, we would have difficulty reading even the Constitution or the Declaration of Independence. Constant spellings help our ever-dynamic language to span gaps of time.

Today's language is no more static than was yesterday's; it would be impossible to maintain a perfect correspondence between pronunciation and spelling. This is not to say that certain reforms would not be helpful. Some "respelling" is already taking place; advertisers often spell *though* as *tho,* *through* as *thru,* and *night* as *nite.* For a period of time the Chicago *Tribune* used such spellings, but in 1975 gave this up. Spelling habits are hard to change.

In the case of homophones, it is very helpful at times to have different spellings for the same sounds, as in the following:

The book was red.   The book was read.

Lewis Carroll once more makes the point with his own inimitable humor:

"And how many hours a day did you do lessons?" said Alice.
"Ten hours the first day," said the Mock Turtle, "nine the next, and so on."
"What a curious plan!" exclaimed Alice.
"That's the reason they're called *lessons,*" the Gryphon remarked, "because they *lessen* from day to day."

There are also reasons for using the same spelling for different pronunciations. In Chapter 4 it was shown that a morpheme may be pronounced differently when it occurs in different contexts, and that in most cases the pronunciation is "regular"; that is, it is determined by rules which apply throughout the language. The identical spelling reflects the fact that the different pronunciations represent the same morpheme.

Similarly, the phonetic realizations of the vowels in the following forms are "regular":

ay/ɪ	i/ɛ	e/æ
divine/divinity	*serene/serenity*	*sane/sanity*
sublime/sublimate	*obscene/obscenity*	*profane/profanity*
sign/signature	*hygiene/hygienic*	*humane/humanity*

The spelling of such pairs thus reflects our knowledge of the sound pattern of the language and the semantic relations between the words.

Other examples provide further evidence. The **b** in *"debt"* may remind us of the related word *debit* in which the **b** is pronounced. The same principle is true of pairs such as *sign/signal, knowledge/acknowledge, bomb/bombadier, gnosis/prognosis/agnostic.*

It is doubtful that anyone would suggest that the plural morpheme should be spelled *s* in *cats* and *z* in *dogs.* The sound of the morpheme is determined by rules, and this is just as true in other cases like those given above.

There are also different spellings that represent the different pronunciations of a morpheme when confusion would arise from using the same spelling. For example, there is a rule in English phonology that changes a /t/ to an /s/ in certain cases: *democrat → democracy.* The different spellings are due in part to the fact that this rule does not apply to all morphemes, so that *art + y* is *arty,* not **arcy.* There are many regular phoneme-to-grapheme rules that determine when a morpheme is to be spelled identically and when it is changed. Notice, also, that a *c* always represents the /s/ sound when it is followed by a *y* or *i* or *e,* as in *cynic* and *citizen* and *censure.* Since it is always pronounced [k] when it is the final letter in a word or when it is followed by any other vowel (*coat, cat, cut,* and so on), no confusion results.

Such rules of orthography can be taught to children learning to read, which would lessen the difficulties they have with the spelling system. For example, by pointing out the alternate pronunciations of morphemes such as the [o] in *melodious* or the [g] in *signal,* students may more easily remember how to spell the related words *melody* or *sign.*

There is another important reason why spelling should not always be tied to the phonetic pronunciation of words. Different dialects of English have divergent pronunciations. Cockneys drop their "haitches" and Bostonians and Southerners drop their "r's"; *neither* is pronounced [niðər] and [niðə] by Americans, [nayðə] by the British, and [neðər] by the Irish; some Scots pronounce *night* as [nɪxt]; one hears "Chicago" and "Chicawgo," "hog" and "hawg," "bird" and "boyd"; *four* is pronounced [fɔ:] by the British, [fɔr] in the Midwest, and [foə] in the South; *orange* is pronounced in at least two ways in the United States: [arənǰ] and [ɔrənǰ].

While dialectal pronunciations differ, the common spellings represent the fact that we can all understand each other. It is necessary for the written language to transcend local dialects. With a uniform spelling system, a native of Atlanta and a native of Glasgow can communicate through writing. If each dialect were spelled according to its own pronunciation, written communication among the English-speaking peoples of the world would suffer more than the spoken communication does today.

Spelling Pronunciations

For pronunciation, the best general rule is to consider those as the most elegant speakers who deviate least from written words.
Samuel Johnson, 1755

Despite the primacy of the spoken over the written language, the written word is often regarded with excessive reverence. Undoubtedly the stability, permanency, and graphic nature of writing cause some people to favor it over ephemeral and elusive speech. Humpty Dumpty expressed a rather typical attitude: "I'd rather see that done on paper," he announced.

Writing has, however, affected speech only marginally, and most notably in the phenomenon of **spelling pronunciation.** Since the sixteenth century, we find that spelling has influenced standard pronunciation to some extent. The most important of such changes stem from the eighteenth century under the influence and "decrees" of the dictionary-makers and the schoolteachers. The struggle between those who demanded that words be pronounced according to the spelling and those who demanded that words be spelled according to their pronunciation generated great heat in that century. The "preferred" pronunciations were given in the many dictionaries printed in the eighteenth century, and the "supreme authority" of the dictionaries influenced pronunciation in this way.

Spelling also has influenced pronunciation in words that are infrequently used in normal daily speech. Many words which were spelled with an initial *h* were not pronounced with any /h/ sound as late as the eighteenth century. Thus, at that time no /h/ was pronounced in *honest, hour, habit, heretic, hotel, hospital, herb.* Frequently used words like *honest* and *hour* continued to be pronounced without the /h/, despite the spelling. But all those other words were given a "spelling pronunciation." Since people did not hear them very often, when they saw them written they concluded that they must begin with an /h/.

Similarly, many words now spelled with a *th* were once pronounced /t/ as in *Thomas;* later most of these words underwent a change in pronunciation from /t/ to /θ/, as in *anthem, author, theater.* It is interesting that "nicknames" often reflect the earlier pronunciations: "Ka*t*e" for "Ca*t*herine," "Be*tt*y" for "Elizabe*th*," "Ar*t*" for "Ar*t*hur." The words *often* and *soften,* which are usually pronounced without a /t/ sound, are pronounced with the /t/ by some people because of the spelling. At one time, however, the /t/ was never pronounced in *often* and *soften.*

The clear influence of spelling on pronunciation is observable in the way place-names are pronounced. *Berkeley* is pronounced [bʌrkli] in California, although it stems from the British [ba:kli]; *Worcester* [wustər] or [wustə] in Massachusetts is often pronounced [wərčɛstər] in other parts of the country.

While the written language thus has some influence on the spoken, it never changes the basic system—the grammar—of the language. The writing system, conversely, reflects, in a more or less direct way, the grammar that every speaker knows.

SUMMARY

Writing is one of the basic tools of civilization. Without it, the world as we know it could not exist.

The first writing was "picture writing," which used **pictograms** to represent objects directly. Pictograms became stylized and people came to associate them with the *word sounds* that represented the object in their language. The Sumerians first developed a pictographic writing system to keep track of commercial transactions. It was later expanded for other uses and eventually evolved into the highly stylized **cuneiform** writing. Cuneiform was borrowed by several nations and was adapted for use in a syllabic writing system by application of the **rebus principle,** which used the symbol of one word to represent any word or syllable with the same sounds.

The Egyptians also developed a pictographic system that became known as **hieroglyphics.** This system was borrowed by many peoples including the Phoenicians, who improved on it, using it as a **syllabary.** In a syllabic writing system one symbol is used for each syllable. The Greeks borrowed this Phoenician system and in adapting it to their own language used the symbols to represent individual sound segments, thus inventing the first **alphabet.**

There are three types of writing systems still being used in the world: **word writing,** where every symbol or character represents a word or morpheme (as in Chinese); **syllable-writing,** where each symbol represents a syllable (as in Japanese); and **alphabetic writing,** where each symbol represents (for the most part) one phoneme (as in English).

Many of the world's languages do not have a written form, but this does not mean the languages are any less developed. We learn to speak before we learn to write, and historically tens of thousands of years went by during which language was spoken before there was any writing.

The writing system may have some small effect on the spoken language. Languages change in time, but writing systems tend to be more conservative. When the spoken and written forms of the language become divergent, some words may be pronounced as they are spelled, sometimes due to the efforts of "pronunciation reformers."

There are advantages to a conservative spelling system. A common spelling permits speakers whose dialects have diverged to communicate through writing, as is best exemplified in China, where the "dialects" are mutually unintelligible. We are also able to read and understand the language as it was written centuries ago. In addition, besides some gross lack of correspondences between sound and spelling, the spelling often reflects speakers' morphological and phonological knowledge.

EXERCISES

1. Discuss the statement quoted in the chapter that "alphabetic writing was not invented, it was discovered." That is, how does the existence of alphabets reflect a linguistic universal?

2. A. "Write" the following words and phrases using pictograms that you invent:

a. eye   e. tree   i. ugly
b. a boy   f. forest   j. run
c. two boys   g. war   k. Scotch tape
d. library   h. honesty   l. smoke

B. Which words are most difficult to symbolize in this way? Why?

C. How does the following sentence reveal the problems in pictographic writing? "A grammar represents the unconscious, internalized linguistic competence of a native speaker."

3. A *rebus* is a written representation of words or syllables using pictures of objects whose names resemble the sounds of the intended words or syllables. For example, ◉ might be the symbol for "eye" or "I" or the first syllable in "idea."

A. Using the rebus principle, "write" the following

a. tearing   b. icicle   c. bareback   d. cookies

B. Why would such a system be a difficult system in which to represent all words in English? Illustrate with an example.

4. A. Construct non-Roman alphabetic letters to replace the letters used to represent the following sounds in English:

t r s k w č i æ f ŋ

B. Use these symbols plus the regular alphabet symbols for the other sounds to write the following words in your "new orthography."

a. character   e. cheat
b. guest   f. rang
c. cough   g. psychotic
d. photo   h. tree

5. Suppose the English writing system were a *syllabic* system instead of an *alphabetic* system. Use capital letters to symbolize the necessary syllabic units for the words listed below and list your "syllabary." Example: Given the words *mate, inmate, intake,* and *elfin,* one might use: A = mate, B = in, C = take, and D = elf. In addition, write the words using your syllabary. Example: *inmate:* BA, *elfin:* DB; *intake:* BC; *mate:* A. (Do not use any more syllable symbols than you absolutely need.)

a. childishness   d. lifelessness   g. witness   j. witless
b. childlike   e. likely   h. lethal   k. lesson
c. Jesuit   f. zoo   i. jealous

6. In the following pairs of English words the boldfaced portions are pronounced the same but spelled differently. Can you think of any reason why the spelling should remain distinct? (Hint: *reel* and *real* are pronounced the same, but *reality* shows the presence of a phonemic /æ/ in *real.*)

a. **I** am   **i**amb
b. **goose**   pro**duce**
c. **fashion**   compli**cation**
d. New**ton**   or**gan**
e. n**o**   kn**ow**
f. hy**mn**   **him**

7. In the following pairs of words the boldfaced portions in the second column are pronounced differently from those in the first column. Try to state some reasons why the spelling of the words in column B should not be changed.

A	B
a. mi**ng**le	lo**ng**
b. li**ne**	**chi**ldren
c. **s**onar	re**s**ound
d. **c**ent	mysti**c**
e. cru**mb**le	bo**mb**
f. cat**s**	dog**s**
g. sta**gn**ant	desi**gn**
h. sere**ne**	obsce**ni**ty

8. Each of the following sentences is ambiguous (can have more than one meaning) in the written form. How can these sentences be made unambiguous when they are spoken?

   a. John hugged Bill and then he kissed him.
   b. What are we having for dinner, Mother?
   c. She's a German language teacher.
   d. They formed a student grievance committee.
   e. Charles kissed his wife and George kissed his wife, too.

9. In the written form, the following sentences are not ambiguous, but they would be if spoken. State the devices used in writing which make the meanings explicit.

   a. They're my brothers' keepers.
   b. He said, "He will take the garbage out."
   c. The red book was read.
   d. The flower was on the table.

10. If you were given the task of making changes in the present spelling system of English, what are some of the changes you would propose? Are there any "silent" letters that should be dropped from the orthography? Should some sounds always have the same letters to represent them? Should some letters with different sounds be given additional symbols? Justify your proposals.

REFERENCES

Diringer, D. 1962. *Writing.* Holt, Rinehart and Winston. New York.
Doblhofer, E. 1961. *Voices in Stone: The Decipherment of Ancient Scripts and Writings.* The Viking Press. New York.
Gelb, I. J. 1952. *A Study of Writing.* University of Chicago Press. Chicago.
Robertson, S., and F. G. Cassidy. 1954. *The Development of Modern English.* Prentice-Hall. Englewood Cliffs, N.J. Pp. 353–374 (on spelling and spelling reform).
Wang, William S-Y. "The Chinese Language," *Scientific American,* vol. 228, no. 2 (Feb. 1973): 50–63.

Chapter 6

Semantics: The Meanings of Language

Language without meaning is meaningless.

Roman Jakobson

B.C.   **Johnny Hart**

By permission of Johnny Hart and Field Enterprises, Inc.

For thousands of years philosophers have been pondering the meaning of "meaning." Yet everyone who knows a language can understand what is said to him or her and can produce strings of words that convey meaning.

Learning a language includes learning the "agreed-upon" meanings of certain strings of sounds and learning how to combine these meaningful units into larger units that also convey meaning. We are not free to change the meanings of these words at will, for if we did we would be unable to communicate with anyone.

Humpty Dumpty, however, refused to be so restricted when he said:

"There's glory for you!"
    "I don't know what you mean by 'glory,'" Alice said.
    Humpty Dumpty smiled contemptuously. "Of course you don't—till I tell you. I meant 'there's a nice knock-down argument for you!'"
    "But 'glory' doesn't mean 'a nice knock-down argument,'" Alice objected.
    "When *I* use a word," Humpty Dumpty said, in rather a scornful tone, "it means just what I choose it to mean—neither more nor less."
    "The question is," said Alice, "whether you *can* make words mean so many different things."

Alice is quite right. You cannot make words mean what they do not mean. Of course if you wish to redefine the meaning of each word as you use it you are free to do so, but this would be an artificial, clumsy use of language, and most people would not wait around very long to talk to you. A new word

163

may be created, but it enters the language with its sound-meaning relationship already determined.

Fortunately there are few Humpty Dumptys—because all the speakers of a language share the basic vocabulary, the sounds and meanings of words. And all speakers know how to combine the meanings of words to get the meanings of phrases and sentences. We have no difficulties in using language to talk to each other. The study of the linguistic meaning of words, phrases, and sentences is called **semantics.**

Semantic Properties

"My name is Alice . . ."

"It's a stupid name enough!" Humpty Dumpty interrupted impatiently. "What does it mean?"

"Must a name mean something?" Alice asked doubtfully.

"Of course it must," Humpty Dumpty said with a short laugh: "my name means the shape I am—and a good handsome shape it is, too. With a name like yours, you might be any shape, almost."

Lewis Carroll, *Through the Looking-Glass*

Not only do we know what the morphemes of our language are, we also know what they *mean*. Dictionaries are filled with words and their meanings. So is the head of every human being who speaks a language. You are a walking dictionary. You know the meaning of thousands of words. Your knowledge of their meanings permits you to use them appropriately in sentences and to understand them when heard, even though you probably seldom stop and ask yourself: "What does *boy* mean?" or "What does *walk* mean?"

Most words and morphemes in the language have their own meanings. We shall talk about the meaning of words, even though we already know that words may be composed of several morphemes.

Suppose someone said:

The assassin was stopped before he got to Thwacklehurst.

If the word *assassin* is in your mental dictionary, you know that it was some *person* who was prevented from *murdering* some *important person* named Thwacklehurst. Your knowledge of the meaning of *assassin* tells you that it was not an animal that tried to kill the man and that Thwacklehurst was not likely to be a little old man who owned a tobacco shop. In other words, your knowledge of the meaning of *assassin* includes knowing that the individual to whom that word refers is *human*, is a *murderer*, and is a killer of *very important people*. These, then, are some of the semantic properties of the word that speakers of the language agree to. The meaning of all nouns, verbs, adjectives, adverbs—the "content words"—and even some of the "function words" such as *with* or *over* can at least partially be defined by such properties, or **semantic features.**

The same semantic property may be part of the meaning of many different words. "Female" is a semantic property that helps to define

bitch	hen	actress	maiden
doe	mare	debutante	widow
ewe	vixen	girl	woman

The words in the last two columns are also distinguished by the semantic property "human." The feature "human" is also found in

doctor   dean   professor   bachelor   parent   baby   child

The last two of these words are also specified as "young." That is, parts of the meaning of the words *baby* and *child* are that they are "human" and "young."

The "meaning" of a word can then be specified by indicating a "plus" or "minus" for the presence or absence of all the semantic properties that define the word, as illustrated in the following way:

ACTRESS	**BABY**	**GIRL**	**BACHELOR**	**MARE**	**COURAGE**
+ human	+ human	+ human	+ human	− human	....
+ female	....	+ female	− female	+ female	....
.	+ young	+ young	− young	− young	....
.	.	.	.	.	+ abstract
.	.	.	.	.	

THE FAMILY CIRCUS

Bil Keane

Copyright 1978.
The Register and Tribune
Syndicate. Inc

"Daddy, am I a bachelor yet?"

Reprinted Courtesy The Register and Tribune Syndicate, Inc.

Of course, words have many more properties which define their meanings than are shown. For example, part of the meaning of *mare* must relate to its "horseness" though whether this is accomplished by including "+horseness" as a feature of *mare* or by some other means is not entirely clear. But note that such semantic properties can be used to classify words into semantic groups—those that are all +human or +abstract and so on. In addition, the presence of certain properties automatically excludes others, so we do not need to indicate that courage is "–human," "–female," and so on, because "+abstract" implies all that. *Baby* is not specified as either "+female" or "+male." A baby can be either sex; this is a fact about the meaning of *baby* that can be indicated by omitting any gender specification. Some properties also mutually exclude each other ("human" and "abstract"), and in some cases one property implies the presence of another ("human" → "animate").

The same semantic property may occur in different parts of speech. "Female" is part of the meaning of the noun *mother*, of the verb *breastfeed*, and of the adjective *pregnant*. Other semantic properties are found usually in words belonging to one particular part of speech. "Cause" is a verbal property, possessed by *darken, kill, uglify*, and so on.

darken	cause to become dark
kill	cause to die
uglify	cause to become ugly

Other semantic properties that help account for the meaning of verbs are shown in this table.

SEMANTIC PROPERTY	VERBS HAVING IT
+motion	bring, fall, plod, walk, run . . .
+contact	hit, kiss, touch . . .
+creation	build, imagine, make . . .
+sense	see, hear, feel . . .

Our linguistic knowledge tells us that for the most part no two words have exactly the same meaning, and this suggests that through semantic properties we can make finer and finer distinctions in meaning. To distinguish *plod* from *walk* we could use the property "slow" and to further distinguish *stalk* from *plod* a property such as "purposeful" is needed.

Evidence for the existence of semantic properties is found in some of the speech errors, or "slips of the tongue," that we all make. In the chapter on phonology some errors were cited that reveal the internalized phonological system of the language. Other errors result in the substitution of a word for an intended word. Consider the following word-substitution errors that some speakers have actually produced:

INTENDED UTTERANCE	ACTUAL UTTERANCE (ERROR)
blond hair	blond eyes
bridge of the nose	bridge of the neck
when my gums bled	when my tongues bled
he came too late	he came too early
Mary was young	Mary was early
the lady with the dachshund	the lady with the Volkswagen
that's a horse of another color	that's a horse of another race
he has to pay her alimony	he has to pay her rent

These errors, and thousands of others we and others have collected, reveal that the incorrectly substituted words are not total random substitutions, but share some semantic properties with the intended words. *Hair* and *eyes, nose* and *neck, gums* and *tongues* are all "body parts" or "parts of the head." *Young, early,* and *late* are related to "time." *Dachshund* and *Volkswagen* are both "German" and "small." The semantic relationship between *color* and *race* and even between *alimony* and *rent* are rather obvious.

Other speech errors are word blends such as in the following:

COMPONENT WORDS	BLEND ERROR
splinters/blisters	splisters
edited/annotated	editated
terrible/horrible	herrible
smart/clever	smever
a tennis player/athlete	a tennis athler
a swinging/hip chick	a swip chick
marijuana/acid	maracid
frown/scowl	frowl
aspect/viewpoint	aspoint

It is almost as if the speakers who produced these errors had the semantic properties or features of the words that would express the meaning they wished to convey and pulled out of their mental dictionaries more than one word that included some of these semantic properties and then couldn't decide between them and so blended them together. Errors in speech thus support what we have been saying about the semantic properties of words.

The meaning of a word, then, is specified in part by a set of semantic properties. Consider, for example, the word *kitten*. Knowing the meaning of this word means knowing that it refers to an animal, a young animal, a young feline animal, and so on. The word does not specify a particular kitten. That is, the meaning of *kitten* does not include the size or color or age of any specific kitten or what its name is or where it lives or who owns it. The meaning signifies what all kittens have in common. It defines "kittenness."

Scientists know that water is composed of hydrogen and oxygen. We know that water is an essential ingredient of lemonade or a bath. But one need not know any of these things to know what the word *water* means, and to be able to use and understand this word in a sentence.

We may know what a word means without knowing anything about the situation in which it is used in an utterance. Some philosophers deny this. Hayakawa believes that "the contexts of an utterance determine its meaning" and that "since no two contexts are ever exactly the same, no two meanings can be exactly the same. . . . To insist dogmatically that we know what a word means in *advance of its utterance* is nonsense."[1]

Nonetheless, we must insist on this "nonsense." It is not important that a word mean *exactly* the same thing each time it is used. What is important is that unless the word has essentially the same meaning from one utterance to another, two people speaking the same language could not understand each other. If we are to understand the nature of language, we must explain the

[1] S. I. Hayakawa. 1964. *Language in Thought and Action,* rev. ed. (Harcourt Brace Jovanovich. New York.)

fact that speakers can and do communicate meaningfully with other speakers of their language.

Hayakawa attempts to support his view by the following example. He writes:

> . . . if John says "my typewriter" today, and again "my typewriter" tomorrow, the . . . meaning is different in the two cases, because the typewriter is not exactly the same from one day to the next (nor from one minute to the next): slow processes of wear, change and decay are going on constantly.[2]

But, we would answer, such minute changes can hardly be said to affect the *linguistic* meaning of the *word*.

We have no trouble comprehending the meaning of *typewriter*. We know that what is being talked about is an object readily recognized as a "typewriter," and that the meaning of the *word* does not include the materials of which it is made, how old it is, whether it works well or not, its color, its location, or whether the owner knows how to type. Such information is not included among the semantic properties of the word.

Linguistic knowledge includes knowing the meaning of words and morphemes. Because you know this you can use these words and combine them with other words and understand them when you hear them. This knowledge is part of the grammar of the language.

Ambiguity

"Mine is a long and sad tale!" said the Mouse, turning to Alice, and sighing.

"It is a long tail, certainly," said Alice, looking down with wonder at the Mouse's tail, "but why do you call it sad?"

Lewis Carroll, *Alice's Adventures in Wonderland*

A smile is the chosen vehicle for all ambiguities.

Herman Melville, *Pierre*, IV

B.C.   **Johnny Hart**

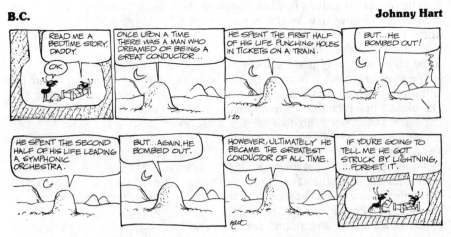

By permission of Johnny Hart and Field Enterprises, Inc.

[2] *Ibid.*

We have already said that knowing a word means knowing its sounds and meanings. Both aspects are necessary, for the same sounds can sometimes mean different things. When different words are pronounced the same but have different meanings, they are called **homonyms** or **homophones.** They may have the same or different spelling. *To, too,* and *two* are homophones since they are all pronounced as /tu/; *will,* as in *last will and testament,* and *Will,* the man's name, and *will* to denote future tense mean different things but are spelled and pronounced identically. Homonyms may create ambiguity. A word or a sentence is **ambiguous** if it can be understood or interpreted in more than one way.

The sentence

She cannot bear children.

may be understood to mean "She is unable to give birth to children" or "She cannot tolerate children." The ambiguity is because there are two words *bear* with two different meanings. Sometimes additional context can disambiguate the sentence, as is illustrated by the following sentences.

She cannot bear children if they are noisy.
She cannot bear children because she is sterile.

Both words *bear* as used in the above sentences are verbs. There is another homonym, *bear,* the animal, which is a noun with very different semantic properties. The adjective *bare,* despite its different spelling, is pronounced like the above words and also has a different meaning.

Homonyms are good candidates for humor, as well as for confusion.

"How is bread made?"
"I know *that!*" Alice cried eagerly. "You take some flour—"
"Where do you pick the flower?" the White Queen asked. "In a garden, or in the hedges?"
"Well, it isn't *picked* at all," Alice explained: "it's *ground*—"
"How many acres of ground?" said the White Queen.

The humor of this passage is based on two sets of homonyms: *flower* and *flour* and the two meanings of *ground.* Alice means *ground* as the past tense of *grind,* while the White Queen is interpreting *ground* to mean "earth." Thus, sentences may be ambiguous because they contain one or more ambiguous words. This is **lexical ambiguity.** Some other examples of such lexically ambiguous sentences are:

(1) (a) The Rabbi married my sister.
    (b) Do you smoke after sex?
    (c) Mary licked her disease.
    (d) Thomas Jefferson ate his cottage cheese with relish.
    (e) The girl found a book on Main Street.

Although (1e) is ambiguous, similar sentences, such as those under (2), are not.

(2) (a) The girl found a glove on Main Street.
(b) The girl found a book on language.
(c) The girl found a book in New York.

Sentence (1e) can mean either:

"The girl found a book which was lying on Main Street."
or
"The girl found a book while she was on Main Street."
or
"The girl found a book whose subject matter concerned Main Street."

The ambiguity is caused by the particular semantic properties of the words *book, on*, and *street*. The meaning of *book* includes something like "contains written information about." *On* is a homonym meaning "on the surface of" or "about" (that is, "on the subject of"). *Street* has "surface on which things may be located" among its semantic properties.

In sentence (2a), *glove* does not include the meaning "contains written information about" and therefore *on* can be assigned only the meaning "on the surface of." In sentence (2b), *language* does not possess any semantic property that would allow it to be used in a phrase of location, and consequently *on* can be interpreted only as meaning "about." In sentence (2c), *in* is not ambiguous in the way *on* is (it lacks the semantic property "about"), so the entire phrase is unambiguous and has to do with where the book was found.

The semantic properties of these various words determine the ambiguity or lack of ambiguity of these sentences. They also reveal why in the sentence *He lectured on semantics, on* must be interpreted to mean "about" or "concerning," since *semantics* cannot be interpreted as a place; but in the sentence *He lectured on Main Street, Main Street* can be interpreted as the topic of his lecture (with *on* meaning "about") or as the place where he lectured.

The semantic properties also explain why

The girl found a glove on Main Street.

is sensible, but

* The girl found a glove on semantics.

is not.

Thus we see that *on* can have two meanings in certain phrases, but only one meaning in other phrases. The semantic properties of the noun that follows it, as well as the semantic properties of the other words in the sentence, are the determining factors.

Such examples of homonyms and ambiguous sentences show that there is no one-to-one relation between sounds and meanings, and that one cannot always determine the precise meaning from the sounds alone. This is further evidence that the sound–meaning relationship in language is arbitrary, and that one must learn how to relate sounds and meanings when learning the language.

METAPHOR

Our doubts are traitors.
Shakespeare

Walls have ears.
Cervantes

*The night has a thousand eyes
and the day but one.*
Frances William Bourdillon

There is another kind of ambiguity in language which creates what is called **metaphor.** Some sentences are ambiguous because they have both a **literal** meaning and a nonliteral or **metaphorical** meaning. The literal meaning is based on the normal semantic properties of the words in the sentence; the metaphorical meaning is based on semantic properties that are inferred or that provide some kind of a resemblance. For example, the literal meaning of the sentence

Dr. Jekyll is a butcher.

is that a physician, named Jekyll, also works as a retailer of meats or a slaughterer of animals used for food.

The metaphorical meaning is that the doctor named Jekyll is harmful, possibly murderous, and may like to operate unnecessarily.

Similarly, the sentence

John is a snake in the grass.

can be interpreted literally to refer to a pet snake on the lawn named John. Metaphorically the sentence has nothing to do with a scaly, limbless reptile.

The literal meaning of some sentences such as

My new car is a lemon.

is anomalous. One could, if driven to the wall (another metaphor), provide some literal interpretation that is plausible if given sufficient context. For example, the *new car* may be a miniature or toy carved out of a piece of citrus fruit. The more common meaning, however, would be metaphorical and interpreted as referring to a new purchased automobile that breaks down and requires constant repairs.

Philosophers and psychologists, as well as linguists, are interested in those aspects of language and language processing that make it possible for us to understand metaphors. The problem is related to our ability to comprehend the literal meaning of sentences. We need to understand what semantic properties of the literal meaning of a word are being related to the metaphorical meaning. To understand the metaphor

Time is money.

it is necessary to know that in our society we are often paid according to the number of hours or days worked. To recognize that the sentence

Jack is a pussy cat.

has a different meaning than " Jack is a tiger."

requires knowledge that the metaphorical meaning of each sentence does not depend on the fact that "feline-ness" is a semantic property common to both *pussy cat* and *tiger;* rather, other semantic properties of these two words are referred to.

Metaphorical ambiguity appears to be even more complex than literal lexical ambiguity. Yet as speakers of a language we have the semantic ability to comprehend both kinds of ambiguous sentences.

STRUCTURAL AMBIGUITY

Not all ambiguity is lexical ambiguity. Sometimes when there are two or more ways of understanding a sentence, the ambiguity is not due to the occurrence of lexically ambiguous words or to the fact that the sentence may be literally or metaphorically interpreted, as shown in the following examples:

(3) (a) I know a man with a dog who has fleas.
(b) They hated the shooting of the hunters.
(c) The horse is ready to ride.
(d) John saw Joan walking to the store this morning.
(e) The invisible man's hair tonic is in the plastic bottle.
(f) The English history teacher is having her tea.

These sentences are **structurally ambiguous.** It is the structure of the sentences that permits more than one interpretation, rather than the words in the sentences. (Such structural aspects will be discussed more fully in Chapter 7.) In (3a) either the man or the dog has the fleas depending on whether *who has fleas* is associated with *man* or *dog.* In (3b) our knowledge of linguistic structure permits us to interpret the sentence as referring to hunters as shooters or as being shot. Try to figure out the different meanings of each of the other sentences in this group.

Context may provide the information needed to disambiguate the sentences. In fact, we usually understand an ambiguous sentence in only one of its meanings and may not notice it to be ambiguous until it is pointed out to us. (The fact that after being told, we do see the ambiguity shows that the several meanings are there.) If (3d) were uttered in circumstances where it was clear that *John* was riding in a car, then clearly the sentence would mean that Joan was walking.

Certain sentences whose written form is ambiguous may be disambiguated in speech. In Chapter 3 we illustrated how phrases such as *hòt dóg* (meaning "dog which is hot") versus *hót dòg* meaning a kind of sausage can be disambiguated depending on which word receives the greater stress. In (3f) if *English* receives greater stress than *history,* with *teacher* being most heavily stressed, the sentence would refer to a teacher of English history, whereas if *history* gets the greatest stress, the teacher would be English.

It is our knowledge of a language that accounts for our ability to assign various possible meanings out of context. If you did not know the different meanings of the sentences above they would not be ambiguous. The existence of homonyms does not mean that words have no meaning as separate entities, nor does the existence of structural ambiguity mean that sentences have no structure. Rather, these two sources of ambiguity reveal our semantic knowledge.

Paraphrase

Does he wear a turban, a fez or a hat?
Does he sleep on a mattresss, a bed or a mat, or a Cot,
The Akond of Swat?
Can he write a letter concisely clear,
Without a speck or a smudge or smear or Blot,
The Akond of Swat?
Edward Lear, "The Akond of Swat"

Not only do languages contain different words that sound the same but have different meanings; they also contain words that sound different but have the same or nearly the same meanings. Such words are called **synonyms.** There are dictionaries of synonyms that contain many hundreds of entries, such as, for example:

apathetic/phlegmatic/passive/sluggish/indifferent
pedigree/ancestry/genealogy/descent/lineage

It has been said that there are no perfect synonyms—that is, that no two words ever have *exactly* the same meaning. Still, the following pairs of sentences have very similar meanings.

I'll be happy to come./I'll be glad to come.
He's sitting on the sofa./He's sitting on the couch.

Some individuals may always use *sofa* instead of *couch*, but if they know the two words they will understand the sentences with either word and interpret them to mean the same thing. The degree of semantic similarity between words depends to a great extent on the number of semantic properties they share. *Sofa* and *couch* refer to the same type of object and share most, if not all, of their semantic properties.

There are words that have many semantic features in common but that are not synonyms or near synonyms. *Man* and *boy* both refer to male humans; the meaning of *boy* includes the additional semantic property of "youth" whereby it differs from the meaning of *man*. Thus the semantic system of English permits you to say *A sofa is a couch* or *A couch is a sofa* but not *A man is a boy* or *A boy is a man*, except when you wish to describe "boylike" qualities of the man or the "manlike" qualities of the boy.

Often a word with several meanings, called a **polysemous** word, will share one of its meanings with another word. Thus *mature* and *ripe* are synonymous when applied to fruit, but only *mature* can apply to animals. In the same sense, *deep* and *profound* are another such pair. Both apply to thought, but only *deep* applies to water. Sometimes words that are ordinarily opposites can mean the same thing in certain contexts; thus a *good* scare is the same as a *bad* scare.

Words that appear to be synonymous may differ in appropriateness, which is also part of meaning. *Croak* in one of its senses means "die," as does *pass on,* but your kindly Great Aunt Therza "passes on," although her crotchety neighbor may "croak." A game called "conjugating adjectives" is based in part on appropriateness and other subtle features of meaning. One attempts to think of words with similar meaning but different social values.

It goes like this:

I'm thrifty, you're tight, he's stingy.
I'm firm, you're rigid, she's obstinate.

When synonyms occur in otherwise identical sentences, the sentences will be paraphrases. Sentences are **paraphrases** if they have the same meaning (except possibly for minor differences in emphasis). Thus the use of synonyms may create **lexical paraphrase,** just as the use of homonyms may create lexical ambiguity.

Sentences may also be paraphrases because of structural differences that are not essential to their meanings. Consider the following pair of sentences.

(4) (a) I handed a turtle that was named Max to Zachary.
  (b) I handed to Zachary a turtle that was named Max.

Although differences in word order often mean differences in meaning (*man bites dog* versus *dog bites man*), in the case of the sentences in (4) this is not so. Sometimes word order can be changed without changing meaning, and our semantic knowledge of the language tells us just when this is the case. Similar examples to those in (4) are:

(5) (a) A man who Carol knows came over to visit.
  (b) A man came over to visit who Carol knows.

(6) (a) Call up your mother right now!
  (b) Call your mother up right now!

Another case of paraphrase involves slight structural, morphological and "function word" differences. If you know English, you recognize that the following groups are paraphrases.

(7) (a) It seems that Dolores is very kind to animals.
  (b) Dolores seems to be very kind to animals.

(8) (a) They loaded the truck with hay.
  (b) They loaded hay onto the truck.

(9) (a) It is easy to play sonatas on this violin.
  (b) This violin is easy to play sonatas on.
  (c) Sonatas are easy to play on this violin.

Because speakers of English agree on these paraphrase relations, they must share semantic rules that assign essentially the same meaning to each of the sentences in (7), (8), and (9).

Yet another kind of paraphrase, unlike previous cases, is illustrated in (10), (11), and (12):

(10) (a) Jack went up the hill and Jill went up the hill.
   (b) Jack and Jill went up the hill.

(11) (a) John expects himself to be rich someday.
   (b) John expects to be rich some day.

(12) (a) She has been dieting and he has been dieting too.
    (b) She has been dieting and he has been too.
    (c) She has been dieting and he has too.

In (10) the two sentences are paraphrases because the semantic rules of the language tell us that *went up the hill* is true of both Jack and Jill even though in (10b) this fact is stated only once. This "deletion of identical material" is found in all languages of the world and may be a result of a general tendency for languages to be more efficient by not repeating information already known or easily deducible. The same principle is at work in (11), where the omission of *himself* doesn't alter the meaning, and in (12), where the successive omission of parts of the "verb phrase" doesn't prevent us from understanding that "he has been dieting." Note that if (12a) had read

She has been dieting and he has been eating like a pig.

then neither (12b) nor (12c) would be a paraphrase because the omitted material would not be identical. We know all this because we know the semantic rules of English.

As mentioned above, all languages have similar deletion rules that "preserve" meaning, that is, result in paraphrase. In the Japanese sentence in (13b) below, the verb in the first clause is omitted, but is still understood to be *tabeta* "ate."

(13) (a) Taroo wa sakana o tabeta, Keiko wa gohan o tabeta.
      Taroo   fish   ate   Keiko   rice   ate
      "Taro ate fish, Keiko ate rice."
    (b) Taroo wa sakana o Keiko wa gohan o tabeta.
      Taro   fish   Keiko   rice   ate
      "Taro ate fish and Keiko, rice."

In fact, the same phenomenon of a missing but understood verb can be seen in the English translation of (13b). In both languages the semantic rules permit us to understand the verbal meaning even in a clause where the verb is not explicitly present.

A similar case to the ones discussed in (10)–(13) is illustrated in (14):

(14) (a) The Secretary of State advises the President on Mondays, whereas the Secretary of the Treasury advises the President on Fridays.
    (b) The Secretary of State advises the President on Mondays, whereas the Secretary of the Treasury advises him on Fridays.

In this pair of paraphrases it may appear that the sameness in meaning is due to the synonymity of *the president* and *him*. By substituting *Attorney General*, or any other appropriate noun for *President*, it is clear that this cannot be the cause, since *him* cannot have indefinitely many synonyms. Rather this shows that a pronoun can be used in place of a repeated noun, and the semantic rules governing pronouns tell us that this results in paraphrase.

Actually this last case is representative of a more general process called **anaphora.** Anaphora is the use of a short form or **proform** in the place of a longer expression. Usually such a proform is used when it is clear from the context what the proform means. A *pronoun* is one kind of proform. Pairs of sentences in which one has a proform substituted are usually paraphrases. The pairs below illustrate this.

(15) (a) I love Disa and Jack loves *Disa* too.
     (b) I love Disa and Jack loves *her* too.   (Pronoun)

(16) (a) Emily acted polite and Zachary *acted polite* also.
     (b) Emily acted polite and Zachary *did* also.   (Pro-verb)

(17) (a) I am sick and *my being sick* makes me sad.
     (b) I am sick, *which* makes me sad.   ("Pro-phrase")

If we did not know the meanings of words, and if we did not know the rules of semantics that combine word meanings into larger units of meaning, we would not be able to know when sentences are paraphrases. That we do recognize paraphrases and ambiguities shows that language is a rule-governed system that relates sounds and meanings.

Antonyms: Different Sounds, Opposite Meanings

As a rule, man is a fool;
When it's hot, he wants it cool;
When it's cool, he wants it hot;
Always wanting what is not.
Anonymous

The meaning of a word may be partially defined by saying what it is *not*. *Male* means *not female*. *Dead* means *not alive*. Words that are opposite in meaning are often called **antonyms**. Ironically, the basic property of two words which are antonyms is that they share all but one semantic property. The property they do not share is present in one and absent in the other. Thus, in order to be opposites, two words must be semantically very similar.

There are several kinds of antonymy. There are **complementary pairs:**

alive/dead   married/single   awake/asleep

They are complementary in that *not alive = dead* and *not dead = alive*.
There are **gradable** pairs of antonyms:

big/small   hot/cold   fast/slow   happy/sad

With gradable pairs the negative of one word is not synonymous with the other. For example, someone who is *not happy* is not necessarily *sad*. It is also true of gradable antonyms that more of one is less of another. More bigness is less smallness; wider is less narrow, and taller is less short. Another characteristic of many pairs of gradable antonyms is that one is **marked** and the other **unmarked**. The unmarked member is the one used in questions of degree. We ask "How *high* is it? (not "How low is it?") or "How *tall* is she?" And we answer "One thousand feet high" or "Five feet tall" but never "Five feet short," except humorously. *High* and *tall* are the unmarked members of *high/low*, and *tall/short*. Notice that the meaning of these adjectives, and other similar ones, is relational. The words themselves provide no information about absolute size. Because of our knowledge of the language, and of things in the world, this normally causes no confusion.

Another kind of "opposite" involves pairs like

give/receive, buy/sell, teacher/pupil.

They are called **relational opposites** and display symmetry in their meaning. If A *gives* X to B, then B *receives* X from A. If A is B's *teacher,* then B is A's *pupil.* Pairs of words ending in *-er* and *-ee* are usually relational opposites. If Mary is Bill's employ*er,* then Bill is Mary's employ*ee.*

Comparative forms of gradable pairs of adjectives often form relational pairs. Thus, if Sally is *taller* than Alfred, then Alfred is *shorter* than Sally. If a Cadillac is *more expensive* than a Ford, then a Ford is *cheaper* than a Cadillac.

If meanings of words were indissoluble wholes, there would be no way to make the interpretations that we do. We know that *big* and *red* are not opposites because they have too few semantic properties in common. They are both adjectives, but *big* possesses a semantic property involving size, whereas *red* involves color. On the other hand, *buy/sell* can be relational opposites because both contain the meaning "transfer of property," differing only in one feature, direction of transfer.

In English there are a number of ways to form antonyms. You can add the prefix *un-:*

likely/unlikely   able/unable   fortunate/unfortunate

Or you can add *non-:*

entity/nonentity   conformist/nonconformist

Or you can add *in-:*

tolerant/intolerant   discreet/indiscreet   decent/indecent

Sometimes by putting a *not* before an adjective we can create a gradable pair. *Far* and *not far* are an example. They are different from *far/near,* also a gradable pair, because *not far* is not necessarily near. We also have *near/not near* and our semantic knowledge even tells us that an object that is *not far* is closer than one that is *not near.* Because we know the semantic properties of words, which define a great part of their meanings, we know when two words are antonyms, synonyms, or homonyms, or are totally unrelated in meaning.

Anomaly: No Sense and Nonsense

Don't tell me of a man's being able to talk sense; everyone can talk sense. Can he talk nonsense?
William Pitt

If in a conversation someone said to you

My brother is an only child.

you might think either that he was making a joke or that he didn't know the meaning of the words he was using. You would know that the sentence was strange, or **anomalous.** Yet it is certainly an English sentence. It conforms to all the grammatical rules of the language. It is strange because it represents a contradiction; the meaning of brother includes the fact that the individual referred to is a male human who has at least one sibling. The sentence

That bachelor is pregnant.

is anomalous for similar reasons; the word *bachelor* includes the fact that the individual is "male" and males cannot become pregnant, at least not on our planet. Such sentences violate semantic rules. If you did not know the meanings of words you could not make judgments of this kind about sentences.

The semantic properties of words determine what other words they can be combined with. One sentence that has been used by linguists to illustrate this is

Colorless green ideas sleep furiously.[3]

The sentence seems to obey all the syntactic rules of English. The subject is *colorless green ideas* and the predicate is *sleep furiously*. It has the same syntactic structure as the sentence

Dark green leaves rustle furiously.

But there is obviously something wrong *semantically* with the sentence. The meaning of *colorless* includes the semantic property "without color," but it is combined with the adjective *green*, which has the property "green in color." How can something be both "without color" and "green in color" simultaneously? Other such semantic violations also occur in the sentence.

Your knowledge of the semantic properties of words accounts for the strangeness of this sentence and sentences such as

John frightened a tree.
Honesty plays golf.

Part of the meaning of the word *frighten* is that it can occur only with animate nouns as objects. Since you know the meaning of *tree*, and know that it is not "animate," the sentence is anomalous. Similarly, *Honesty plays golf* is anomalous because *honesty* is neither "animate" nor "human" and therefore cannot be the subject of a predicate like *play golf*.

The linguist Samuel Levin has shown that in poetry we find just such semantic violations forming strange but interesting esthetic images. He cites Dylan Thomas's phrase *a grief ago* as an example. *Ago* is a word ordinarily used with words specified by some temporal semantic feature:

a week ago		*a table ago
an hour ago	but not	*a dream ago
a month ago		*a mother ago
a century ago		

[3] Noam Chomsky. 1957 *Syntactic Structures*. (Mouton. The Hague.)

When Thomas used the word *grief* with *ago* he was adding a durational-time feature to *grief* for poetic effect.

In the poetry of E. E. Cummings one finds phrases like

the six subjunctive crumbs twitch
a man . . . wearing a round jeer for a hat
children building this rainman out of snow.

Though all of these phrases violate some semantic rules, one can understand them. In any case, it is the breaking of the rules that actually creates the imagery desired. The fact that you can understand these phrases and at the same time recognize their anomalous or deviant nature shows your knowledge of the semantic system and semantic properties of the language.

Sentences that are anomalous in this way are often known as "nonsense":

As I was going up the stair
I met a man who wasn't there
He wasn't there again today—
I wish to God he'd go away.

Nonsense sentences of verses are not strings of random words put together. The words are combined according to regular rules of syntax. Random strings have no meaning and are also not funny. The ability to recognize "nonsense" depends on knowledge of the semantic system of the language and the meanings of words.

There are other sentences that sound like English sentences but make no sense at all because they include words that have no meaning; they are **uninterpretable.** One can only interpret them if one dreams up some meaning for each "no-sense" word. Lewis Carroll's "Jabberwocky" is probably the most famous poem in which most of the content words have no meaning— they do not exist in the lexicon of the grammar. Yet all the sentences "sound" as if they should be or could be English sentences:

'Twas brillig, and the slithy toves
    Did gyre and gimble in the wabe;
All mimsy were the borogoves,
    And the mome raths outgrabe.

. . .

He took his vorpal sword in hand:
    Long time the manxome foe he sought—
So rested he by the Tumtum tree,
    And stood awhile in thought.

And as in uffish thought he stood,
    The Jabberwock, with eyes of flame,
Came whiffling through the tulgey wood,
    And burbled as it came!

One, two! One, two! And through and through
    The vorpal blade went snicker-snack!
He left it dead, and with its head
    He went galumphing back.

You probably do not know what *vorpal* means. Nevertheless, you know that

He took his vorpal sword in hand

means the same thing as

He took his sword, which was vorpal, in hand
It was in his hand that he took his vorpal sword

Knowing the language, and assuming that *vorpal* means the same thing in the three sentences (since the same sounds are used), you can decide that the "truth value" of the three sentences is identical. In other words, you are able to decide that two things mean the same thing even though you don't know for sure what either one means. You do this by assuming that the semantic properties of *vorpal* are the same whenever it is used.

We now see why Alice commented, when she had read "Jabberwocky":

"It seems very pretty, but it's *rather* hard to understand!" (You see she didn't like to confess, even to herself, that she couldn't make it out at all.) "Somehow it seems to fill my head with ideas—only I don't exactly know what they are! However, *somebody* killed *something:* that's clear, at any rate—"

The semantic properties of words show up in other ways in sentence construction. For example, if the meaning of a word includes the semantic property "human" in English we can replace it by one sort of pronoun but not another. We have already seen that a "nonhuman" noun cannot be the subject of a predicate like *play golf*. Similarly, this semantic feature determines that we call a boy *he*, and a table *it*.

According to Mark Twain, our maternal ancestor Eve also had such knowledge in her grammar, for she writes in her diary:

If this reptile is a man, it ain't an *it*, is it? That wouldn't be grammatical, would it? I think it would be *he*. In that case one would parse it thus: nominative *he*; dative, *him;* possessive, *his'n*.

These kinds of restrictions based on semantic properties are found in all languages. In one dialect of the Ghanaian language Twi, different numerals are used with human nouns than with nonhuman nouns. The word *baanu* meaning "two" is used exclusively with human nouns, and the word *abieŋ* meaning "two" is used exclusively with nonhuman nouns. Similarly, the words for "three" are *baasã* with humans and *abiesã* with nonhuman objects. Starred phrases are deviant:

HUMAN NOUNS	NONHUMAN NOUNS
nnipa baanu, "two people"	*ŋkokɔ baanu
*nnipa abieŋ	ŋkokɔ abieŋ, "two chickens"
asɔfoɔ baasã, "three priests"	*nsem baasã
*asɔfoɔ abiesã	nsem abiesã, "three things"

Examples like these from English and Twi show the importance of semantic properties in the formation of sentences. It is not that one cannot understand a sentence like

*I stumbled into the table, who fell over.

A Twi speaker would know what is meant by

*nnipa abieŋ, "two people,"

with the wrong form of "two." The point is that these sentences are deviant. They violate rules based on the semantic properties of words.

The discussion in this chapter so far has attempted to show how much speakers of a language know about the meanings of words and sentences— that is, the semantic system of their language.

Idioms

DENNIS THE MENACE   **Hank Ketcham**

"WELL, THAT'S ANOTHER THING UP WITH WHICH SHE WON'T PUT!"

Courtesy Field Newspaper Syndicate

Knowing a language obviously means knowing the morphemes, simple words, compound words, and their meanings. But in addition there are fixed phrases, consisting of more than one word, with meanings that cannot be inferred by knowing the meanings of the individual words. Such expressions are called **idioms.** All languages contain many idiomatic phrases. We have in English, for example:

sell down the river
haul over the coals
eat one's hat
let one's hair down
put one's foot in one's mouth
throw one's weight around

snap out of it
cut it out
hit it off
get it off
bite one's tongue
give a piece of one's mind

Idioms are similar in structure to ordinary phrases except that idioms tend to be frozen in form and do not readily enter into other combinations or allow the word order to change. Thus

(18) She put her foot in her mouth.

has the same structure as

(19) She put her bracelet in her drawer.

But whereas

The drawer in which she put her bracelet was hers.
Her bracelet was put in her drawer.

are sentences related to (19)

The mouth in which she put her foot was hers.
Her foot was put in her mouth.

are not ordinarily thought of as related to (18), unless humor is intended.
On the other hand some idioms do occur in several patterns without affecting the idiomatic sense, such as these:

The FBI kept tabs on radicals.
Tabs were kept on radicals by the FBI.
Radicals were kept tabs on by the FBI.

Great heed should be taken to prevent oil spills.
The heed taken to prevent oil spills should be great.

Often idioms break the rules on combining semantic properties. The object of *eat* must usually be something with the semantic property [+ edible], but in

he ate his hat
eat your heart out

this restriction is violated.
Idioms, grammatically as well as semantically, have very special characteristics. They must be entered into one's mental dictionary as single "items," with their meanings specified, and one must learn the special restrictions on their use in sentences.

The "Truth" of Sentences

. . . having Occasion to talk of Lying and false Representation, it was with much Difficulty that he comprehended what I meant. . . . For he argued thus: That the Use of Speech was to make us understand one another and to receive Information of Facts; now if any one said the Thing which was not, these Ends were defeated; because I cannot properly be said to understand him. . . . And these were all the Notions he had concerning that Faculty of Lying, so perfectly well understood, and so universally practised among human Creatures.
Jonathan Swift, Gulliver's Travels

We comprehend sentences because we know the meaning of individual words, *and we know rules for combining their meanings.* Jonathan Swift's Gulliver seems to be unaware of this:

. . . I placed all my words with their interpretations in alphabetical order. And thus in a few days, by the help of a very faithful memory, I got some insight into their language.

If you ever study a foreign language, you'll have to learn both word meanings and how to combine them into sentence meanings. Memorizing the words won't get you very far. In acquiring your native language, of course, you learn these semantic rules unconsciously.

We all know the meaning of *red* and *brick*. The combination *red brick* is simply what "redness" and "brickness" have in common. Add *the* to form *the red brick* and the meaning becomes "a particular instance of redness and brickness, presumably known to speaker and audience." If we had begun with *large* and *brick*, the semantic rule for *large brick* could not have been what "largeness" and "brickness" have in common, for what is large for a brick may be small for a house and gargantuan for a cockroach. Yet we correctly understand *large house* and *large cockroach*. The rule needs to specify that *large brick* means "brickness" plus "largeness insofar as bricks go," just as *large house* means "houseness" plus "largeness insofar as houses go," and so on. Had we begun with *false* and *brick*, the combination *false brick* would involve "a resemblance to brickness that is not true brickness." Thus different semantic rules are needed for different adjective–noun combinations.

In understanding the expression *sees a red brick,* we understand that some object which is a combination of "redness" and "brickness" exists and has been perceived as a visual impression. In *John sees a red brick,* we understand the perceiver to be an individual male human being named John. Had we examined *John seeks a red brick* instead, we could not have concluded that a red brick exists, for one can seek for nonexistent objects. This shows that the semantic rules governing combinations with *see* differ from those of *seek*.

The semantic rules allow us to assign a meaning to any well-formed sentence of our language. For example, one could assign a meaning to the sentence

(20) The Declaration of Independence was signed in 1776.

whether it was shouted from the top of a mountain, read from a slip of paper, picked up in a muddy gutter, whispered during a movie, or spoken with a mouth full of bubblegum. One can also understand the meaning of the sentence

(21) The Declaration of Independence was signed in 1700.

even though it is a false statement. Your ability to recognize the "falseness" of the statement depends upon your understanding of its meaning and also on your knowledge of history.

A minority of sentences can be recognized as true by virtue of linguistic knowledge alone. Such sentences are called **analytic.** The following statements are examples of analytic sentences:

(22) Dogs are animals.
　　　John is as tall as himself.
　　　Babies are not adults.
　　　My uncle is male.

There are also contradictory sentences, which are always false. The negative forms of the preceding sentences are all contradictory, as are:

(23) Adults are children.
　　　Kings are female.

Part of the meaning of a sentence, then, is knowledge of its "truth conditions," the conditions under which it can be said to be true. Philosophers talk about the "truth value" of a sentence. In this sense, sentence (20) is true and sentence (21) is false. Sentence (21) is false because the particular event to which it refers occurred at a time other than that stated.

Consider this sentence:

(24) Rufus believes that the Declaration of Independence was signed in 1700.

This sentence is true if some individual named Rufus does indeed believe the statement, and it is false if he does not.

It does not matter that a subpart of the sentence, corresponding to sentence (21), is false. An entire sentence may be true even if one or more of its parts are false, and vice-versa. All this is determined by the semantic rules, which permit you to state under what conditions a sentence is true or false. One can understand any "well-formed" sentence—one can assign a meaning to it—even if one is unable to decide on its "truth value." Its meaning, however, partially depends on knowing what conditions would make it a true statement or a false one.

Knowledge of the external world may help you decide if a sentence is true or false, but in addition you must be able to use your linguistic knowledge to understand its meaning. You may never have heard of the Declaration of Independence and may therefore not know whether such a declaration was signed in 1776, 1700, or 1492. But your knowledge of the language permits you to say that sentence (20) means that some document called *The Declaration of Independence* was signed by someone or other in the year 1776. Notice that your linguistic knowledge, not your knowledge about the particular event referred to, also permits you to say that sentence (25) means the same thing as sentence (20):

(25) It was in the year 1776 that the Declaration of Independence was signed.

and means the same thing as sentence (26):

(26) Some person or persons signed the Declaration of Independence in 1776.

The sentence doesn't tell you who signed the document. That fact is not included in the linguistic meaning of the sentence.

Sentences (20), (25), and (26), you probably recall, are paraphrases. They mean approximately the same thing, differing only in emphasis. A more precise definition of paraphrase can now be given: **Sentences are paraphrases if they have the same truth conditions.**

Knowing a language includes knowing the semantic rules for combining meanings and the conditions under which sentences are true or false.

Names

What's in a name? That which we call a rose
By any other name would smell as sweet.
Shakespeare, *Romeo and Juliet*, II, ii

Her name was McGill and she called herself Lil
But everyone knew her as Nancy.
John Lennon and Paul McCartney, "Rocky Raccoon"[4]

"What's in a name?" is a question that has occupied philosophers of language for centuries. Plato was concerned with whether names were "natural," though the question didn't bother Adam when he named the animals; Humpty Dumpty thought his name meant his shape, and in part it does.

Usually, when we think of names we think of names of people or places, which are **proper names.** We do not think of *Canis familiaris* as being named "dog." Still, the old view persists that all words name some object, though that object may be abstract. This view presents difficulties. We are unable to identify the objects named by *sincerity* or *forgetfulness,* not to mention *into, brave,* and *think.* In this book, then, "name" will always mean "*proper name.*"

Proper names can refer to objects. The objects may be extant, such as those designated by

Disa Karin Viktoria Lubker
Lake Michigan
The Empire State Building

or extinct, such as

Socrates
Troy

or even fictional

> Sherlock Holmes
> Dr. John H. Watson
> Wonderland
> Oz

Proper names are **definite,** which means they refer to a unique object insofar as the speaker and listener are concerned. If I say

> Mary Smith is coming to dinner.

my spouse understands Mary Smith to refer to our friend Mary Smith, and not to one of the dozens of Mary Smiths in the phone book.

The article *the* is used to make words definite. If someone says

> I saw the dog.

it is assumed that all participants in the discourse can identify which specific dog is meant. The indefinite article *a* usually involves no such assumption, and the sentence

> I saw a dog.

is generally intended to be a description of the kind of object I saw rather than which particular object. However, in the sentence

> Bobby wants to marry a dancer.

the phrase *a dancer* may refer to a particular individual. This is a different use of *a*, and the sentence is ambiguous, because there may or may not be a particular dancer that Bobby wants to marry.

Because they are inherently definite, proper names are not in general preceded by *the:*

> *The John Smith
> *The California

There are some exceptions, such as the names of rivers, ships, and erected structures:

> The Mississippi
> The Queen Mary
> The Empire State Building
> The Eiffel Tower
> The Golden Gate Bridge

Proper names cannot usually be pluralized, though they can be plural, like *The Great Lakes* or *The Pleiades*. Sometimes, however, to make necessary distinctions, we may talk about "the two fat Johns" and "the two skinny Johns," given a room full of people named John. For clarity some proper names may be pluralized and even preceded by an article or adjective, although this is not usually done.

Giving names to things is an act that often reveals linguistic creativity. One need only look at the names of Kentucky Derby winners (*Cañonero II, Secretariat*) to realize this. Although the naming of children is more conventional and the language provides a stock of personal names, many parents coin a name for their child that they hope (usually in vain) to be original. But once a proper name is coined, it cannot be pluralized or preceded by *the* or any adjective (except for cases like those cited above), and it will be used to refer uniquely, for these are among the many rules already in the grammar, and speakers know they apply to all proper names, even new ones.

Sense and Reference

You mentioned your name as if I should recognize it, but beyond the obvious facts that you are a bachelor, a solicitor, a Freemason, and an asthmatic, I know nothing whatever about you.
Sir Arthur Conan Doyle, "The Norwood Builder,"
The Memoirs of Sherlock Holmes

Take care of the sense, and the sounds will take care of themselves.
Lewis Carroll, *Alice's Adventures in Wonderland*

We hinted in the last section that the name *Humpty Dumpty* not only referred to a fictional object, but had some further meaning, something like "a good round shape." This raises the interesting question of whether proper names have a meaning over and above the fact of pointing out objects. Certainly, the name *Sue* has the semantic property "female" as evidenced by the humor in Johnny Cash's song "A Boy Named Sue." *The Pacific Ocean* has the semantic properties of *ocean,* and even such names as *Fido* and *Bossie* have become associated with dogs and cows respectively.

Words other than proper names both have a meaning and can be used to refer to objects. The German philosopher and mathematician Gottlob Frege proposed a distinction between the **reference** of a word, which is the object designated, and the **sense** of a word, which is the additional meaning. Frege reasoned that if meaning were equated with reference, then two different expressions with the same reference could be substituted for one another in a sentence without changing its meaning. As an example, he used expressions like *the evening star* and *the morning star,* the reference of both being the planet Venus. He considered the question

Is the evening star the evening star?

to which the answer is obviously "yes." Then, for the second occurrence of *the evening star,* he substituted *the morning star* to produce a new question:

Is the evening star the morning star?

This question is quite different from the first question, and its correct answer follows only from careful astronomical observation. Frege concluded that the meaning of words involves more than just reference. He called that "something extra" *sense*. Hayakawa, in his discussion of "typewriter," was referring to its reference rather than its sense.

Phrases, like words, normally both have sense and can be used to refer. Thus the phrase

The man who is my father

refers to a certain individual and has a certain sense which is different from that of

The man who married my mother

although both expressions usually have the same reference. Phrases may, however, have sense, but no reference. If this were not so we would be unable to understand sentences like these:

The present king of France is bald.
By the year 3000, our descendants will have left Earth.

Speakers of English have no trouble comprehending the meaning of these sentences, even though France now has no king, and our descendants of a millennium from now do not exist.

Speech Acts, Pragmatics, World Knowledge

You can do things with speech. You can make promises, lay bets, issue warnings, christen boats, place names in nomination, offer congratulations, swear testimony. By saying *I warn you that there is a sheepdog in the closet,* you not only say something, you *warn* someone. Verbs like *bet, promise, warn,* and so on are **performative verbs.** Using them in a sentence may sometimes be tantamount to performing some nonlinguistic act.

There are hundreds of performative verbs in every language. The following sentences illustrate their usage:

I *bet* you five dollars the Yankees win.
I *challenge* you to a match.
I *dare* you to step over this line.
I *fine* you $100 for possession of oregano.
I *move* that we adjourn.
I *nominate* Batman for mayor of Gotham City.
I *promise* to improve.
I *resign!*

Notice that in all these sentences the speaker is the subject (that is, they are in "first person") and in uttering the sentence is performing some nonlinguistic act, such as daring, nominating, resigning. Also, all these sentences are affirmative, declarative, and in the present tense. All this is typical of **performative sentences.**

Actually, every utterance is some kind of speech act. Even when there is no performative verb, as in *It is raining,* we recognize an implicit performance of *stating*. On the other hand, *Is it raining?* is a performance of *questioning*, just as *Leave!* is a performance of *ordering*. In all these we could use, if we chose, an actual performative verb: *I **state** that it is raining; I **ask** if it is raining; I **order** you to leave.*

Language is full of implicit promises, toasts, warnings, and so on. *I will marry you* is an implicit performance of a promise and, under appropriate circumstances, is as much a promise as *I promise I will marry you*. Plainly, to arise from your seat, glass in hand, and shout *The health of our host* is as genuinely a toast as if you said *I toast the health of our host*.

The study of how we do things with sentences is the study of **speech acts.** In studying speech acts, we are acutely aware of the importance of the context of the utterance. In some circumstances *There is a sheepdog in the closet* is a warning, but the very same sentence may be a promise or even a mere statement of fact, depending on circumstances.

Speech act theory aims to tell us when it is that we ask questions but mean orders, or when we say one thing with special (sarcastic) intonation and mean the opposite. Thus, at a dinner table, the question *Can you pass the salt?* means the order *Pass the salt!* It is not a request for information, and *yes* is an inappropriate response. Still, much humor is achieved by characters who take everything literally:

HAMLET: Whose grave's this, sirrah?
CLOWN (gravedigger): Mine, sir . . .
HAMLET: What man dost thou dig it for?
CLOWN: For no man, sir.
HAMLET: What woman then?
CLOWN: For none neither.
HAMLET: Who is to be buried in't?
CLOWN: One that was a woman, sir; but, rest her soul, she's dead.
HAMLET: How absolute the knave is! We must speak by the card, or equivocation will undo us.[5]

The general study of how context influences the way we interpret sentences is called **pragmatics.** The theory of speech acts is part of pragmatics, and pragmatics itself is part of what we have been calling linguistic performance.

We have already noted that we can understand a sentence even if we are unable to tell whether it is true or false. Often we do know the truth value of a sentence, and the knowledge we use to decide is knowledge about the world (assuming of course that the sentence is neither analytic nor contradictory). Knowledge of the world is part of context, and so pragmatics includes how language users apply knowledge of the world to interpret utterances.

Speakers often make explicit assumptions about the real world and the sense of an utterance may depend on those assumptions, which some linguists term **presuppositions.**[6] Consider the following:

(27) (a) Have you stopped hugging your sheepdog?
     (b) Who bought the badminton set?

[5] *Hamlet,* V, i.
[6] Other linguists describe the same phenomenon as **implication.** *Presupposition* is used here because it seems to be a more widely accepted usage.

(c) John doesn't write poems in the bathroom.
(d) The present King of France is bald.
(e) Would you like another beer?

In (27a) the speaker has *presupposed* that the listener has at some past time hugged his sheepdog. In (27b) there is the presupposition that someone has already bought a badminton set and in (27c) it is assumed that John writes poetry. We have already run across (27d), which we decided we could understand even though France does not presently have a king. The use of a definite term usually presupposes an existing referent. When presuppositions are inconsistent with the actual state of the world, the utterance is felt to be strange.

If someone were to say (27e) to you, the meaning of that sentence presupposes or implies that you have already had at least one beer. Part of the meaning of the word *another* includes this presupposition. The Hatter in *Alice's Adventures in Wonderland* would not agree with us.

> "Take some more tea," the March Hare said to Alice, very earnestly.
> "I've had nothing yet," Alice replied in an offended tone, "so I can't take more."
> "You mean you can't take *less*," said the Hatter: "It's very easy to take *more* than nothing."

The humor in this passage comes from the fact that knowing the language includes knowing the meaning of the word *more*. *More* does not mean "more than nothing" but "more than something." In other words, *more*, in this usage, presupposes something previously.

Anomaly, as discussed in a previous section, results partly from world knowledge. The anomalous character of *The worm has bad intentions* arises not because *worm* has the semantic property "lacks intentional ability," but because our knowledge of zoology does not ascribe intentions to worms. Pragmatic considerations also work to make semantically anomalous utterances meaningful. Thus *Golf plays John*, when spoken in the clubhouse just after John has played golf miserably, may be interpretable.

In all languages there are many words and expressions whose references rely entirely on the circumstances of the utterance and can only be understood if one knows these circumstances. This aspect of pragmatics is called **deixis**. Pronouns are often deictic.

I　my　mine　you　your　yours

These pronouns require identification of speaker and listener for interpretation.

Proper names as well as expressions such as

this person
that man
these women
those men

are deictic for they require pragmatic information in order for the listener to make a "referential connection" and understand what is meant. The above examples illustrate **person deixis**.

There are also **time deixis** and **place deixis**. The following are all deictic expressions of time.

now	then	tomorrow/yesterday
this time	that time	seven days ago
two weeks from now	last week	next April

In order to understand what specific times are referred to when such expressions are used, one needs to know when the utterance was said. Clearly, *next week* has a different reference when uttered today than a month from today. If, for example, you found an advertising leaflet on the street that said "BIG SALE NEXT WEEK" with no date given, you would not know if the sale had already taken place.

Expressions of place deixis require contextual information of the place of the utterance, as shown by the following:

here	there	this place	that place
this city	these parks	yonder mountain	those towers over there

The Dennis the Menace cartoon indicates what can happen if the deictic conventions are not observed.

DENNIS THE MENACE   **Hank Ketcham**

Courtesy Field Newspaper Syndicate

Directional terms such as

before/behind   left/right   front/back

are deictic insofar as you need to know which way the speaker is facing. In Japanese the verb *kuru* "come" can only be used for motion toward the place of utterance. A Japanese speaker cannot call up a friend and ask

May I "kuru" *to your house?*

The correct verb is *iku*, "go," which indicates motion away from the place of utterance. These verbs thus have a deictic aspect to their meaning.

When we examine deixis in language the role of pragmatic knowledge in apprehending the full meaning of utterances is clearly revealed.

Contrary to what we have claimed, some linguists have said that pragmatic knowledge is as much a part of linguistic competence as grammatical knowledge. Another position is taken by other language scholars, who believe that knowledge of speech acts is part of linguistic performance. Whichever position one adopts, it is clear that linguistic knowledge is so vast and complex that it interacts with other kinds of knowledge.

The Meaning of "Meaning"

"The name of the song is called 'Haddocks' Eyes.'"
"Oh, that's the name of the song, is it?" Alice said. . . .
"No, you don't understand," the Knight said. . . .
"That's what the name is called. The name really is 'The Aged Aged Man.'"

Lewis Carroll, *Through the Looking-Glass*

To define the meaning of a morpheme or a word we find ourselves using other words in the definition. If the meaning of the prefix *in-* is "not," what does *not* mean? If the meaning of *man* is defined by such semantic properties as "male," "human," and so on, what is the meaning of *human* and *male?* It is clear that at some point we have to stop and assume that everyone "knows" the definitions of the describing terms. Those words left undefined are the basic **primitive semantic elements.** Anyone who has studied geometry is acquainted with this procedure. One reads a definition: "A line is the shortest distance between two points." What is a point? One assumes the knowledge of a point. "Point" is a primitive concept in geometry, just as "male," "human," "abstract," "morpheme," "phoneme," and so on are primitive terms in linguistics.

Though we are not ordinarily aware of it, language has infected us with a kind of cerebral schizophrenia. We constantly (and effortlessly) deal with the world on two levels: the level of actual objects, thoughts, and perceptions and the level of *names of* objects, thoughts, and perceptions. That is, we perceive reality on the one hand and talk about it on the other. Linguists have a tendency to become three-way schizophrenics. They not only have objects and language, but in addition they must treat language itself as an object. Anthropologists might describe a man by saying he is a bipedal, hairless primate. They are using language to talk about certain objects. Linguists wish to describe the language used to talk about these objects. Thus, they might say that *man,* the word, is a "noun," has three "phonemes," or possesses the semantic feature "human."

A language used for describing a language is called a **metalanguage.** Ordinary English can be the metalanguage used by anthropologists or botanists or physicists to describe the objects of interest to them. Linguists also have to use ordinary language as a metalanguage to describe ordinary language.

We offer an elementary illustration of these concepts which we hope will clarify the problem:

OBJECT (Real World)	LANGUAGE (Object for Linguists)	METALANGUAGE
	man is a bipedal, hairless primate	*man* is a *noun*
		man is composed of three *phonemes*
		the meaning of *man* includes the semantic property "human"

The terms *noun, phoneme, male,* and *human* are terms in the linguistic metalanguage, in the theory of language. This book is filled with such terms: *phone, allophone, phoneme, syntax, grammar, morpheme, word, sentence.* . . . Thus, while the word *man* is part of our language, when we say "*man* is a word" we are using language to discuss language, and *word* is part of the metalanguage.

One can see why language has intrigued philosophers from the beginning of history. The complexities discussed only punctuate the miracle that all normal human beings learn a language, use the language to express their thoughts, and understand the meanings of sentences used by others.

SUMMARY

Knowing a language is knowing how to produce and understand sentences with particular meanings. The study of linguistic meaning is called **semantics.** Semantics concerns the study of word and morpheme meanings, as well as the study of rules for combining meanings.

The meanings of morphemes and words are defined in part by their **semantic properties** or **features.** When two words have the same sounds but differ semantically (have different meanings), they are **homonyms,** or **homophones** (for example, *bear* can mean either "give birth to" or "tolerate"). The use of homophones in a sentence may lead to **ambiguity,** which occurs when a single utterance has more than one meaning. Ambiguity may also occur because of the structure of the sentence. *Flying planes can be dangerous* is both structurally and lexically ambiguous. *Planes* can refer to special woodworking tools or airplanes. If the *airplane* meaning is intended, then the sentence can be interpreted to mean "To fly planes can be dangerous" or "Planes that are flying can be dangerous." These two meanings result from the sentence structure.

Sentences with the same truth conditions are **paraphrases.** Sentences may be paraphrases of one another because they contain **synonyms** (different words that mean the same thing, such as *couch* and *sofa*) or because they differ structurally in ways that do not affect meaning.

A word that has several meanings, depending on context, is **polysemous.** (For example, the word *good* has somewhat different meanings in *good child, good knife, good check.*)

Two words that are "opposite" in meaning are **antonyms.** There are antonymous pairs that are **complementary** (*alive/dead*), there are **gradable** pairs of antonyms (*hot/cold*) and there are **relational** pairs (*buy/sell, employer/employee*).

Some sentences are strange or **anomalous** in that they deviate from what we expect. *The red-haired girl has blond hair* and *The stone ran* are anomalous. Other sentences are **uninterpretable** because they contain "words" which are "nonexistent" (for example, *An orkish sluck blecked nokishly*). The semantic properties of words play a crucial role in determining whether a sentence is anomalous.

Words may be combined to form phrases with meanings assigned to the whole unit; such phrases are **idioms** and their meanings are not the sums of their parts (for example, *put one's foot in one's mouth*). Idioms often violate co-occurrence restrictions of semantic properties.

When you know a language you know many rules for combining meanings of words. We have only studied a few such rules. For example, you know a *good king* is a king, but a *former king* is not a king. When you know the meaning of a sentence you are able to tell under what conditions the sentence is true or false. You can understand the sentence even if it is a false statement; in fact, if you didn't understand it you could not make this judgment. Some sentences are **analytic**; that is, true by virtue of linguistic knowledge alone. *Mothers are female* is an analytic sentence. **Contradictory sentences** are the opposite of analytic sentences and are always false by virtue of linguistic meaning alone (for example, *My aunt is a man*).

Proper names are special morphemes used to designate particular objects uniquely; that is, they are **definite**. Proper names are normally not preceded by an article or adjective, and they cannot be pluralized.

Words have **sense** and can be used to **refer**. Larger expressions like phrases and sentences also have sense and reference. Frege showed that meaning is more than reference alone. In fact, some meaningful expressions (for example, *the present king of France*) have sense but no reference.

Performative verbs like *bequeath* allow us to do things with sentences. One doesn't even need a performative verb; for example, shouting *Look out!* may have the effect of a warning (*I warn you to look out!*). The study of how we do things with utterances is the study of **speech acts.** Context is needed to determine the nature of the speech act.

Deictic terms such as *you, now, there* require knowledge of the circumstances (the person, place, or time) of the utterance to be interpreted referentially. The general study of how context affects linguistic interpretation is **pragmatics.** Speech act theory is part of pragmatics, which itself is part of linguistic performance.

Linguists have to use language to describe language. The language used for description is called a **metalanguage.** Using language to describe objects in the world, we may talk about a man, child, ostrich, and so on. But when we say *man* is a "word" or a "noun," these descriptive terms are part of the metalanguage of linguistics.

Everything one knows about linguistic meaning is included in the semantic system of one's grammar.

EXERCISES

1. Although language could not function properly if those who conversed failed to agree on the meanings of the words used, there are many situations where one person does not know all the words used in a sentence. Identify some of these situations and in each case imagine what the person might do to increase understanding. (For example, in a conversation with a linguist, a reference is made to your "organs of articulation," but you aren't really sure what *articulation* means.)

2. For each group of words given below, state what semantic property or properties are shared by the (a) words and the (b) words, and what semantic property or properties distinguish between the classes of (a) words and (b) words.
   Example: a. widow, mother, sister, aunt, seamstress
              b. widower, father, brother, uncle, tailor
   The (a) and (b) words are "human"
   The (a) words are "female" and the (b) words are "male"

A. a. bachelor, man, son, paperboy, pope, chief
   b. bull, rooster, drake, ram

B. a. table, stone, pencil, cup, house, ship, car
   b. milk, alcohol, rice, soup, mud

C. a. book, temple, mountain, road, tractor
   b. idea, love, charity, sincerity, bravery, fear

D. a. pine, elm, ash, weeping willow, sycamore
   b. rose, dandelion, aster, tulip, daisy

E. a. book, letter, encyclopedia, novel, notebook, dictionary
   b. typewriter, pencil, ballpoint, crayon, quill, charcoal, chalk

F. a. walk, run, skip, jump, hop, swim
   b. fly, skate, ski, ride, cycle, canoe, hang-glide

G. a. ask, tell, say, talk, converse
   b. shout, whisper, mutter, drawl, holler

H. a. alive, asleep, dead, married, pregnant
   b. tall, smart, interesting, bad, tired

I. a. alleged, counterfeit, false, putative, accused
   b. red, large, cheerful, pretty, stupid

(*Hint:* is an alleged murderer always a murderer?)

3. We passed lightly over the distinction between homophony (different words with the same pronunciation) and polysemy (one word with more than one meaning). In practice, it is not always easy to make this distinction. For instance, is a human *face* and the *face* of a clock an instance of homophony or polysemy? Dictionary writers must make thousands of decisions of this kind. In a dictionary, homophonous words have separate entries, whereas the various meanings of a polysemous word occur in the same entry.[7] Using any up-to-date dictionary, look up ten sets of homophones (some homophones have four or five entries; for example, *peak*). Then look up ten polysemous words with five or more given meanings (for example, *gauge*).

4. Explain the semantic ambiguity of the following sentences by providing two sentences which paraphrase the two meanings. Example: *She can't bear children* can mean either *She can't give birth to children* or *She can't tolerate children.*

   a. He waited at the bank.
   b. Is he really that kind?
   c. The proprietor of the fish store was the sole owner.
   d. The long drill was boring.
   e. When he got the clear title to the land it was a good deed.
   f. It takes a good ruler to make a straight line.

5. We gave a few examples of "conjugating" adjectives. Actually, there are hundreds. Besides the one in the cartoon, here are a few more: I'm intelligent, you're overeducated, he's a smart-ass; I'm generous, you're extravagant, she's prodigal; I'm easy-going, you're lazy, he's slovenly. The idea is expressed in the Dennis the Menace cartoon on page 196.

---

[7] Often, word etymologies are used as the basis for decision. If two different meanings of a form come from historically different sources, the forms are considered to be homophones and receive separate entries.

"HE CALLS IT MED'TATION, MOM CALLS IT A EXERCISE...BUT I CALL IT GOOFIN' OFF."

Courtesy Field Newspaper Syndicate

Try to think up five more sets.

6. The following sentences are ambiguous when seen written. After figuring out the ambiguity see which ones can be disambiguated in speech by special intonation or pauses.

   a. The lamb is too hot to eat.
   b. Old men and women will be served first.
   c. Kissing girls is what Stephen likes best.
   d. They are moving sidewalks.
   e. Becky left directions for Jack to follow.
   f. John loves Richard more than Martha.

7. There are several kinds of antonymy. Indicate which among the following are complementary pairs, which are gradable pairs, and which are relational opposites:

A	B
good	bad
expensive	cheap
parent	offspring
beautiful	ugly
false	true
lessor	lessee
pass	fail
hot	cold
legal	illegal
larger	smaller
poor	rich
fast	slow
asleep	awake
husband	wife
rude	polite

8. Not all scholars agree with the view that proper names can have sense as well as reference. They believe that if a proper name has meaning at all, that meaning is the reference. They argue that the sentence *All Davids are male* is not analytic in the way that the sentence *All dogs are animals* is. Their reason is that a word like *dog* has as part of its sense "is an animal," but the name *David* is male merely by convention. Thus, a girl could be named David, but a dog must be an animal. Therefore, according to them, male is not part of the meaning of *David*. Write a short essay stating your views. (You may want to consider whether a sentence like *Paris is a city* is analytic. What if someone names her baby *Paris?* What if someone names her baby *dog?* A hit song of the 1960s was "Walkin' My Cat Named Dog.")

9. A. Which of the following sentences are analytic, and which are merely synthetically true?

   a. Kings are monarchs.
   b. Kings are rich.
   c. Dogs are four-legged.
   d. Cats are felines.
   e. George Washington is George Washington
   f. George Washington was the first President of the United States.
   g. Uncles are male.
   h. An uncle has at least one brother or one sister.

   B. Which of the following are contradictory, and which are merely synthetically false?

   a. My aunt is a man.
   b. Aunts are always wicked.
   c. The evening star isn't the morning star.
   d. The evening star isn't the evening star.
   e. Babies can lift one ton.
   f. Puppies are human.
   g. My bachelor friends are all married.
   h. My bachelor friends are all lonely.

10. In sports and games many expressions are "performative." By shouting *you're out*, the first-base umpire performs an act. Likewise for *checkmate* in chess. Think up a half-dozen or so similar examples and explicate their use.

11. Which of the following contain deictic expressions? (*Hint:* which ones require you to know the circumstances [participants, time, place, and so on] of the utterance in order to be understood?)

    a. I saw you standing there.
    b. Dogs are animals.
    c. Yesterday all my troubles seemed so far away.
    d. Abraham Lincoln was the sixteenth President of the United States.
    e. He was born in a log cabin.
    f. It was then that she pulled him toward her.
    g. Both authors of this book were born in May.
    h. The Declaration of Independence was signed in 1776.
    i. Germany invaded Poland on September 1, 1939.
    j. Once you're inside, the treasure will be found on your right.

12. One suggested criterion of a "performance sentence" is whether you can begin it with *I hereby*. Notice that if you say sentence *a* aloud it sounds like a genuine apology, but to say sentence *b* aloud sounds funny because you cannot perform an act of knowing:

   a. I hereby apologize to you.
   b. I hereby know you.

   It is clear that Snoopy, in the following cartoon, understands this point.

© 1961 United Feature Syndicate, Inc.

   One can test a sentence to see if it is a performance sentence by inserting *hereby* and seeing whether it sounds "right." Using such a test, determine which of the following sentences are performance sentences.

   c. I testify that she met the agent.
   d. I know that she met the agent.
   e. I suppose the Yankees will win.
   f. He bet her $2500 that Reagan would win.
   g. I dismiss the class.
   h. I teach the class.
   i. We promise to leave early.
   j. I owe the I.R.S. $1,000,000.
   k. I bequeath $1,000,000 to the I.R.S.
   l. I swore I didn't do it.
   m. I swear I didn't do it.

13. The following sentences make certain presuppositions. What are they?

   a. The police stopped the minors from drinking.
   b. Please take me out to the ball game again.
   c. Valerie regretted not receiving a new T-bird for Labor Day.
   d. That her pet turtle ran away made Emily very sad.
   e. The administration regrets that the professors support the students. (Compare this to: *The administration believes that the professors support the students,* in which there is no such presupposition.)
   f. It is strange that the U.S. invaded Cambodia in 1970.
   g. It isn't strange that the U.S. invaded Cambodia in 1970.

14. Which of the following sentences illustrate language, and which metalanguage?

   a. Yellow is the color of my true love's hair.
   b. *Yellow* is a color word.
   c. *Dog* contains the semantic property "animal."
   d. A dog is an animal.
   e. *Halitosis* is spelled h-a-l-i-t-o-s-i-s.
   f. Halitosis is smelled by everyone.

REFERENCES

Austin, J. L. 1962. *How to Do Things with Words*. Harvard University Press. Cambridge, Mass.

Davidson, D., and G. Harman, eds. 1972. *Semantics of Natural Languages*. Reidel. Dordrecht, The Netherlands.

Dillon, G. L. 1977. *Introduction to Contemporary Linguistic Semantics*. Prentice-Hall. Englewood Cliffs, N.J.

Katz, J. 1972. *Semantic Theory*. Harper & Row. New York.

Lyons, J. 1977. *Semantics*. Cambridge University Press. Cambridge, England.

Palmer, F. R. 1976. *Semantics: A New Outline*. Cambridge University Press. Cambridge, England.

Searle, John R. 1969. *Speech Acts: An Essay in the Philosophy of Language*. Cambridge University Press. Cambridge, England.

Chapter 7

Syntax: The Sentence Patterns of Language

Grammatical or Ungrammatical

"Then you should say what you mean," the March Hare went on.

"I do," Alice hastily replied: "at least—I mean what I say—that's the same thing, you know."

"Not the same thing a bit!" said the Hatter. "You might just as well say that 'I see what I eat' is the same thing as 'I eat what I see'!"

"You might just as well say," added the March Hare, "that 'I like what I get' is the same thing as 'I get what I like'!"

"You might just as well say," added the Dormouse . . . "that 'I breathe when I sleep' is the same thing as 'I sleep when I breathe'!"

"It is the same thing with you," said the Hatter.

Lewis Carroll, *Alice in Wonderland*

In the previous chapters we have discussed how the grammar of a language represents the speaker's linguistic knowledge, including knowledge of *phonetics* (the sounds of language), *phonology* (the sound patterns of language), *morphology* (the structure of words), and *semantics* (the meanings of words and sentences). Knowing a language also means being able to put words together to form sentences to express our thoughts. That part of our linguistic knowledge which concerns the structure of sentences is called **syntax.**

Part of the meaning of a sentence is revealed by the particular morphemes of which it is composed, but sentence meaning is more than the sum of the meanings of morphemes. The sentence

The dentist hurt my teeth.

does not have the same meaning as

My teeth hurt the dentist.

and the string of morphemes

my the hurt teeth dentist

has no linguistic meaning, even though it is made up of meaningful elements. Although a sentence is a string of morphemes, every string of morphemes is not a sentence. There are rules in one's grammar that determine how morphemes and words must be combined to express a particular meaning. These are the *syntactic rules* of the language, and like the phonological rules and morphological rules, they constitute part of a speaker's linguistic knowledge.

When you know a language, then, you know which combinations or strings of morphemes are permitted by the syntactic rules and which are not. Those that conform to the syntactic rules are called the **sentences** or **grammatical sentences** of the language, and strings of morphemes that do not are called **ungrammatical.**[1]

You don't have to study grammar or linguistics to know which sentences are grammatical and which are ungrammatical. Even very young English-speaking children know that

(1) The boy kissed the girl.

is a "good" sentence but that something is wrong or funny with the string of words

(2) *Girl the boy the kissed.

In Chapter 1 you were asked to distinguish between grammatical and ungrammatical strings of words by marking the ungrammatical strings with an asterisk. Here is a similar list. According to *your* knowledge or intuitions about English, which of these sentences would you "star"?

(3) (a) Sylvia wanted George to go.
    (b) Sylvia wanted George go.
    (c) Sylvia heard George to go.
    (d) Sylvia heard George go.
    (e) Sylvia hoped George go.
    (f) Clarence looked up the number.
    (g) Clarence looked the number up.
    (h) Morris walked up the hill.
    (i) Morris walked the hill up.
    (j) John put the bread.
    (k) John put the bread in the cupboard.
    (l) John cut the bread.
    (m) Last night John was crying the baby.
    (n) Last night John was crying.
    (o) Last night John was drying the baby.
    (p) Last night John was making the baby cry.
    (q) Last night John was making the baby dry.

We predict that speakers of English would "star" sentences (3b, 3c, 3e, 3i, 3j, 3m) as ungrammatical. If we are right, this shows that grammaticality judgments are not quixotic but are rule-governed. Notice that the syntactic

---

[1] In this chapter we will use the term **ungrammatical sentence** to mean "a string of words that is not a (grammatical) sentence." Strictly speaking this is a "contradiction in terms," since all sentences are by definition grammatical, but it is a convenient locution that we will use when no confusion can result.

rules which account for our intuitions about these sentences are not merely "ordering" rules like those which determine that *boy the* is an ungrammatical phrase while *the boy* is grammatical. Syntactic rules do determine the order of morphemes in a sentence but they also do much more. The rules must specify, for example, that *to* is required with the verb *want*, as illustrated by sentences (3a, 3b), but is not permitted after *heard* as shown by (3c, 3d). Our knowledge of syntax also permits us to "move" the word *up* in (3f) to produce (3g), but not in (3h). Moreover we recognize that in (3j) either some word is missing, which is present in sentence (3k), or that a wrong word was used and something like (3l) would be better. For English speakers (3m) would be considered strange, although any of the four sentences that follow it would seem correct.

These examples show that sentences are not simply words and morphemes strung together randomly. Sentences conform to specific patterns and these patterns are dictated by the syntactic rules of the language. This is true of all the world's languages. The fact that all speakers can distinguish grammatical from ungrammatical combinations of words in their own language, and sometimes even know how to "fix up" these combinations to make them grammatical sentences, demonstrates their knowledge of the rules of syntax.

Remember that grammaticality is *not* based on what you were taught in a class in grammar, but on the rules you and the other speakers of your language learned or constructed while acquiring the language as children.

Furthermore, your ability to make "correct" grammaticality judgments (according to your rules) does not depend on your having heard the sentence before. You may never have heard or read the sentence

A pigeon-toed sloth won the beauty contest wearing a purple tutu.

but your syntactic knowledge will "tell" you that the string of morphemes is a grammatical sentence. Nor do grammaticality judgments depend on whether the sentence is meaningful or not. Consider the following sentences.

Colorless green ideas sleep furiously.
A verb crumpled the milk.

As we pointed out in Chapter 6, such sentences are semantically *anomalous*. They are, however, syntactically well formed or grammatical. While they sound "funny," they differ in their "funniness" from the following strings:

*Furiously sleep ideas green colorless.
*Milk the crumpled verb a.

In the discussion on nonsense, we also demonstrated that grammatical sentences can even include words with *no* meaning. If this were not so, the "Jabberwocky" and other such poems would not be amusing. They sound like good English sentences, because your syntactic knowledge judges them to be grammatical. If they were ungrammatical strings of nonsense words they would have little effect, as shown by:

*Toves slithy the and brillig twas
wabe the in gimble and gyre did . . .

We also saw in the previous chapter that the grammaticality of sentences does not depend on whether a sentence is true or not, or whether it has a referent in the real world.

This ability to make grammaticality judgments reflects speakers' unconscious knowledge of the syntactic rules of their grammars.

What Else Do You Know About Syntax?

TUMBLEWEEDS

Tom K. Ryan

© 1978 United Features Syndicate, Courtesy of Field Newspaper Syndicate

Your syntactic knowledge goes beyond your being able to decide which strings are grammatical and which are not. It accounts for the **structural ambiguity** of expressions like the one illustrated in the cartoon. The humor of the cartoon depends on the ambiguity of the phrase *synthetic buffalo hides*. The ambiguity results from the fact that *synthetic* can modify *buffalo hides* or simply *buffalo*. That is, you may interpret (*synthetic buffalo*) and (*hides*) to be the structural parts or constituents of the phrase, or, instead, (*synthetic*) and (*buffalo hides*) to be the **structural constituents**. The syntactic rules of English allow either interpretation. It is therefore due to the syntactic structure that the expression has two meanings and not due to any ambiguous words. The same is true of the following sentences.

It's a miracle that the old magician was able to work.
Visiting professors can be interesting.
He decided on the train.

Note that there are sentences which appear to be similar in structure to these sentences but which have only one meaning, as determined by the rules of syntax.

It's a miracle that the old magician was able to walk.
Laughing professors can be interesting.
He traveled on the train.

Syntactic knowledge, together with knowledge of semantics, also underlies your ability to determine whether sentences are paraphrases. English speakers usually agree on whether sentences are paraphrases or not:

PARAPHRASES

Pleasing Disa is fun for Vicki.
It is fun for Vicki to please Disa.
Disa is fun for Vicki to please.

NOT PARAPHRASES

Pleasing Disa is fun for Vicki.
It is fun for Disa to please Vicki.
Vicki and Disa are fun to please.

Because of your knowledge of English syntax, you are also able to determine how different parts of a sentence are related, that is, *who* does *what* to *whom*. These are the **grammatical relations** of a sentence and they reveal how each part of the sentence functions grammatically, or syntactically. Sentences such as

Disa is eager to please.
Disa is easy to please.

appear to be similar in structure, yet speakers of English know that in the first sentence, Disa is the one who would be pleasing someone else, and in the second sentence someone would be pleasing Disa. In the first sentence *Disa* functions as the "subject" of *please* and in the second sentence as the "object."

Finally, syntactic rules permit speakers to produce and understand an infinite set of sentences never produced or heard before—the creative aspect of language we mentioned in Chapter 1.

We thus see that syntactic rules in a grammar must at the very least account for

1. the "grammaticality" of sentences;
2. the ordering of words and morphemes;
3. our knowledge of structural ambiguity;
4. our knowledge that sentences may be paraphrases of each other;
5. our knowledge of the grammatical function of each part of a sentence, that is, of the grammatical relations;
6. speakers' ability to produce and understand an infinite set of possible sentences.

A major goal of linguistics is to show clearly and explicitly how syntactic rules can account for this knowledge. A theory of grammar must provide a complete characterization of what speakers tacitly know about their language. In keeping with this goal, in this chapter we will discuss some aspects of this kind of knowledge and the kinds of rules that account for it. A full description of syntax goes beyond the scope of the book, however.

Sentence Structure

Who climbs the grammar-tree distinctly knows
Where noun and verb and participle grows.
John Dryden, "Juvenal's Satire," vi

Syntactic rules determine the correct order of words in a sentence. But sentences are more than merely words placed one after another like beads on a string. As the discussion of *synthetic buffalo hides* showed, the words of a sentence can be divided into two or more groups, and within each group the words can be divided into subgroups, and so on, until only single words remain. The groups and subgroups are "natural" groupings of the words. What is meant by "natural" will be clarified in the section below on Syntactic Rules. For now, we appeal to your intuition to divide the sentence

The child found the puppy.

into the two groups:

(The child)   (found the puppy)

By continuing this "division" process, the sentence could be represented in the following branching diagram.

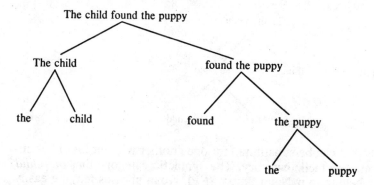

Such a diagram is called a **constituent structure tree.** The "tree" is upside down with the "root" at the top and the "leaves" at the bottom. At each point where the tree "branches" there is a group of words that form a part or *structural constituent* of the sentence. At the bottom of the tree are the individual words or morphemes. In addition to revealing the linear order of the words and other structural parts of the sentence, a constituent structure tree has **hierarchical structure.** This means that the groups and subgroups of words comprising the structural constituents are shown by the level on which they appear in the tree. If your intuition agrees with this analysis, then your grammar, like ours, specifies that the phrase *found the puppy* is correctly divided into the two parts, *found* and *the puppy*, as shown in the diagram, and that this division is more natural than a division into *found the* and *puppy*, because *the puppy* is a **structural constituent** whereas *found the* is not.

The expression *synthetic buffalo hides* has two possible constituent structure tree representations:

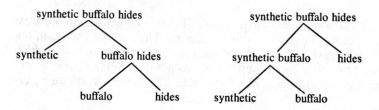

Each tree represents one of the possible meanings. Thus constituent structure can explicitly account for our intuitive knowledge of some ambiguities.

All sentences in all languages can be represented by constituent structure trees, and all languages have syntactic rules which determine the linear order of words and their hierarchical structure, that is, how the words are grouped into structural constituents.

Your knowledge of constituent structure also tells you that certain constituents can be substituted for other constituents without affecting the grammaticality of the sentence (although the meaning may change). For example, the constituents *the child* and *the puppy* can be substituted for each other in the sentence we diagrammed above to produce:

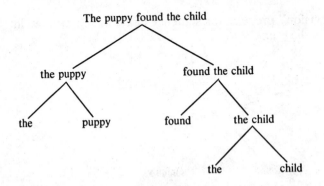

Constituents that can be substituted for one another without loss of grammaticality form a **syntactic category**. The syntactic category that *the child* and *the puppy* belong to is **Noun Phrase (NP)**. Noun phrases may be easily identified because they can function as "subject" or "object" in a sentence, and only noun phrases may do so. Noun phrases often, but not always, contain a noun or pronoun. Part of your syntactic knowledge is knowing the syntactic categories of your language. And you know what a noun phrase is even if you have never heard the term before. You can identify which of the following expressions are noun phrases by substituting each into the spaces in "Who found _____?" and "_____ was lost." The ones that "feel right" will be the noun phrases:

(4) (a) a bird
    (b) the red banjo
    (c) have a nice day
    (d) with a balloon
    (e) the woman who was laughing
    (f) it
    (g) John
    (h) run

We assume that you were able to identify (4a, 4b, 4e, 4f, 4g) as noun phrases.

There are, of course, other syntactic categories. The constituent *found the puppy* is a **Verb Phrase (VP)**. Verb phrases always contain a verb, which may be followed by other constituents, such as a noun phrase. Thus, a syntactic category can include in it other syntactic categories. You can determine which of the following are verb phrases by trying to substitute each one into "The child _____."

(5) (a) saw a duck
    (b) a bird
    (c) slept
    (d) smart
    (e) is smart
    (f) found the cake
    (g) found the cake in the cupboard

The verb phrases are (5a, 5c, 5e, 5f, 5g).
    Other syntactic categories, with a few examples, are:

Sentence (S): *The puppy found the child.*
Prepositional Phrase (PP): *in the cupboard, by the brook*
Adjective Phrase (AP): *smart, very large, quaint old*
Noun (N): *child, puppy, woman, cake, bird, cupboard*
Verb (V): *find, have, sleep, bite, cry*
Adjective (Adj): *red, smart, lazy, small*
Pronoun (Pro): *it, he, she*
Preposition (P): *at, in, on, to, with*
Article (Art): *the, a*

All languages have syntactic categories, and although different languages may have different syntactic categories, the speakers of any language know the syntactic categories of their language.
    We can now be more explicit in representing the constituent structure of *The child found the puppy* by indicating to what syntactic category each constituent belongs:

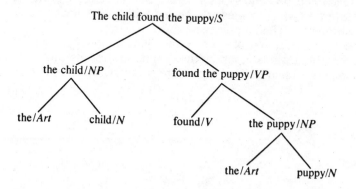

This kind of diagram is appropriate for representing sentences of any language. Three aspects of our syntactic knowledge of sentence structure are revealed in this kind of constituent structure tree:

(6) (a) linear order of words;
    (b) grouping of words into structural constituents;
    (c) the syntactic category of each structural constituent.

Although the above diagram is correct, it is redundant, and can instead be drawn as follows:

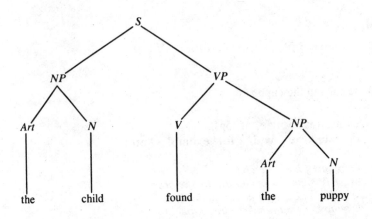

No information is lost by this "streamlining." If you trace each word up the tree you will see that *puppy* is a noun, *the puppy* is a noun phrase, *found the puppy* is a verb phrase, *the child found the puppy* is a sentence, and that *child* is also a noun and *the child*, like *the puppy*, is also a noun phrase, and so on. The tree diagram also shows that the sentence *The child found the puppy* consists of two structural constituents: a noun phrase *the child* and a verb phrase *found the puppy;* and that the verb phrase *found the puppy* consists of two structural constituents: the verb *found* and the noun phrase *the puppy*, and so on. The article *the* and the noun *puppy* are constituents contained in a larger constituent noun phrase *the puppy*, but by themselves neither is a noun phrase. A constituent includes *all* the smaller constituents beneath it in the tree. Each branching point in the tree is called a **node.** A constituent structure tree whose nodes are labeled with the syntactic category of each constituent is called a **phrase marker.**

Every sentence of English, and of every other human language, can be similarly represented by a phrase marker that explicitly reveals the three kinds of information mentioned in (6) above. Here are a few other examples from English.

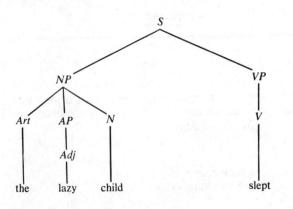

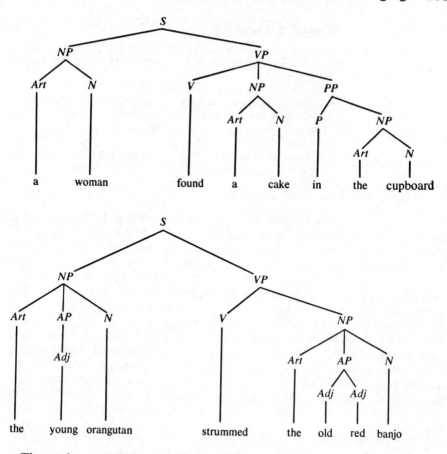

These phrase markers reveal that some noun phrases of English are:

the child	the puppy	the lazy child	the old red banjo
a woman	the cake	the cupboard	the young orangutan

Some verb phrases are:

found the puppy	found a cake in the cupboard
slept	strummed the old red banjo

A prepositional phrase is:

in the cupboard

Some sentences are:

The child found the puppy	A woman found a cake in the cupboard
The lazy child slept	The young orangutan strummed the old red banjo

The phrase markers further reveal that an article plus an adjective or an adjective phrase plus a noun combine to form a noun phrase; a verb alone can be a verb phrase, and so on.

Word Classes

We next went to the School of Languages, where three Professors sat in Consultation upon improving that of their own Country.

The first Project was to shorten Discourse by cutting Polysyllables into one, and leaving out Verbs and Participles; because in Reality all things imaginable are but Nouns.

The other was a Scheme for entirely abolishing all Words whatsoever; and this was urged as a great Advantage in Point of Health as well as Brevity. For it is plain, that every Word we speak is in some degree a Diminution of our Lungs by Corrosion. . . .

Jonathan Swift, *Gulliver's Travels*

The learned professors of languages in Laputa proposed a scheme for abolishing all words, thinking it would be more convenient if "Men [were] to carry about them, such Things as were necessary to express the particular Business they are to discourse on." We doubt that this scheme could ever come to fruition even in Laputa, not only because it would be difficult to carry around an unobservable *atom* or an abstract *loyalty* but because our thoughts are expressed in sentences that have structure and cannot be represented by Things pulled from a sack. Instead, words occur at the bottom of phrase markers under the node labeled with the **word class** (or *syntactic category* or "part of speech") of that word. All languages have word classes. This is a universal fact about languages. There even appear to be universal word classes in all languages, such as verb and noun. Speakers of a language know both the words and the classes into which they fall even if they do not know the technical (linguistic) names for these word classes.

The syntactic categories of words and groups of words are revealed by the way they pattern in sentences. If you didn't have knowledge of these syntactic categories, you would be unable to form grammatical sentences or distinguish between grammatical and ungrammatical sentences.

The vocabulary items—the morphemes and words—of a language, together with their phonological, semantic, and syntactic specifications, are contained in the **lexicon,** one component of the grammar of that language.

The lexicon contains more syntactic information than simply the syntactic category of each word. If it did not, speakers of English would be unable to distinguish the ungrammatical sentences *John found* and *John found in the house* from grammatical sentences like *John found the ball*. What accounts for this is that the verb *find* must be followed by a noun phrase, its "direct object." That is, when specified as a verb (rather than a noun) *find* is a **transitive verb** which means that it has a **co-occurrence restriction** which limits its occurrence to sentences with direct objects. Information about such co-occurrence restrictions on a word must also be in the lexicon, thus accounting for the ungrammaticality of:

(7) (a) *John put the meat.
(b) *John cried the baby.
(c) *A milk is in the glass.

The verb *put* in (7a) must co-occur with a prepositional phrase of location as in *John put the meat in the refrigerator*. In (7b) the verb *cry* co-occurs with a noun phrase direct object, but it should not, since it is an **intransitive** verb. The noun *milk* is a **mass noun** like *information* and *money* and cannot co-occur with the indefinite article *a*, which is why (7c) is "starred." All of this is known by speakers of English and is reflected in the grammar as co-occurrence restrictions that are stated in the lexicon for each word.

Co-occurrence restrictions may be optional. The verb *eat* is specified as optionally occurring with or without a direct object:

John ate.
John ate lunch.

There are other co-occurrence restrictions that are somewhat different from the ones we have been discussing. Consider

*The house found the boy.
*The rock cried.
*Lunch ate John.

According to one theory of grammar these sentences are semantically deviant. The semantic rules of the language, discussed in the previous chapter, will indicate the anomaly of such sentences. These rules are similar to co-occurrence restrictions in that they must state, for example, that the verb *cry* must co-occur with an "animate" subject.

Even though such sentences are semantically anomalous, they are syntactically well formed, as they can be represented by phrase markers similar to normal sentences:

The boy found the house.
The child cried.
John ate lunch.

Some of the excerpts from E. E. Cummings' poetry that we cited earlier illustrate that sentences in a language may be syntactically well formed but semantically deviant. The noun phrase *the six subjunctive crumbs* can be diagrammed as:

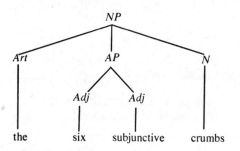

This is how we might diagram the more meaningful NP *the six subjunctive sentences*. But since *subjunctive* normally refers to some grammatical concept, and *crumbs* never does (unless we speak metaphorically of "sentence crumbs"), the result is semantic deviance, or oddness, or anomaly.

Nonsense poetry, such as Carroll's "Jabberwocky," also shows that phrases and sentences can be syntactically well formed, yet semantically un-

interpretable, since the "lexical items" selected are possible but nonoccurring forms, having no "agreed-on" meaning. This is further shown by the
following poem, "Uffia" by Harriet R. White:

When sporgles spanned the floreate mead
  And cogwogs gleet upon the lea,
  Uffia gopped to meet her love
Who smeeged upon the equat sea.

The Rules of Syntax

*Everyone who is master of the language he speaks . . . may
form new . . . phrases, provided they coincide with the genius
of the language.*
Michaelis, *Dissertation* (1769)

When you know a language you know how to form all
kinds of sentences—negative sentences, declarative sentences (that make
statements), interrogative sentences (that ask questions), imperative sentences (that give commands), passive sentences, and so on. This knowledge
is contained in syntactic rules that determine how such sentences are constructed. We can illustrate this by the rule in English for forming "yes–no"
questions from corresponding declarative statements.

Form the yes–no question that corresponds to each of the declarative sentences below:

(8) (a) Disa is dancing.
    (b) She has already bathed the dog.
    (c) Beavers can build dams.

If you know English (and understood our request) you produced:

(9) (a) Is Disa dancing?
    (b) Has she already bathed the dog?
    (c) Can beavers build dams?

In stating the rule, the simplest statement consistent with the available
evidence might be something like this:

QUESTION RULE (first tentative version)
To form a yes–no question from its corresponding declarative sentence, move the
second word of the sentence to the beginning of the sentence.

This rule will "work" for all the above examples. If it were the correct rule
(it isn't!) we might conclude that sentences are structured merely by num-
bering or renumbering the words.

Disa can dance.   Can Disa dance?
 1   2   3   →   2   1   3

But we have already seen that the words of a sentence are not like beads on a
string. They form constituents, and the constituents are of a certain type or
category such as noun phrase or verb.

To discover that the rule will not work in all cases consider the following:

(10) (a) The girl is taking ballet lessons.
(b) Most beavers can build dams.
(c) Jack and Jill have already gone up the hill.

If the rule is applied as stated, it will produce the clearly ungrammatical:

(11) (a) *Girl the is taking ballet lessons?
(b) *Beavers most can build dams?
(c) *And Jack Jill have already gone up the hill?

The rule as stated is inadequate. It should refer to the *first verb of the sentence* rather than the second word. We must revise the rule:

QUESTION RULE (second tentative version)
To form a yes–no question from the corresponding declarative sentence, move the first verb of the sentence to the beginning of the sentence.

If we apply the second version of the rule, we would form:

(12) (a) Is the girl taking ballet lessons?
(b) Can most beavers build dams?
(c) Have Jack and Jill already gone up the hill?

This version of the question rule is an improvement. It covers all of the sentences the first rule covers, and additional sentences that the first version could not handle. It is still not entirely adequate, as we shall see below. But this rule is interesting because rules for deriving other types of sentences than yes–no questions are similar to it. For example, to form the corresponding negative sentences of the declarative sentences of (8) and (10), we could state:

NEGATIVE RULE (first tentative version)
To form a negative sentence from the corresponding positive sentence, insert the word *not* after the first verb of the sentence.

The corresponding negatives of (8) and (10) follow this rule:

(13) (a) Disa is not dancing.
(b) She has not already bathed the dog.
(c) Beavers cannot build dams.
(d) The girl is not taking ballet lessons.
(e) Most beavers cannot build dams.
(f) Jack and Jill have not already gone up the hill.

When two or more rules make reference to the same structural item or category or constituent—in this case "the first verb of the sentence"—the generalization provides some evidence that we are on the right track. This may help explain how children learn languages. If many rules refer to the same constituents, a child learning them need only learn them once—for example, "the first verb of the sentence." The same concept can be used in learning how to make both yes–no questions and negative sentences. Grammars have many such generalizations, which helps explain how children construct their grammars but, of course, cannot explain all aspects of this complex process, which will be discussed in greater detail in Chapter 10. What is important to note here, however, is that the rule refers to a structure of a certain type. However, the second tentative version of the question rule will still not work, and has to be revised further, as shown by the sentences under (14).

(14) (a) The girl who loves John is pretty.
(b) Jack and Jill who climbed the hill are twins.

Applying the second tentative version of the question rule we get the ungrammatical sentences under (15).

(15) (a) *Loves the girl who John is pretty?
(b) *Climbed Jack and Jill who the hill are twins?

The difficulty is that the sentences in (14) are complex sentences; that is, the subject NPs include **embedded sentences** called *relative clauses*. Thus, the first verb in each sentence is part of the sentence embedded in the first NP and is not the verb in the main or highest sentence, as the following phrase marker reveals.

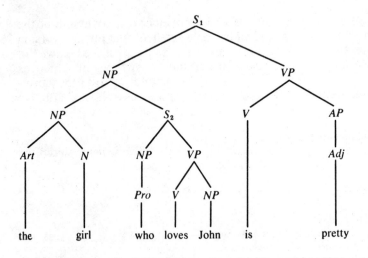

It is the first verb in S_1, the main sentence or the highest S node, that must be moved. We can therefore reformulate the question rule to state this fact.

QUESTION RULE (third tentative version)
To form a yes–no question from the corresponding declarative sentence, move the first verb of the highest S (S_1 or main sentence) immediately before the first NP of that sentence.

We can illustrate the operation of the rule using an abbreviated or simplified phrase marker for (14a).

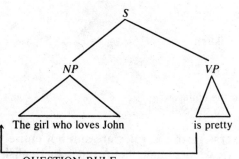

QUESTION RULE

By applying this new version of the rule, the following grammatical yes–no questions for the sentences in (14) would be derived.

(16) (a) Is the girl who loves John pretty?
(b) Are Jack and Jill who climbed the hill twins?

As further support for this formulation of the rule we can see that the negative rule requires a similar modification. If we applied the rule as previously stated to (14) we would get:

(17) (a) *The girl who loves not John is pretty.
(b) *Jack and Jill who climbed not the hill are twins.

The correct negative sentences are:

(18) (a) The girl who loves John is not pretty.
(b) Jack and Jill who climbed the hill are not twins.

We can reformulate the negative rule to refer to the verb in S_1 (the main sentence) exactly as we reformulated the question rule and we will then get the results we want.

NEGATIVE RULE (second tentative version)
To form a negative sentence from the corresponding positive sentence, insert the word *not* after the first verb of the highest or main sentence.

What we have been trying to illustrate by these examples and these rules is that syntactic knowledge depends on knowing the structure of sentences, even when these structures or phrase markers are very complex. It is *in principle* impossible to account for the rules that all of us as speakers of English know without reference to such notions as syntactic categories such as NP, V, VP, and without reference to the hierarchical structure of the sentences.
Although our aim is not to present all the details of English syntax, some further discussion of the question and negative rules will further clarify the extent of your syntactic knowledge. The tentative versions of both rules will apply to the sentence in (19) to derive the sentences in (20).

(19) Santa Lucia will give toys to the children.

(20) (a) Will Santa Lucia give toys to the children?   QUESTION RULE
(b) Santa Lucia will not give toys to the children.   NEGATIVE RULE

However, if we apply the rules to

(21) Santa Lucia gives toys to the children.

we get the ungrammatical sentences in (22)

(22) (a) *Gives Santa Lucia toys to the children?
(b) *Santa Lucia gives not toys to the children.

Thus we see that the previous versions of the rules are still not entirely correct: rules of syntax must not yield ungrammatical results. In English, there is a distinction between the syntactic category of verb and the syntactic category of **auxiliary verb** or "helping verb." Auxiliary verbs form a closed class and include *can, is, have, do, will,* and a few others. In stating the question and negative rules, we should have referred to "the first auxiliary verb of the main sentence" instead of simply the first verb. Our final revision of these rules is then:

QUESTION RULE (fourth version)
To form a yes–no question from the corresponding declarative sentence, move the first auxiliary verb of the highest S (or main sentence) immediately before the first NP of that sentence.

NEGATIVE RULE (third version)
To form a negative sentence from the corresponding positive sentence, insert the word *not* after the first auxiliary verb of the highest or main sentence.

These rules will still produce the correct question and negative forms of sentence (19) but they will (correctly) fail to apply to sentence (21) because there is no auxiliary verb. Thus the ungrammatical strings in (22) will not be generated.

The question and negative forms of (21) are:

(23) (a) Does Santa Lucia give toys to the children?
(b) Santa Lucia does not give toys to the children.

Speakers of English know that, under certain circumstances, they must insert the auxiliary verb *do* in its correct morphological shape *does* when no other auxiliary verb is present. In terms of the grammar, there is a syntactic rule that inserts the morpheme *do* into sentences that meet certain conditions.

It is beyond the scope of this introductory book to discuss fully the specifics of these syntactic rules and the sentences they help account for. What is clear is that the question and negative rules should apply to sentences such as (21) only after the rule inserting *do* has applied.

To derive (23a) from (21), therefore, *do* must first be inserted, and then the question rule applied. It is significant that more than one rule may apply to a given sentence, and when this happens the rules can apply in order, just as in the phonological rules.

In this section we have tried to support our claim that speakers of a language have knowledge of syntactic rules. We have also attempted to illustrate the way linguists approach the problem of constructing the rules of grammar. We started with some sentences and formulated as simple a rule as possible to account for the data. We then examined more data (sentences of English) and found the rule was not adequate since it failed to account entirely for what English speakers know. We revised the rule to account for the new data, being sure that it still accounted for the previous sentences. We then continued to revise it until it seemed to be adequate for all sentences of English. The adequacy of any of the formulations can only be tested by trying out the rule on new sentences. This is in general how science proceeds. Observations are made and principles are tentatively formulated based on them. The principles are tested on all possible data to see if they are adequate. If they prove to be inadequate they are reformulated in such a way as to continue to encompass more and more observations. Linguistics is the scientific study of language and therefore proceeds in this way in the attempt to discover and formulate the rules of grammar and the principles that underlie the specific rules of any grammar. The major principle we have been discussing is that the rules of syntax apply to structures of a general sort, not to specific examples or words, and that you, as speakers of a language, know the rules and the structures to which they apply.

The Function of Constituents

When you know a language, you not only know what the constituents of the sentences are but you also know how they **function** in the language. We noted this earlier when we discussed the difference between

Disa is easy to please.
Disa is eager to please.

This may be further illustrated in the following sentences.

(24) (a) The team promised the coach to exercise during vacation.
(b) The team persuaded the coach to exercise during vacation.

In (24a) *the team* functions as the **subject** of the verb *exercise;* it is the team that will exercise (if the promise is kept). However, in (24b) *the coach* functions as the subject of *exercise.*

Knowledge of a language permits one to distinguish between the structural and the functional relations of constituents.

Consider, for example, the following sentences:

(25) (a) The dog bit the man.
(b) The man was bitten by the dog.
(c) John loved Mary.
(d) It was Mary John loved.

In both (25a) and (25b) the **logical subject**—the doer of the action—is the dog, but *the dog* in (25a) is the **structural subject** (the first NP of the highest sentence) whereas in (25b) *the man* is the structural subject. We therefore see that our knowledge of the language permits us to distinguish between structural subject and logical subject.

(25c) and (25d) are paraphrases but with a different **focus.** By moving *Mary* from the position of object of the verb to the first part of the sentence, our attention is focused on who it was that John loved. This can also be done for contrastive purposes, as in

It was Mary John loved, not Susan.

Contrast or emphasis can also be reflected phonologically by stressing the word to be focused or contrasted or emphasized.

Many sentences can be thought of as being divided into a **topic**—what is being talked about—and a **comment**—what is being said about the topic. The topic often corresponds to the *structural* subject of a sentence. In (25a) the topic is *the dog* and the comment is *bit the man*, whereas in (25b) the topic is *the man* and the comment is *was bitten by the dog*. One of the functions of passive sentences is to make the topic the structural subject, even when it is not the logical subject. The topic of a sentence is also called the **old information,** because it represents something already under discussion. The comment, on the other hand, is **new information,** because it represents information added to the discourse. In many languages there is a tendency to state old information at the beginning of the sentence followed by the new information: In English, the structural subject occurs first in the sentence.

Some languages have grammatical morphemes or particles that explicitly mark the topic of the sentence. In Japanese this particle is *wa*, and nouns followed by *wa* in Japanese generally occur at the beginning of the sentence. The tendency for old information to occur first in a sentence may be universal.

Knowledge of language includes ways of contrasting, focusing, and topicalizing different parts of a sentence, as well as determining "who did what to whom," which is illustrated by sentence (25a) and its corresponding passive (25b). This was also illustrated by our discussion of sentences like those in (24) above.

The Infinitude of Language

Big fleas have little fleas
That on their bodies bite 'em
And little fleas have littler fleas
And so ad infinitum
Anonymous

Normal human minds are such that . . . without the help of anybody, they will produce 1000 (sentences) they never heard spoke of . . . inventing and saying such things as they never heard from their masters, nor any mouth.
Huarte De San Juan, c. 1530–1592

We have already noted that there is no longest sentence in any language. Speakers have the ability to make any sentence even longer by various means, such as adding an adjective or preceding the entire sentence by an expression such as *Did you know that . . .* Even children know how to produce and understand very long sentences, and know how to make them even longer, as illustrated by the children's rhyme about the house that Jack built.

This is the farmer sowing the corn,
That kept the cock that crowed in the morn,
That waked the priest all shaven and shorn,
That married the man all tattered and torn,
That kissed the maiden all forlorn,
That milked the cow with the crumpled horn,
That tossed the dog
That worried the cat
That killed the rat
That ate the malt
That lay in the house that Jack built.

Children begin this rhyme with the line *This is the house that Jack built,* and continue by lengthening it to *This is the malt that lay in the house that Jack built,* and so on.

You can add any of the following to the beginning of the rhyme and still have a grammatical, even longer, sentence:

I saw that . . .
What is the name of the unicorn that noticed that . . .
Ask someone if . . .
Do you know whether . . .

What is it about sentence structure and syntactic rules that allows a speaker to make any sentence longer? A clue is found in the B.C. cartoon.

B.C.   **Johnny Hart**

By permission of Johnny Hart and Field Enterprises, Inc.

The sentence in the final box consists of five sentences combined together as shown below:

You mean   you didn't know   that I knew   she didn't know   you knew that.

If we attempt to represent the entire sentence by a phrase marker (thus revealing the hierarchical structure), we would get, omitting inessential details, the following:

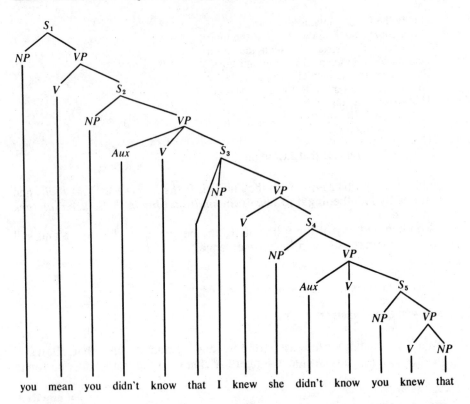

you mean you didn't know that I knew she didn't know you knew that

In this phrase marker sentences are contained within sentences are contained within sentences; S_5 is **embedded** in S_4; S_4 is embedded in S_3 and so on. When a constituent is embedded within another constituent of the same category, that constituent **recurs** (occurs again) and the structure or phrase marker containing the recurring constituents is **recursive**. The rules of sentence formation in all languages allow recursive structures. As the same type of structural constituent can occur over and over there is no limit to the potential length of sentences.

Because the number of different syntactic categories or constituent types is limited in all languages, recursive structures are necessary for producing very long sentences. If speakers had to keep choosing new constituent types as they made a sentence longer and longer, they would eventually exhaust the supply and sentence length would be limited. Recursive sentence structures are very common and most sentences of more than several words involve recursion.

Noun phrases, verb phrases, prepositional phrases and adjective phrases, in addition to sentences, commonly recur in English sentence structures. The following sentences exemplify such recursion.

(26) (a) I visited my wife's mother's father's cousin's friend's store. (NP recursion)
(b) The very seedy battered rundown old red wooden shack fell down. (AP recursion)
(c) I want to begin to try to learn to play the saxophone. (VP recursion)

(d) I like the brightness of the coloring of the lettering on the cover of the report. (PP and NP recursion)

The phrase marker of the long noun phrase in (26d) is shown in the tree diagram below. Note that NPs occur within PPs, which occur within NPs, and so on. This shows that more than one type of constituent can recur in a single structure.

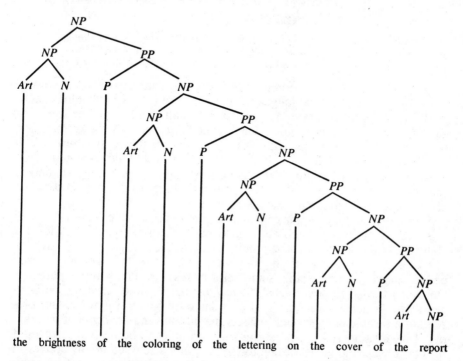

Some of these phrases and sentences may be hard to follow, but that is due to performance limitations. All the examples of recursion represent the *types* of expressions that English speakers are capable of producing and understanding.

We also noted in Chapter 1 and at the beginning of this chapter that speakers of any language can produce and understand an unlimited number of sentences they have never heard or spoken previously. The grammar must also, then, account for this **creative aspect** of language.

The basis of this creative aspect is also recursion. As sentences become longer and longer they can become more and more varied. If there is no longest sentence there is no limit to the number of different sentences that can be produced. Thus, by the simple means of recursion, the rules of sentence formation permit an infinite set of different sentences, which can be produced and understood by all speakers of the language. Note that any particular sentence must be finite in length. But since no limit can be placed on sentence length it is the set of sentences that are infinite in principle. Also note that no individual speaker can produce or understand infinitely many sentences. We are, rather, pointing to the linguistic capacity to do so in theory. Speakers "pick and choose" the sentences (or more correctly form them, as they are not stored anywhere to be chosen) needed to express their thoughts, and they use the rules (unconsciously of course) to understand the sentences produced by other speakers of their language.

Transformational-Generative Grammars

. . . the only thing that is important is whether a result can be achieved in a finite number of elementary steps or not.
John Von Neumann

Since a grammar of a language is an *explicit* characterization of all the rules of that language, including the rules of phonology, morphology, semantics, and syntax, it must reflect all aspects of a speaker's linguistic knowledge. This requires that it specify *all* and *only* the grammatical sentences of the language with descriptions of sentence structures. If it failed to specify all the possible sentences it would not account for a speaker's ability to do this; if it was not restricted to *only* the grammatical sentences it would not account for speakers' ability to distinguish between grammatical and nongrammatical strings.

A grammar that meets this goal in an explicit and testable fashion is called a **generative grammar.** Such a grammar must account equally well for our ability to both understand and produce sentences.

As we saw in the chapter on phonology, formalizing the rules of grammar permits explicit generalizations and helps us test the claims of the grammar. One such formal theory of generative grammar is called **transformational-generative grammar,** a theory first postulated by Noam Chomsky. Our presentation throughout the book reflects the notions and concepts of this theory. Like all scientific theories, this one continues to be revised to account for new observations, according to the methods discussed briefly above. In the future there may be a fully developed alternative theory that will supplant it. In the version of transformational-generative grammar presented here, the syntactic component of the grammar contains two kinds of syntactic rules: phrase-structure rules and transformational rules, both of which will be discussed in the following sections.

PHRASE-STRUCTURE RULES

[The professor had written] all the words of their language in their several moods, tenses and declensions [on tiny blocks of wood, and had] emptied the whole vocabulary into his frame, and made the strictest computation of the general proportion there is in books between the numbers of particles, nouns, and verbs, and other parts of speech.
Jonathan Swift, Gulliver's Travels

The rules that determine the basic constituent structure of sentences are called **phrase-structure rules.** These rules state what every constituent can be composed of. Some are combinations of other constituents, while others consist of a single word or morpheme.

In English a noun phrase (NP) can be an article (Art) followed by a noun (N):

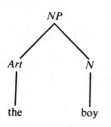

The phrase structure rule that states this is:

(27) NP → Art   N

and it has two meanings:

(a) A noun phrase **may be** an article followed by a noun.

(b) An article followed by a noun **is always** a noun phrase.

The right side of the arrow shows the linear order of the component constituents. The single constituent named on the left side of the arrow is the node from which all the righthand-side nodes branch down in a tree diagram. Phrase-structure rules are explicit. They state exactly what a constituent can be. Therefore, insofar as (27) is concerned, an NP is *not* a noun followed by an article, nor does it occur in any of the following structures:

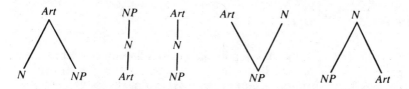

All phrase-structure rules specify precisely the hierarchical structure of constituents and the linear order of the elements they contain.

Although an NP can be made up of an article plus a noun, among other things, neither an article nor a noun can contain further constituents. Articles and nouns occur at the bottom of trees and eventually have words or morphemes attached to them.

If there were no other phrase-structure rules stating what an NP in English "may be" no sentence could include NPs like

the big dog
it

since neither of these is simply an article plus a noun. We need other rules:

NP → Art   AP   N
NP → Pro

where AP stands for adjective phrase. An adjective phrase may be a single adjective, which is revealed by the rule

AP → Adj

These rules now specify that the following constituent structures are well-formed in English:

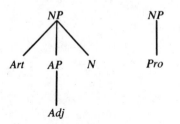

By implication, strings such as *the dog big* and *the it* are not NPs because such structures as

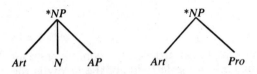

do not correspond to any NP phrase-structure rule in both linear order and hierarchical structure.

We now have three rules for the NP constituent, which we abbreviate in the following manner:

(28) NP → $\left\{ \begin{array}{l} \text{Art} \quad (\text{AP}) \quad \text{N} \\ \text{Pro} \end{array} \right\}$

The braces indicate that either the top or the bottom line may be chosen to be the right side of the arrow. If the top line is chosen, the constituent in parenthesis may be present or absent. Thus, (28) is a more convenient way of writing the three rules:

NP → Art N
NP → Art AP N
NP → Pro

We have already discussed similar rule abbreviations in phonology.

We noted previously that a noun could be preceded by any number of adjectives in a noun phrase. We need a **recursive** rule to capture this fact.

AP → AP Adj

A rule is recursive if the constituent to the left of the arrow is repeated as one of the constituents to the right of the arrow. This rule can be abbreviated or collapsed with

AP → Adj

to give

(29) AP → (AP) Adj

The constituent structure of the noun phrase *a large red ancient building* is shown as follows:

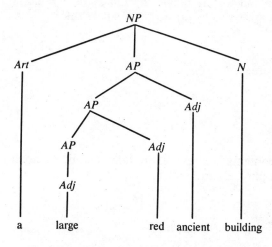

The NP node branches into an article followed by an adjective phrase followed by a noun, as allowed by the rules in (28). The first two APs are themselves APs followed by adjectives, and the bottommost AP is a single adjective, all of which is allowed by the recursive rules in (29). To be "correct" every constituent in the tree can contain only constituents permitted by the phrase-structure rules, except for bottommost constituents, which have words of the corresponding syntactic category attached. The same constituent may be repeated in a tree as long as the rules are adhered to. It is by means of recursive rules that the length of sentences cannot be limited. The recursive use of a rule is illustrated in this tree by the repetition of AP nodes that result in the sequence of adjectives *large, red, ancient.*

Phrase-structure rules must reflect precisely the linguistic knowledge that speakers have about the constituent structures of their language. Grammars of all languages have phrase-structure rules because all sentences in all languages conform to certain constituent structures. There are, of course, many other phrase-structure rules in the grammar of English:

In English a verb phrase may consist of:

(a) A verb alone: The boy *slept.*
VP → V

(b) A verb followed by a noun phrase: The child *found the puppy.*
VP → V NP

(c) A verb followed by a noun phrase followed by a prepositional phrase: The woman *put the cake in the cupboard.*
VP → V NP PP

(d) A verb followed by a prepositional phrase: The child *laughed at the puppy*.

VP → V PP

We have presented four separate phrase-structure rules for the VP. In each there is a verb after the arrow, which shows that every VP must have a verb; the verb may *optionally* be followed by an NP, or a PP, or both. If we again use parentheses around a category to mean "optional" (as we did in the NP and AP rules) we can express rules (a)–(d) as a single rule:

VP → V (NP) (PP)

Some prepositional phrases are:

in the cupboard
to the store
with a light touch
beneath a red blanket

Every prepositional phrase contains a preposition followed by a noun phrase. This fact is stated in a phrase-structure rule as:

PP → P NP

An important phrase-structure rule of English is:

S → NP VP

This rule corresponds to what many schoolchildren learn as "Every sentence has a subject and a predicate." The rule explains why we recognize that the following are not sentences of English:

The man   (lacks a VP)
Found it   (lacks an NP)
Found it the man (NP and VP in wrong order)

The node S is always the top or *root* node of the phrase marker of a complete sentence, and it may occur within the tree also, as in the following:

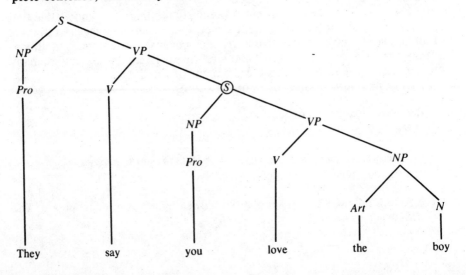

In this phrase marker an embedded sentence follows the verb in a verb phrase. Such a sentence functions as a **complement**. The sentence *you love the boy* is a complement of the verb *say*. Both sentence nodes in the tree have an NP VP below them, conforming to the phrase-structure rule for sentences.

This phrase marker is a *recursive structure*. The constituents S and VP both recur. This recursion results from another phrase-structure rule:

$$VP \rightarrow V \quad S$$

which is needed because the first VP node has a V and an S immediately below it. If we look at this rule together with the rule for S, we can see the source of recursion.

(a) $S \rightarrow NP \quad VP$ $\qquad$ *recursive pair*

(b) $VP \rightarrow V \quad S$

Rule (a) has S on the left and VP on the right side of the arrow; Rule (b) is just the opposite: it has VP on the left and S on the right side of the arrow. When two rules are such that two constituents occur on both the left and right side of the arrow they form a **recursive pair** of rules. It is such rules that allow phrase markers to be very large (with no limit on size).

We now summarize all the phrase-structure rules for the grammar of English we have presented so far:

$$S \rightarrow NP \quad VP$$
$$NP \rightarrow \begin{Bmatrix} Art & (AP) & N \\ Pro & & \end{Bmatrix}$$
$$AP \rightarrow (AP) \quad Adj$$
$$VP \rightarrow V \begin{Bmatrix} (NP) & (PP) \\ S & \end{Bmatrix}$$
$$PP \rightarrow P \quad NP$$

These rules tell us among other things that the basic sentences of English have a noun-phrase subject followed by a verb and possibly followed by a noun-phrase object. We find in all languages that sentences contain a noun-phrase subject (Sub), a verb (V), and possibly a noun-phrase object (O). In some languages the basic or "preferred" order of these elements is subject-verb-object (SubVO). Many familiar languages, such as French, Spanish, and English, are examples. Other languages, such as Japanese and Korean, have the preferred order subject-object-verb (SubOV). Others, such as classical Hebrew and Welsh, are VSubO languages; and, rarely, one finds a language like Malagasy (spoken on Madagascar), which is VOSub, or Dyirbal, an Australian language, which is OSubV. No language has been discovered that has the preferred word order OVSub.

Although German is a language closely "related" (see Chapter 9) to English, it has SubOV word order in sentences that function as complements. This particular characteristic of German inspired Mark Twain to say:

Whenever the literary German dives into a sentence, that is the last you are going to see of him till he emerges on the other side of the Atlantic with his verb in his mouth.[2]

Languages may differ in the details of their phrase-structure rules and syntactic categories, but grammars of all languages have the *type* of rule we are calling phrase-structure rules that determine the structure of phrase markers, and all grammars make use of the notion "syntactic category." Knowing this may help when trying to learn a foreign language. An English speaker studying French for the first time may have to learn that the NP expansion rule in French is NP → Art N (AP), whereas the English rule he already knows says NP → Art (AP) N, but he already intuitively knows what an NP is, what an article is, and how nouns differ from adjectives.

TRANSFORMATIONAL RULES

Our life passes in transformation
Rainer Maria Rilke, *Duineser Elegien*, vii

THE WIZARD OF ID　　　　　　　　　　　　**Brant Parker and Johnny Hart**

By permission of Johnny Hart and Field Enterprises, Inc.

Phrase-structure rules such as those discussed above account for much of the syntactic knowledge that speakers possess about their language, including the linear order of words and morphemes, the constituent structure of sentences, and the creative and open-ended nature of language. The lexicon accounts for the co-occurrence restrictions between words. Yet syntax is even more complex than this, and our syntactic knowledge must include rules that relate certain kinds of sentences to one another.

With the exception of structurally ambiguous sentences, it might appear that each sentence of the language should be represented by exactly one phrase marker. A phrase or sentence that is structurally ambiguous should have as many different phrase markers as it has meanings. This is how the grammar accounts for this kind of ambiguity. Are there reasons that sentences that are not structurally ambiguous should be represented by more than one phrase marker?

Consider the pair of sentences in (30):

(30) (a) The detective tracked *down* the missing heiress.
　　　 (b) The detective tracked the missing heiress *down*.

---

[2] Mark Twain, *A Connecticut Yankee at King Arthur's Court*.

In these sentences *down* belongs to the class of **verbal particles** (Prt), and although they often have the same form as prepositions they are different in that they can occur on either side of the direct object NP. Prepositions cannot undergo such "movement," as the following examples show:

(31) (a)   She sped down the alley.
      (b) *She sped the alley down.

In (31a) *down* is a preposition, and (31b) shows that prepositions cannot be moved as particles can.

If English speakers agree with these grammaticality judgments then the grammar of English must reflect the difference between verbal particles and prepositions, and account for the special properties associated with the particles. Based on (30) it might be supposed that the phrase-structure rules of English include, in addition to the rules already discussed, rules such as

(32) VP → V   Prt   NP

to account for sentences like (30a), and

(33) VP → V   NP   Prt

to account for sentences like (30b).

These rules would permit the following phrase marker to represent sentence (30a):

(34) Tentative phrase marker of sentence (30a)

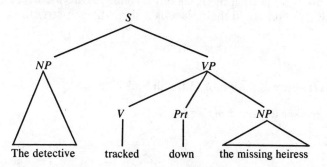

This phrase marker would represent sentence (30b):

(35) Phrase marker of sentence (30b)

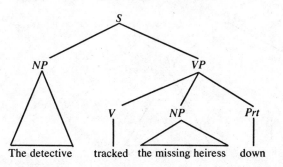

The rules in (32) and (33) permit seemingly correct phrase markers, but speakers of English know that the sentences in (30) are related: they mean the same thing and each seems to be a stylistic variant of the other. The rules we have formulated do not reveal speakers' knowledge of the relatedness of these sentences, since the phrase marker (34) that represents sentence (30a) is generated by a different phrase-structure rule than the phrase marker (35) that represents sentence (30b). In other words, they are generated *independently* of each other.

Another problem with rules (32) and (33) is they do not reflect the fact that the verb + particle combination is a single constituent (rather than two constituents under the VP). Evidence for this is found in the following sentence:

(36) Detectives track down heiresses, and police, criminals.

The meaning of this sentence includes "police track down criminals" even though the second occurrence of *track down* is absent. English allows verbal *constituents* to be missing in contexts such as (36), and this suggests that *track down* is a single constituent.

Another reason to suppose that *track down* is a single constituent is that *track* and *down* are "dependent" on each other in the sense that *track* cannot co-occur with any random verbal particle—**track over, *track out* are ungrammatical. Nor can the particle *down* occur with any verb—**follow down* is also ungrammatical. Some linguists analyze verb + verbal particle combinations as single units in the lexicon, which would ensure that they are single constituents when they appear in a phrase marker.

If these arguments are correct then the rules of (32) and (33) are incorrect and should not be in the grammar. In their place is a single phrase-structure rule:

(37) $V \rightarrow V_{prt}$ Prt

Now the phrase-marker representation of (30) will look like:

(38) Revised phrase marker for sentence (30a)

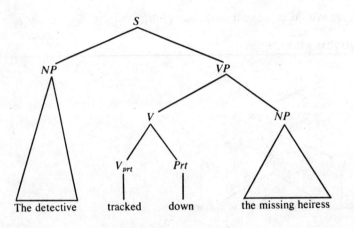

In revising the phrase-structure rules for verbal particles, we have mentioned a new syntactic category, V_{prt}. This is a subcategory of verbs that can combine with verbal particles. They are generally common words of Germanic origin (see Chapter 9).

The phrase marker in (38) is an adequate representation of sentence (30a), but (35), the phrase marker that represents sentence (30b), is inadequate because the verb and verbal particle are not a single constituent. Since (30b) is a variant of (30a) we have just as strong reasons to want a single constituent. Only in (30b) it is impossible because the verb and particle are not next to each other in the phrase marker. When the verb and verbal particle occur separated as in (35) they form a **discontinuous dependency,** sometimes called a **discontinuous constituent.**

Discontinuous dependencies occur elsewhere in English, and apparently occur in all languages. For example there is a discontinuous dependency in the following sentence:

(39) A review will soon appear of Chomsky's new book.

The expressions *a review* and *of Chomsky's new book* "belong together," as in a variant of this sentence shown in (40):

(40) A review of Chomsky's new book will soon appear.

But they do not occur together in (39) much in the same way that the verb and particle belong together but are separated in sentences like (30b).

The problem that discontinuous dependencies pose is that it is not possible to represent both the correct linear order and the apparently correct constituent structure of sentences like (30b) or (39) in a single phrase marker. One way to account for sentences containing discontinuous dependencies is to represent them by two phrase markers. The two phrase markers will be structurally related in the sense that one can be "derived" from the other by a relatively simple operation. Such an operation is called a **transformation.**

The concept of allowing more than one phrase marker to represent a single sentence, and relating one phrase marker to another by a transformation, is the basis of transformational grammar.

Sentences like (30a) will continue to be represented by a single phrase marker like (38). Sentences like (30b) will be represented both by (38), which reveals its underlying constituent structure, and (35), which reveals the linear order of its morphemes. To relate (38) to (35) we have a structural operation—a transformation—that describes precisely how phrase marker (35) is derived from phrase marker (38). We can state the transformation informally:

PARTICLE MOVEMENT TRANSFORMATION
If in a phrase marker there is a V_{prt} followed immediately by a verbal particle followed immediately by a noun phrase, then the verbal particle can be moved to the immediate righthand side of the noun phrase.

Note that no particular V_{prt}'s are mentioned in the rule. The particle movement transformation applies to *any* phrase marker that meets the condition of application. In general, transformations apply to *classes* of phrase markers. Because sentences containing verb-plus-particle structures have, like all other sentences, no upper limit on their potential length, the particle movement transformation can apply to an infinite set of phrase markers, as can all transformations. To each phrase marker it applies to, the particle movement transformation changes it into a phrase marker in which the particle is to the right of the direct object NP.

Examples of sentences containing verbal particles show that in some cases a transformational rule is **optional**; it may or may not apply. This is why

> He looked up the word in the dictionary.
> He looked the word up in the dictionary.

are both grammatical.

Sometimes, however, transformational rules are **obligatory**; if they are not applied the sentence will be ungrammatical, as shown in (41)

> **(41)** (a) *He looked up it in the dictionary.
>   (b) He looked it up in the dictionary.

When the NP object is a pronoun the particle movement transformation *must* apply. The statement of the particle movement transformation above is therefore inadequate as it stands and needs revision.

Any phrase marker to which a transformation applies is called an **underlying structure.** The *first* underlying structure to which a transformation applies is called the **deep structure.** In the derivation of (30b), the underlying structure (38) is also (with details omitted) the deep structure. It is generated by the phrase-structure rules, including the rule in (37). The result of applying a transformation to an underlying phrase marker is always a new phrase marker that, if no further transformations apply, is called the **surface structure.** The phrase marker in (35) is *derived* transformationally from (38) and since it does not undergo any further transformations (in this oversimplified presentation) it is the surface structure of (30b). The actual pronunciation of a sentence is based on its surface structure.

Since the publication in 1957 of Noam Chomsky's *Syntactic Structures*, which is generally considered the beginning of transformational grammar, linguists have postulated hundreds if not thousands of different transformations. For example, a transformation has been proposed that relates the phrase markers of underlying declarative statements to the phrase markers of the corresponding yes–no questions. It is called the *question transformation* and an informal statement of it would be similar to our question rule of a previous section. Similarly, a transformation has been suggested that relates the phrase markers of nonnegative sentences to those of the corresponding negatives. This *negative transformation* is similar to our negative rule discussed earlier. The insertion of *do* into phrase markers that lack an auxiliary verb has also been thought by some linguists to be a transformational process.

Although the field of transformational grammar is in flux, and there are divergent versions of Chomsky's original theory, the aim of the theory is still to reveal in explicit detail the knowledge that speakers have about the syntactic structures of their language.

The grammars of all languages have transformations. And although the details of particular transformations may differ from language to language, the kinds of operations transformations perform are the same. We find transformations that move or delete constituents in all languages. But we never find in any language a transformation that relates two phrase markers by deleting every other word or reversing the order of the words. There are universal constraints on what can occur. This is consistent with the thesis that we have been putting forth throughout this book: that human languages are far more similar than their "accidental" differences make them appear.

We have stated phonological rules formally, and we have stated the rules that determine the form of phrase markers formally as phrase-structure rules. We can also state transformations formally.

If we examine the informal statement of the particle movement transformation we see that it has an "if–then" clause. Transformations are basically of the form "If phrase markers are of such and such a form, then do such and such to them." That is, the transformation first states the class of phrase markers it applies to, and then tells what changes it makes to any phrase marker in that class. Formally, the statement of what kind of phrase marker the transformation applies to is called the **Structural Description** (SD). What it does to the phrase marker is called the **Structural Change** (SC).

The structural description (SD) appears formally as a sequence of syntactic category names such as NP or V, and "variables" (to be discussed below). Each symbol in the sequence has a number written below it. Any phrase marker that has constituents "matching up" to the sequence has the structural change (SC) applied to it. The structural change is expressed by recombining the numbers below each symbol of the structural description to indicate how one phrase marker is changed structurally into another. The formal statement of the particle movement transformation looks like this:

PARTICLE MOVEMENT TRANSFORMATION

SD: $X - V_{prt} - Prt - NP - Y$

    1   2   3   4   5

SC: 1   2 $\emptyset$ 4+3   5

The variables X and Y state that *anything* to the left of the verb or to the right of the NP is irrelevant to this transformation. Variables stand for parts of the phrase marker that have nothing to do with the transformation. The entire SD says that any phrase marker that contains a V_{prt} followed by a particle followed by an NP "qualifies" for the SC. The SD defines a class of phrase markers, and the use of variables makes this class infinite, since any amount of phrase-marker "material" can be covered by X or Y. This reflects our informal statement that transformations apply to infinite sets of phrase markers, in accordance to what we know about speakers' linguistic competence.

The SC tells us to leave the verb and everything to its left alone—the "1" and the "2" remain the same; move the particle to the right of the NP—indicated by the "$\emptyset$" and "4 + 3"; and leave everything else alone—the "5" remains the same. The "$\emptyset$" indicates that the particle is no longer in its original position—that is, it has been actually *moved,* and not just *copied.*

The SD does not mention any particular string of morphemes such as *track down* or *look up* because it defines a class of phrase markers of infinite size. The transformation is general and applies to the infinite number of phrase markers that include a V_{prt} followed by a particle followed by an NP. For each of these phrase markers a new phrase marker is produced in which the particle is moved to the right of the NP. Transformations are responsible for the generation of infinitely many phrase markers not generated directly by the phrase-structure rules, and as such contribute to the open-endedness and creativity that characterize all languages.

Because of its generality the particle movement transformation would apply to the phrase markers underlying all the sentences in (42), to give derived phrase markers that correspond (in the linear ordering of the nodes) to the sentences in (43):

(42) (a) Aladdin cleaned up his lamps.
  (b) A cow kicked over the bucket.
  (c) The guys brought in the beer.

(43) (a) Aladdin cleaned his lamps up.
  (b) A cow kicked the bucket over.
  (c) The guys brought the beer in.

We have presented only a fraction of the transformational formalism that has developed since 1957. Our purpose has been to provide a brief introduction to formal syntactic theory for those readers who wish to read further in the field and who may encounter this formalism in other works.

Ambiguity Revisited

THE WIZARD OF ID   **Brant Parker and Johnny Hart**

By permission of Johnny Hart and Field Enterprises, Inc.

The rules of syntax account for all our knowledge of sentence structure. In particular they account for our ability to recognize sentences that are structurally ambiguous, as we saw in the earlier discussion of "synthetic buffalo hides." Each "reading" of the expression *synthetic buffalo hides* is represented by a different phrase marker. Further examples of this kind of ambiguity are illustrated by such sentences as

(44) Mary and Joe or Bill frightened the sheepdog.

This sentence has the two meanings shown in (45a) and (45b):

(45) (a) Mary and Joe frightened the sheepdog or Bill frightened it.
(b) Mary and Joe frightened the sheepdog or Mary and Bill frightened it.

The double meaning of sentence (44) is not due to any ambiguous words, but rather to the fact that there are two different phrase-marker representations of (44) allowed by the rules of English syntax. These are shown in (46) and (47):

(46) Phrase-structure tree of sentence (44) as paraphrased by sentence (45a)

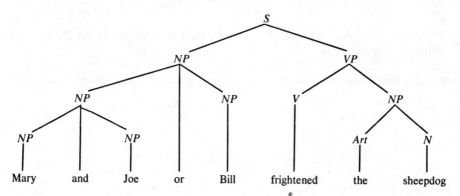

(47) Phrase-structure tree of sentence (44) as paraphrased by sentence (45b)

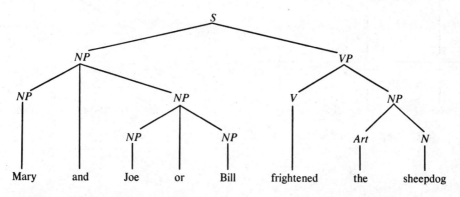

The ambiguity of (44), and the other examples of structural ambiguity we have studied so far, can all be accounted for by assigning to each meaning a different *surface structure* phrase marker. All structural ambiguity, however, cannot be represented this way.

Consider a sentence such as (48):

(48) The horse is ready to ride.

The two meanings correspond to (49a) and (49b):

(49) (a) The horse is ready to ride (in his trailer to the track).
(b) The horse is ready (for someone) to ride.

There is only one surface structure that can possibly correspond to (48) in either of its meanings, and that is (50):

(50)

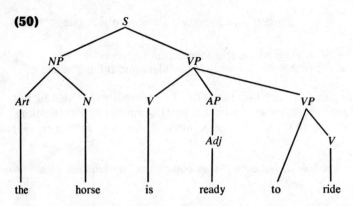

the   horse   is   ready   to   ride

To account for the fact that (48) is syntactically ambiguous we assign two different phrase markers to its *deep structure*, rather than to its surface structure. Here are the two deep structures. (Don't worry about the fact that you are unfamiliar with some of the rules that specify these phrase markers.)

(51) Deep structure of sentence (48) with the meaning of (49a)

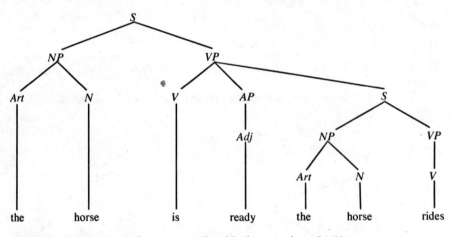

the   horse   is   ready   the   horse   rides

(52) Deep structure of sentence (48) with the meaning of (49b)

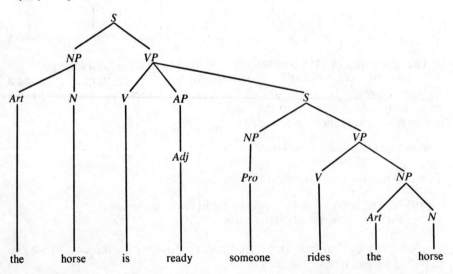

the   horse   is   ready   someone   rides   the   horse

The basic meaning difference between the two readings of (48) is explicitly revealed in the two deep structures. In (51), the fact that it is the horse that will do the riding is expressed in the subordinate clause (the embedded S) by making *horse* the subject of *ride*. In (52) *horse* is the object of *ride* in the embedded S, which corresponds to the fact that someone will ride the horse. Of course, in both cases *horse* is the subject of *ready*, which is shown by its being the first NP in both deep-structure trees.

As discussed in the previous section, transformational rules will relate the deep structure phrase markers in (51) and (52) to the corresponding surface structure, which in both cases is the same phrase marker, namely (50).

It may appear that there are two different kinds of structural ambiguity: one in which there are multiple surface-structure phrase markers, and the other in which there is a single surface-structure but multiple deep-structure phrase markers. In fact sentences that have multiple surface-structure phrase-marker representations also have multiple deep-structure phrase-marker representations that reflect the same kinds of differences present in surface structure. Structural ambiguity is always the result of the fact that the rules of syntax allow more than one phrase marker to underlie the same *string* of words in surface structure, irrespective of whether or not the structural differences are also revealed by the surface-structure phrase markers.

There are some differences between ambiguous sentences whose ambiguities are revealed in surface structure, and those whose ambiguities are revealed only in the underlying structure. The former can sometimes be disambiguated by pronouncing them one way or the other, depending on the intended meaning, whereas the latter usually cannot be so disambiguated. If you pronounce *synthetic buffalo* (pause) *hides,* the meaning is generally heard as "the hides of a 'synthetic' buffalo," whereas if you pronounce *synthetic* (pause) *buffalo hides,* it is most likely to be perceived as "buffalo hides that are synthetic." Further examples of ambiguous sentences whose ambiguities are revealed in surface structure (as well as deep structure) are as follows:

(53) They are moving sidewalks.
I know a man with a dog who has fleas.
They said she would go yesterday.

Some ambiguous sentences whose ambiguities are revealed only by their underlying structures are:

(54) It is too old to eat.
John loves Martha more than Dick.
We deplore the shooting of the hunters.

The ambiguities of such sentences as (48) or those in (54) could not be explained if sentences had only surface-structure representations. Underlying representations, which are needed independently of considerations of ambiguity, are the only way certain kinds of structural ambiguities can be revealed, and this is further support for the theory that allows underlying representations.

SUMMARY

Speakers of a language recognize the grammatical sentences of their language and know how the morphemes in a grammatical sentence must be arranged. All speakers are capable of producing and understanding an unlimited number of new sentences never before spoken or heard. They also recognize ambiguities, know when different sentences are paraphrases, and correctly perceive the grammatical relations in a sentence. All this knowledge, and much more, is accounted for in the grammar by the **rules of syntax.**

Sentences have structure and can be represented by **constituent-structure** trees whose nodes are labeled with **syntactic-category** names. Such a representation is called a **phrase marker** and reveals three kinds of structural information about sentences:

1. Linear order of words;
2. Grouping of words into structural constituents;
3. The syntactic category of each structural constituent.

Linguists often describe sentences in terms of phrase markers.

Speakers have much knowledge of the words and morphemes of their language. This knowledge is contained in the **lexicon.** The lexicon contains information about the meaning and pronunciation of every word and morpheme. In addition each lexical item is specified as to its syntactic category ("part of speech") and its **co-occurrence restrictions.** For example, a **transitive** verb must be followed by a noun phrase, but an **intransitive** must not.

Speakers know when two sentences are related to each other. For example, the declarative sentence *John can go* is related to its corresponding yes—no question *Can John go?* in a regular way that can be expressed informally by a rule. Such rules necessarily make reference to constituent structure and such structural notions as "highest S." We therefore conclude that such structural information must be present in the grammar.

There is no longest sentence in any language. Speakers of a language can always make any sentence longer. To account for this aspect of language phrase markers can be **recursive structures:** constituents of the same category may **recur** within the same phrase marker allowing the size of phrase markers to be potentially unlimited, hence the length of sentences to be likewise.

A grammar of a language is an explicit characterization of all the rules of that language. When a grammar accounts for sentences in a totally explicit way it is called a **generative grammar.** Generative grammars account equally well for the production and the comprehension of sentences. To be explicit, rules must be stated formally. Phrase-structure rules are formal statements as to what kinds of basic or underlying phrase markers are allowed. A phrase-structure rule is always of the form

$$A \rightarrow B_1 \cdots B_n \qquad \text{(where } n \text{ is 2 or more)}$$

and means two things:

(a) The category A **may be** a B_1 followed by a B_2 . . . followed by a B_n.

(b) A B_1 followed by a B_2 . . . followed by a B_n **is always** an A.

To account for the occurrence of **recursive structures,** phrase-structure rules can be **recursive.** A single phrase-structure rule is recursive if the category to the left of the arrow is mentioned on the right of the arrow. A set of phrase-structure rules is recursive if there are two categories, each mentioned on the left and right sides of the arrows of two or more rules. Recursive rules reflect the fact that there is no upper limit to sentence length, and therefore the sentences of the language are an infinite set. This helps to account for the open-endedness and creativity that all speakers of all languages exhibit.

Some kinds of sentences must be represented by multiple phrase markers, for example sentences that exhibit **discontinuous dependencies.** One phrase marker reveals the underlying constituent structure, and the other reveals the linear order of words as the sentence is actually pronounced. The two phrase markers are related by a **structural operation** called a **transformation.** The notion that multiple phrase markers, related in a pairwise fashion to each other by transformations, can represent a single sentence is the basis of **transformational grammar.** Any phrase marker to which a transformation applies is called an **underlying structure.** The **deep structure** is a special underlying structure: it is the first phrase marker to which any transformation applies, and itself is not the result of a transformation. The **surface structure** is the end result of the application of transformations. No further transformation applies to it, but the pronunciation of the sentence is based on the surface structure.

Structurally ambiguous sentences such as *The horse is ready to ride* are accounted for in the grammar by assigning different deep-structure phrase markers, one for each meaning. Some kinds of ambiguous sentences such as *They sell synthetic buffalo hides* also have different surface-structure phrase markers that reveal each meaning.

The syntax of human language is sufficiently complex to require phrase-structure rules, a lexicon, and transformations to account for speakers' knowledge.

EXERCISES

1. We stated that the rules of syntax specify all and only the grammatical sentences of the language. Why is it important to say "only"? That is, what would be wrong with a grammar that specified as grammatical sentences all of the truly grammatical ones plus a few that were not grammatical?

2. Besides distinguishing grammatical from ungrammatical strings, the rules of syntax account for other kinds of linguistic knowledge such as
   a. When a sentence is structurally ambiguous.
   b. When two sentences are paraphrases.
   c. What the grammatical relations are in sentences.

(*Exercise 2 continued on p. 240*)

(*Exercise 2 continued from p. 239*)
   In each case a–c, draw on your own linguistic knowledge of English to provide an example different than the ones we presented, and explain why your example illustrates the point. If you know a language other than English, can you provide examples in that language?

3. Consider the following sentences:

   a. I hate war.
   b. You know that I hate war.
   c. He knows that you know that I hate war.
   A. Write another sentence that includes sentence *c*.
   B. What does this reveal about the nature of language?
   C. How is this characteristic of human language related to the difference between linguistic competence and performance?

4. Paraphrase each of the following sentences in two different ways to show that you understand the ambiguity involved:

   a. Smoking grass can be nauseating.
   b. Dick finally decided on the boat.
   c. The professor's appointment was shocking.
   d. Old men and women are hard to live with.
   e. That sheepdog is too hairy to eat.
   f. Could this be the invisible man's hair tonic?
   g. The governor is a dirty street fighter.
   h. I cannot recommend him too highly.
   i. Terry loves his wife and so do I.
   j. They said she would go yesterday.

5. Following the examples on pages 208–209 draw phrase markers for the surface structures of the following sentences:

   a. The puppy found the child.
   b. A frightened passenger landed the crippled airplane.
   c. He died.
   d. The ice melted.
   e. The hot sun melted the ice.
   f. A quaint old house appeared on the grassy knoll.
   g. The old tree swayed in the wind.
   h. The children put the toys in the large red box.

6. In all languages, sentences can occur within sentences. For example, in Exercise 3, sentence *b* contains sentence *a*, and sentence *c* contains sentence *b*; or sentence *a* is *embedded* in sentence *b*, and sentence *b* is embedded in sentence *c*. Sometimes embedded sentences appear slightly changed from their "normal" form, but you should be able to recognize and write down the embedded sentences in the sentences below:

   a. Becky said that Jake would play the piano.
   b. Yesterday I noticed my accountant repairing the toilet and my plumber computing my taxes.
   c. I deplore the fact that bats have wings.
   d. That Guinevere loves Lorian is known to all my friends.
   e. Who promised the teacher that Maxine wouldn't be absent?
   f. It's ridiculous that he washes his own Rolls-Royce.

   g. The woman asked for the waiter to bring a glass of ice water.
   h. The person who answers this question will win $100.
   i. The idea of Romeo marrying a 13-year-old is disconcerting.
   j. I gave my hat to the nurse who was helping me cut my hair.
   k. For your children to spend all your royalty payments on tuition is a shame.
   l. Give this fork to the person whom I'm getting the pie for.
   m. khăw   chỹa wăa   khruu   maa.
       he   believe   teacher come
       He believes the teacher is coming.
   n. Je me demande quand il   partira.
       I me ask   when he will leave
       I wonder when he'll leave.

7. Because languages have recursive properties there is no limit to the potential length of sentences, and the set of sentences of any language is infinite. Give two examples (different from the ones in the text) of:

   A. Adjective recursion
   B. Noun recursion
   C. Noun phrase recursion
   D. Verb phrase recursion
   E. Sentence recursion

In one example the relevant category should appear twice in the phrase marker and in the other example at least three times. Diagram one of the phrase markers in each case, being careful to illustrate the recursion.

8. Co-occurrence restrictions ensure that a verb is surrounded by the "right" constituents. For example, a transitive verb like *find* must have a direct object NP. An intransitive verb like *fall* must not have a direct object NP. Many verbs "go both ways," so *melt* may or may not have a direct object: *The ice melted* or *The sun melted the ice.*

   A. Think of five verbs whose co-occurrence restrictions are similar to *fall*—that is, which are strictly intransitive.
   B. Think of five verbs whose co-occurrence restrictions are similar to *find*—that is, which are strictly transitive.
   C. Think of five verbs whose co-occurrence restrictions are similar to *melt*—that is, which take an optional direct object. What do you notice *semantically* about verbs like *melt* insofar as the semantic properties of its subject and object are concerned when the verb is transitive and when the verb is intransitive? (Hint: concentrate on the semantic properties of the object when the verb is transitive, and of the subject when the verb is intransitive.)

9. Consider these pairs of related sentences:

The parent gave the money to the child.
The parent gave the child the money.

I wrote a letter to the senator.
I wrote the senator a letter.

   A. Using a different verb, think up another such pair.
   B. State as precisely as possible in terms of constituent structure the rule that relates the sentences. (Some linguists call this rule "*dative shift.*")

10. Here is a set of made-up phrase-structure rules. The "initial symbol" is still S, and the "terminal symbols" (that is, the ones that don't appear to the left of an arrow) are actual words:

  (i) S → A B C
  (ii) A → the
  (iii) B → children
  (iv) C → ran
  (v) C → C and D
  (vi) D → ran and D
  (vii) D → ran

  A. Give three phrase-structure trees that these rules characterize.
  B. How many phrase-structure trees could these rules characterize? How do you know? (Hint: Look for recursive rules.)

11. Using the convention that parentheses mean "optional element," and each line contained in braces can occur separately to the right of the arrow, expand the following collapsed phrase-structure rules into the individual rules that they abbreviate:

  A. $VP \rightarrow V \begin{Bmatrix} (NP) & (PP) \\ S & \end{Bmatrix}$

  B. $A \rightarrow \begin{Bmatrix} B & (A) \\ C & E & F \\ (H) & D \end{Bmatrix}$

  C. $AUX \rightarrow T \ (M) \ (have) \ (be)$

12. Using the abbreviatory conventions of the previous exercise, collapse the following sets of rules into a single rule.

A.	B.	C.
A → A B	A → B	W → X
A → B	A → C	W → X Y
	C → D	W → Y Z
		W → X Y Z

REFERENCES

Akmajian, A., R. A. Demers, and R. M. Harnish. 1979. *Linguistics: An Introduction to Language and Communication.* M.I.T. Press. Cambridge, Mass.

Chomsky, Noam. 1957. *Syntactic Structures.* Mouton. The Hague.

Chomsky, Noam. 1965. *Aspects of the Theory of Syntax.* M.I.T. Press. Cambridge, Mass.

Chomsky, Noam. 1972. *Language and Mind,* rev. ed. Harcourt Brace Jovanovich. New York.

Culicover, Peter. 1976. *Syntax.* Academic Press. New York.

Newmeyer, Frederick J. 1981. *Linguistic Theory in America: The First Quarter Century of Transformational-Generative Grammar.* Academic Press. New York.

Stockwell, R. P. 1977. *Foundations of Syntactic Theory.* Prentice-Hall. Englewood Cliffs, N.J.

Stockwell, R. P., M. Bean, and D. Elliot. 1977. *Workbook for Foundations of Syntactic Theory.* Prentice-Hall. Englewood Cliffs, N.J.

PART THREE

Social Aspects of Language

The distribution of human beings into races and tribes and the variation in their languages and dialects are certainly closely related, but both of these result primarily from the productivity of human intellectual power in all its forms.

Wilhelm von Humboldt (1765–1835), *Linguistic Variability & Intellectual Development*

Children raised in isolation do not use language; it is used by human beings in a social context, communicating their needs, ideas, and emotions to one another . . .

William Labov, *Sociolinguistic Patterns*

Chapter 8

Language in Society

Dialects

I have noticed in traveling about the country a good many differences in the pronunciation of common words. . . . Now what I want to know is whether there is any right or wrong about this matter. . . . If one way is right, why don't we all pronounce that way and compel the other fellow to do the same? If there isn't any right or wrong, why do some persons make so much fuss about it?

Letter quoted in "The Standard American" in J. V. Williamson and V. M. Burke, eds., *A Various Language*

All speakers of English can talk to each other and pretty much understand each other. Yet no two speakers speak exactly alike. Some differences are due to age, sex, state of health, size, personality, emotional state, and personal idiosyncrasies. That each person speaks somewhat differently from all others is shown by our ability to recognize acquaintances by hearing them talk. The unique characteristics of the language of an individual speaker are referred to as the speaker's **idiolect.** English may then be said to consist of 400,000,000 idiolects, or the number equal to the number of speakers of English.

Beyond these individual differences, the language of a group of people may show regular variations from that used by other groups of speakers of that language. When the English spoken by speakers in different geographical regions and from different social groups shows *systematic* differences, the groups are said to speak different **dialects** of the same language. The *dialects* of a single language may thus be defined as mutually intelligible forms of that language which differ in systematic ways from each other.

It is not always easy to decide whether the systematic differences between two speech communities reflect two dialects or two different languages. A rule-of-thumb definition can be used: "When dialects become mutually unintelligible—when the speakers of one dialect group can no longer understand the speakers of another dialect group—these 'dialects' become different languages." But to define "mutually intelligible" is itself a difficult task. Danes speaking Danish and Norwegians speaking Norwegian and Swedes speaking Swedish can converse with each other. Yet Danish and Norwegian and Swedish are considered separate languages because they are spoken in separate countries that are distinct political nations and because there are regular

245

differences in their grammars. Similarly, Hindi and Urdu are mutually intelligible "languages" spoken in Pakistan and India, although the differences between them are not much greater than the English spoken in America and the English spoken in England (or parts of England) and the English spoken in Australia. On the other hand, the various languages spoken in China such as Mandarin and Cantonese have been referred to as "dialects" of Chinese because they are spoken within a single country and have a common writing system, although in spoken form they are mutually unintelligible.

Since neither mutual intelligibility nor the existence of political boundaries is decisive, it is not surprising that a clear-cut distinction between language and dialects has evaded linguistic scholars. We shall, however, use the rule-of-thumb definition and refer to dialects of one language as mutually intelligible versions of the same basic grammar, with systematic differences between them.

However "dialect" is defined, what is certain is that systematic variations do occur within a language community, as pointed out by William Bright:[1]

> Within any recognizable speech community, variations are normally found on all levels of linguistic structure—phonological, grammatical, and lexical. Some of the variations are correlated with geographical location . . . some . . . may . . . depend on the identity of the person spoken to or spoken about . . . Other variations are correlated with the identity of the speaker. These include cases of difference between men's and women's speech . . . linguistic variation may also be correlated with the social status of the speakers [or] . . . with other facts in the social and cultural context (p. 32).

REGIONAL DIALECTS AND ACCENTS

The educated Southerner has no use for an r *except at the beginning of a word.*
Mark Twain, *Life on the Mississippi*

Dialectal diversity tends to increase proportionately to the degree of communicative isolation between the groups. **Communicative isolation** refers to a situation such as existed between America, Australia, and England in the eighteenth century. There was some contact through commerce and emigration, but an Australian was less likely to talk to an Englishman than to another Australian. Today the isolation is less pronounced because of the mass media and jet airplanes. But even within one country, regionalisms persist. Children learn the language spoken to them and reinforce the unique features characteristic of the dialect used.

The changes that occur in the language spoken in one area are not necessarily spread to another area. Within a single group of speakers who are in regular contact with one another, the changes are spread among the group and "relearned" by their children. When some communication barrier separates groups of speakers—be it a physical barrier such as an ocean or a mountain range, or social barriers of a political, racial, class, or religious kind—linguistic changes are not easily spread and dialectal differences are reinforced.

Dialect changes in the grammar do not take place all at once within the

[1] W. Bright. 1976. *Variation and Change in Language: Essays by William Bright.* A. S. Dil. ed. Stanford University Press. Stanford, California.

speech community. Rather, they take place gradually, often originating in one region and slowly spreading to others, and often taking place throughout the lives of several generations of speakers.

A change that occurs in one region and fails to spread to other regions of the language community gives rise to the **dialect differences** we have referred to. When enough such differences give the language spoken in a particular region (for example, the city of Boston or the Brooklyn section of New York) its own "flavor," that version of the language is referred to as a **regional dialect.** The phonological or phonetic distinctions are often referred to as different **accents.** A person is said to have a Boston accent, a Southern accent, a Brooklyn accent, a Midwestern drawl, and so on. Thus, *accent* refers to the characteristics of speech that convey information about the speaker's dialect—that reveal if the speaker comes from a certain part of the country, or belongs to a particular sociolinguistic group, or grew up in another country. Americans often refer to someone as having a British accent or an Australian accent; in Britain they refer to an American accent. The term *accent* is also used to refer to the speech of someone who speaks a language non-natively; for example, a French person speaking English is described as having a French accent. *Accent* most often is used to refer to phonological differences or *"interference"* from a different dialect or second language.

A humorous *Language Guide to Brooklyn* illustrates the pronunciation characteristics of a Brooklyn accent:

earl: a lubricant
oil: an English nobleman
tree: the numeral that precedes four
doze: the ones yonder
fodder: male parent

A similar glossary was published to "translate" a Southern dialect:

sex: one less than seven, two less than eh-et, three less than noine, foe less than tin.

American regional dialects are a constant source of humor. A sports writer, Jim Murray, discussing the Southern regional dialect in a column entitled "Berlitz of the South," begins: "When the North conquered the South in the late unpleasantness between the two, it tore down the rebel flag, broke up the Confederacy, sent the carpetbaggers in, but it never could do much about the language."[2] He then provides "a few common translations you may want to have" if you are ever in the South, including:

watt: primary color, as in "the flag is raid, watt, and blue"
height: where you don't like someone
pa: something good to eat
bike: what you do with a pa
mine: principal or chief
mane: Homo sapiens, your best friend is your mine mane
rod: what you do in auto

[2] Los Angeles *Times*, April 5, 1973.

These regional dialects tell us a great deal about how languages change, which will be discussed at greater length in the next chapter. But it is interesting to note here that the origins of many regional dialects of English can be traced to the people who first settled America. To a great extent, the varieties of American English arose from the English spoken in southern England in the seventeenth and eighteenth centuries.

An example of how regional dialects developed may be illustrated by examining changes in the pronunciation of words with an *r*.

The English colonists who first settled this country pronounced an *r* wherever it was spelled. In the seventeenth century, Londoners and Jamestowners pronounced *farm* as [farm] and *father* as [faðər]. By 1800 the citizens of London no longer pronounced *r* in places where it was formerly pronounced; an *r* was now pronounced only when it occurred before vowels. *Farm* had become [fa:m] and *father* [fa:ðə] and *far* [fa:]. In New England and along the Southern Atlantic Seaboard, close commercial (and linguistic) ties with England were maintained. In these areas, American English reflected the same "*r*-dropping" that occurred in England, but in other regions the change did not enter the language, which is why most Americans today

Table 8-1 Comparison between Seventeenth- and Nineteenth-Century London English

Seventeenth-century London	Nineteenth-century London
1. *r* was pronounced wherever it was spelled: *farm* [farm], *father* [faðər], *farther* [farðər] (Standard American English of today retains this pronunciation)	1. *r* was only pronounced when it occurred before a vowel: *farm* [fa:m], *father* [fa:ðə], *farther* [fa:ðə] (In New England and the South, a similar change occurred)
2. The vowel in words like *half, last, path,* and *laugh* was [æ] (This is the vowel still used in these words in Standard American)	2. The vowel [æ] in these words changed to the back vowel [a:] (A similar change occurred in New England: *laugh*: British [la:f], New England [laf]
3. The vowel in *due, duty, true* was a diphthong: *due* [dyu]	3. The diphthong was maintained except after *r* (The [yu] was also maintained in New England and the South; in Standard American the [yu] became [u] after an alveolar: *due* [du])
4. The *h* in *which, when, what, where* signified a voiceless *w* /ʍ/; *which* contrasted with *witch* (The contrast was maintained in areas of the Midwest and West)	4. The voiceless /ʍ/ was lost; all *wh* words were pronounced with a voiced /w/; *which* and *witch* became homophones (This change spread to many regions of America)
5. Words like *laboratory, dictionary, cemetery* were given both primary and secondary stress: *laboratory* [læbərətòri] (American dialects preserved this stress pattern)	5. Secondary stress was lost in some of these words with subsequent syllable loss, and stress shifted to the second syllable: *laboratory* [ləbórətri]

pronounce *r* before consonants as did our English ancestors two hundred years ago.

By the time of the American Revolution, there were three major dialect areas in America: the Northern dialect spoken in New England and around the Hudson River; the midland dialect spoken in Pennsylvania; and the Southern dialect. These dialects differed from each other, and from the English spoken in England, in systematic ways. Some of the changes that occurred in British English spread to America; others did not. Pioneers from all three dialect areas spread westward. The intermingling of their dialects "leveled" or "submerged" many of their dialectal differences, which is why the English used in large sections of the Midwest and the West is very similar. Many of the features that characterized seventeenth-century British persisted in the States long after they were changed in England, as is shown in Table 8-1.

Other regional changes took place in the United States, further separating American regional "accents." In the Southern dialect, for example, when the *r* was dropped it was replaced by a "schwa-like" glide: *farm* is pronounced as two syllables [faəm], as are *four* [foə] and *poor* [poə]. This led Jim Murray to end his column cited above with the admonition: "Also remember, there is no such thing as a one-syllable word." This, of course, is not so, as his own examples show, but it is true that many words which are monosyllabic in Standard American are disyllabic in the Southern dialect: the word *right*, pronounced as [rayt] in the Midwest, New England, and the Middle Atlantic states and in British English, is pronounced [raət] in many parts of the South.

Regional dialects also may differ in the words people use for the same object. Hans Kurath, an eminent American dialectologist, opens his paper "What Do You Call It?" by asking: "Do you call it a *pail* or a *bucket?* Do you draw water from a *faucet* or from a *spigot?* Do you pull down the *blinds,* the *shades,* or the *curtains* when it gets dark? Do you *wheel* the baby, or do you *ride* it or *roll* it? In a *baby carriage,* a *buggy,* a *coach,* or a *cab?*"[3] One takes a *lift* to the *first floor* (our *second floor*) in England, but an *elevator* in America; one gets five gallons of *petrol* (not *gas*) in London; in Britain a *public school* is "private" (you have to pay) and if a student showed up there wearing *pants* ("underpants") instead of *trousers* he would be sent home to get dressed. If you ask for a *tonic* in Boston you will get a drink called a *soda* or *soda-pop* in Los Angeles, and a *freeway* in Los Angeles is a *thruway* in New York, a *parkway* in New Jersey, a *motorway* in England, and an *expressway* or *turnpike* in other dialect areas.

Kurath produced **dialect maps,** on which dialect differences were geographically plotted. For instance, he might use black dots to mark every village whose speakers retained the voiceless *w* pronunciation of *wheelbarrow,* and a white dot where voiced *w* was pronounced. Often in such cases, the black dots fall together, as do the white dots. These define dialect areas. When a line can be drawn on the map between the areas, it is called an **isogloss.** When you "cross" an isogloss, you are passing from one dialect area to another. Sometimes several isoglosses will coincide, usually at a political

---

[3] Hans Kurath, 1971. "What Do You Call It?" in Juanita V. Williamson and Virginia M. Burke, eds. *A Various Language: Perspective on American Dialects* (Holt, Rinehart and Winston. New York.)

boundary, or at a natural boundary such as a river or mountain range. Linguists call these a **bundle of isoglosses,** and the regional dialects thereby defined are particularly distinctive.

Systematic syntactic differences also distinguish dialects. In most American dialects sentences may be conjoined as follows:

John will eat and Mary will eat → John and Mary will eat.

But in the Ozark dialect this transformation is also possible:

John will eat and Mary will eat → John will eat and Mary.

Some American speakers use *gotten* in a sentence such as *He should have gotten to school on time;* in British English, only the form *got* occurs. In a number of American dialects the pronoun *I* occurs when *me* would be used in British English and in other American dialects.

Am.	between you and I	*Br.*	between you and me
Am.	Won't he permit you and I to swim?	*Br.*	Won't he permit you and me to swim?

In British English a syntactic transformation permits the deletion of the pronoun in the sentence *I could have done it* to form *I could have done,* which is not permitted in the American grammar.

With all such differences we still are able to understand the speakers of another dialect. Even though regional dialects differ as to pronunciation, vocabulary, and syntactic rules, these are minor differences when compared with the totality of the grammar. The largest part of the vocabulary, the sound-meaning relations of words, and the syntactic rules, are shared, which is why the dialects are mutually intelligible.

THE "STANDARD"

We don't talk fancy grammar and eat anchovy toast. But to live under the kitchen doesn't say we aren't educated.
Mary Norton, *The Borrowers*

Standard English is the customary use of a community when it is recognized and accepted as the customary use of the community. Beyond this . . . is the larger field of good English, any English that justifies itself by accomplishing its end, by hitting the mark.
George Philip Krapp, *Modern English: Its Growth and Present Use*

Even though every language is a composite of dialects, many people talk and think about a language as if it were a "well-defined" fixed system with various dialects diverging from this norm.

Mario Pei, a professor of Romance languages and the author of a number of books on language that were quite popular at one time, supported such a view. In his discussion of *Webster's Third New International Dictionary,* published in 1961, Pei[4] accused the editors of the dictionary of confusing "to the point of obliteration the older distinction between standard, substan-

[4] M. Pei. "A Loss for Words." *Saturday Review,* November 14, 1964, pp. 82–84.

dard, colloquial, vulgar, and slang." Pei attributed to the editors the view that "Good and bad, right and wrong, correct and incorrect no longer exist" (p. 82).

In light of our discussion in Chapter 1, it is obvious that Pei was a *prescriptive* rather than a *descriptive* grammarian. Prescriptive grammarians, or language "purists," usually consider the dialect used by political leaders and the upper socioeconomic classes, the dialect used for literature or printed documents, the dialect taught in the schools and propagated by the mass media, as the *correct* form of the language.

But how does one dialect become so prestigious? Once a dialect gets a head start, it often builds up momentum. The more "important" it gets, the more it is used; the more it is used, the more important it becomes. Such a dialect may be that spoken in the political or cultural center of a country and may spread into other regions. The dominance in France of the Parisian dialect, and in England (to a lesser extent) of the London dialect, is attributable to this cause.

The ridiculousness of the view that a particular dialect is better than any other was revealed by the great Danish linguist Otto Jesperson[5] when he wrote: "We set up as the best language that which is bound in the best writers, and count as the best writers those that best write the language. We are therefore no further advanced than before."

The dominant or prestige dialect is often called the **standard dialect. Standard American English (SAE)** is a dialect of English that many Americans *almost* speak; divergences from this "norm" are labeled "Philadelphia dialect," "Chicago dialect," "Black English," and so on.

SAE is an idealization. Nobody speaks this dialect, and if somebody did, we wouldn't know it because SAE is not defined precisely. Several years ago there actually was an entire conference devoted to one subject: a precise definition of SAE. This convocation of scholars did not succeed in satisfying everyone as to what SAE should be. The best hint we can give you is to listen to national broadcasters (though nowadays some of these people may speak a regional dialect).

When two languages are compared, it is necessary to compare one of the dialects of each language. The "standards" are usually used. When American and British English are compared, SAE and the British spoken by educated British people, called Received Pronunciation (RP),[6] are the dialects used for this purpose. The standard dialect is taught to nonnative speakers and is usually the most widespread; speakers of all dialects usually understand it easily even if they do not use it. Speakers of different dialects use the standard as the written form, since this dialect is the accepted literary language.

In France, a notion of the "standard" as the only correct form of the language is propagated by an official academy of "scholars" who determine what usages constitute the "official French language." This Academy enacted a law forbidding the use of "Franglais" words in advertising (words of English origin like *le parking*). The Parisian dialect is considered the "standard" at the expense of the hundreds of local village dialects (called *patois*

[5] O. Jesperson. 1925 (reprinted, 1964). *Mankind, Nation and Individual.* Indiana University Press. Bloomington.

[6] Received Pronunciation (commonly called RP) is the British pronunciation that is "received" (accepted as "proper") at the royal court.

[patwa] by the Academy). Many of these *patois* are actually separate languages, derived from Latin (as are French, Spanish, and Italian). In the past (and to some extent in the present) a Frenchman or Frenchwoman from the provinces who wished to succeed in French society nearly always had to be bidialectal. In recent years in France the regional "nationalist" movements have placed as a major demand the right to use their own languages in their schools and for official business. In the section of France known as l'Occitanie, the popular singers sing in the regional language, Languedoc, both as a protest against the official "standard language" policy and as part of the cultural revival movement. One of the most popular of these singers, Marti, has recorded a very popular song concerned with just this question. The final chorus in Languedoc, French, and English reveals this:

LANGUEDOC	FRENCH	ENGLISH
Mas perqué, perqué	Mais pourquoi, pourquoi	But why, why
M'an pas dit à	Ne m'a-t-on pas dit à	Did they not speak to
l'escóla	l'école	me at school
La lenga de mon pais?	La langue de mon pays?	The language of my country?

In the province of Brittany in France there is also a strong movement for the use of Breton in the schools, as opposed to the "standard" French. Breton is not even in the same language family as French, which is a Romance language like Italian, Spanish, and Portuguese deriving from Latin; Breton is a Celtic language in the group with Irish, Gaelic, and Welsh. We will discuss such family groupings in Chapter 9. It is not, however, the structure of the language or the genetic family grouping that has led to the popularity of the Breton singer Gilles Servat in Brittany and in other sections of France where this Breton movement is supported. It is rather the pride of a people who speak a language or a dialect not considered as good as the "standard," and their efforts to change this political view of language use.

Those who interpret "standard" literally and consider other dialects as inferior are not confined to Paris. Although a standard dialect is in no *linguistic* way "superior," we still find self-appointed guardians of "the purity of the language" in practically all countries, and certainly in the United States.

In April 1977 the State Transportation Director of California became incensed because she would receive memos that she believed included "improper" English. She sent a memorandum to all the employees of the Department of Transportation: "I would . . . like to point out two words which are frequently used around here are plural and not singular; those words are 'criteria' and 'data.'" She goes on to say she hopes never again to see these incorrectly used. The problem of course is that language changes but such change does not mean corruption. For the great majority of American English speakers, *criteria* and *data* are now mass nouns, like *information*. Information can include one fact or many facts, but one would still say "The information is. . . ." For some speakers it is equally correct to say "The criteria is . . ." or "The criteria are. . . ." Those who say "The data are . . ." would or could say "The datum (singular) is. . . ."

A difficulty faced by those who wish to dictate the correct forms of words and syntax is that it is not always clear, even to the users of standard language, which forms are correct. A letter from a farmer to a zoo, described in an article in the Los Angeles *Times,* reveals this confusion:[7]

> Would you send me a couple of mongooses to kill off the snakes on my farm?"
> That didn't sound right and he began again: "Would you send me a couple of mongeeses. . . ?"
> That didn't sound right, either, and, on the third try, this plain man of the land found the answer to a dilemma that has been vexing linguists for centuries:
> "Would you send me a mongoose to kill off the snakes on my farm? And, while you're at it, you might as well send me another one."

The idea that language change equals corruption goes back at least as far as the Greek grammarians at Alexandria, circa 100–200 B.C. They were concerned that the Greek spoken in their time was different from the Greek of Homer, and they believed that the earlier forms were purer. They also tried to "correct" the imperfections but failed as miserably as do any modern counterparts. Similarly, the Moslem Arabic grammarians in the eighth and ninth centuries A.D. working at Basra attempted to purify Arabic in order to restore it to the perfection of the Koran Arabic.

A standard dialect (or prestige dialect) may have social functions—to bind people together or to provide a common written form for multidialectal speakers. It is, however, neither more expressive, more logical, more complex, nor more regular than any other dialect. Any judgments, therefore, as to the superiority or inferiority of a particular dialect are social judgments, not linguistic or scientific ones.

BLACK ENGLISH

> *For some blacks and some whites (notice the infamous all has been omitted) it is not a matter of you say e-ther and we say i-ther, but rather:*
> *. . . You kiss your children, and we give 'em some sugar. . . . You cook a pan of spinach, and we burn a mess of greens. You wear clothes, and we wear threads. . . . You call the police, and we drop a dime. You say wow! We say ain't that a blip. You care, love and hurt, and we care, love and hurt. The differences are but a shade.*
> Sandra Haggerty, "On Digging the Difference" (Los Angeles *Times,* April 2, 1973)

LUTHER   **Brumsic Brandon, Jr.**

© 1982, Los Angeles Times Syndicate. Reprinted with permission

[7] Los Angeles *Times,* April 17, 1977.

While the majority of U.S. dialects are free from stigma to a great extent, especially the many regional dialects, one dialect of North American English has been a victim of prejudicial ignorance. This is the dialect spoken by a large section of non-middle-class U.S. blacks; it is usually referred to as Black English (BE) or Negro English or Nonstandard Negro English. The distinguishing features of this English dialect persist for social, educational, and economic reasons. The historical discrimination against black Americans[8] has created ghetto living and segregated schools. Where social isolation exists, dialect differences are intensified. In addition, particularly in recent years, many blacks no longer consider their dialect to be inferior and it has become a means of positive black identification.

Since the onset of the civil-rights movement in the 1960s, Black English has been the focus of national attention. There are those who attempt to equate the use of Black English with inferior "genetic" intelligence and "cultural deprivation," and justify these incorrect notions by stating that BE is a "deficient, illogical, and incomplete" language. Such epithets cannot be applied to any language and are as unscientific in reference to BE as to Russian, Chinese, or Standard American English. The cultural-deprivation myth is as false as the idea that some dialects or languages are inferior. A person may be "deprived" of one cultural background but very rich in another.

There are people, white and black, who think they can identify an unseen person's race by hearing him talk, believing that different races inherently speak differently. This assumption is equally false; a black child raised in an upper-class British household will speak RP English. A white child raised in an environment where Black English is spoken will speak Black English. Children construct grammars based on the language they hear.

There are, however, systematic differences between BE and SAE, just as there are systematic differences between Australian and American English. Dialect differences may show up in the phonological rules of the grammars. British grammar has a rule that can be stated as "Delete the /r/ except before a vowel." Black English has the same rule (as do some nonblack Southern dialects). Words like *guard* and *god, nor* and *gnaw, sore* and *saw, poor* and *pa, fort* and *fought,* and *court* and *caught* are pronounced identically in BE because of the presence of this phonological rule in the grammar.

Other words that do not rhyme in SAE do rhyme in BE: *yeah* and *fair, idea* and *fear.* In BE (and other Southern dialects) the "*r*-deletion" rule has been extended in some cases, so that it is also deleted between vowels. *Carol* is pronounced identically with *Cal,* and *Paris* with *pass.* It is possible, however, that in these words no deletion rule applies but the lexical representations of *Carol* and *Cal,* for example, are identical, without the *r*.

For some speakers of BE an "*l*-deletion" rule also occurs, creating homophones like *toll* and *toe, all* and *awe, help* and *hep* [hɛp]. (Again, some of these may not include the *l* as part of their phonological representations.)

A regular phonological rule in BE and not in SAE simplifies consonant clusters, particularly at the end of words and when one of the two consonants is an alveolar (/t/, /d/, /s/, /z/). The application of this rule may delete the past-tense morpheme so that *past* and *passed* (*pass + ed*) are both pronounced *pass.* When speakers of this dialect say *I pass the test yesterday,*

---

[8] As used here, "American" refers to the United States.

they are not showing an ignorance of past and present, but are pronouncing the past tense according to the rule present in their grammar:

"passed" /pæs + t/ → apply rule → [pæs]

Because of this consonant rule, *meant* and *mend* are both pronounced the same as *men*. And when combined with the "*l*-deletion" rule, *told, toll,* and *toe* have identical pronunciations.

	told	*toll*	*toe*
Phonemic Representation	/told/	/tol/	/to/
Consonant cluster simplification rule	ø	NA	NA
l-deletion rule	ø	ø	NA
Phonetic Representation	[to]	[to]	[to]

The merging of the past and present tense forms in words such as *pass* [pʰæs] and *passed* [pʰæs] is clearly due to a phonological deletion rule rather than a syntactic merging of tenses. The deletion rule is optional; it does not always apply, and studies have shown that it is more likely to apply when the final [t] or [d] does *not* represent the past tense morpheme, as in nouns like *past* [pʰæs] or *paste* [pʰes] as opposed to verbs like *passed* or *chased* where the final past tense [t] will not always delete. This has also been found true with final [s] or [z], which will be retained more often by speakers of BE in words like *seats* [sit + s] where the [s] represents "plural" than in words like *Keats* [kʰit] where it is more likely to be deleted.

There are other systematic differences between the phonology of BE and SAE. BE shares with many regional dialects the lack of any distinction between /ɪ/ and /ɛ/ before nasal consonants, producing identical pronunciations of *pin* and *pen*, *bin* and *Ben*, *tin* and *ten*, and so on. The vowel used in these words is roughly between the [ɪ] of *pit* and the [ɛ] of *pet*.

In BE the phonemic distinction between /ay/ and /aw/ has been lost, both having become /a/. Thus *why* and *wow* are pronounced [wa]. Another change has reduced the /ɔy/ (particularly before /l/) to the simple vowel [ɔ] without the glide, so that *boil* and *boy* are pronounced [bɔ]. One other regular feature is the change of a final /θ/ to /f/ so that *Ruth* is pronounced [ruf] and *death* [dɛf]. It is interesting that this [θ]–[f] correspondence also is true of some dialects of British English where, in fact, /θ/ is not even a phoneme in the language. *Think* is regularly /fiŋk/ in Cockney English.

Notice that these are all systematic changes and "rule-governed." The kinds of changes that have occurred are very similar to sound changes that have taken place in languages all over the world, including Standard English. Some dialects of Black English drop final nasal consonants. The preceding vowel, however, retains its nasalization, so the words end in nasalized vowels. (Note the rule in Standard English that nasalizes a vowel before a nasal consonant, discussed in Chapter 3.) This is precisely how French developed nasal vowels. Linguistic change caused final nasal consonants to be dropped, leaving behind a nasal vowel to distinguish the word.

Every dialect of every language has its own lexical items and its own phonological rules. The preponderance of likenesses of Black English to Standard English—the two dialects share most lexical forms and rules—is what makes the differences so conspicuous. If Black English were as incomprehensible as Russian, many Americans would probably have more respect for it.

Syntactic differences, as noted above, also exist between dialects. Linguists such as William Labov have investigated the syntactic structures of Black English. It is the syntactic differences that have often been used to illustrate the "illogic" of BE, and yet it is just such differences that point up the fact that BE is as syntactically complex and as "logical" as SAE.

Following the lead of early "prescriptive" grammarians, some "scholars" and teachers conclude that it is illogical to say *he don't know nothing* because two negatives make a positive. Since such negative constructions occur in BE, it has been concluded by some "educators" that speakers of BE are deficient because they use language "illogically." Consider the following sentences from BE and SAE:

	SAE	BE
Affirmative:	He knows something.	He know something.[9]
Negative:	He doesn't know anything.	He don't know nothing.
	He knows nothing.	He know nothing.
Affirmative:	He likes somebody.	He like somebody.
Negative:	He doesn't like anybody.	He don't like nobody.
	He likes nobody.	He like nobody.
Affirmative:	He has got some.	He got some.
Negative:	He hasn't got any.	He ain't got none.
	He's got none.	He got none.

In Black English when the verb is negated the indefinites *something, somebody,* and *some* become the negative indefinites *nothing, nobody,* and *none.* The rule is simple and elegant and of a type quite common in the world's languages. This was the rule that existed in earlier periods for all dialects of English. In Standard English, if the verb is negated the indefinites become *anything, anybody,* and *any.* If in the negative sentences in SAE the forms *nothing, nobody,* and *none* are used, then the verb is not negated. The speakers of both SAE and BE know how to negate sentences. The rules are essentially the same, but differ in detail. Both dialects are strictly rule-governed, as is every syntactic process of every dialect in the world.

It has also been said that BE is "illogical" because the copula (that is, the verb *to be*) is deleted in sentences such as *He nice.* Consider the following sentences from SAE and BE:

SAE	BE
He is nice/He's nice.	He nice.
They are mine/They're mine.	They mine.
I am going to do it/I'm gonna do it.	I gonna do it.

[9] As the examples in this list show, Black English also regularizes the present tense verb forms. In SAE the third person singular verb forms are inflected by adding to the verb the particular phonetic form that is the same as the plural ending (for example, [z] as in *loves* or *knows,* [s] as in *kicks,* or [əz] as in *kisses*). The absence of this ending in Black English may be the result of the application of phonological rules such as those discussed above.

Note that wherever the standard can use a contraction (he + is → he's), Black English can delete the copula. The following sentences, however, will show that where a contraction *cannot* be used in SAE, the copula *cannot* be deleted in BE:[10]

SAE	BE
*He is as nice as he says he's.	*He as nice as he say he.
*How beautiful you're.	*How beautiful you.
*Here I'm.	*Here I.

These examples further illustrate that syntactic rules may operate slightly differently from one dialect to another, but that the surface forms of the sentences are derived by rule—they are not strings of words randomly put together. It is interesting to note that many languages allow such copula deletion. In Russian the copula is never used in such sentences. In Swahili, *mimi ni mwanafunzi* "I am a student" is grammatical and so is *mimi mwanafunzi* "I a student" with the copula, *ni*, missing.

In BE, the possessive morpheme -'s is absent whenever possession is redundantly specified by word order:

SAE	BE	
That is John's house.	That John house.	
That is your house.	That you house.	
That house is John's.	That house John's.	
	(but not	*That house John.)
That house is yours.	That house yours.	
	(but not	*That house your.)

There is nothing "illogical" about the presence of such a rule; when word order suffices to indicate possession, the possessive ending is "superfluous."

Other BE sentences that are formed by syntactic rules different from those in the grammar of SAE are:

He done told me.
I been seen it.
I ain't like it.
I been washing the car.

These are not "corruptions" of the standard but dialect sentences that appear strange to nonspeakers of the dialect, although not as strange as the following sentence appears to a nonspeaker of French:

Il me l' a   donné.
he me it has given
He has given it to me.

There have also been studies of vocabulary differences between BE and SAE. Edith Folb[11] conducted a comparative study of Los Angeles urban

---

[10] Sentences taken from W. Labov. 1969. "The Logic of Nonstandard English" (Georgetown University, 20th Annual Round Table, No. 22).

[11] E. Folb. 1980. *Runnin' Down Some Lines: The Language and Culture of Black Teenagers.* Harvard University Press. Cambridge, Mass.

black and white vocabularies. She demonstrated that there is a class of words shared by blacks of various socioeconomic and social groups and by blacks in different sections of the city, such as Watts and Venice. She also found that there are differences among these groups that reveal differences of experience and outlook. Reed[12] points out that many of the terms Folb found in use in different black communities in Los Angeles could also be found in Chicago's Black Belt, New York's Harlem, or Boston's Roxbury section, pointing to a shared black lexicon across the country that he suggests "may owe something to modern communication between black groups." He adds, "A striking uniformity in basic characteristics . . . has evidently resulted from mass labor migration from specific areas of the South, beginning after World War I, but having its greatest impact following World War II."

There are many more differences between the grammars of BE and SAE than those we have discussed. But the ones we have listed are enough to show the "regularity" of BE and to dispel the notion that there is anything "illogical" or "primitive" about this dialect.

The study of Black English is important for linguists, of course, but it is also important for nonlinguists. When teachers in an American school teach French or German or Russian, we expect them to know both English and the language they are teaching. Yet in many schools in our country where the students are primarily speakers of Black English, instruction seldom if ever takes place in Black English. There is nothing wrong with attempting to teach the standard dialect in all schools for nonlinguistic reasons, but the standard will be learned much more easily by speakers of other dialects if teachers are aware of the systematic differences and permit children to use their own dialect to express themselves. Certainly, there would be less of a communication breakdown between students who speak Black English (not to mention other speakers of nonstandard dialects) and their teachers if these nonstandard dialects were not considered to be inferior versions of the standard. Children who read *your brother* as *you bruvver* are using their own pronunciation rules. They would be more likely to respond positively to the statement "In the dialect we are using, the "th" sound is not pronounced [v], as it is in yours" than they would be to a teacher who expressed an attitude of contempt toward their grammar. To give another example, when speakers of BE do not add the *-'s* in possessive phrases like *Mary hat* (instead of *Mary's hat*), an attempt to "correct" them which assumes that they do not understand possession as a *concept* creates serious problems for both the children and their teachers. The children know perfectly well what they mean, but their teachers may not know that they know, and the children do not know why the teachers cannot understand them and keep telling them they are "wrong." Thus, a linguistic study of the systematic differences between dialects may, hopefully, repair some of the damage that has been done in situations like these—whatever the motivations of those involved.

Another important reason for studying these dialects is that such study provides rich data for an understanding of the extent to which dialects differ

[12] C. E. Reed. 1977. *Dialects of American English,* revised edition. University of Massachusetts Press. Amherst, Mass.

and leads to a better knowledge of human language. Furthermore, the history of any dialect reveals important information about language change in general.

History of Black English Take the history of Black English as an example. It is simple enough to date its beginning—the first blacks arrived in Virginia in 1619. There are, however, different theories as to the factors that led to the systematic differences between Black English and other American English dialects.

One view suggests that the origins of Black English can be traced to the fact that the Negro slaves learned English from their white masters as a second language. The difficulties of second-language learning for an adult are all too clear to anyone who has attempted to do this. The basic grammar may be learned, but many surface differences persist. These differences, it is suggested, were reflected in the grammars constructed by the children of the slaves, since they heard English primarily from their parents. Had they been exposed to the English spoken by the whites as children, their grammars would have been less different from regular Southern speech. The dialect differences persisted and grew because the black in America was isolated by social and racial barriers as important as the geographic barriers that isolated the New Zealander from other English speakers. The proponents of this theory point to the fact that Black English and Standard American are basically identical in their deep structures; that is, they suggest that the phrase-structure rules are the same but transformational rules and phonological rules change sentences to produce surface differences.

A second view suggests that many of the particular features found in Black English are traceable to influences of the African languages spoken by the slaves. During the seventeenth and eighteenth centuries, Africans who spoke different languages were purposefully grouped together by the slave traders to discourage communication between the slaves, the idea being to prevent slave revolts. This theory suggests that in order to communicate with each other the slaves were forced to use the one common language all had access to, namely, English, and used a simplified form—called a *pidgin* —with various features from West African languages. According to this view, the differences between BE and other dialects are due more to "deep" syntactic differences than to surface distinctions.

That Black English is closer to the Southern dialect of English than to other dialects is quite apparent. This fact does not favor either of the opposing views. The theory which suggests that the Negro slaves imitated the English of their white Southern masters explains the similarities in this way. One might also explain the similarities by the fact that for many decades a large number of Southern white children were raised by black women and played with black children. It is not unlikely that many of the distinguishing features of Southern dialects were acquired from Black English in this way. A publication of the American Dialect Society in 1908–1909 makes this point clearly:

For my part, after a somewhat careful study of east Alabama dialect, I am convinced that the speech of the white people, the dialect I have spoken all my life and the one I tried to record here, is more largely colored by the language of the negroes than by any other single influence.[13]

The two-way interchange still goes on. Standard American English is constantly enriched by words, phrases, and usage originating in Black English, and Black English, whatever its origins, is one of the many dialects of English, influenced by the changes which go on in the other dialects.

LINGUA FRANCAS

Language is a steed that carries one into a far country.
Arab proverb

Many areas of the world are populated by people speaking divergent languages. In such areas, where groups desire social or commercial communication, one language is often used by common agreement. Such a language is called a **lingua franca.**

In medieval times, a trade language came into use in the Mediterranean ports. It consisted of Italian mixed with French, Spanish, Greek, and Arabic, and was called Lingua Franca, "Frankish language." The term *lingua franca* was generalized to other languages similarly used. Thus, any language can be a lingua franca.

English has been called "the lingua franca of the whole world," French, at one time, was "the lingua franca of diplomacy," and Latin and Greek were the lingua francas of Christianity in the West and East, respectively, for a millennium. Among Jews, Yiddish has long served as a lingua franca.

More frequently, lingua francas serve as "trade languages." East Africa is populated by hundreds of tribes, each speaking its own language, but most Africans of this area learn at least some Swahili as a second language, and this lingua franca is used and understood in nearly every marketplace. A similar situation exists in West Africa, where Hausa is the lingua franca.

Hindi and Urdu are the lingua francas of India and Pakistan, respectively. The linguistic situation of this area of the world is so complex that there are often regional lingua francas—usually the popular dialects near commercial centers. The same situation existed in Imperial China. An old Chinese saying still quoted today notes that two people separated by a blade of grass cannot understand each other. In modern China, the Chinese language as a whole is often referred to as *Zhongwen,* which technically refers to the written language, while *Zhongguo hua* refers to the spoken language. Ninety-four percent of the people living in the People's Republic of China are said to speak Han languages, which can be divided into eight major dialects (or language groups) that for the most part are mutually unintelligible. Within each group there are hundreds of dialects. In addition to these Han languages there are more than fifty "national minority" languages, including the five principal ones: Mongolian, Uighur, Tibetan, Zhuang, and Korean. The situation is clearly very complex and for this reason an extensive language reform policy was inaugurated in the People's Republic to spread a standard language, called Putonghua, which embodies the pronunciation of the Peking dialect, the grammar of Northern Chinese dialects, and the vocabulary of modern colloquial Chinese. The Linguistics Delegation spon-

---

[13] L. W. Payne, "A Word-List from East Alabama," *Dialect Notes.* 3:279–328, 343–391.

sored by the American Academy of Sciences, which visited the People's Republic in 1974, was very impressed by the program, which aims at making all Chinese conversant in Putonghua, as a second dialect or language. The native languages and dialects are not considered inferior; rather, the approach is to spread the "common speech" (the literal meaning of *putonghua*) so that all may communicate with each other in this lingua franca.[14]

Certain *lingua francas* arise naturally; others are developed due to government policy and intervention. In many places of the world, however, there are still areas where people cannot speak with neighbors only a few miles away.

PIDGINS AND CREOLES

> *Padi dɛm; kɔntri; una ɔl we de na Rom.*
> *Mɛk una ɔl kak una yes. A kam bɛr Siza,*
> *a nɔ kam prez am.*
> *Dɛn kin mɛmba bad we pɔsin kin du*
> *lɔŋtem afta pɔsin kin dɔn dai;*
> *bɔt plɛnti tɛm di gud we pɔsin du*
> *kin bɛr wit im bon dɛm.*
> *Mɛk i bi so wit Siza.*
> Julius Caesár III, ᵢᵢ, translated to Krio by Thomas Decker

A lingua franca is typically a language with a broad base of native speakers, likely to be used and learned by persons whose native language is in the same language family. Often in history, however, missionaries and traders from one part of the world have visited and attempted to communicate with peoples residing in another area. In such cases the contact is too specialized, and the cultures too widely separated for the usual kind of lingua franca to arise. Instead, the two (or possibly more) groups use their native languages as a basis for a rudimentary language of few lexical items and "straightforward" grammatical rules. Such a "marginal language" is called a *pidgin*.

A notable pidgin that exists today is called **Tok Pisin**. It was once called Melanesian Pidgin English. It is widely used in Papua, New Guinea. Like most pidgins, many of its lexical items and much of its structure are based on only one language of the two or more contact languages, in this case English. Tok Pisin has about 1,500 lexical items, of which about 80 percent are derived from English.

Although pidgins are in some sense rudimentary, they are not devoid of grammar. The phonological system is rule-governed, as in any human language. The inventory of phonemes is generally small, and each phoneme may have many allophonic pronunciations. In Tok Pisin, for example, [č], [š], and [s] are all possible pronunciations of the phoneme /s/; [masin], [mašin], and [mačin] all mean *machine*. When a New Guinean says [masin] and an Englishman says [mašin], the difference in Pidgin is nondistinctive and no more serious than the different *p*'s in *gap* [gæp] and [gæpʰ], that is, they are freely variant.

Although case, tense, mood, and voice are generally absent from pidgins (as from many nonpidgin languages), one cannot speak an English pidgin by

---

[14] For further information, see W. P. Lehmann, ed. 1975. *Language and Linguistics in the People's Republic of China* (Texas: Texas University Press. Austin.). One of the authors of this book, V. Fromkin, was a member of this delegation.

merely using English without inflecting verbs or declining pronouns. Pidgins are not "baby talk" or Hollywood "Injun talk." *Me Tarzan, you Jane* may be understood, but it is not pidgin as it is used in West Africa.

Pidgins are simple, but are rule-governed. In Tok Pisin, verbs that take a direct object must have the suffix -*m*, even if the direct object is absent in surface structure; this is a "rule" of the language:

Mi driman long kilim wanpela snek.
I dreamed that I killed a snake.

Bandarap em i kukim.
Bandarap cooked (it).

Other rules determine word order, which, as in English, is usually quite strict in pidgins because of the lack of case endings on nouns.

With their small vocabularies, pidgins are not very good at expressing fine distinctions of meaning. Many lexical items bear a heavy semantic burden, with context being relied upon to remove ambiguity. Much circumlocution and metaphorical extension is necessary. All of these factors combine to give pidgins a unique flavor. What could be a friendlier definition of friend than the Australian aborigine's *him brother belong me*, or more poetic than this description of the sun: *lamp belong Jesus*? A policeman is *gubmint catchum-fella*, whiskers are *grass belong face*, and when a man is thirsty *him belly allatime burn*. And who can top this classic announcement by a Chinese servant that his master's prize sow had given birth to a litter: *Him cow pig have kittens*?

Pidgin has come to have negative connotations, perhaps because the best-known pidgins are all associated with European colonial empires. The *Encyclopaedia Britannica* once described Pidgin English as "an unruly bastard jargon, filled with nursery imbecilities, vulgarisms and corruptions." It no longer uses such a definition, since in recent times there is greater recognition of the fact that pidgins reflect human creative linguistic ability. Tok Pisin has its own writing system, its own literature, and its own newspapers and radio programs, and it has even been used to address a United Nations meeting.

Some people would like to eradicate Tok Pisin. A pidgin spoken on New Zealand by the Maoris was replaced, through massive education, by Standard English, and the use of Chinese Pidgin English was forbidden by the government of China. It, too, has died out. Pidgins have been unjustly maligned; we must realize that they may serve a useful function. The linguist Robert A. Hall points out that a New Guinean can learn Tok Pisin well enough in six months to begin many kinds of semiprofessional training.[15] To learn English for the same purpose might require ten times as long. In an area with well over 500 mutually unintelligible languages, Tok Pisin plays a vital role in unifying similar cultures.

During the seventeenth, eighteenth, and nineteenth centuries many pidgins sprang up along the coasts of China, Africa, and the New World to accommodate the Europeans. Chinook Jargon is a pidginized American Indian language used by various tribes of the Pacific Northwest to carry on trade.

---

[15] Robert A. Hall. 1955. *Hands Off Pidgin English* (Pacific Publications. New South Wales.).

The original Lingua Franca was an Italian-based pidgin used in Mediterranean ports, and Malay, the language of Indonesia and Malaysia, has been highly influenced by a Dutch-based pidgin. Some linguists have even suggested that Proto-Germanic was originally a pidgin, arguing that ordinary linguistic change cannot account for certain striking differences between the Germanic tongues and other Indo-European languages. They theorized that in the first millennium B.C. the primitive Germanic tribes that resided along the Baltic Sea traded with the more sophisticated, seagoing cultures. The two people communicated by means of a pidgin, which either grossly affected Proto-Germanic, or actually became Proto-Germanic. If this is true, English, German, Dutch, and Yiddish had humble beginnings as a pidgin.

One distinguishing characteristic of pidgin languages is that no one learns them as native speakers. When a pidgin comes to be adopted by a community as its native tongue, and children learn it as a first language, that language is called a **creole**; the pidgin has become **creolized**. Creoles become fully developed languages, having more lexical items and a broader array of grammatical distinctions than pidgins. In time, they become languages as complete in every way as other languages.

Creoles often arose on slave plantations in certain areas where Africans of many different tribes could communicate only via the plantation pidgin. Haitian Creole, based on French, developed in this way, as did the "English" spoken in parts of Jamaica. Gullah is an English-based creole spoken by the descendants of African slaves on the islands off the coast of Georgia and South Carolina. Louisiana Creole, related to Haitian Creole, is spoken by large numbers of blacks and whites in Louisiana. Krio, the language spoken by as many as 200,000 Sierra Leoneans, developed, at least in part, from an English-based pidgin.

The development of pidgins with subsequent creolization may account for both a reduction in the number of the world's languages (for many languages may be replaced by a single Creole, as is happening today on New Guinea) and much of the linguistic diversity—the multiplicity of languages—in the world today.

Styles, Slang, and Jargon

Slang is language which takes off its coat, spits on its hands—and goes to work.
Carl Sandburg

STYLE

You were probably not surprised to learn that your language is "spoken differently" in the different parts of the world; dialects are a common phenomenon. But you may not be aware that you speak two or more "dialects" of your own language. When you are out with your friends, you talk one way; when you go on a job interview, you talk differently. These "situation dialects" are called **styles**.

Nearly everybody has at least an informal and a formal style. In an informal style the rules of contraction are used more often, the syntactic rules of negation and agreement may be altered, and many words are used that do not occur in the formal style. Many speakers have the ability to use a number of different styles, ranging between the two extremes of formal and informal. Speakers of minority dialects sometimes display virtuosic ability to slide back and forth along a continuum of styles that may range from the informal patterns learned in a ghetto to "formal standard." When William Labov was studying Black English used by Harlem youths he encountered difficulties because the youths (subconsciously) adopted a different style in the presence of white strangers. It took time and effort to gain their confidence to the point where they would "forget" that their conversations were being recorded and so use their normal style.

Many cultures have rules of social behavior that strictly govern style. In some Indo-European languages there is the distinction between "*you* familiar" and "*you* polite." German *du* and French *tu* are to be used only with "intimates"; *Sie* and *vous* are more formal and used with nonintimates. French even has a verb *tutoyer* which means "to use the 'tu' form," and German uses the verb *duzen* to express the informal, or less-honorific style of speaking.

Other languages have a much more elaborate code of style usage. In Thai one uses *kin* "eat" to his intimates, and very informally; but he uses *thaan* "eat" informally with strangers, and *rábpràthaan* on formal occasions or when conversing with dignitaries or esteemed persons (such as one's parents). Thai also has a style for talking about Buddhist monks. The verb "eat" is *chăn* when said of a monk. The ordinary third-person pronoun in Thai is *khăw* "he, she, it, they," but if the person referred to is a monk a Thai must use *thăn*. Japanese and Javanese are also languages with elaborate styles that must be adhered to in certain social situations.

One mark of an informal style is the frequent occurrence of **slang.** Almost everyone uses slang on some occasions, but it is not easy to define the word. One linguist has defined slang as "one of those things that everybody can recognize and nobody can define."[16] The use of slang, or colloquial language, introduces many new words into the language, by recombining old words into new meanings. *Spaced out, right on, hangup,* and *rip-off* have all gained a degree of acceptance. More rarely, slang will come up with an entirely new word for the language, such as *barf, flub,* and *pooped.* Slang often consists of using old words with totally new meanings ascribed to them. *Grass* and *pot* have widened their meaning to "marijuana"; *pig* and *fuzz* are derogatory terms for "policeman"; *rap, cool, dig, stoned, bread,* and *split* have all extended their semantic domain. The words we have cited sound "slangy" because they have not gained total acceptability. Words such as *dwindle, freshman, glib,* and *mob* are former slang words that in time overcame their "unsavory" origin. It is not always easy to know where to draw the line between "slang" words and "regular" words. This seems always to have been true. In 1890, John S. Farmer, coeditor with W. E. Henley of *Slang and Its Analogues,* remarked: "The borderland between slang and the 'Queen's English' is an ill-defined territory, the limits of which have never been clearly mapped out."

Hippie and *pot* are no longer recognized as slang by some persons, but are by others. Also, one generation's slang is not another generation's slang.

---

[16] Paul Roberts. 1958. *Understanding English* (Harper & Row. New York.), p. 342.

Fan (as in "Dodger fan") was once a slang term, short for *fanatic*. *Phone*, too, was once a slangy, clipped version of *telephone*, as *TV* was of *television*. In Shakespeare's time, *fretful* and *dwindle* were slang, and recently *goof*, *blimp*, and *hot dog* were all hard-core slang.

The use of slang varies from region to region, as one would expect, so slang in New York and slang in Los Angeles are not the same. Interestingly, the word *slang* is slang in British English for "scold."

Slang words and phrases are often "invented" in keeping with new ideas and customs. They may represent "in" attitudes better than the more conservative items of the vocabulary. Their importance is shown by the fact that it was thought necessary to give the returning Vietnam prisoners of war a glossary of eighty-six new slang words and phrases, from *acid* to *zonked*. The words on this list—prepared by the Air Force—had come into use during only five years. Furthermore, by the time this book is published, many of these terms may have passed out of the language, and many new ones will have been added.

A number of slang words have entered English from the "underworld," such as *snow* for "cocaine," *payola, C-note, G-man, to hang paper* ("to write 'bum' checks"), *sawbuck*, and so forth.

JARGON AND ARGOT

Practically every conceivable science, profession, trade, and occupation has its own set of words, some of which are considered to be "slang" and others "technical," depending on the status of the people using these "in" words. Such words are sometimes called **jargon** or **argot**. Linguistic jargon, some of which is used in this book, consists of terms such as *phoneme, morpheme, case, lexicon, rule, style,* and so on. The existence of argots or jargons is illustrated by the story of a seaman witness being cross-examined at a trial, who was asked if he knew the plaintiff. Indicating that he didn't know what *plaintiff* meant brought a chide from the attorney: "You mean you came into this court as a witness and don't know what *plaintiff* means?" Later the sailor was asked where he was standing when the boat lurched. "Abaft the binnacle," was the reply, and to the attorney's questioning stare he responded: "You mean you came into this court and don't know where *abaft the binnacle* is?"

Many jargon terms pass into the standard language. Jargon spreads from a narrow group until it is used and understood by a large segment of the population, similar to slang. Eventually, it may lose its special status as either jargon or slang and gain entrance into the respectable circle of formal usage.

This is true of the now ordinary French word meaning "head," *tête*, which was once a slang word derived from the Latin *testa*, which meant "earthen pot." But some slang words seem to hang on and on in the language, never changing their status from slang to "respectable." Shakespeare used the expression "beat it" to mean "scram" (or more politely, "leave!"), and "beat it" would be considered by most English speakers to still be a slang expression. Similarly, the use of the word *pig* for policeman goes back at least as far as 1785, when Grose called a Bow Street police officer a China Street pig.

Taboo or Not Taboo

Sex is a four-letter word.
Bumper-sticker slogan

An item in a newspaper included the following paragraph (the names have been deleted to protect the guilty):

"This is not a Sunday school but it is a school of law," the judge said in warning the defendants he would not tolerate the "use of expletives during jury selection." "I'm not going to have my fellow citizens and prospective jurors subjected to filthy language," the judge added.

How can language be filthy? In fact, how can it be clean? The filth or beauty of language must be in the ear of the listener, or in the collective ear of society.

There can't be anything about a particular string of sounds which makes it intrinsically clean or dirty, ugly or beautiful. If you tell someone that you pricked your finger when sewing, it would not raise an eyebrow, but if you refer to your professor as a prick, the judge quoted above would undoubtedly consider this a "dirty" word.

Certain words in all societies are considered **taboo**—words that are not to be used, or, at least, not to be used in "polite society." The word *taboo* was borrowed from Tongan, a Polynesian language, and in that society it refers to acts which are forbidden or which are to be avoided. When an act is taboo, reference to this act may also become taboo. That is, first you are forbidden from doing something; then you are forbidden from talking about it.

What acts or words are forbidden reflect the particular customs and views of the society. Some words may be used in certain circumstances and not in others. Peter Farb reports that among the Zuñi Indians it is improper to use the work *takka*, meaning "frogs," during a religious ceremony; what must be used instead is a complex compound word which literally translated would be "several-are-sitting-in-a-shallow-basin-where-they-are-in-liquid."[17]

In certain societies, words which have religious connotations are considered profane if used outside of formal or religious ceremonies. Christians are forbidden to "take the Lord's name in vain" and this has been extended to the use of curses, which are believed to have magical powers. Thus *hell* and *damn* are changed to *heck* and *darn*, perhaps with the belief or hope that this will fool the "powers that be." In England the word *bloody* is a taboo word, perhaps because it originally referred to the blood of Christ. In the Oxford English Dictionary it states that it has been in general colloquial use from the Restoration and is "now constantly in the mouths of the lowest classes, but by respectable people considered 'a horrid word' on a par with obscene or profane language, and usually printed in the newspapers . . . 'b____y.'" It further states that its origin is not quite certain. This itself gives us a clue about "dirty" words; people who use these words often do not know why they are taboo, only that they are, and, to some extent, this is why they remain in the language, to give vent to strong emotional feelings.

[17] Peter Farb. 1975. *Word Play* (Bantam Books. New York.), p. 85.

Words relating to sex, sex organs, and natural bodily functions make up a large part of the set of taboo words of many cultures. Some languages have no native words to mean "sexual intercourse" but do borrow such words from neighboring people. Other languages have many words for this common and universal act, most of which are considered taboo.

What is rather surprising is that two words or expressions can have the identical linguistic meaning and one can be acceptable for use and the other strictly forbidden or the cause of embarrassment or horror. In English, words which we have borrowed from Latin and French seem to carry with them a "scientific" connotation and thus appear to be technical terms and "clean," while good old native Anglo-Saxon words are taboo. This seems to reflect the view that the vocabulary used by the upper classes was clearly superior to that used by the lower classes, a view that was, of course, held and propagated by the upper classes. Peter Farb points out that this distinction must go back at least as far as the Norman conquest in 1066, when "a duchess *perspired* and *expectorated* and *menstruated*—while a kitchen maid *sweated* and *spat* and *bled.*"[18]

There doesn't seem to be any good reason why the word *vagina* is "clean" while *cunt* is "dirty"; or why *prick* or *cock* is taboo, but *penis* is acknowledged as referring to part of the male anatomy; or why everyone clearly *defecates,* but only vulgar people *shit.* For many people, of course, even words like *breast, intercourse, testicles,* and so on are avoided as much as are words like *tits, fuck,* and *balls.* But this is because of nonlinguistic attitudes, not because of the words or language.

EUPHEMISMS

> Banish the use of the four letter words
>   whose meaning is never obscure
> The Anglos, the Saxons, those bawdy old birds
>   Were vulgar, obscene, and impure.
> But cherish the use of the weasling phrase
>   That never quite says what it means;
> You'd better be known for your hypocrite ways
>   Than vulgar, impure, and obscene.
> Ogden Nash, "Ode to the Four Letter Words"

The existence of taboo words or taboo ideas stimulates the creation of **euphemisms.** A euphemism is a word or phrase that replaces a taboo word, or that is used in the attempt to avoid either fearful or unpleasant subjects. Probably because in so many societies, including our own, death is something feared, there are a number of euphemisms that have been created to deal with this subject. People are less apt to *die* and more apt to *pass on* or *pass away.* And those who take care of your *loved ones* who have *passed away* are more likely to be *funeral directors* than *morticians* or *undertakers* these days.

Ogden Nash's poem, quoted above, exhorts against such euphemisms, as another verse of this poem clearly demonstrates:

When in calling, plain speaking is out;
When the ladies (God bless 'em) are milling about,

[18] Ibid., p. 89.

You may wet, make water, or empty the glass;
You can powder your nose, or the "johnny" will pass.
It's a drain for the lily, or man about dog
When everyone's drunk, it's condensing the fog;
But sure as the devil, that word with a hiss
It's only in Shakespeare that characters _____.

There are scholars who are as upset as Ogden Nash with the attitudes revealed by the use of euphemisms in society. A journal, *Maledicta,* subtitled "The International Journal of Verbal Aggression" and edited by Reinhold Aman, "specializes in uncensored glossaries and studies of all offensive and negatively valued words and expressions, in all languages and from all cultures, past and present." A review of this journal by Bill Katz in the *Library Journal* (November 1977) points out, "The history of the dirty word or phrase is the focus of this substantial . . . journal [whose articles] are written in a scholarly yet entertaining fashion by professors . . . as well as by a few outsiders."

One such scholarly study of euphemisms used by Australian speakers of English was conducted by the linguist Jay Powell.[19] The expressions which revolve around the idea "toilet" or the functions connected with it show that there is more than "prudery" involved, as is illustrated by the Australian euphemisms which replace the verb *urinate:*

drain the dragon
syphon the python
water the horse
squeeze the lemon
drain the spuds
see if the horse has kicked off his blanket
wring the rattlesnake
shake hands with wife's best friend
point Percy at the porcelain
train Terence on the terracotta

Similar "metaphors" exist for *have intercourse:*

shag
root
crack a fat
dip the wick
play hospital
hide the ferret
play cars and garages
hide the egg roll (sausage, salami)
boil bangers
slip a length
go off like a beltfed motor
go like a rat up a rhododendron
go like a rat up a drain pipe
have gin on the rocks
have a northwest cocktail

[19] Paper delivered at the Western Conference of Linguistics, University of Oregon, 1972.

These euphemisms, as well as the differences between the accepted Latinate "genteel" terms and the "dirty" Anglo-Saxon terms, show that a word or phrase not only has a linguistic **denotative** meaning, but also has what some linguists call a **connotative** meaning, an implication representing a feeling, an emotion, or a value judgment. In learning a language, children learn which words are "taboo," and these taboo words differ from one child to another, depending on the value system accepted in the family or group in which the child grows up.

Thus, while we maintain that words or phrases or language cannot be bad or dirty in themselves, they can be used to express particular values of the speaker. The taboo words reflect society's values, or the opinions of parts of society.

The use of epithets for people of different religions, nationalities, or color tell us something about the users of these words. The word *boy* is not a taboo word when used generally, but when a 20-year-old white man calls a 40-year-old black man "boy," the word takes on an additional meaning; it reflects the racist attitude of the speaker. So also words like *kike, wop, nigger,* and so forth express racist and chauvinist views of society. If racial and national and religious bigotry and oppression did not exist, then in time these words would either die out or lose their racist connotations.

Language and Sexism

doc•tor, n. . . . a man of great learning.
The American College Dictionary, 1947

A businessman is aggressive, a businesswoman is pushy. A businessman is good on details, she's picky. . . . He follows through, she doesn't know when to quit. He stands firm, she's hard. . . . His judgments are her prejudices. He is a man of the world, she's been around. . . . He isn't afraid to say what is on his mind; she's mouthy. He exercises authority diligently; she's power mad. He's closemouthed; she's secretive. He climbed the ladder of success; she slept her way to the top.
From "How to Tell a Businessman from a Businesswoman," Graduate School of Management, UCLA, The Balloon, vol. XXII, no. 6

In the discussion of obscenities, blasphemies, taboo words, and euphemisms, we have seen that the language used, and the words introduced into a language, reflect the views and values of society. We also suggested that a language or words of a language cannot be intrinsically either good or bad but can only be viewed as such by the people who use it. One word may have positive connotations, while another word with the identical linguistic meaning may have negative connotations. Thus we find the same individual referred to as a terrorist by one group and as a freedom fighter by another. A woman may be referred to as a castrating female (or ballsy women's libber) or as a courageous feminist advocate.

The question as to whether the language we use affects the culture and views of society is still being debated. But there is pretty much a unanimous opinion that the language we use is affected by the views and values of society. This is very apparent when we look at how the sexism in society is reflected in our language. Language cannot be sexist in itself, just as it can't be "dirty," but it can reflect sexist attitudes just as it can reflect attitudes as to what is or is not considered "taboo."

PEANUTS   **Charles Schulz**

© 1977 United Feature Syndicate, Inc.

The fact that on hearing someone say *My cousin is a professor* (or *a doctor*, or *a lawyer*, or *a CPA*, or *the Chancellor of the University*, or *the President of the country*, or *the delegate to the U.N.*) most people would conclude that the cousin was a man has nothing to do with the English language but a great deal to do with the fact that, historically, women have not been prominent in these professions. Similarly, if you heard someone say *My cousin is a nurse* (*elementary school teacher, model, whore, prostitute*), you would no doubt conclude that the cousin was a woman. The linguist Sol Saporta pointed out that it is less easy to understand why the sentence *My neighbor is a blond* brings the response that the speaker is referring to a woman.[20] This could be due to the fact that the physical characteristics of women in our society assume greater importance than those of men because women are constantly exploited as sex objects. This is further borne out by studies analyzing the language used by men in reference to women, which often has derogatory or sexual connotations. Such terms go very far back into history and sometimes enter the language with no pejorative implications but gradually gain them. Thus, from Old English *huswif*, "housewife," the word *hussy* was derived. Muriel Schulz points out, for example, "In

---

[20] Sol Saporta, "Language in a Sexist Society." Paper delivered at a meeting of the Modern Language Association, New York, December 1974.

their original employment, a *laundress* made beds, a *needlewoman* came to sew, a *spinster* tended the spinning wheel, and a *nurse* cared for the sick. But all apparently acquired secondary duties in some households, because all became euphemisms for a mistress or a prostitute at some time during their existence.''[21]

Words for women—all with abusive or sexual overtones—abound: *dish, tomato, piece, piece of ass, chick, piece of tail, bunny, pussy, pussycat, bitch, doll, slut, cow,* to name just a few. Many fewer such pejorative terms exist for men.

One striking fact about the asymmetry between male and female terms in many languages is that when there are male/female pairs it is the male form which for the most part is *unmarked* and the female term which is created by adding a bound morpheme or by compounding. We have many such examples in English:

MALE	FEMALE
prince	princess
count	countess
host	hostess
heir	heiress
hero	heroine
Paul	Pauline

One talks of a *male nurse* because it is expected that a nurse will be female, and for parallel reasons we have the compounds *lady doctor, career woman,* and *woman athlete.*

The unmarked, or male, nouns also serve as the general terms, as do the male pronouns. The *brotherhood of man* includes women, but *sisterhood* does not include men.

Changes in the language are taking place, however, and reflect the growing consciousness of sexism in society. Thus today at the University of California at Santa Cruz not only are there *chairpersons* of departments but a *freshperson* class as well as sophomore, junior, and senior classes. Changes in the language follow changes in society; hopefully, they may also affect male attitudes toward women. But the language is not responsible for the sexism; it merely reflects it.

It is, however, unfortunate that the asymmetries mentioned above do exist. The fact that the woman adopts the man's name in marriage can be traced back to early (and to a great extent, current) legal practices. Thus we often refer to a woman as Mrs. Jack Fromkin but seldom refer to a man as Mr. Vicki Fromkin. We talk of Professor and Mrs. John Smith but seldom, if ever, of Mr. and Dr. Mary Jones. Furthermore, it is insulting to be called a *spinster* and even more so an *old maid* but certainly not to be called a *bachelor.* There is nothing inherently pejorative about the word *spinster.* The connotations reflect the different views society has about an unmarried woman as opposed to an unmarried man. It isn't the language that is sexist; it is society.

An increasing number of researchers have been investigating language and

[21] Muriel R. Schulz, "The Semantic Derogation of Woman," in B. Thorne and N. Henley, eds. *Language and Sex.* 1975. (Newbury House Publishers. Rowley, Mass.), pp. 66–67.

sex and language and sexism. One area of research concerns the differences between male and female speech styles. In Japanese, male and female speech comprise two distinct dialects of the language. So different are these two styles that "seeing eye" guide dogs in Japan are trained in English because the sex of the owner is not known in advance and it is easier and more socially acceptable for a blind person to use English than the "wrong" sex's language style.

There is nothing inherently wrong in the development of different styles, which may include intonation, phonology, syntax, and lexicon. What has been stressed throughout this chapter is that the language is neither good nor bad but its use may be for good or bad. If one views women as inferior, then special speech characteristics will be viewed as inferior. When everyone in society is indeed created equal, and treated as such, there will be little concern for the sexual asymmetries which exist in language.

Artificial Languages

La inteligenta persono lernas la interlingvon Esperanton rapide kaj facile. (Esperanto for: "The intelligent person learns the international language Esperanto rapidly and easily.")

Since the scattering at Babel, many people have hoped for a return to the blissful state when everyone would speak a universal language. Lingua francas are a step in that direction, but none has gone far enough. Since the seventeenth century, scholars have been inventing artificial languages with the hope that they would achieve universal acceptance and that universal language would bring universal peace. With stubborn regularity the world has rejected every attempt. Perhaps the world has seen too many civil wars to accept this idea.

The obituary column of artificial languages indicates the constant attempts and regular failures: Bopal, Kosmos, Novial, Parla, Spokil, Universala, and Volapük are but a few of the deceased hundreds. Most artificial languages never get beyond their inventors, because they are abstruse and difficult and uninteresting to learn.

One artificial language has enjoyed some success. **Esperanto** was invented by the Polish scholar Zamenhof, who wrote under the pseudonym of Dr. Esperanto ("one who hopes"). He gave his "language" the advantages of extreme grammatical regularity, ease of pronunciation, and a vocabulary based mainly on Latin-Romance, Germanic, and Greek. Esperanto is spoken, it is claimed, by several million speakers throughout the world, including some who learned it as one of their native languages. There is a literature written in it, a number of institutions teach it, and it is officially recognized by some international organizations.

Esperantists claim that their language can be learned easily by any intelligent person. But despite the claims of its proponents, it is not maximally simple. There is an obligatory accusative case (*Ni lernas Esperanto***n** "We're learning Esperanto"), and adjectives and nouns must agree in number (*inteligenta persono* "intelligent person," but *inteligentaj personoj* "intelligent persons"). Speakers of Chinese or Malaysian (and even English) would find this very different from the rules of their grammars. Esperanto is regular insofar as all nouns end in -*o*, with plural -*oj*; all adjectives end in -*a*, with plural -*aj;* the present tense of all verbs ends in -*as,* the future in -*os,* and the past in -*is;* and the definite article is always *la.* But to speakers of Thai, a language that does not have a definite article at all, Esperanto is far from "simple," and speakers of the many languages that indicate tenses without verb endings (as English indicates the future tense with *shall* or *will*) may find that aspect of Esperanto difficult to learn.

A modification of Esperanto, called **Ido** ("offspring" in Esperanto), has further simplified the language by eliminating the accusative case and abolishing adjective and noun agreement, but the basic problem remains. Esperanto is essentially a Romance-based pidgin with Greek and Germanic influence, albeit a highly developed one with an immense vocabulary. It therefore remains "foreign" to speakers of most languages; a Russian or a Hungarian or a Nigerian or a Hindu would find Esperanto as unfamiliar as French or Spanish.

The problems besetting the world community are basically nonlinguistic, despite the linguistic problems that do exist. Language problems may intensify social and economic problems, but they do not generally cause wars, unemployment, poverty, pollution, disease.

SUMMARY

Every person has his or her own way of speaking. The unique and often idiosyncratic features of an individual's language are called an **idiolect.** The language used by a group of speakers may show, in addition, systematic differences called a **dialect.** The dialects of a language are the mutually intelligible forms of that language which differ in *systematic* ways from each other. Dialects develop and are reinforced because languages change, and the changes that occur in one group or area may differ from those that occur in another. **Regional dialects** and **social dialects** develop for this reason. Some of the differences in the regional dialects of America may be traced to the changes that took place historically in British English after the American colonization. The colonists who maintained close contact with England reflected the changes occurring in British English while earlier forms were preserved among Americans who spread westward and broke communication contact with England.

Dialect differences include pronunciation differences (often called "accents"), vocabulary distinctions, and syntactic rule differences. The grammar differences between dialects are not as great as the parts that are shared, thus permitting speakers of different dialects to communicate with each other.

In most countries one dialect assumes the role of being the **standard.** While this particular dialect is not linguistically superior, it may be considered by some to be the only "correct" form of the language. Such a view has unfortunately led to the idea that some nonstandard dialects are "deficient," as is erroneously suggested regarding **Black English** (**BE** as distinguished from **Standard American English—SAE**), the dialect used by large numbers, but by no means all, black Americans. A study of Black English shows it to be as logical, complete, rule-governed, and expressive as any other dialect.

In areas where many languages are spoken, the people often use one language as a **lingua franca** to communicate with each other. In other cases, the languages spoken by two or more groups may be simplified lexically, phonologically, and syntactically to become a **pidgin.** When a pidgin becomes the language learned natively, it is **creolized.** Such **creole languages** exist in many parts of the world.

Besides regional and social dialects, speakers may use different **styles** of their dialect depending on the particular context. **Slang** is used infrequently in formal papers or situations, but is widely used in speech; **argot** and **jargon** are words used to describe the special terms of a professional or trade group.

In all societies certain acts or behaviors are frowned on, forbidden, or considered **taboo.** The words or expressions referring to these taboo acts are then also avoided, or considered "dirty." Language itself cannot be clean or dirty; the views toward parts of the language reflect the views of society toward the acts or behaviors referred to by the language. Taboo words and acts give rise to **euphemisms,** which are words or phrases that replace the expressions to be avoided. Thus, *powder room* is a euphemism for *toilet,* which itself is a euphemism for *lavatory.*

Just as the use of some words may reflect society's views toward sex or natural bodily functions, so also some words may reflect racist, chauvinist, and sexist attitudes in society. The language itself is not racist or sexist but reflects these views of various sectors of a society.

The communication barriers that exist because of the thousands of languages used in the world have led to the invention of artificial languages, which, the inventors hope, could be used universally. All such attempts have failed. Most such languages, including the most widely known, Esperanto, are not "universal" in any sense but are pidgins based on a small number of languages from one language family, and may still be difficult to learn.

EXERCISES

1. Each pair of words below is pronounced as shown phonetically in at least one American dialect. State whether you pronounce each word in the way it is given here. If not, state how your pronunciation differs.

a.	"horse"	[hɔrs]	"hoarse"	[hors]
b.	"morning"	[mɔrnɪ̃ŋ]	"mourning"	[mornɪ̃ŋ]
c.	"for"	[fɔr]	"four"	[for]
d.	"ice"	[ʌys]	"eyes"	[ayz]
e.	"knife"	[nʌyf]	"knives"	[nayvz]
f.	"mute"	[myut]	"nude"	[nyud]
g.	"pin"	[pʰĩn]	"pen"	[pʰẽn]
h.	"hog"	[hɔg]	"hot"	[hat]
i.	"marry"	[mæri]	"merry"	[mɛri]
j.	"merry"	[mɛri]	"Mary"	[meri]
k.	"cot"	[kʰat]	"caught"	[kʰɔt]
l.	"father"	[faðə]	"farther"	[fa:ðə]
m.	"(to) lease"	[lis]	"(to) grease"	[griz]
n.	"what"	[ʌwat]	"watt"	[wat]
o.	"ant"	[ænt]	"aunt"	[ãnt]
p.	"creek"	[kʰrik]	"sick"	[sɪk]

2. In the period from 1890 to 1904, the book *Slang and Its Analogues* by J. S. Farmer and W. E. Henley was published in seven volumes. The following entries are included in this dictionary. For each item: (1) state whether the word or phrase still exists; (2) if not, state what the modern slang term would be; (3) if the word remains but its meaning has changed, provide the modern meaning.

all out —entirely, completely, as in "All out the best." (The expression goes back to as early as 1300.)

to have apartments to let —to be an idiot; one who is empty-headed.

been there —as in "Oh, yes, I've been there." Applied to a man who is shrewd and who has had many experiences.

belly-button —the navel.

berkeleys —a woman's breasts.

bitch —the most offensive appellation that can be given to a woman, even more provoking than that of whore.

once in a blue moon —extremely seldom.

boss —a master; one who directs.

bread —employment. (1785—"out of bread" = "out of work.")

claim —to steal.

cut dirt —to escape.

dog cheap —of little worth. (Used in 1616 by Dekker: "Three things there are Dog-cheap, learning, poorman's sweat, and oathes.")

funeral —as in "It's not my funeral." "It's no business of mine."

to get over —to seduce, to fascinate.

grub —food.

groovy —settled in habit; limited in mind.

head —toilet (nautical use only).

hook —to marry.

hump —to spoil.

hush money —money paid for silence; blackmail.

itch —to be sexually excited.

jam —a sweetheart or a mistress.

to lift a leg on —to have sexual intercourse.

leg bags —stockings.

looby —a fool

to lie low —to keep quiet; to bide one's time.

malady of France —syphilis (used by Shakespeare in 1599).

nix —nothing

noddle —the head.

old —money. (1900—"Perhaps it's somebody you owe a bit of the old to, Jack.")

to pill —to talk platitudes.

pipe layer —a political intriguer; a schemer.

poky —cramped, stuffy, stupid.

pot —a quart; a large sum; a prize; a urinal; to excel.

puny —a freshman.

puss-gentleman —an effeminate.

3. Suppose someone said, "I don't got nothin'" and you heard someone reply, "That's an illogical statement, since two negatives make a positive." How would you argue with the "corrector"?

4. We repeat below the part of the speech by Mark Antony from Shakespeare's *Julius Caesar* that we presented before as translated into Sierra Leone Krio by Thomas Decker. See how much of it you can understand. Then see if you can find this particular passage in the play. What are some of the ways in which Krio resembles English? List some of the obvious differences between Krio and English as exemplified in this passage.

> Padi dem; kɔntri; una ɔl we de na Rom.
> Mɛk una ɔl kak una yes. A kam bɛr Siza,
> a nɔ kam prez am.
> Den kin mɛmba bad we pɔsin kin du
> lɔŋtɛm afta pɔsin kin dɔn dai;
> bɔt plɛnti tɛm di gud we pɔsin du
> kin bɛr wit im bon dɛm.
> Mɛk i bi so wit Siza.

5. In Edith Folb's study of black argot, she includes a glossary of terms with their definitions. Some of these slang terms are listed in Column I. Their definitions are given in random order in Column II—that is, as presented they are paired incorrectly. Try to match the term in I with its correct definition. (Answers are presented upside down below the lists.)

I.	II.
a. back to back	1. smooth and round wheel covers
b. ace	2. knowledgeable about
c. down with	3. small bottle of wine or devoted lover
d. moons	4. convey important information
e. blow heavy	5. side-by-side
f. puppy	6. succeed in life
g. shine on	7. black person
h. whup the game	8. ignore
i. sling shot	9. best friend
j. blood	10. Cadillac El Dorado

Answers: a-5, b-9, c-2, d-1, e-4, f-3, g-8, h-6, i-10, j-7

6. Suppose someone asked you to help compile items for a new dictionary of slang. List ten "slang" words that you use regularly and provide a dictionary definition for each.

7. Below are given some words used in British English for which different words are usually used in American English. See if you can find the American equivalents.

a. clothes peg	k. biscuits
b. braces	l. queue
c. lift	m. torch
d. pram	n. underground
e. waistcoat	o. high street
f. shop assistant	p. crisps
g. sweets	q. chips (fish and chips)
h. boot (of car)	r. lorry
i. bobby	s. holiday
j. spanner	t. tin
	u. knock up

8. This chapter has discussed various types of dialects that represent mutually intelligible systematic variations of a single language. In addition to such dialects, which arise historically, "secret" languages are invented that "distort" the language, often to prevent understanding by those who have not learned the language "game."

Pig Latin is a common language game of English. But even Pig Latin has dialects, forms of the "language game" with different rules.

A. Consider the following data from three dialects of Pig Latin, each with its own rule applied to words beginning with vowels:

	DIALECT 1	DIALECT 2	DIALECT 3
"eat"	[itme]	[ithe]	[ite]
"arc"	[arkme]	[arkhe]	[arke]

(1) State the rule that accounts for the Pig Latin forms in each dialect.
(2) How would you say "honest," "admire" and "illegitimate" in each dialect? Give the phonetic transcription of the Pig Latin forms.

B. In one dialect of Pig Latin, the word "strike" is pronounced [aykstre], and in another dialect it is pronounced [traykse]. In the first dialect "slot" is pronounced [atsle] and in the second dialect, it is pronounced [latse].

(1) State the rules for each of these dialects that account for these different Pig Latin forms of the same words.
(2) Give the phonetic transcriptions for the following words in both dialects.
"spot," "crisis," "scratch," "please," "break."

9. Thousands of language games such as Pig Latin exist in the world's languages. In some, a suffix is added to each word; in others a syllable is inserted after each vowel; there are rhyming games and games in which phonemes are reversed. There is a game used by the Walbiri, natives of central Australia, in which the meanings of words are distorted rather than the phonological forms. In this language, all nouns, verbs, pronouns, and adjectives are replaced by their semantic opposites. Thus, the sentence *Those men are small.* means *This woman is big.* It is interesting to see that these language games provide evidence for the phonemes, words, morphemes, semantic features, and so on that are posited by linguists for descriptive grammars.

Below are some sentences representing different English language games. Write each sentence in its undistorted form; state the language-game "rule."

a. /ay-o tʊk-o may-o dɔg-o awt-o tu-o ðə-o kʌntri-o/
b. /ðɪsli ɪzli əli mɔrli kamliplɪliketliədli gemli/
c. Mary-shmary can-shman talk-shmalk in-shmin rhyme-shmyme.
d. betpetterper latepate thanpan nevpeverper.
e. thop-e fop-oot bop-all stop-a dop-i opum blop-ew dap-own
/ðapə faput bapɔl stape dapi apəm blapu dapawn/
f. [kʌbən yʌbu spʌbik thʌbəs kʌbaynd ʌbəv ʌbənglʌbɪš
(This is in "ubby dubby," from a well-known children's television show popular in the 1970s.)

10. Compile a list of argot (or jargon) terms from some profession or trade (for example, *lawyer, musician, doctor, longshoreman,* and so forth). Give a definition for each term in "nonjargon" terms.

11. "Translate" the first paragraph of any well-known document or speech —such as the Declaration of Independence, the Gettysburg Address, or the Preamble to the Constitution—into informal, colloquial language.

REFERENCES

Burling, Robbins. 1970. *Man's Many Voices.* Holt, Rinehart and Winston. New York.

Dillard, J. L. 1972. *Black English: Its History and Usage in the United States.* Random House. New York.

Hymes, Dell, ed. 1964. *Language in Culture and Society.* Harper & Row. New York.

Hymes, Dell, ed. 1971. *Pidginization and Creolization of Languages.* Cambridge University Press. Cambridge, England.

Labov, W. 1969. "The Logic of Nonstandard English." Georgetown University 20th Annual Round Table, Monograph Series on Languages and Linguistics, No. 22.

Shopen, Timothy, and Joseph M. Williams, eds. 1981. *Style and Variables in English.* Winthrop Publishers. Cambridge, Mass.

Trudgill, Peter. 1974. *Sociolinguistics.* Penguin Books, Middlesex, England. (Reprinted 1977.)

Williamson, Juanita V., and Virginia M. Burke. 1971. *A Various Language: Perspectives on American Dialects.* Holt, Rinehart and Winston. New York.

Chapter 9

The Syllables of Time: Language Change

> The language of this country being always upon the flux, the Struldbruggs of one age do not understand those of another, neither are they able after two hundred years to hold any conversation (farther than by a few general words) with their neighbors the mortals, and thus they lie under the disadvantage of living like foreigners in their own country.
>
> Jonathan Swift, *Gulliver's Travels*

All languages change with time. It is fortunate for us that though languages change, they do so rather slowly compared to the human life span. It would be inconvenient to have to relearn our native language every twenty years. In the field of astronomy we find a similar situation. Because of the movement of individual stars, the stellar configurations we call constellations are continuously changing their shape. Fifty thousand years from now we would find it difficult to recognize Orion or the Big Dipper. But from year to year the changes are not noticeable. Linguistic change is also slow, in human, if not astronomical, terms. If we were to turn on a radio and miraculously receive a broadcast in our "native language" from the year 3000, we would probably think we had tuned in some foreign-language station. Yet from year to year, even from birth to grave, we hardly notice any change in our language.

Where languages have written records it is possible to see the actual changes that have taken place. We know quite a bit about the history of the English language, because about a thousand years of English is preserved in writing. Old English, spoken in England around the end of the first millennium, is scarcely recognizable as English. (Of course our linguistic ancestors didn't call their language Old English!) A speaker of modern English would find the language unintelligible. There are college courses in which Old English is studied in much the same way as any foreign language such as French or Swahili.

The following example from *Caedmon's Hymn* in Old English spoken and written in the period between A.D. 658 and 680 will reveal why it must be studied as a "foreign" language:

Nū sculon herian	heofon-rīces Weard,
Now we must praise	heaven-kingdom's Guardian
Meotodes meahte	and his mōd-ġeþanc
the Creator's might	and his mind-plans,
weorc Wuldor-Fæder,	swā hē wundra ġehwæs,
the work of the Glory-Father,	when he of wonders of every one
ēċe Dryhten	ōr astealde
eternal Lord,	the beginning established.

The tenth-century epic *Beowulf,* written in Old English, further exemplifies the need for a translation, as students of English literature well know (the letter þ is pronounced like the *th* in *think*):

Wolde guman findan þone þe him on sweofote sare geteode.
He wanted to find the man who harmed him while he slept.

Almost 400 years later, Chaucer wrote *The Canterbury Tales.* The language used by Chaucer, now called Middle English, was spoken from around 1100 to 1500; as one might expect, it is more easily understood by present-day readers, as is seen by looking at the opening of the *Tales:*

Whan that Aprille with his shoures soote
The droghte of March hath perced to the roote . . .

When April with its sweet showers
The drought of March has pierced to the root . . .

Two hundred years after Chaucer, in a language that can be considered an earlier dialect of Modern English, Shakespeare's Hamlet says:

A man may fish with the worm that hath eat of a king, and eat of the fish that hath fed of this worm.

Shakespeare wrote in the sixteenth century. A passage from *Everyman,* written about 1485, further illustrates why it is claimed that Modern English was already spoken by 1500:

The Summoning of Everyman called it is,
That of our lives and ending shows
How transitory we be all day.
The matter is wonder precious,
But the intent of it is more gracious
And sweet to bear away.

The division of English into Old English (449–1100 A.D.), Middle English (1100–1500), and Modern English (1500–present) is somewhat arbitrary, being marked by the dates of events in English history that profoundly influenced the English language. Thus the history of English and the changes that occurred in the language reflect, to some extent, nonlinguistic history.

An examination of the changes that have occurred during the 1500 years since the "birth" of English shows that the sound system has changed, the syntactic rules have changed, and the semantic system has changed. Because speakers' knowledge of their language is represented by their grammar, the changes that occur in a language are changes in the grammar; all parts of the grammar may change. Although we have discussed linguistic change only in relation to English, the histories of other languages show that similar changes occur in all languages.

Regularity of Sound Change

That's not a regular rule: you invented it just now.
Lewis Carroll, *Alice's Adventures in Wonderland*

New York City offers a variety of surprises to its visitors, not the least of which is linguistic. You will not be on the streets of Manhattan for long before you hear a reference to "thoid" avenue, or discover that our little winged friends are called "boids" by many natives.

What you are hearing is a dialect difference, sometimes called an "accent." Remarkably enough, those New Yorkers who speak this dialect pronounce *all* words like *third, bird, first, heard,* and so forth as "thoid," "boid," "foist," "hoid." This is an example of a **regular sound correspondence.** Wherever a Californian, say, pronounces [ər] at the beginning or in the middle of a word, speakers of this New York dialect pronounce [ɔy] ("oi").[1] To a great extent, it is such differences in pronunciation that define different dialects. In a dialect other than our own, many hundreds of words may be pronounced differently, but because the differences are due to a small number of regular sound correspondences, we are able to figure out what is said.

The different pronunciations of *third, bird,* and so on did not always exist in English. We will investigate how such dialectal differences arose, and why the sound differences are usually regular, and not confined to just a few words.

A similar situation occurs in the history of the English language. In Chaucer's time, 600 years ago, the small rodent we call a mouse [maws] was called a *mūs* [mu:s], and this mūs may have lived in someone's *hūs* [hu:s], which is the way *house* [haws] was pronounced. In general, where we now pronounce [aw], speakers of Chaucer's time pronounced [u:]. This is a regular correspondence, like the one between [ər] and [ɔy]. For example, *out* [awt] was pronounced *ūt* [u:t] and *south* [sawθ], *sūð* [su:ð]. Many other such regular correspondences can be found, relating older and newer forms of English. In general, all languages exhibit similar correspondences in their history.

We also find regular sound correspondences among different languages. If you ever studied a Romance language such as French or Spanish, you may have noticed that where an English word begins with *f*, the corresponding word in a Romance language often has a *p*. Thus *father*, French *père*, Spanish *padre;* or English *fish*, French *poisson*, Spanish *pescado*. This *f-p* correspondence is another example of a regular sound correspondence.[2]

Many languages exhibit such correspondences. For instance, the American Indian languages Cree and Ojibwa show a *t-n* correspondence: Cree *atim*, Ojibwa *anim*, "dog"; Cree *nitim*, Ojibwa *ninim*, "my sister-in-law."

---

[1] Some speakers of this dialect use the diphthong [ʌy] or [əy].

[2] The individual histories of English and the Romance languages have somewhat obscured the regularity of this correspondence, but even so it is quite striking.

Languages change in time, and the regular sound correspondences we observe between older and modern forms of a language are due to changes in the language's phonological system that affect certain sounds, or classes of sounds, rather than individual words. English underwent the sound shift; [u:] became [aw] centuries ago. The regularity we observe is precisely because it is the *sound* that undergoes the change, not the lexical item.

The process of sound shift can account for dialect differences. At an earlier stage of English a sound change of [ər] to [ɔy] took place among certain speakers. The change did not spread, perhaps because these speakers were isolated in some ways, or perhaps because the pronunciation of [ɔy] became a "regionalism" that others did not imitate. Whatever the case, we are quite sure that many dialect differences in pronunciation result from a sound shift whose spread is limited.

Regional dialect differences in pronunciation arise from the natural linguistic phenomenon of sound change. Many of the world's modern languages were at first regional dialects that became widely spoken and survived as separate languages. The Romance languages were once dialects of Latin spoken in the Roman Empire. There is nothing "degenerate" or "illiterate" about regional pronunciations. They are simply a result of natural sound change that failed to spread beyond certain limits. Language change is inevitable, and while it may be desirable to maintain a certain literary standard that spans a number of different dialects, it is absurd to label all change, and all regional variations, as signs of the corruption of the tongue.

When one dialect undergoes many sound shifts that other dialects of the language do not, that dialect may no longer be intelligible to speakers of the other dialects. At that point, often after centuries, that dialect is considered a separate language. Thus dialects of a language may in time develop into separate languages. These languages are said to be **genetically related** because they developed from the same ("parent") language. (See below for some language "families.") All genetically related languages were dialects of the same language at an earlier stage.

Regular sound correspondences between languages indicate that the languages are genetically related. To see why this is so, consider the diagram in Figure 9-1. Speakers of language L, for whatever reasons, split into two groups. One group undergoes a sound shift A → B. The other group undergoes a sound shift A → C. When the sound shifts are complete, the two languages display the sound correspondence B ↔ C, which can only be explained by positing for each the same parent language, having some sound A wherever L_1 has B and L_2 has C. For the same reason, if we compare L_1 with its older form L, we discover the regular correspondence B ↔ A.

It is this kind of situation that resulted in the *f-p* correspondence, mentioned above, that is found between English and the Romance languages. Speakers of Indo-European, the language that both English and French descended from, once broke up into smaller groups. One of those groups underwent a sound shift of $p \rightarrow f$. Their descendants eventually spoke "Germanic" languages (for example, English and German). The other Indo-Europeans, in particular the ones whose descendants spoke Romance languages, did not experience the change. Today we see the result of this ancient sound change in the *f-p* sound correspondence.

One way in which languages change in time is in the phonological system. These changes show up as regular sound correspondences between older

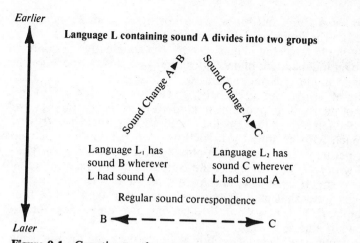

Earlier

Language L containing sound A divides into two groups

Sound Change A▶B

Sound Change A▶C

Language L₁ has
sound B wherever
L had sound A

Language L₂ has
sound C wherever
L had sound A

Regular sound correspondence

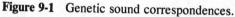

B ◀ ─ ─ ─ ─ ─ ─ ▶ C

Later

Figure 9-1 Genetic sound correspondences.

and more modern forms of a language, as dialect differences, and as differences between languages that are related genetically by having come from a common ancestor.

Phonological Change

Etymologists . . . for whom vowels did not matter and who cared not a jot for consonants.
Voltaire

In earlier chapters we discussed the kinds of knowledge one has about the phonological system. This includes knowledge of the phonological units in the language, the phonetic pronunciation of morphemes, and the phonological rules. Any of these aspects of the phonology is subject to change.

INVENTORY OF SOUNDS

If you know modern English you know that /x/, the velar fricative, is not part of the English sound system. One of the changes that occurred in the history of our language was the loss of this particular sound. *Night* was once pronounced [nıxt], *drought* was pronounced [druxt], and *saw* was pronounced [saux]. A phonological change—the loss of /x/—took place between the times of Chaucer and of Shakespeare. All the words that were once pronounced with a /x/ no longer include this sound. In some cases the /x/ became /f/, as in *rough* and *tough*. In other cases it disappeared, as in *night* and *light*. In other cases the /x/ became a /k/, as in *elk* (Old English *eolh* [ɛlx]). In some cases it was "vocalized"—that is, it became a vowel, as in *hollow* (Old English *holh* [holx]) or *sorrow* (Old English [sorx]). There are British dialects, such as Scottish, that have kept the /x/ sound in some of these words.

This example shows that the **inventory** of sounds can be changed. English *lost* a phoneme. The inventory can also change by the *addition* of new phonemes to the language. Old English did not have the phoneme /ž/. When words like *azure, measure,* and *rouge* were borrowed from French, this sound was added to the inventory of phonological units.

A phonetically predictable sound may also become distinctive or contrastive and become an independent phonological unit—that is, a phoneme. In Old English, for example, the phoneme /f/ was pronounced as [f] in initial and final position of words, but as [v] between two vowels. Just as [p] and [pʰ] are variants of the same /p/ phoneme in modern English, [f] and [v] were variants of the phoneme /f/ in Old English. Later, when English borrowed words from French with an initial [v], such as *veal*, [v] was pronounced rather than [f], perhaps because English already had a phonetic [v]. *Veal* now contrasted with *feel;* the voicing of the labiodental consonant in initial position became distinctive, and [v] became a separate phoneme /v/.

These examples show that phonemes may be lost (for example, /x/), or added (for example, /ž/), or may "split" to become two phonemes (for example, /f/ became /f/ and /v/).

Such changes occur in all languages. For example, in Latin the phoneme /k/ had allophones [č] and [k]. By the time Italian had developed from Latin, both *č* and *k* had achieved phonemic status /č/ and /k/, as exhibited in modern Italian *ciarpa* [čarpa] "scarf" and *carpa* [karpa] "carp." An older stage of Russian had the phoneme /æ/, but in modern Russian [æ] is merely an allophone of /a/ and so has lost its phonemic status.

PHONOLOGICAL RULES

As discussed in Chapters 3 and 4, the phonological system includes more than the set of sounds in the language; it also includes the rules that show the different pronunciations of the same morpheme when these morphemes occur in different contexts. These rules "tell" us to pronounce the /t/ that occurs at the end of *democrat* as a [t] but to pronounce it as an [s] in *democracy*.

In the course of linguistic change, such rules can be made more general. At one time, for example, the nouns *house* and *bath* were differentiated from the verbs *house* and *bathe* by the fact that the verbs ended with a short vowel sound (still reflected in the spelling). Furthermore, there was a rule in English (mentioned above in relation to [f] and [v]) that said: "When a voiceless consonant phoneme occurs between two vowels, make that consonant voiced." Thus the /s/ in the verb *house* was pronounced [z] and the /θ/ in the verb *bathe* was pronounced [ð]. Then a rule was added to the grammar of English that first "weakened" and then "deleted" unstressed short vowels in certain contexts. The final vowel sound was thus deleted from the verb *house* (that is, we do not pronounce it [hawzə] but [hawz]) and also from *bathe*. The deletion of the vowels also resulted in the new phonemes /z/ and /ð/, which prior to this change were simply the phonetic realizations of the phonemes /s/ and /θ/ between vowels, but which now contrasted with these sounds at the end of words, e.g. [haws] / [hawz].

Eventually, the "intervocalic-voicing" rule was "dropped" from the grammar of English, showing that the set of phonological rules can change by loss of a rule.

Five hundred years ago, Fante, a language of Ghana, did not have the sounds [ts] or [dz]. The *addition* of a phonological rule to the language "created" these sounds; this rule said: "pronounce a /d/ as [dz] and a /t/ as [ts] when these phonemes occur before /i/." The addition of this rule to the grammar of Fante did not create new phonemes; [dz] and [ts] are predictable phonetic realizations of the underlying phonemes /d/ and /t/. The grammar, however, was changed—a new rule was added.

The colonial settlers of America, like their countrymen who remained in England, pronounced the *r* wherever it was spelled: *farm, mother,* and *margin* were pronounced [farm], [mʌðər], and [marjən]. Between 1607 and 1900 a phonological rule was added to the grammar of British English. The same rule was added to the grammars of the English spoken by the American settlers in Boston, perhaps because of the close commercial contact that was maintained between the British and Boston merchants, but it was not added to the grammars of many other Americans. This rule said: "Pronounce an *r* only when the *r* occurs before a vowel."

Thus by 1900, British and Bostonian speakers pronounced *farm* [fam], *mother* [mʌðə], and *margin* [majən]: this pronunciation is part of what we call a "Boston accent," or Boston dialect. All English speakers continued to pronounce the *r* in words like *Mary* and *breakfast*. This additional rule did not change the phonological representation of all the words where the /r/ was not pronounced. When *four* [fɔ], for example, is followed by a word that begins with a vowel, the /r/ shows up, as in *four acts* [fɔrækts]. Thus the word must be phonemically /fɔr/. The new phonological rule in the grammars of speakers of this "*r*-less" dialect "deletes" the *r* only when it does not precede a vowel.

The addition of phonological rules can affect the pronunciation of words, resulting in dialect differences, and may cause changes in the phonological inventory as well.

All phonological changes like those cited above took place gradually over the course of many generations of speakers. Those speakers didn't plan the changes, any more than we are presently planning on what changes will take place in English by the year 2300. They would have been aware of the changes only through dialect differences. "Progressive" dialects would have shown the changes sooner than "conservative" dialects, though no one could predict whether the changes would sweep the entire language.

Repatterning of Sounds The "*r*-dropping" rule referred to above did not affect all phonemic representations. In some cases, however, sound changes do result in a basic repatterning of sounds in words and morphemes. *Farm* in the "*r*-less" dialects lost the *r* to become rephonemicized as /fam/ since the "*r*" never occurs before a vowel. The new rule thus affected this word differently than it did the word *far* /far/, which phonetically would be pronounced [fa] in the expression *far more* /far mɔr/ [fa mɔ] but would be pronounced [far] in *far off* /far ɔf/ [far ɔf], since in the latter phrase it is followed by a vowel. Sound changes may therefore result in phonemic repatterning as well as phonetic changes of words and morphemes.

A major change in the history of English that resulted in new phonemic representations of words and morphemes took place approximately between 1400 and 1600 and is known as **the Great Vowel Shift.** The seven long, or tense, vowels of Middle English underwent the following change:

MIDDLE ENG.		MODERN ENG.	MIDDLE ENG.		MODERN ENG.	
[i:]	→	[ay]	[mi:s]	→	[mays]	*mice*
[u:]	→	[aw]	[mu:s]	→	[maws]	*mouse*
[e:]	→	[i:]	[ge:s]	→	[gi:s]	*geese*
[o:]	→	[u:]	[go:s]	→	[gu:s]	*goose*
[ɛ:]	→	[e:]	[brɛ:ken]	→	[bre:k]	*break*
[ɔ:]	→	[o:]	[brɔ:ken]	→	[bro:k]	*broke*
[a:]	→	[e:]	[na:mə]	→	[ne:m]	*name*

By diagraming the Great Vowel Shift on a vowel chart (Figure 9-2), we can see that each long vowel underwent an increase in tongue height, with the highest vowels [i:] and [u:] "falling off" to become the diphthongs [ay] and [aw]. In addition, [a] was "fronted."

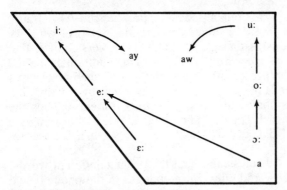

Figure 9-2 The Great Vowel Shift.

These changes are among the most dramatic examples of regular sound shift. The phonemic representation of many thousands of words changed. Today, some reflection of this vowel shift is seen in the alternating forms of morphemes in English: *please, pleasant; serene, serenity; sane, sanity; crime, criminal; sign, signal;* and so on.

The Great Vowel Shift is a primary source of many of the spelling "inconsistencies" of English, because our spelling system still reflects the way words were spelled before the Great Vowel Shift took place.

Morphological and Syntactic Change

Of all the words of witch's doom
There's none so bad as which and whom.
The man who kills both which and whom
Will be enshrined in our Who's Whom.
Fletcher Knebel

Changes in the phonological component of the grammar are by far the most studied type of language change. This is due to the relative ease with which phonological changes can be recognized. More recently, there has been an increasing interest in change other than phonological. Morphological and syntactic changes in the grammar also take place.

Rules of morphology and syntax may be lost, added, or changed. We can observe some of these changes by comparing older and newer forms of the language, or by looking at different dialects.

For example, an advertising slogan once caused a great deal of furor among language "purists" in America. They insisted that "Winston tastes good like a cigarette should" is "bad" English, because they said that there is a "rule" in our grammar stating that *like* can only be followed by a "noun phrase" and cannot be used as a "conjunction" to introduce an embedded sentence. According to them, the slogan should read "Winston tastes good *as* a cigarette should." But the grammar of many speakers of English has changed, so that *like* is now a conjunction, and for them the Winston jingle is a perfectly grammatical sentence.

For a number of centuries, English speakers had no trouble deciding when to use *who* and *whom*. The rule that once governed the occurrence of *who* and *whom* is slowly fading out of the language. Some speakers say *I don't know who to give it to;* others still use *whom*. Some speakers are not quite sure which pronoun to use. We are able to witness this change in progress.

Another change taking place before our eyes (or ears) is the use of the pronoun *I* in expressions like *between John and I, They gave it to Mary and I*, instead of the pronoun *me*. This may have started as a **hypercorrection** since the prescriptivists would correct those who said *It is me* instead of *It is I*, and eventually *I* began to be used more and more after prepositions and verbs in phrases where nouns and pronouns are conjoined.

The suffix *-ize*, which changes nouns and adjectives into verbs meaning "make . . ." is also gradually becoming "productive" in American English. Speakers are attaching this suffix to more and more words that previously did not take this suffix. Words like *privatize* "to make private," *rigidize* "to make rigid" are achieving the status of *optimize, stabilize,* and *finalize*. This represents a change in the morphology of American English that results in an expansion of the lexicon, as discussed below. The change seems to be upsetting the neoprescriptivists. In his book *A Civil Tongue*[3] Edwin Newman devotes an entire chapter, entitled "Ize Front," lamenting this change in the use of *-ize*.

The syntactic rules relating to the English negative construction underwent a number of changes from Old English to the present. In Modern English, negation is expressed by adding *not* or *do not*. One may also express negation by adding words like *never*[4] or *no*:

I am going → I am not going.
I went → I did not go.
I go to school → I never go to school.
I want meat → I don't want any meat; I want no meat.

In Old English the main negation element was *ne*. It usually occurred before the "helping verb" or **auxiliary** (or before the main verb if there was no auxiliary), as illustrated by these examples from Old English manuscripts:

(1) þæt he *na*   siþþan geboren *ne* wurde
that he never after born   not would-be
that he should never be born after that

---

[3] E. Newman. 1976. *A Civil Tongue*. (New York. The Bobbs-Merrill Co.)
[4] From a contraction of *not ever*.

(2) ac hie *ne* dorston þær on cuman
but they not dared there on come
but they dared not land there[5]

Notice in example (1) that not only is the word order different from that in Modern English, but that there are two negatives: *na* (a contraction of *ne* + *a*; "not" + "ever" = "never") and *ne*. This use of a "double negative" in Old English is considered by some present-day grammarians to be "substandard" and "ungrammatical" today. Whether it is grammatical depends upon the rules of one's own grammar; it was grammatical in Old English, as it is in certain English dialects of modern times.

In addition to the contraction of *ne* + *a* → *na*, other negative contractions occurred in Old English: *ne* could be attached to *habb-* "have," *wes-* "be," *wit-* "know," and *will-* "will" to form *nabb-*, *nes-*, *nyt-*, and *nyll-*, respectively.

We also have "contraction" rules that change *do* + *not* or *did* + *not* into *don't* and *didn't;* other contraction rules are similar to those found in Old English: *not* + *ever* → *never; will* + *not* → *won't; can* + *not* → *can't;* and so on. In our contractions the phonetic form of the negation element in *won't, can't, haven't, isn't,* and *wasn't* always comes at the end of the word. This is because in modern English the grammatical word order puts the *not* after the auxiliary. In Old English the negative element shows up at the beginning, since it typically preceded the auxiliary. The rules of word order have changed.

As late as the fifteenth and sixteenth centuries, one could merely add *not* at the end of an affirmative sentence to negate it. Such sentences are found in the writings of Malory and Shakespeare:

He saw you not.
I love thee not, therefore pursue me not.

In modern English, *not* must precede the main verb of the clause, and a *do*, marked for the proper tense, must be inserted, in ordinary use:

He saw you → He did not see you (or He didn't see you).
I love you, therefore pursue me → I do not love you, therefore do not pursue me (I don't love you).

Another change in English since Malory's time affected the rules of "comparative" and "superlative" constructions. Today we form the comparative by adding *-er* to the adjective or by inserting *more* before it; the superlative is formed by adding *-est* or by inserting *most*. In Malory's writing there are many examples of double comparatives and superlatives, which are now ungrammatical: *more gladder, more lower, moost royallest, moost shamefullest*. These would be "starred" forms today.

When we study a language whose only source is written records, such as Elizabethan English, we see only sentences that are grammatical unless the author is *deliberately* using ungrammatical sentences. There being no native speakers of Elizabethan English around for us to query, we can only infer

[5] From E. C. Traugott. 1972. *The History of English Syntax* (Holt, Rinehart and Winston. New York.). *Note:* þ, or "thorn," was pronounced [θ].

what sentences were ungrammatical. Such inference leads us to believe that expressions like *the Queen of England's crown* were ungrammatical in former versions of English. The occurrence of *The Wife's Tale of Bath* (rather than *The Wife of Bath's Tale*) in *The Canterbury Tales* supports this inference. Modern English, on the other hand, allows some rather complex constructions that involve the possessive marker. An English speaker can use possessive constructions such as

The girl whose sister I'm dating's roommate is very pretty.
The man from Boston's hat fall off.

Older versions of English would have to resort to an *of* construction to express the same thought (*The hat of the man from Boston fell off*). It is clear that a syntactic change took place that accounts for the extended use of the possessive morpheme *'s*.

To appreciate fully the extent to which the morphological component of a grammar may change, we can look beyond English, or even the family of Germanic languages, and consider other Indo-European languages. These changes often resulted in changes in the syntax. In Classical Latin, as well as in Russian, Lithuanian, and other languages, one finds an extensive system of *case endings* on nouns. Whenever speakers of Latin used a noun, they had to add the correct case suffix to the noun stem, according to the function of the noun in the sentence (all of which a native speaker would do without thinking, of course). Latin had six cases. Below are the different forms (the declension) for the noun *lupus*, "wolf":

CASE	NOUN STEM		CASE ENDING		
nominative	lup	+	us	lupus	The *wolf* runs.
genitive	lup	+	i	lupi	A sheep in *wolf's* clothing.
dative	lup	+	ō	lupō	Give food *to the wolf*.
accusative	lup	+	um	lupum	I love the *wolf*.
ablative	lup	+	ō	lupō	Run *from a wolf*.
vocative	lup	+	e	lupe	*Wolf,* come here!

In *Alice's Adventures in Wonderland*, Lewis Carroll has Alice give us a brief lesson in grammatical case. Alice, greatly shrunken, is swimming around in a pool of her own tears with a mouse, whom she wishes to befriend:

"Would it be of any use, now," thought Alice, "to speak to this mouse? Everything is so out-of-the-way down here, that I should think very likely it can talk: at any rate, there's no harm in trying." So she began: "O Mouse, do you know the way out of this pool? I am very tired of swimming about here, O Mouse!" (Alice thought this must be the right way of speaking to a mouse: she had never done such a thing before, but she remembered having seen in her brother's Latin Grammar, "A mouse—of a mouse—to a mouse—a mouse—O mouse!")

Alice gives us an English "translation" of the nominative, genitive, dative, accusative, and vocative cases (she omits the ablative).

Such an extensive case system (of which we have seen only part) was present in Latin, Ancient Greek, and Sanskrit. It was also present in Indo-European, the ancestor of all these languages. Modern languages such as

Lithuanian and Russian retain much of the Indo-European case system, but these languages are in the minority. In most modern Indo-European languages, changes have all but obliterated the case system. English still retains the genitive case, calling it possessive (in a *a sheep in wolf's clothing*, the noun *wolf* is in the genitive case). Pronouns retain a few more traces: *he* is nominative, *him* is accusative and dative (note the *m* in the Latin accusative), and *his* is genitive.

English has replaced its depleted case system with an equally expressive system of prepositions, and stricter constraints on word order. For example, in Latin *lupus dat dōnum virō* means "the wolf gives a gift to the man." The dative ending *ō* on virō "man" indicates the dative case, or the receiver. In English this same meaning is conveyed either by the proposition *to*, and the word order **accusative object-*to*-dative object,** or by the word order **dative object-accusative object** without the preposition: *The wolf gives the man a gift*. And in English, word order is stricter than in Latin, for in Latin *lupus dōnum virō dat*—literally "the wolf a gift to the man gives,"—is a grammatical sentence, which it is not in English.

Old English also had a rich case-ending system, as illustrated by the following:

1.

CASE	MODERN ENGLISH	OE SINGULAR	OE PLURAL
nominative	stone/stones	stān	stānas
genitive	stone's/stones'	stānes	stāna
dative	stone/stones	stāne	stānum
accusative	stone/stones	stān	stānas

2.

CASE	MODERN ENGLISH	OE SINGULAR	OE DUAL	OE PLURAL
nominative	I/we two/we	ic [ɪč]	wit [wɪt]	wē [we:]
genitive	my-mine/our-ours	min [mɪn]	uncer [unker]	ūre/ūser
dative	me/us	mē [me:]	unc [unk]	ūs [u:s]
accusative	me/us	mec [meč]	uncit [unkit]	ūsic [u:sɪč]

In these examples, *stone* represents the principal "strong" masculine noun declension. There were "weak" declensions also. The plural of this "strong" declension in the nominative and accusative cases became generalized to all the English regular nouns, another example of historical change.

We have mentioned a phonological rule that weakened certain short unstressed vowels. When the vowel was dropped in the plural form of "stones" [stɔ:nəs] (the stem vowel had changed by this time), it became [stɔwnz], and when the "weak" syllables representing case endings in the forms of the singular, genitive plural, and dative plural were dropped, English lost much of its case system.

With the loss of these case endings, new syntactic rules regulating word order entered the language, possibly so that excessive ambiguity would not result. In Old English, word order was not as crucial, because the language was so highly inflected. The doer of the action and the object of the action were revealed unambiguously by various case endings. This does not mean that there was no preferred word order, but even if the normal order was violated, the sentence meaning was perfectly clear. The following sentences all meant "The man slew the king":

Se man sloh þone kyning.
þone kyning sloh se man.
Se man þone kyning sloh.
þone kyning se man sloh.
Sloh se man þone kyning.
Sloh þone kyning se man.

Se was a definite article used only with the subject noun, and *þone* was the definite article used only with the object noun.

In modern English only the first literal (word-for-word) translation of these Old English sentences would mean what the original meant:

The man slew the king.
The king slew the man.
*The man the king slew.
*The king the man slew.
*Slew the man the king.
*Slew the king the man.

Furthermore, the last four examples would not be grammatical in Modern English as whole sentences—the syntactic rules that determine proper word order are violated.

Thus we see that the morphological and syntactic parts of grammars undergo change just as do the phonological components.

Lexical Change

Curl'd minion, dancer, coiner of sweet words.
Matthew Arnold, "Sohrab and Rustum"

As noted in the previous chapters, knowing a language means knowing what words and morphemes are in the language, and that means knowing what they "mean." These basic units of meaning constitute the vocabulary, or **lexicon,** which is part of the grammar. Changes in the lexicon can include the addition of new words, changes in the meanings of words, or the loss of words.

When speakers start to use a new word—that is, when a word is **added** to the lexicon—the change may be quite obvious and relatively abrupt. When speakers fail to use a word—that is, when a word is **lost** from the lexicon—the process takes place gradually over the course of several generations.

There are a number of ways in which new words can enter the language. In Chapter 5 we discussed *compounding,* the recombining of old words to form new ones, with new meanings. Thousands of common English words entered the language via this process, as the earlier examples showed. A few others may be cited: *afternoon, bigmouth, chickenhearted, do in, egghead, force feed, g-string, icecap, jetset, longshoreman, moreover, nursemaid, offshore, pothole, railroad, sailboat, takeover, undergo, water cooler, x-axis, zoo-ecology.*

We also saw that new words may be formed by derivational processes, as in *uglification* or *finalize* (from which we get a "bonus" *finalization*). In Chapter 4 on morphology we discussed other methods for enlarging the vocabulary. These included word coinage, deriving words from names, blends, back formations, acronyms, and abbreviations or clippings.

Borrowings

Neither a borrower nor a lender be.
Polonius, *Hamlet*

Borrowing is the "process by which one language or dialect takes and incorporates some linguistic element from another."[6] Most languages do not follow Polonius' advice when it comes to words. Borrowing is an important source of language change, and loans from other languages are an important source of new words. Most languages are borrowers, and the lexicon of any language can be divided into native and nonnative words (often called **loan words**). A *native word* is one whose history (or **etymology**) can be traced back to the earliest-known stages of the language.

A language may borrow a word *directly* or *indirectly*. A *direct* borrowing means that the borrowed item is a native word in the language it is borrowed from. The native Middle French word *festa* (Modern French *fête;* the Old French was *feste*, from Latin *festa*) was directly borrowed by Middle English, and has become Modern English *feast*. On the other hand, the word *algebra* was borrowed from Spanish, which in turn had borrowed it from Arabic. English borrowed *algebra* indirectly from Arabic, with Spanish as an intermediary.

Some languages are heavy borrowers; Albanian has borrowed so heavily that few native words are retained. On the other hand, many American Indian languages have borrowed but lightly from their neighbors.

English has borrowed extensively. Of the 20,000 or so words in common use, about three-fifths are borrowed. However, the figure is misleading. Of the 500 most frequently used words, only two-sevenths are borrowed, and since these "common" words are used over and over again in sentences, the actual frequency of appearance of native words is much higher than the statistics on borrowing would lead one to believe. "Little" words such as *and, be, have, it, of, the, to, will, you, on, that,* and *is* are all native to English, and constitute about one-fourth of the words regularly used. Thus it is not unreasonable to suppose that more than four-fifths of the words commonly used in speaking English are native to the language.

One can almost trace the history of the English-speaking peoples by studying the kinds of loan words in the language and when they entered the language. Until the Norman Conquest in 1066, England was inhabited chiefly by the Angles, the Saxons, and the Jutes, peoples of Germanic origin who came to England in the fifth century A.D. and remained to eventually become the English. (The word *England* is derived from *Angles*.) Originally, they spoke Germanic dialects, from which Old English developed directly, and these contained a number of Latin borrowings, but were otherwise undiluted by foreign elements. These Germanic tribes, who had displaced by force the earlier Celtic inhabitants of the islands, adopted a few Celtic place names, which were borrowings in Old English alongside the Latin, but the

---

[6] Antony Arlotto. 1972. *Introduction to Historical Linguistics.* (Houghton Mifflin. Boston.) p. 184. Note that the "borrowee" does not give up the borrowed element.

Celts were so thoroughly vanquished that their language had little effect on the language of the invaders.

For three centuries after the Norman Conquest, French was the language used for all affairs of state and for most commercial, social, and cultural matters. The West Saxon literary language was abandoned, but regional varieties of English did continue to be used in the homes of the people, and in their churches when they worshipped, and even in the market places of their small villages. During these three centuries, vast numbers of French words entered English, of which these are but a few:

government	crown	prince	state	parliament
nation	jury	judge	crime	sue
attorney	property	miracle	charity	court
lechery	virgin	saint	pray	mercy
religion	value	royal	money	society

Until the Norman invasion, when an Englishman slaughtered an ox for food, he ate *ox*. If it was a pig, he ate *pig*. If it was a sheep he ate *sheep*. But "ox" served at the Norman tables was *beef* (*boeuf*), "pig" was *pork* (*porc*), and "sheep" was *mutton* (*mouton*). The French language also gave English the food-preparing words *boil, broil, fry, stew,* and *roast*.

Many languages supplied words for English to borrow and assimilate. Between 1500 and 1700, the time of the Renaissance in England, there was much study of the Greek and Roman classics, and "learned" words from these sources entered our lexicon. In 1476 the printing press was introduced to England by William Caxton, and by 1640, 55,000 books had been printed in English. The authors of these books used many Greek and Latin words and as a result, many words of Ancient Greek and Latin came into the language.

From Greek came *drama, comedy, tragedy, scene, botany, physics, zoology, atomic,* and many other words. Greek roots have also provided English with a means for coining new words. *Thermos* "hot" plus *metron* "measure" give us *thermometer*. From *akros* "topmost" and *phobia* "fear" we get *acrophobia* "dread of heights." An ingenious American cartoonist, Robert Osborn, has "invented" some phobias, to each of which he gives an appropriate name:

logizomechanophobia	"fear of reckoning machines" from Greek *logizomai* "to reckon or compute" + *mekhane* "device" + *phobia*
ellipsosyllabophobia	"fear of words with a missing syllable" from Greek *elleipsis* "a falling short" + *syllabē* "syllable" + *phobia*
pornophobia	"fear of prostitutes" from Greek *porne* "harlot" + *phobia*[7]

Here is a sampling of words borrowed by English from Latin:

bonus	alumnus	quorum	exit
scientific	orthography	describe	advantage
rape	violent		

---

[7] From *An Osborn Festival of Phobias.* Copyright © 1971 by Robert Osborn. Text Copyright © 1971 by Eve Wengler. Reprinted by permission of Liveright Publishers, New York.

Latin, like Greek, has also provided prefixes and suffixes that are used productively with both native and nonnative roots. The prefix *ex-* comes from Latin:

ex-husband	ex-wife	ex-sister-in-law	exhibit
extend	export	exhale	exterminate
exclude	exalt	exhibit	

The suffix *-able/-ible* is also Latin, borrowed via French, and can be attached to almost any English verb:

writable	readable	answerable	movable
kissable	intelligible	trainable	laughable
typewritable	operable	questionable	

During the ninth and tenth centuries, the Scandinavian raiders who first raided and then settled on the British Isles left their traces in the English language. In fact, the pronouns *they, their,* and *them* are loan words from the Scandinavians. This is the only time that English ever borrowed pronouns. Many English words beginning with [sk] are of Scandinavian origin: *scatter, scare, scrape, skirt, skin, sky.*

Bin, flannel, clan, slogan, and *whiskey* are all words of Celtic origin, borrowed at various times from Welsh, Scots-Gaelic, or Irish.

From Dutch we borrowed such words as *buoy, freight, leak, pump, yacht.*

From German, *quartz, cobalt,* and—as we might guess—*sauerkraut* and *beer.*

From Italian, many musical terms, including words describing opera houses, have been borrowed: *opera, piano, virtuoso, balcony,* and *mezzanine.*

Words having to do with mathematics and chemistry were borrowed from Arabic, for early Arab scholarship in these fields was quite advanced. *Alcohol, algebra, cipher,* and *zero* are a representative sample. Often Arabic loan words enter English through Spanish, the original borrower. Such indirect borrowing is common, and sometimes it is difficult to trace the history of a borrowed word accurately. This is especially true in the case of French and Latin. English has borrowed extensively from both, and since French descended from Latin, confusion may arise as to the actual source. Borrowing from both a language and its ancestor leads to the kind of unusual situation that we find in the etymology of *animal,* which as a noun is borrowed from Latin, but as an adjective (for example, *animal magnetism*) is borrowed from French.

Spanish has loaned us *barbecue, cockroach, guitar,* and *ranch,* as well as *California,* literally "hot furnace."

With the settlement of the "New World," the English-speaking Americans borrowed from Indian languages as well as from Spanish. American Indian languages provided us with *pony, hickory,* and *squash,* to mention a few, and nearly half the state names of the United States are Indian.

Hundreds of "place names" in America are of non-English origin. One certainly can't call Indian names "foreign," except in the sense that they were foreign to English.

American Indian place names:

Connecticut	Potomac	Ohio	Mississippi
Erie	Huron	Michigan	Alleghenies
Appalachians	Ozarks	Massachusetts	Kentucky
Wisconsin	Oregon	Texas	Chattanooga
Chicago	Milwaukee	Omaha	Hackensack

Spanish place names:

Rio Grande	Colorado	Sierra Nevada	Santa Fe
Los Angeles	San Francisco	Santa Barbara	San Jose

Dutch place names: *Brooklyn* and *Harlem*.

The influence of Yiddish on English is interesting when one realizes that Yiddish words are used by many non-Jews, as well as non-Yiddish-speaking Jews in America. There was even a bumper sticker once quite popular (at least in Los Angeles) reading "Marcel Proust is a yenta." *Yenta* is a Yiddish word meaning "gossipy woman" or "shrew." *Lox* "smoked salmon," *bagel* "a hard roll resembling a doughnut," and *matzo* "unleavened cracker" belong to American English, as well as a number of Yiddish expressions introduced by comedians: *schmaltz, schlemiel, schmoe, kibbitz.*

Other languages also borrow words, and many of them have borrowed extensively from English. Twi speakers drank palm wine before the white man arrived in Africa. Now they also drink [bia] "beer," [hwiski] "whiskey," and [gɔrdɔn ǰin] "Gordon's gin."

Italian is studded with "strange" words like *snack, poster,* and *puzzle* (pronounced "pootsle"), and Italian girls use *blushes* and are warned by their mothers against *petting*.

Young Russians, intently aware of western culture, have incorporated into the Russian language words like *jazz, rock,* and the *twist,* which they dance in their *blue jeans* to *rock music*. When former President Nixon was about to be impeached *Pravda,* the official Communist Party newspaper, used the word *impeechmente* instead of the previously used Russian word *ustraneniye* "removal." The borrowing of non-Russian words is not, however, a new one. Fedorenko, the former Soviet delegate to the United Nations, was quoted in the Los Angeles *Times* (August 7, 1974) as saying, "Usage of a foreign word when there is an adequate Russian term is insulting to common sense and taste." In support of his view, he refers to Lenin, whom he quotes as saying, "We are spoiling the Russian language using foreign words without necessity. In addition, we use them wrongly." We are not sure whether Lenin was more concerned about the use or the misuse of foreign words in Russian.

Hebrew, used primarily as a religious language for centuries, seems to have lost a number of the obscenities it once had, and so today Israeli citizens have been forced to borrow some of their "four-letter words" from Arabic, which like most spoken languages possesses a wealth of them. One Arabic obscenity used in Hebrew is *kuss ummak,* meaning "your mother's cunt."

French, a language from which English once borrowed heavily, now borrows from English. *Le weekend, le picnique, le bar, le club, le hit parade, les hot dogs,* or *le after shave* may not, however, be as freely used as they were before 1977. A law went into effect on January 4, 1977, prohibiting the use of any foreign expression where an equivalent French term exists; and if a French term does not exist, then advertisers are forced to provide an explanation in French. This law applies to all advertisements and documents relating to the sale of goods in France, and lawbreakers will be fined. This attempt to purge borrowed words from the "pure" French language will undoubtedly fail, as all other such efforts have failed in the past, since language and the users are the final arbiters.

Colombia also has declared a war on non-Spanish words, and along with the French purists who shout "down with Franglais" (in French, of course) there are Italian purists who are upset with the "Italish" (English/Italian) besmirching the language of Dante.

As we noted in Chapter 5 on writing systems, the Japanese have a special syllabary just for loan words. For thousands of years Japanese borrowed heavily from Chinese (to which it is unrelated). Because Japanese uses Chinese characters in its writing system, many native Japanese words are paired with a Chinese word that is used in place of the native Japanese word in various situations, most notably in word compounds. Japanese even has two ways of counting, one using native Japanese words for the numbers and the other using Chinese loan words.

In the past 100 years Japanese has borrowed heavily from European languages, especially American English, which has provided Japanese with many thousands of loan words including technical vocabulary, sports terms, and many ordinary words of daily life.

Loss of Words So far in this section we have discussed how words are *added* to a language. It is also true that words can be *lost* from a language, though a word's departure is never as striking as a new word's arrival. When a new word comes into vogue, its very presence draws attention. But a word is lost by the act of inattention—nobody thinks of it; nobody uses it; and it fades out of the language.

English has lost many words, which a reading of any of Shakespeare's works will quickly make obvious. Here are a few taken from *Romeo and Juliet: beseem* "to be suitable," *mammet* "a doll or puppet," *wot* "to know," *gyve* "a fetter," *fain* "gladly" or "rather," *wherefore* "why."

Semantic Change

His talk was like a stream which runs
with rapid change from rocks to roses.
It slipped from politics to puns;
It passed from Mahomet to Moses.
Winthrop Mackworth Praed, The Vicar

We have seen that a language may gain or lose lexical items. It is also common for lexical items to shift in meaning, providing yet another way in which languages change. There are three ways in which a lexical item may change semantically. Its meaning may become broader; its meaning may become narrower; its meaning may shift.

Broadening When the meaning of a word becomes broader, that word means everything it used to mean, and then some. The Middle English word *dogge* meant a specific breed of dog, much like the word *dachshund* in Modern English. The meaning of *dogge* was **broadened** to encompass all members of the species *Canis familiaris*. The word *holiday* originally meant "holy day," a day of religious significance. Today, of course, the word signifies any day on which we don't have to work. *Butcher* once meant "slaughterer of goats" (and earlier "of bucks"), but its modern usage is more general. Similarly, *picture* used to mean "painted representation," but today you can take a picture with a camera. A *companion* used to mean a person with whom you shared bread, but today it's a person who accompanies you. *Quarantine* once had the restricted meaning "forty days' isolation," and *bird* once meant "young bird." The invention of steam-powered boats gave the verb *sail* an opportunity to extend its dominion to boats without sails, just as the verb *drive* widened in meaning to encompass self-propelled vehicles.

Narrowing In the King James version of the Bible (1611), God says of the herbs and trees, "to you they shall be for meat" (Genesis 1:29). To a speaker of seventeenth-century English, *meat* meant "food," and *flesh* meant "meat." Since that time, semantic change has **narrowed** the meaning of meat to what it is in Modern English. The word *deer* once meant "beast" or "animal," as its German related word *Tier* still does. The meaning of *deer* has been narrowed to a particular kind of animal. Similarly, the word *hound* used to be the general term for "dog," like the German *Hund*. Today *hound* means a special kind of dog. Before the Norman Conquest, as we have pointed out before, the words *ox, pig, calf,* and *sheep* meant both the animal and the meat of that animal. The Normans brought with them the words *beef, pork, veal,* and *mutton,* which were borrowed into English, thus narrowing the meaning of *ox, pig, calf,* and *sheep.* The Old English word that occurs as modern *starve* once meant "to die." Its meaning has narrowed to become "to die of hunger," and in colloquial language "to be very hungry," as in "I'm starved." *Token* used to have the broad meaning "sign," but long ago was specialized to mean a physical object that is a sign, such as a *love token.* *Liquor* was once synonymous with *liquid, reek* used to mean "smoke," and *girl* once meant "young person of either sex."

Meaning Shifts The third kind of semantic change that a lexical item may undergo is a shift in meaning. The word *bead* originally meant "prayer." During the Middle Ages the custom arose of repeating one's prayers (that is, *beads*) over and over and counting them by means of little wooden balls on a rosary. The meaning of *bead* shifted from "prayer" to the visible manifestation of a prayer. The word *knight* once meant "youth" but was elevated in meaning in time for the age of chivalry. *Lust* used to mean simply "pleasure," with no negative or sexual overtones. *Lewd* was merely "ignorant," and *immoral* meant "not customary." *Silly* used to mean "happy" in Old English. By the Middle English period it had come to mean "naive," and only in Modern English does it mean "foolish." The overworked Modern English word *nice* meant "ignorant" a thousand years ago. When Juliet tells Romeo, "I am too *fond*," she is not claiming she likes Romeo too much. She means "I am too *foolish.*"

Reconstructing "Dead" Languages

. . . Philologists who chase
A panting syllable through time and space,
Start it at home, and hunt it in the dark,
To Gaul, to Greece, and into Noah's Ark.
Cowper, *Retirement*

That branch of linguistics which deals with how languages change, what kinds of changes occur, and why they occurred is called **historical and comparative linguistics.** It is *historical* because it deals with the history of particular languages; it is *comparative* because it deals with relations between languages.

The main linguistic work in the nineteenth century was historical-comparative research. In that century, Darwin's theory of evolution had a profound influence on all areas of science, linguistics included, which led to theories of language and language development that were analogous to biological theories. Language was considered to have a "life cycle" and to develop according to evolutionary laws. In addition, it was believed that language, like the human animal, has a "genealogical tree"—that is, that each language can be traced back to a common ancestor. This theory of biological naturalism is known by the name of the *Stammbaum* ("family tree") theory.

The nineteenth-century historical and comparative linguists based their theories on the observations that there is a resemblance between certain languages, and that the *differences* among languages showing such resemblance are *systematic:* in particular, that there are regular sound correspondences. They also assumed that languages displaying systematic differences, no matter how slight in resemblance, had descended from a common source language—that is, were genetically related.

The chief goal of the nineteenth-century historical-comparativists was to develop and elucidate the genetic relationships that exist among the world's languages. They aimed to establish the major language families of the world and to define principles for the classification of languages. Their work grew out of earlier research.

In 1786 Sir William Jones (a British scholar who found it best to reside in India because of his sympathy for the rebellious American colonists) delivered a paper in which he observed that Sanskrit bore to Greek and Latin "a stronger affinity . . . than could possibly have been produced by accident." Jones suggested that these three languages had "sprung from a common source" and that probably Germanic and Celtic had the same origin. The classical philologists of the time attempted to disprove the idea that there was any genetic relationship between Sanskrit, Latin, and Greek, since if such a relationship existed it would make their views on language and language development obsolete. A Scottish philosopher, Dugall Stewart, for example, put forth the hypothesis that Sanskrit and Sanskrit literature were inventions of Brahmans, who used Greek and Latin as models to deceive Europeans. This "scholar" wrote on this complex question without knowing a single Sanskrit character, whereas Jones was an eminent Sanskritist.

The work of Jones was supported by many scholars. About thirty years after Jones delivered his important paper, the German linguist Franz Bopp pointed up the relationship between Sanskrit, Latin, Greek, Persian, and Germanic. At the same time, a young Danish scholar named Rasmus Rask corroborated these results, and brought Lithuanian and Armenian into the relationship as well. Rask was the first scholar to describe formally the regularity of certain phonological differences between related languages.

Rask's investigation of these regularities was followed up by the German linguist Jakob Grimm (of fairy-tale fame), who published a four-volume treatise (1819–1822) that specified the regular sound correspondences between Sanskrit, Greek, Latin, and the Germanic languages. It was not only the similarities that intrigued Grimm and the other linguists, but the systematic nature of the differences. Where Latin has a [p], English often has a [f]; where Latin has a [t], English often has a [θ]; where Latin has a [k], English often has a [h].

Grimm pointed out that certain phonological changes must have occurred early in the history of the Germanic languages, which did not take place in Sanskrit, Greek, or Latin. Because the changes were so strikingly regular, they became known as "Grimm's law," which is illustrated in Figure 9-3.

Earlier stage:[8]   bh dh gh b d g p t k
                     ↓   ↓   ↓   ↓ ↓ ↓ ↓ ↓ ↓
Later stage: b   d   g   p t k f θ x (or h)

Figure 9-3 Grimm's Law (an early Germanic sound shift).

By observing **cognates,** which are words in related languages that developed from the same word (and hence often, but not always, have the same meaning), we can observe sound correspondences and from them deduce sound changes. Thus, from the cognates shown in Figure 9-4 of Sanskrit, Latin, and English (representing Germanic), we observe the regular correspondence *p-p-f* which indicates that the languages are genetically related. We posit Indo-European *$*p$*[9] as the reflex of the *p-p-f* correspondence:

INDO-EUROPEAN	SANSKRIT		LATIN		ENGLISH	
*p	p	pitar-	p	pater	f	father
		pad-		pēs		foot
		No cognate		piscis		fish
		pasu		pecu		fee

Figure 9-4 Cognates of Indo-European ***p**.

A more complete chart of correspondences is given in Figure 9-5. Here we give but a single representative example of each regular correspondence. In most cases there are *many cognate sets* exhibiting the same correspondence. These cognate sets lead us to reconstruct the Indo-European sound shown in the first column.

---

[8] This "earlier stage" is the original parent of Sanskrit, Greek, the Romance and Germanic languages, and other languages—namely, Indo-European. The symbols *bh, dh,* and *gh* are "breathy voiced" stop phonemes, often called "voiced aspirates."

[9] The asterisk before a letter indicates a "reconstructed" sound. It does not mean an unacceptable form. This is the only other use of the asterisk in this book and occurs only in this chapter.

INDO-EUROPEAN	SANSKRIT		LATIN		ENGLISH	
*p	p	pitar-	p	pater	f	father
*t	t	trayas	t	trēs	θ	three
*k	ś	śun[10]	k	canis	h	hound
*b	b	No cognate	b	labium	p	lip
*d	d	dva-	d	duo	t	two
*g	j	ajras	g	ager	k	acre
*bh	bh	bhrātar-	f	frāter	b	brother
*dh	dh	dhā	f	fē-ci	d	do
*gh	h	vah-	h	veh-ō	g	wagon

Figure 9-5 Some Indo-European sound correspondences.

Sanskrit underwent the fewest consonant sound changes in its history, while Latin underwent somewhat more, and Germanic (under Grimm's law) underwent almost a complete restructuring. Still, the fact that it was the phonemes and phonological rules which changed, and not individual words, has resulted in the remarkably regular correspondences that allow us to reconstruct much of the sound system of Indo-European.

Exceptions can be found to these regular correspondences, and Grimm was aware of this. He stated: "The sound shift is a general tendency; it is not followed in every case." Karl Verner in 1875 was able to explain some of the exceptions to Grimm's law; "Verner's law" explained why Indo-European **p**, **t**, and **k** failed to correspond to **f**, **θ**, and **x**, in some cases:

When the preceding vowel was unaccented, f, θ, and x underwent a further change to b, d, and g.

A group of young linguists who became known as the Neo-Grammarians went beyond the idea that such sound shifts represented only a tendency, and claimed that sound laws have no exception. They viewed linguistics as a natural science, and therefore believed that laws of sound change were unexceptionable natural laws. The "laws" they put forth often had exceptions, however, which could not always be explained as dramatically as Verner's law explained the exceptions to Grimm's law. But the work of these linguists provided important data and insights into language change and why such changes occur. And the assumption that sound change is exceptionless is an important concept in modern historical linguistics.

When the differences among two or more languages are systematic and regular, as exemplified by regular sound correspondences, the languages are probably related. We often find languages that we suspect are related, but whose "parent" has long since disappeared. This is certainly the case for the languages studied by Bopp, Rask, Grimm, and those scholars who followed them. It is possible that by comparing the "daughter" languages we may deduce many facts about the parent language. The method of **reconstruction** of a parent language from a comparison of its daughters is called the **comparative method.**

A brief example will illustrate how the comparative method works. Consider these words in four Romance languages.[11]

---

[10] ś is a sibilant different from s.

[11] Data from Winfred P. Lehmann. 1973. *Historical Linguistics*, 2nd ed. (Holt, Rinehart and Winston. New York.) *Note: ch* = [š]; *c* = [k].

FRENCH	ITALIAN	SPANISH	PORTUGUESE	
cher	caro	caro	caro	"dear"
champ	campo	campo	campo	"field"
chandelle	candela	candela	candeia	"candle"

In French we find *š* where we find *k* in the three other languages. This regular sound correspondence, *š-k-k-k*, along with other facts, supports the view that French, Italian, Spanish, and Portuguese descended from a common language. The comparative method leads us to reconstruct a *k* in "dear," "field," and "candle" of the parent language. More important, it tells us the *k* underwent a change to *š* in French, which did not occur in Italian, Spanish, and Portuguese. Those languages retained the original *k* of the parent language, Latin.

To use the comparative method, analysts identify regular sound correspondences (not always easy to do) in what they take to be "daughter" languages, and for each correspondence, they reconstruct a sound of the parent language. In this way the entire sound system of the parent may be reconstructed. The various phonological changes that occurred in the development of each "daughter" language as it descended and changed from the parent are then identified. Sometimes the sound that analysts choose in their reconstruction of the parent language will be the sound that appears most frequently in the correspondence. This was illustrated above with the four Romance languages.

It is not unusual for other considerations to outweigh the "majority rules" principle. The likelihood of certain phonological changes to occur may persuade the analyst to reconstruct a "minority" sound, or even a sound that doesn't occur at all in the correspondence. For example, consider data in these four hypothetical languages.

LANGUAGE A	LANGUAGE B	LANGUAGE C	LANGUAGE D
hono	hono	fono	vono
hari	hari	fari	veli
rahima	rahima	rafima	levima
hor	hor	for	vol

Wherever Languages A and B have an *h*, Language C has an *f* and Language D has a *v*. Therefore we have the sound correspondence *h-h-f-v*. Because of this we might be tempted by the comparative method to reconstruct *h* in the parent language. But from other data on historical change, and from phonetic research, we know that *h* seldom becomes *f* or *v*. Generally the reverse is the case. Thus linguists reconstruct an **f* in the parent, and posit the sound change "*f* becomes *h*" in languages A and B, and "*f* becomes *v*" in Language D. The other correspondences are not problematic insofar as these data are concerned. They are:

o-o-o-o   n-n-n-n   a-a-a-e   r-r-r-l   m-m-m-m

These lead us to reconstruct the forms **o, *n, *a, *r, *m* for the parent language, and to posit the sound change "*a* becomes *e*" and "*r* becomes *l*" in language D. These are "natural" sound changes often found in the world's languages. Language D, in this example, is the most *innovative* of the three languages, as it has undergone three sound changes.

It is by means of the comparative method that nineteenth-century linguists, beginning with August Schleicher in 1861, were able to initiate the reconstruction of the long-lost parent language so aptly conceived by Jones, Bopp, Rask, and Grimm. This language, which we believe flourished about 6000 years ago, we have been calling **Indo-European.**

Historical Evidence

You know my method. It is founded upon the observance of trifles.
Sir Arthur Conan Doyle, "The Boscombe Valley Mystery"

How do we discover phonological changes? How do we know how Shakespeare or Chaucer or the writer of *Beowulf* pronounced their versions of English? Obviously, we have no phonograph records or tape recordings that would give us direct knowledge.

For many languages there are historical records that go back more than a thousand years. These records are studied to find out how languages were once pronounced. The spelling in early manuscripts tells us a great deal about the sound systems of older forms of modern languages. If certain words are always spelled one way, and other words another way, it is logical to conclude that the two groups of words were pronounced differently, even if the precise pronunciation is not known. For example, if you didn't know English, but you consistently found that the word which meant "deep hole" was written as *pit,* and the word for a domesticated animal was written as *pet,* it would be safe to assume that these two words were pronounced differently. Once a number of orthographic contrasts are identified, good guesses can be made as to actual pronunciation. These guesses are supplemented by common words that show up in all stages of the language, allowing their pronunciation to be traced from the present, step by step, into the past.

Another clue to earlier pronunciation is provided by non-English words used in the manuscripts of English. Suppose a French word that scholars know contains the vowel [o:] is borrowed into English. The way the borrowed word is spelled reveals a particular spelling-sound correspondence. A number of spelling symbols were related to certain sounds in this way.

Other documents can be examined for evidence. Private letters are an excellent source of data. Linguists prefer letters written by "naive" spellers, since they will misspell words according to the way they pronounce them. For instance, at one point in English history all words spelled with *er* in their stems were pronounced as if they were spelled with *ar.* Some poor speller kept writing *clark* for *clerk,* which helped linguists to discover the older pronunciation.

Clues are also provided by the writings of the prescriptive grammarians of the period. Between 1550 and 1750 a group of prescriptivists in England known as **orthoepists** attempted to preserve the "purity" of English. In prescribing how people should speak, they told us how people actually spoke. If an orthoepist were alive in America today he might write in his manual: "It is incorrect to pronounce *Cuba* with a final *r.*" Future scholars would know that there were speakers of English who pronounced it that way.

Some of the best clues to earlier pronunciation are provided by puns and rhymes in literature. Two words rhyme if the vowels and final consonants of these words are the same. When a poet rhymes the verb *found* with the noun *wound*, it strongly suggests that the vowels of these two words were identical:

BENVOLIO: . . . 'tis in vain to seek him here that means to not be found.
ROMEO: He jests at scars that never felt a wound.

Shakespeare's rhymes are very helpful in reconstructing the sound system of Elizabethan English:

Where's the place? Upon the heath
There to meet with Macbeth

In the speech of Shakespeare's Elizabethan audience, *heath* [hɛ:θ] rhymed with *Macbeth* [məkbɛθ]. The pronunciation of *heath* has changed as a result of changes in the sound system of English.

Dialect differences may provide clues as to what earlier stages of a language were like. There are many dialects of English spoken around the world, including the United States. By comparing the pronunciation of various words in several dialects, we can "reconstruct" earlier forms and see what changes took place in the inventory of sounds and in the phonological rules. When we study different dialects it becomes apparent that all language change is not "hidden." We can actually observe some changes in progress.

For example, since some speakers of English pronounce *Mary, merry,* and *marry* with three different vowels (that is, [meri], [mɛri], and [mæri], respectively), we suspect that at one time all speakers of English did so. (The different spellings are also a clue.) For some dialects, however, only one of these sounds can occur before /r/, namely the sound [ɛ], so we can "see" a change taking place. This same change can also be seen in this "drinking song" of the University of California.

They had to carry Harry to the ferry
And the ferry carried Harry to the shore
And the reason that they had to carry Harry to the ferry
Was cause Harry couldn't carry any more.

This song was written by someone who rhymed *Harry, carry,* and *ferry.* It doesn't sound quite as good to those who do not rhyme *Harry* and *ferry.*

The historical-comparativists working on Indo-European languages, and other languages with written records, had a difficult job, but not nearly so difficult as those scholars who are attempting to discover genetic relationships among languages with no written history. Linguists have, however, been able to establish language families and reconstruct the histories of such individual languages. They first study the grammars of the languages and dialects spoken today and compare the sound systems, the vocabularies, and the syntax, seeing what correspondences exist. By this method, Major John W. Powell, Franz Boas, Edward Sapir, Mary Haas, and others have worked out the complex relationships of American Indian languages. Other linguists have worked with African languages and have established a number of major and minor language families in Africa, each containing many subgroups. It has also been established that over a thousand different languages are spoken in Africa.

The Genetic Classification of Languages

The Sanskrit language, whatever be its antiquity, is of a wonderful structure, more perfect than the Greek, more copious than the Latin, and more exquisitely refined than either, yet bearing to both of them a stronger affinity, both in the roots of verbs and in the forms of grammar, than could possibly be produced by accident; so strong, indeed, that no philologer could examine all three, without believing that they have sprung from some common source, which, perhaps, no longer exists . . .

Sir William Jones, 1786

We have discussed how different languages descend from one language, and how historical and comparative linguists classify languages into families and reconstruct earlier forms of the ancestral language. When we examine the languages of the world, we perceive similarities and differences among them that provide further evidence for the "genetic" relatedness we know exists.

Counting to five in English, German, and Pima (a southwestern American Indian language) shows similarities between English and German not shared by Pima:

ENGLISH	GERMAN	PIMA
one	eins	hermako
two	zwei	gohk
three	drei	waik
four	vier	giik
five	fünf	hetasp

This similarity between English and German is pervasive. Sometimes it is extremely obvious (*man/Mann*), at other times a little less obvious (*child/Kind*).

Because German and English are human languages, we expect to find certain similarities between them. But there are more similarities than in other languages. It is not the case that they are related because they are highly similar, however. Rather, they are highly similar because they are related. They are related because at one time in history they were the same language, the language spoken by the German tribes, some of which settled in Britain in the fifth century. Languages that are related were, at some point in the past, one language.

Fifth-century Germanic is the parent of Modern English and Modern German, which are its "daughters"; English and German are "sisters." Sisterhood is the fundamental genealogical relationship between languages. Similarly, the Romance languages of French, Spanish, Portuguese, Italian, and Romanian are daughters of Latin and sisters to one another.

Where there are mothers and sisters, there must be *cousins*. At one time, well over 2000 years ago, an early form of the Germanic, from which English ultimately descended, and an early form of Latin were sisters. The respective offspring are cousins. The five Romance languages listed above are cousins to English. The numbers from one to three in the three languages reveal this relationship:

SPANISH	FRENCH	ENGLISH
uno	un	one
dos	deux	two
tres	trois	three

Norwegian, Yiddish, Danish, Icelandic, and Dutch are all close relatives of English. They, like English, are Germanic. Greek is a somewhat more distant cousin. The Celtic language gave birth to Irish, Scots Gaelic, Welsh, and Breton, all cousins of English. Breton is spoken by the people living in the northwest coastal regions of France called Brittany. It was brought there by Celts fleeing from Britain in the seventh century and has been preserved as the language of some Celtic descendants in Brittany ever since. Russian is also a distant cousin, as are its sisters, Bulgarian, Serbo-Croatian, Polish, Czech, and Slovak. The Baltic language Lithuanian is related to English, as is its sister language, Latvian. A neighboring language, Estonian, however, is not a relative. Sanskrit, as pointed out by Sir William Jones, as far removed from the European languages as it appears to be, is a distant cousin of these languages, as are its daughters, Hindi, spoken in India, and Bengali, spoken primarily in Bangladesh. Even Modern Persian, spoken in Iran, is a distant cousin of English.

All the languages mentioned in the last paragraph, except for Estonian, are related, more or less distantly, because they descended from Indo-European.

Figure 9-6, an abbreviated "family tree" of the Indo-European family of languages, gives a genealogical and historical classification of the languages shown. All the languages of the world may be similarly classified. This diagram is somewhat simplified. For one thing, the "dead-ends"—languages that evolved and died, leaving no offspring—are not included. A language dies when no children learn it. This may come about in two ways: either all the speakers of the language are annihilated by some tragic event or, more commonly, the speakers of the language are absorbed by another culture that speaks a different language. The children, at first bilingual, grow up using the language of the dominant culture. Their children, or their children's children, fail to learn the old language, and so it dies. This is what has become of many American Indian languages. Cornish, a Celtic language akin to Breton, met a similar fate in England in the seventeenth century. Today, however, there are "revival" movements among some people to "resurrect" their old languages. In Brittany, for example, many of the popular singers use only Breton. Hebrew is an example of a nearly "dead" language —it was used only in religious ceremonies—that was revived for everyday use. It is now the national language of Israel and is spoken natively by a large number of people.

The family tree also fails to show a number of intermediate stages that must have existed in the evolution of modern languages. Languages do not evolve abruptly. It is difficult to determine precisely when a "new" language appears. There is evidence that Germanic had at first three daughters. From the northernmost daughter, the Scandinavian languages evolved; English, German, and Dutch evolved from the westernmost daughter.

Finally, the diagram fails to show a number of Indo-European languages because of lack of space.

Obviously, most of the world's languages do not belong to the Indo-European family. Linguists have also attempted to classify the non-Indo-Euro-

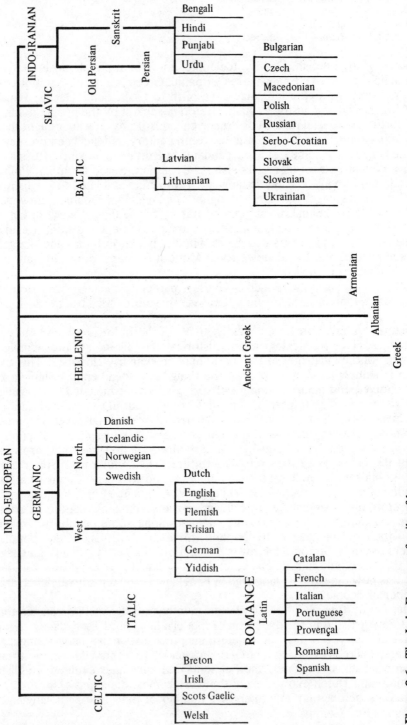

Figure 9-6 The Indo-European family of languages.

pean languages according to their genetic relationships. The task is to identify the languages that constitute a family, and the relationships that exist among those languages.

The results of this research are often surprising; faraway Bengali is an Indo-European language, whereas Hungarian, surrounded on all sides by Indo-European languages, is not.

For linguists interested in the nature of human language, the number of languages in the many different language families provides necessary data. Although these languages are diverse in many ways, they are also remarkably similar in many ways. We find that the languages of the "wretched Greenlanders," the Maoris of New Zealand, the Hottentots of Africa, and the people of North America have similar sounds, similar phonological and syntactic rules, and similar semantic systems. There is evidence, then, that we need a theory of language which aims at universality as well as specificity.

At the end of this chapter we have included a table of some languages of the world showing genetic relationships, the principal geographic areas where the language is spoken and the number of speakers (as nearly as that can be determined).

Why Do Languages Change?

Stability in language is synonymous with rigor mortis.
Ernest Weekley

No one knows exactly how or why languages change. Certainly linguistic changes do not happen suddenly. It is not the case that all speakers of English awoke one morning and decided to use the word *beef* for "ox meat." Nor is it true that all the children of one particular generation grew up to adopt this new word usage. Changes are more gradual, particularly changes in the phonological and syntactic system.

Of course, certain changes may occur instantaneously for any one speaker. For example, when a speaker acquires a new word, he doesn't "gradually" acquire it. Even when a new rule is incorporated into his grammar, the rule is either in or not in his grammar. It may at first be an optional rule; he may use it only some of the time, its use perhaps being determined by social context. What is gradual is the spread of certain changes over the entire speech community.

A basic cause of change can be attributed to the way children acquire the language. No one teaches the child the rules of the grammar; each child constructs her grammar on her own, generalizing rules from the linguistic input she receives. As will be discussed in Chapter 10, the language used by children shows stages in the development of their grammars. The early simple grammars become more and more complex until they approximate the grammars used by adults. The child's grammar is never exactly like that of the adult community. Children receive input from many dialects used around them and from many individual styles, and so on. The features of these grammars may then merge. Certain rules may be simplified or overgeneralized.

The older generation may be using "variable" rules. For example, at certain times they may say "It's I" and at other times "It's me." The less formal style is usually used with children. The next generation may use only the "me" form of the pronoun in this construction. In such cases, the grammar will have changed.

The reasons for some changes are relatively easy to understand. Before television there was no such word as *television* in the language. It soon became a common lexical item. We have already seen how words may be coined or borrowed, and their entry into the language is not mysterious. Other changes are more difficult to explain. For example, no one knows why vowels shifted in English.

We have also discussed how borrowing from other languages can affect the phonological system of a language as well as the lexicon. Thus, when English borrowed French words containing /ž/ and /v/, they were eventually added to the inventory of English phonemes. Metaphorically, we can say that English borrowed /ž/ and /v/ from French.

We have some plausible explanations for some of the phonological changes in languages. Some of these changes are due to physiological mechanisms. Some sounds and combinations of sounds are "easier to pronounce" than others. For example, it is universally the case that vowels are nasalized before nasal consonants. This is because it is difficult to time the lowering of the velum to produce the nasal sound so that it coincides exactly with the production of the consonant. In anticipation of the nasal consonant, then, the velum is lowered during the vowel and the result is a nasalized vowel. As stated in Chapter 3, the effect of one sound on another is called **assimilation;** the vowel **assimilates** to the nasality of the nasal consonant. Once the vowel is nasalized, the contrast that the nasal consonant provided can be equally well provided by the nasalized vowel alone, and the redundant consonant may be deleted. The contrast between oral and nasal vowels that exists in many languages of the world today results from just such a historical sound change.

In French, at one time, *bol* "basin," *botte* "high boot," *bog* "a card game," *bock* "Bock beer," and *bon* "good" were [bɔl], [bɔt], [bɔg], [bɔk], and [bɔ̃n], respectively. Notice that in *bon* there was a final nasal consonant which *conditioned* the nasalization of the preceding vowel. Today, *bon* is pronounced [bɔ̃]; the nasal vowel effectively maintains the contrast with the other words.

Another example from English illustrates how such assimilative processes can change a language. In English when we say *key*, the /k/ is articulated forward in the mouth in anticipation of the high front "palatal" vowel /i/. But when we say the /k/ in *cot*, the [k] is backed in anticipation of the low back vowel [a]. The /k/ in *key* is thus "palatalized." In Old English there were a number of words that began with a palatalized /kʸ/. When these were followed by /i/ they developed into our modern palatal affricate /č/, as is illustrated by the following:

OLD ENGLISH [k]	MODERN ENGLISH [č]
ciese	→ cheese
cinn	→ chin
cild	→ child

The same process that produced the /č/ in English—the palatalization of the /k/—is also found in many other languages. In Twi, for example, the word meaning "to hate" was once pronounced [ki]. The [k] became [kʸ] and then finally a [č], so that today it is pronounced [či].

Such assimilative processes at work in languages gave rise to a "theory of least effort" to explain linguistic change. According to this theory, sound changes are primarily due to linguistic "laziness"; we exert as little effort as possible in speaking. We might call this the "mumbling tendency." We tend to assimilate one sound to another, to drop out unstressed syllables, and so on.

Linguistic history reveals that many exceptional morphemes lost their special status because of a different kind of "laziness." This kind of change has been called **internal borrowing**—that is, we "borrow" from one part of the grammar and apply the rule generally. It is also called **analogic change.** One could say that it is by analogy to *foe/foes* and *dog/dogs* that speakers started saying *cows* as the plural of *cow* instead of the earlier plural *kine*. By analogy to *reap/reaped*, *seem/seemed*, and *ignite/ignited*, children and adults are presently saying *I sweeped the floor*, *I dreamed that I went to the Presidential Ball in my Maidenform Bra*, *She lighted the bonfire*, instead of using *swept*, *dreamt*, and *lit*.

The same kind of analogic change is exemplified by our "regularization" of exceptional plural forms. We borrowed words like *datum/data*, *agendum/agenda*, *curriculum/curricula*, *memorandum/memoranda*, *medium/media*, *criterion/criteria*, *bandit/banditti*, *virtuoso/virtuosi*, to name just a few. The irregular plurals of these nouns have been replaced by regular plurals among many speakers: *agendas, curriculums, memorandums, criterias, virtuosos*. In some cases the borrowed original plural forms were considered to be the singular (as in *agenda* and *criteria*) and the new plural is therefore a "plural-plural." Also, many speakers now regard *data* and *media* as nouns that do not have plural forms, like *information*.

The "theory of least effort" does seem to account for some linguistic changes, but it cannot account for others. Simplification of grammars occurs, but so does elaboration or complication.

Simplification often reduces redundancies, but some redundancy is required to make language efficient. When case endings are lost, confusion can result unless the grammar compensates for the loss; stricter word-order constraints are thus placed on the grammar. While one sees a tendency toward greater simplification, one also finds a countertendency, the desire to be intelligible.

We find many factors that contribute to linguistic change—simplification of grammars, elaboration (to maintain intelligibility), borrowing, lexical additions. But it is the children learning the language who finally incorporate the ongoing changes or create new changes in the grammar of the language. The exact reasons for linguistic change are still elusive. Perhaps language changes for the same reason all things change: that it is the nature of things to change. As Heraclitus pointed out, thousands of years ago, "All is flux, nothing stays still. Nothing endures but change."

Linguistic Paleontology

History is too serious to be left to historians.
Iain Macleod, in the *Observer* (July 16, 1961)

A fascinating application of historical linguistics is deducing information about the culture and location of an ancient civilization for which we have no written history, using as data its partially reconstructed language. Such studies are known as **linguistic paleontology,** and have been carried out extensively on Indo-European.

We have no direct written knowledge of the Indo-European peoples. They are prehistoric. Yet linguists have deduced quite a few things about the Indo-Europeans. For instance, in reconstructing Proto-Indo-European, we find a word for "daughter-in-law," but no word for "son-in-law." This leads us to believe that when a couple "married," they lived in the man's family. This in turn indicates that these people did not form matriarchal families.

We find that the Indo-Europeans had terms for "cow," "sheep," "goat," "pig," "dog," "wolf," "duck," "bee," "oak," "beech," "willow," and "grain." But the lack of terms for vegetables or for special kinds of grain indicates a people that relied heavily on animal sources for food.

The words for "beech," "oak," "salmon," and "wolf," which are known to have existed in Proto-Indo-European, have been used in an attempt to pinpoint the geographical location of the Indo-European speech community. The lack of terms for trees of the Mediterranean or Asiatic areas, such as the olive, cypress, and palm, coupled with the presence of terms for beech and oak trees, which are indigenous to eastern and central Europe, suggests an Indo-European homeland near those places, though this homeland might well have extended as far east as the Volga River. This hypothesis is supported by the presence of terms for "wolf" and "salmon," creatures of that geographic area, and the lack of terms for animals indigenous to Asia. Archeological discoveries in Rumania and the Ukraine support this hypothesis.

Knowing that Proto-Indo-European had no terms for silver, gold, and iron, we can deduce, though not without some doubts, that they were pre-iron-age peoples, placing them in time before 4000 B.C.

For language families without any written history, the attempt to reconstruct an earlier language from several modern languages shown to be related may be the only way of gaining any information about the history of the speakers of those languages. This method has proved to be modestly effective in the case of American Indian languages, although detailed knowledge is still lacking. But we do get a rough picture of where the various American Indian people were at what point in time. Knowing that two languages are closely related, but widely separated geographically, tells us that one or the other group of speakers migrated (or that they both migrated in opposite directions). By linguistic means it is sometimes possible to determine approximately when the languages separated, and therefore when the peoples themselves separated.

By this means, scholars have now concluded that the ancestors of the African Bantu people began their migration about 2,300 years ago, spreading from a small region in Africa throughout much of the continent. Archeologists and linguists have worked together to trace the migration of these people. The historical search started in the nineteenth century, when European explorers found that many of their porters, cooks, and escorts were able to speak a language which was understood in wide areas of Africa. Although there were many differences among the languages the explorers encountered, there were also many similarities, and it appeared that all these languages were related. This family of languages was named Bantu by the nineteenth-century German scholar Wilhelm H. I. Bleek, when he found that *mu-ntu* meant "man" and *ba-ntu* meant "men" in many of these languages. It is now generally believed that more than 130 million Africans speak languages derived from a common Bantu ancestor. Through archeological evidence and linguistic evidence the history of these people has been traced. Professor Christopher Ehret of the University of California at Los Angeles has conducted intensive research on the non-Bantu words that have entered the Bantu languages, words that illustrate the sequence of events in the migration of the Bantu people.

Linguistic paleontology thus shows that the study of linguistic change brings with it auxiliary rewards of knowledge in other fields.

A study of linguistic change could have been the inspiration for Shelley, who pointed out in his poem "Mutability" that:

Man's yesterday may ne'er be like his morrow:
Nought may endure but Mutability.

LANGUAGES OF THE WORLD

How many people of the world can be brought together so that no one person understands the language spoken by any other person? Considering that there are billions of people in the world, the number of mutually unintelligible languages is rather small—"only" about 3,000, according to one suggestion, and as many as 8,000, according to another. The following table lists some of these languages. Despite the seemingly large number of languages spoken in the world today, one-half of the world's population (2,100,000,000 people) speak but fifteen languages. As the figures in the table show, if you spoke Mandarin Chinese, English, Hindi, and Russian, you could speak with more than one billion people.

Table 9-1   Some Languages of the World

Language Subfamily	Language	Principal Geographic Areas Where Spoken	Number of Speakers (Rank in Parentheses)	
INDO-EUROPEAN FAMILY (see Figure 9-6)				
Germanic	Danish	Denmark		5,000,000
	Dutch	Netherlands, Indonesia		13,000,000
	English	North America, Great Britain, Australia, New Zealand	(2)	300,000,000
	Frisian	Northern Holland		400,000
	Flemish	Belgium		5,000,000
	German	Germany, Austria, Switzerland	(7)	100,000,000
	Icelandic	Iceland		200,000
	Norwegian	Norway		4,300,000
	Swedish	Sweden		8,000,000
	Yiddish	(diffuse)		4,000,000
Romance (Latin)	Catalan	Andorra, Spain		5,000,000
	French	France, Belgium, Switzerland, Canada	(11)	75,000,000
	Italian	Italy, Switzerland	(12)	60,000,000
	Portuguese	Portugal, Brazil	(7)	100,000,000
	Provençal	Southern France		9,000,000
	Romanian	Rumania		20,000,000
	Spanish	Spain, Latin America	(3)	200,000,000

Table 9-1 Some Languages of the World—*continued*

Language Subfamily	Language	Principal Geographic Areas Where Spoken	Number of Speakers (Rank in Parentheses)	
INDO-EUROPEAN FAMILY (see Figure 9-6)				
Celtic	Breton	Brittany (France)		1,000,000
	Irish	Ireland		500,000
	Scots Gaelic	Scotland		500,000
	Welsh	Wales		750,000
Hellenic	Greek	Greece, Cyprus		10,000,000
Baltic	Latvian	Latvia (USSR)		2,000,000
	Lithuanian	Lithuania (USSR)		3,000,000
Slavic	Bulgarian	Bulgaria		8,000,000
	Byelorussian	Western USSR		10,000,000
	Czech	Czechoslovakia		10,000,000
	Macedonian	Southern Yugoslavia		1,000,000
	Polish	Poland	(22)	35,000,000
	Russian	USSR	(3)	200,000,000
	Serbo-Croatian	Yugoslavia		15,000,000
	Slovak	Czechoslovakia		4,000,000
	Slovenian	Yugoslavia		1,500,000
	Ukrainian	Southwest USSR	(20)	40,000,000
Indo-Iranian	Bengali	Bangladesh, India	(6)	110,000,000
	Hindi	Northern India	(5)	180,000,000
	Marathi	Western India	(17)	45,000,000
	Persian	Iran		25,000,000
	Punjabi	Northern India	(13)	50,000,000
	Urdu	Pakistan	(20)	40,000,000
Armenian	Armenian	Southwest USSR		4,000,000
Albanian	Albanian	Albania		4,000,000
OTHER THAN INDO-EUROPEAN				
Afro-Asiatic (includes Semitic languages)	Amharic	Ethiopia		8,000,000
	Arabic	North Africa, Middle East	(7)	100,000,000
	Berber	Morocco		6,000,000
	Galla	Somaliland, Ethiopia		7,000,000
	Hausa	Northern Nigeria		20,000,000
	Hebrew	Israel		3,000,000
	Somali	Somalia		2,000,000
Altaic	Japanese	Japan	(7)	100,000,000
	Korean	Korea	(23)	34,000,000
	Mongolian	Mongolia		1,600,000
	Tartar	Western USSR		5,000,000
	Turkish	Turkey		24,000,000
	Uzbek	Southwest USSR		9,000,000
Austro-Asiatic	Cambodian	Cambodia		6,000,000
	Vietnamese	Vietnam	(26)	28,000,000
Austro-Tai	Batak	Sumatra		2,000,000
	Chamorro	Mariana Islands (Guam)		50,000
	Fijian	Fiji Islands		200,000
	Hawaiian	Hawaii		250
	Indonesian	Indonesia	(13)	50,000,000
	Javanese	Java	(17)	45,000,000

Table 9-1   Some Languages of the World—*continued*

Language Subfamily	Language	Principal Geographic Areas Where Spoken	Number of Speakers (Rank in Parentheses)	
OTHER THAN INDO-EUROPEAN				
	Lao	Laos		10,000,000
	Malagasy	Madagascar		6,500,000
	Malay	Malaysia, Singapore		10,000,000
	Maori	New Zealand		100,000
	Samoan	Samoa		130,000
	Tagalog	Philippines		10,000,000
	Tahitian	Tahiti		66,000
	Thai	Thailand	(24)	30,000,000
Caucasian	Avar	Southwest USSR		270,000
	Georgian	Southwest USSR		2,700,000
Dravidian	Kannada	Southwest India		22,000,000
	Malayalam	Southwest India		22,000,000
	Tamil	Southeast India, Sri Lanka	(17)	45,000,000
	Telugu	Southeast India	(13)	50,000,000
Niger-Kordofanian†	Efik	Southeast Nigeria		2,000,000
	Ewe	Ghana		1,700,000
	Fulani	Northeast Nigeria		8,000,000
	Igbo	Southeast Nigeria		6,000,000
	Luganda	Uganda		1,500,000
	Nupe	Nigeria		325,000
	Shona	Rhodesia		118,000
	Swahili	East Africa		15,000,000
	Twi	Ghana, Ivory Coast		2,000,000
	Yoruba	Nigeria		12,000,000
	Zulu	South Africa		2,000,000
Sino-Tibetan	Burmese	Burma		16,000,000
	Cantonese	South China (Canton)		27,000,000
	Hakka	Southeast China	(23)	30,000,000
	Mandarin	North China	(1)	387,000,000
	Taiwanese	Formosa		15,000,000
	Tibetan	Tibet		4,000,000
	Wu	East central China	(16)	46,000,000
Uralic‡	Estonian	Estonia (USSR)		1,000,000
	Finnish	Finland		5,000,000
	Hungarian	Hungary		12,000,000
	Lapp	Northern parts of Norway, Finland, Sweden, USSR		30,000

Amerindian Subfamily	Language	Principal Geographic Areas Where Spoken	Number of Speakers
Algonquian	Arapaho	Wyoming	2,000
	Blackfoot	Montana	5,000
	Cheyenne	Montana	3,000
	Cree	Ontario (Canada)	62,000
	Menomini	Wisconsin	300
	Ojibwa	Ontario	40,000

Table 9-1   Some Languages of the World—*continued*

Amerindian Subfamily	Language	Principal Geographic Areas Where Spoken	Number of Speakers (Rank in Parentheses)
		OTHER THAN INDO-EUROPEAN	
Athapaskan	Apache	Oklahoma	10
	Chipewyan	Alberta (Canada)	5,000
	Navajo	Arizona	120,000
	Sarsi	Alberta	50
Iroquoian	Cherokee	Oklahoma, North Carolina	10,000
	Mohawk	Northern New York	1,000
Mayan	Maya	Guatemala	300,000
Quechumaran	Quechua (Incan)	Bolivia, Peru	6,000,000
Uto-Aztecan	Hopi	Northwest Arizona	4,800
	Nahuatl (Aztec)	Southern Mexico	1,000,000
	Pima	Southern Arizona	18,000
Yuman	Diegueño	Southern California	185
	Mohave	Western Arizona	850

Much of this data is from Merritt Ruhlin. 1976. *A Guide to the Languages of the World.* Language Universals Project, Stanford University. Stanford, California. The number of speakers is the number of native speakers. Languages such as Dutch/Flemish or Norwegian/Danish, which are close enough to be considered dialects, are nonetheless listed as separate languages out of political considerations. Similarly for Hindi/Urdu and Malay/Indonesian.

† All languages given belong to the subfamily of Niger-Congo. Of these Swahili, Luganda, Shona, and Zulu are Bantu languages.

‡ All languages given belong to the subfamily Finno-Ugric. The other Uralic subfamily is Samoyed.

NOTE: Obviously, we have omitted thousands of languages. These are given merely to provide some examples of some of the languages in some of the language families and subfamilies.

SUMMARY

In this chapter we discussed the fact that all languages change through time. Evidence of linguistic change is found in the history of individual languages, and in the **regular correspondences** that exist between different languages and dialects. **Genetically related** languages "descend" from a common "parent" through linguistic change. An early stage in the history of related languages is that they are dialects of the parent language.

All parts of the grammar may change. That is, **phonological, morphological, syntactic, lexical,** and **semantic** changes occur. The particular types of changes were discussed: phonemes, phonological and syntactic rules, and words may be added, lost, or altered. The meanings of words also change.

No one knows all the causes for linguistic change. Basically, change comes about through children's restructuring of the grammar. Grammars are both simplified and elaborated; the elaborations may arise to counter the simplifications that could lead to unclarity and ambiguity.

It was shown that some sound changes result from physiological, **assimilative** processes. Others, like the Great Vowel Shift, are more difficult to explain. Grammatical changes may be explained, in part, as **analogic** changes.

External borrowing from other languages also affects the grammar of a language.

The study of linguistic change is called **historical and comparative linguistics.** Linguists of the eighteenth and nineteenth centuries studied the internal changes that occurred in a language. They also compared languages, reconstructed earlier forms of particular language families, and classified languages according to their "family trees."

Historical-comparative linguists use many methods and a wide variety of data. Old written records are studied. Differences between related dialects and languages provide important clues to earlier stages. A particularly effective technique for reconstructing "dead" languages is the **comparative method.** By comparing the various "daughter" languages (or "daughter" dialects, as the case may be) it is possible to partially reconstruct the linguistic history of a people.

Languages are classified genealogically according to their "life history." The ancestors of the language are specified, including the source or "mother" language. Sisters and cousins, which all sprang up at different points in time from the original source language, are also noted in a "family tree" similar to Figure 9-6. Different language types may be found in a single language family.

In spite of the differences between languages, which we are acutely aware of when we try to learn a foreign language, there are a vast number of ways in which languages are alike. That is, there are language universals as well as language differences.

Finally, we saw that knowledge of the linguistic prehistory of peoples may provide clues to knowledge in other areas of prehistory.

EXERCISES

1. Many changes in the phonological system have occurred in English since 449 A.D. Below are some Old English words (given in their spelling and phonetic forms), and the same words as we pronounce them today. They are typical of regular sound changes that took place in English. What sound changes have occurred in each case?

   Example: OE: hlūd [xlu:d] → Mod. Eng.: loud
   Change: (1) the [x] was lost.
   (2) the long vowel [u:] became [aw].

OE			MOD E
a. crabbe	[krabə]	→	crab
b. fisc	[fɪsk]	→	fish
c. fūl	[fu:l]	→	foul
d. gāt	[ga:t]	→	goat
e. læfan	[læ:van]	→	leave
f. tēþ	[te:θ]	→	teeth

2. At one time in English, the final *g* of the following words was pronounced: *sing, long, bring*. Did a change take place in the phonemic inventory? the phonetic inventory? the phonological rules? Why?

3. The Great Vowel Shift in English left its traces in modern English in such meaning-related pairs as:

   a. ser*e*ne/ser*e*nity [i] / [ɛ]
   b. div*i*ne/div*i*nity [ay] / [ɪ]
   c. s*a*ne/s*a*nity [e] / [æ]

   List as many such meaning-related pairs as you can that relate [i] and [ɛ] as in example *a*, [ay] and [ɪ] as in example *b*, and [e] and [æ] as in example *c*.

4. Below are given some sentences taken from Old English, Middle English, and early Modern English texts, illustrating some changes that have occurred in the syntactic rules of English grammar. (Note: In the sentences, the earlier spelling forms and words have been changed to conform to modern English. That is, the OE sentence *His suna twegen mon brohte to þæm cynige* would be written as *His sons two one brought to that king*, which in Modern English would be *His two sons were brought to the king*.) Underline the parts of each sentence that differ from Modern English. Rewrite the sentence in Modern English. State, if you can, what changes must have occurred. Example:

   > It *not* belongs to you.
   > —SHAKESPEARE, *Henry IV*

   > Mod. Eng.: *It does not belong to you.*

   > Change: It was once possible to negate a sentence by merely adding the negative morpheme *not* before the verb. Today, one must insert a *do* (in its proper morphological form) in addition to the *not*.

   a. It nothing pleased his master.
   b. He hath said that he would lift them whom that him please.
   c. I have a brother is condemned to die.
   d. I bade them take away you.
   e. I wish you was still more a Tartar.
   f. Christ slept and his apostles.
   g. Me was told.

5. A. The vocabulary of English consists of "native" words and also thousands of borrowed words. Look up the following words in a dictionary which provides the etymologies (history) of words. In each case speculate as to how the particular word came to be borrowed from the particular language.

a. size	h. robot	o. skunk	v. pagoda
b. royal	i. check	p. catfish	w. khaki
c. aquatic	j. banana	q. hoodlum	x. shampoo
c. heavenly	k. keel	r. filibuster	y. kangaroo
e. skill	l. fact	s. astronaut	z. bulldoze
f. ranch	m. potato	t. emerald	
g. blouse	n. muskrat	u. sugar	

   B. The *Encyclopaedia Britannica Yearbook* has usually published a new-word list, which is, in the *Britannica's* editors' view, a list of those words that had entered the language during the year. In 1976 a number of entries were noted, among them *galacto-chemistry*, *hoolifans* (to describe rowdy fans at a sports event), and *chairperson*.

Would you expect a yearbook to publish a "lost-word list," recording the words dropped from the language during the year? Defend
your answer.

6. The following pairs show different pronunciations of the same utterances. How do these illustrate some possible causes for language
change? What happens in each case?

   a. lots of money   lota money
   b. I've got to   I gotta
   c. John and Mary   John an Mary
   d. why don't you?   whyncha?
   e. do you want to eat?   wanna eat?
   f. how would you?   howdja [hawǰə]
   g. how do you do   [hadu]
   h. did you eat?   [ǰit]

7. Below is a passage from Shakespeare's *Hamlet,* Act IV, scene iii:

   HAMLET: A man may fish with the worm that hath eat of a king, and eat
            of the fish that hath fed of that worm.
   KING: What dost thou mean by this?
   HAMLET: Nothing but to show you how a king may go a progress through
            the guts of a beggar.
   KING: Where is Polonius?
   HAMLET: In heaven. Send thither to see. If your messenger find him not
            there, seek him i' the other place yourself. But indeed, if you
            find him not within this month, you shall nose him as you go up
            the stairs into the lobby.

   Study these lines and identify every difference in expression between
   Elizabethan and Modern English that is evident. (For example, in line 3,
   thou is now *you*.)

8. Each pair of words below is pronounced as shown phonetically in at
least one American dialect. State whether you pronounce them in this
way. If not, state how your pronunciations would differ.

   a. "horse"   [hɔrs]   "hoarse"   [hors]
   b. "morning"   [mɔrnɪ̃ŋ]   "mourning"   [mornɪ̃ŋ]
   c. "for"   [fɔr]   "four"   [for]
   d. "ice"   [ʌys]   "eyes"   [ayz]
   e. "knife"   [nʌyf]   "knives"   [nayvz]
   f. "mute"   [myut]   "nude"   [nyud]
   g. "pin"   [pʰɪ̃n]   "pen"   [pʰɛ̃n]
   h. "hog"   [hɔg]   "hot"   [hat]
   i. "marry"   [mæri]   "merry"   [mɛri]
   j. "cot"   [kʰat]   "caught"   [kʰɔt]
   k. "father"   [faðə]   "farther"   [faðə]
   l. (to) "lease"   [lis]   (to) "grease"   [griz]
   m. "what"   [ʍat]   "watt"   [wat]
   n. "ant"   [ænt]   "aunt"   [ãnt]
   o. "creek"   [krik]   "sick"   [sɪk]

9. State at least three differences between English and the following languages, using just the sentence(s) given. Ignore lexical differences—that is, the different vocabulary. Example:

Thai: dèg khon   nii   kamlang   kin
     boy *classifier*   *this*   *progressive*   eat
                                      aspect

     'This boy is eating'

     *m*ǎa tua   nán   kin   khâaw
     dog *classifier*   *that*   eat   rice
     'That dog ate the rice.'

Three differences are: (1) Thai has "classifiers." They have no English equivalent. (2) The demonstratives "this" and "that" follow the noun in Thai, but precede the noun in English. (3) The "progressive" is expressed by a separate word in Thai. The verb doesn't change form. In English, the progressive is indicated by the presence of the verb *to be* and the adding of *-ing* to the verb.

a. French:

     cet   homme   intelligent   arrivera
     this   man   intelligent   will arrive
     This intelligent man will arrive.

     ces   hommes   intelligents   arriveront
     these   men   intelligent   will arrive
     These intelligent men will arrive.

b. Japanese:

     watashi ga   sakana   o   tabete   iru
     I   *subject*   fish   *object*   eat *(ing)*   am
            marker   *marker*
     I am eating fish.

c. Swahili:

     mtoto   alivunja   kikombe
     m-   toto   a-   li-   vunja   ki-   kombe
     class   child   he   *past*   break   *class*   cup
     marker   *marker*
     The child broke the cup.

     watoto   wanavunja   vikombe
     wa-   toto   wa-   na-   vunja   vi-   kombe
         child   they   *present* break   cup
     The children break the cups.

d. Korean:

     kɨ   sonyɔn-nɨn   wɨyu-lɨl   masi-ass-ta
     kɨ   sonyɔn- nɨn   wɨyu- lɨl   masi- ass- ta
     the   boy   *subject*   milk   *object*   drink   *past*   *assertion*
                   marker   *marker*
     The boy drank milk.

kɨ-nɨn	muɔs-lɨl	mɔk-ass-nya

kɨ	nɨn	muɔs-	lɨl	mɔk-	ass-	nya
he	subject marker	what	object marker	eat	past	question

What did he eat?

10. Here is a table showing, in phonemic form, the Latin ancestors of ten words in modern French:

LATIN	FRENCH	
kor	kør	"heart"
kantāre	šãte	"to sing"
klārus	kler	"clear"
kervus	sɛrf	"hart" (deer)
karbō	šarbɔ̃	"coal"
kwandō	kã	"when"
kentum	sã	"hundred"
kawsa	šoz	"thing"
kinis	sãdrə	"ashes"
kawda⎫ koda⎭	kø	"tail"

Are the following statements true or false?

a. The modern French word for "thing" shows that a [k], which occurred before the vowel [o] in Latin, became an [š] in French.

b. The French word for "tail" probably derived from the Latin word [koda] rather than from [kawda].

c. One historical change illustrated by these data is that [s] became an allophone of the phoneme /k/ in French.

d. If there was a Latin word *kertus*, the modern French word would probably be *sert*. (Consider only the initial consonant.)

11. Here is how to count to five in a dozen languages. Six of these languages are Indo-European and six are not. Identify which is which.

	LG. 1	LG. 2	LG. 3	LG. 4	LG. 5	LG. 6
1	en	jedyn	i	eka	ichi	echad
2	twene	dwaj	liang	dvau	ni	shnayim
3	thria	tři	san	trayas	san	shlosha
4	fiuwar	štyri	ssu	catur	shi	arbaʔa
5	fif	pjeć	wu	pañca	go	chamishsha

	LG. 7	LG. 8	LG. 9	LG. 10	LG. 11	LG. 12
1	mot	ün	hana	yaw	uno	nigen
2	hai	duos	tul	daw	dos	khoyar
3	ba	trais	set	dree	tres	ghorban
4	bon	quatter	net	tsaloor	cuatro	durben
5	nam	tschinch	tasǒt	pindze	cinco	tabon

12. More than 3,000 languages exist in the world today. State one reason why this number might grow larger and one reason why it might grow smaller. Do you think the number of languages will increase or decrease in the next 100 years? Why?

13. Consider these data from two American Indian languages:

YERINGTON PAVIOTSO = YP	NORTHFORK MONACHI = NM	GLOSS
mupi	mupi	"nose"
tama	tawa	"tooth"
piwɨ	piwɨ	"heart"
sawaʔpono	sawaʔpono	"a feminine name"
nimɨ	niwɨ	"liver"
tamano	tawano	"springtime"
pahwa	pahwa	"aunt"
kuma	kuwa	"husband"
wowaʔa	wowaʔa	"Indians living to the west"
mɨhɨ	mɨhɨ	"porcupine"
noto	noto	"throat"
tapa	tape	"sun"
ʔatapɨ	ʔatapɨ	"jaw"
papiʔi	papiʔi	"older brother"
patɨ	petɨ	"daughter"
nana	nana	"man"
ʔatɨ	ʔetɨ	"bow," "gun"

A. Identify each sound correspondence. (Hint: There are ten different correspondences of consonants and six different correspondences of vowels; e.g., p-p   m-w   a-a   a-e, etc.)

B. a. For each correspondence you identified in A not containing an *m* or *w*, reconstruct a proto-sound. (For example, for *h-h*, *h; *o-o*, *o.)

   b. If the proto-sound underwent a change, indicate what the change is and in which language it took place.

C. a. Whenever a *w* appears in YP, what appears in the corresponding position in NM?

   b. Whenever an *m* occurs in YP, what two sounds may correspond to it in NM?

   c. On the basis of the position of *m* in YP words, can you predict which sound it will correspond to in NM words? How?

D. a. For the three correspondences you discovered in A involving *m* and *w*, should you reconstruct two or three proto-sounds?

   b. If you chose three proto-sounds in D(a), what are they and what did they become in the two "daughter" languages, YP and NM?

   c. If you chose two proto-sounds in D(a), what are they and what did they become in the "daughter" languages? What further statement do you need to make about the sound changes? (Hint: One proto-sound will become two different pairs, depending on its phonetic environment. This is an example of a **conditioned** sound change.)

E. Based on the above, reconstruct all the words given in the common ancestor from which both YP and NM descended. (For example, "porcupine" is reconstructed as *mɨhɨ.)

REFERENCES

Anttila, Raimo. 1972. *An Introduction to Historical and Comparative Linguistics.* Macmillan. New York.

Baugh, A. C. 1957. *A History of the English Language,* 2nd ed. Appleton-Century-Crofts. New York.

Hoenigswald, Henry M. 1960. *Language Change and Linguistic Reconstruction.* University of Chicago Press. Chicago.

Jeffers, Robert J., and Ilse Lehiste. 1979. *Principles and Methods for Historical Linguistics.* M.I.T. Press. Cambridge, Mass.

Lehmann, W. P. 1973. *Historical Linguistics: An Introduction,* 2nd ed. Holt, Rinehart and Winston, New York.

Pedersen, H. 1962. *The Discovery of Language.* University of Indiana Press, Bloomington.

Pyles, Thomas. 1964. *The Origins and Development of the English Language.* Harcourt, Brace & World. New York.

Robertson, Stuart, and Frederick G. Cassidy. 1969. *The Development of Modern English.* Prentice-Hall. Englewood Cliffs, N.J.

Ruhlen, Merritt. *A Guide to the Languages of the World.* 1976. Language Universals Project, Stanford University. Stanford, California.

Traugott, Elizabeth Closs. 1972. *A History of English Syntax.* Holt, Rinehart and Winston. New York.

PART FOUR

The Biological Aspects of Language

The common neurological belief, since the work of Broca over a hundred years ago, is that innate anatomical structures determine the capacity for language in humans.
Norman Geschwind, "Some Comments on the Neurology of Language."

Chapter 10

From the Mouths of Babes: Child Language Acquisition

From this golden egg a man, Prajapati, was born. . . . A year having passed, he wanted to speak. He said bhur *and the earth was created. He said* bhuvar *and the space of the air was created. He said* suvar *and the sky was created. That is why a child wants to speak after a year. . . . When Prajapati spoke for the first time, he uttered one or two syllables. That is why a child utters one or two syllables when he speaks for the first time.*

Hindu myth

Every aspect of language is extremely complex, as we have already seen in the discussions on phonetics, phonology, morphology, syntax, and semantics. Yet, as noted above and as Descartes pointed out: "There are none so depraved and stupid, without even excepting idiots, that they cannot arrange different words together, forming of them a statement by which they make known their thoughts." Perhaps even more remarkable is the fact that children—before the age of 5—learn most of the intricate system we have been calling the grammar of a language. Before they can add 2 + 2 children are conjoining sentences, asking questions, selecting appropriate pronouns, negating sentences, using the syntactic, phonological, morphological, and semantic rules of the grammar. Yet, children are not taught language as they are taught arithmetic.

A normal human being can go through life without having learned to read or write. Millions of people in the world today prove this. But these same millions all speak and understand and can discuss complex and abstract ideas as well as literate speakers can. Thus, learning a language and learning to read are somehow different. Similarly, millions of humans grow to maturity without ever having learned algebra or chemistry or how to use a typewriter. They must in some sense be taught these skills or systems, but they do not have to be taught to walk or to talk.

We are far from completely understanding the language-acquisition process. We are just beginning to grapple with those aspects of the human neurological and biological makeup that explain the child's ability to acquire language. Certainly it is clear that the child is equipped from birth with the neural prerequisites for language and language use.

Our knowledge of the nature of human language tells us something about what the child does and does not do when learning or acquiring a language. The earlier chapters provide some of this information:

1. Children do not learn a language by storing all the words and all the sentences in some giant mental dictionary. The list of words is finite, but no dictionary can hold all the sentences, which are infinite in number.
2. Children learn to construct sentences, most of which they have never produced before.
3. Children learn to understand sentences they have never heard before. They cannot do this by matching the "heard utterance" with some stored sentence.
4. Children must therefore learn "rules" that permit them to use language creatively.
5. No one teaches them these rules. Their parents are no more aware of the phonological, syntactic, and semantic rules than are the children. Children, then, seem to act like very efficient linguists equipped with a perfect theory of language, who use this theory to construct the grammar of the language they hear.

Even if you remember your early years, you will not remember anyone telling you to form a sentence by adding a verb phrase to a noun phrase, or the class of sounds that are followed by an [s] to form plurals. In St. Augustine's *Confessions,* written around 400 A.D., he writes of how he learned to speak:

> . . . for I was no longer a speechless infant; but a speaking boy. This I remember; and have since observed how I learned to speak. It was not that my elders taught me words . . . in any set method; but I . . . did myself . . . practice the sounds in my memory. . . . And thus by constantly hearing words, as they occurred in various sentences . . . I thereby gave utterance to my will.

In addition to acquiring the complex rules of the grammar (that is, linguistic competence), children must also learn the complex rules of the appropriate social use of language, what certain scholars have called communicative competence. These include, for example, the greetings that are to be used, the "taboo" words, the polite forms of address, the various styles that are appropriate to different situations, and so forth.

Stages in Language Acquisition

Children do not wake up one morning with a fully formed grammar in their heads or with all the "rules" of social and communicative intercourse. The language is acquired by stages, and, it is suggested, each successive stage more closely approximates the grammar of the adult language. Observations of children in different language areas of the world reveal that the stages are very similar, possibly universal. Some of the stages last for a short time; others remain longer. Some stages may overlap for a short period, though the transition between stages has often been observed to be quite sudden.

The earliest studies of child language acquisition come from diaries kept by parents. More recent studies include the use of tape recordings, video-

DENNIS THE MENACE   **Hank Ketcham**

"JOEY'S BABY SISTER SAID HER FIRST WORD TODAY, BUT NOBODY KNOWS WHAT IT MEANS."

DENNIS THE MENACE (R) used by permission of Hank Ketcham and © by Field Enterprises, Inc.

tapes, and planned experiments. Spontaneous utterances of children are recorded and in addition various elicitation techniques have been developed so that the child's production and comprehension can be studied under controlled conditions.

Some linguists divide the stages of language acquisition into prelinguistic and linguistic stages. Most scholars agree that the earliest cries and whimpers of the newborn, or neonate, cannot be considered early language. Such noises are completely stimulus-controlled; they are the child's involuntary responses to hunger, discomfort, the desire to be cuddled, or the feeling of well-being. A major difference between human language and the communication systems of other species is that human language is creative, as we discussed earlier, in the sense of being free from either external or internal stimuli. The child's first noises are, however, stimulus responses.

THE BABBLING STAGE

In the first few months, usually around the six-month period, the infant begins to **babble.** The sounds produced in this period (apart from the continuing stimulus-controlled cries and gurgles) seem to include the sounds of human languages. Most linguists believe that in this babbling period infants produce a large variety of sounds, many of which do not occur in the language of the household. Deaf children also babble and it is reported that their early babbling seems very similar to that of normal children. Nondeaf children born of nonspeaking deaf parents also babble. Thus, babbling does not depend on the presence of acoustic, auditory input.

One view suggests that it is during this period that children are learning to distinguish between the sounds of their language and the sounds which are not part of the language. During the babbling period children learn to maintain the "right" sounds and suppress the "wrong" ones.

During the babbling stage the pitch, or intonation contours, of infants' utterances begin to resemble the intonation contours of sentences spoken by adults. It has been suggested that the semantically different intonation contours are among the first linguistic contrasts that children perceive and produce.

THE HOLOPHRASTIC STAGE

Sometime after one year (it varies from child to child and has nothing to do with how intelligent the child is), children begin to use the same string of sounds repeatedly to "mean" the same thing. At this point they have learned that sounds are related to meanings and they are producing their first "words." Most children seem to go through the "one word = one sentence" stage. These one-word sentences (if one can call them sentences at all) are called **holophrastic** sentences (from *holo* "complete" or undivided" plus *phrase* "phrase" or "sentence").

Perhaps a picture of one child, J. P., at this stage will illustrate how much the young child has already learned. J. P.'s words of April 1977, age 16 months, were as follows:[1]

[ʔaw]	"not" "no" "don't"	[baw] ~ [daw]	"down"
[bʌʔ] ~ [mʌʔ]	"up"	[dæ]	"daddy"
[da]	"dog"	[s:]	"aerosol, etc. spray"
[iʔo] ~ [šiʔo]	"Cheerios"	[sʸu:]	"shoe"
[sa]	"sock"	[hay]	"hi"
[ay] ~ [ʌy]	"light"	[sr̩]	"shirt," "sweater"
[ma]	"mommy"		
[sæ:] ~ [əsæ:]	"what's that?" "hey, look!"		

J. P.'s mother reports that before April he also used the words [bʊ) for "book," [ki] for "kitty," and [tsi] for "tree" but seemed to have "lost" them.

What is more interesting than merely the list of J. P.'s vocabulary is the way he used these words. "Up" was originally restricted to mean "get me up" when he was either on the floor or in his high chair, but later was used to mean "get up!" to his mother as well. His word for "Cheerios" was first used to label or ask for Cheerios only when they were visible; then he began to use it to ask for Cheerios even when he could not see them. J. P. used his word for "sock" when pointing to anyone's socks as well as other undergarments that go on over the feet, which illustrates how a child may extend the meaning of a word from a particular referent to encompass a larger class.

When he first began to use these words, the stimulus had to be present. But by May this was no longer true. "Dog," for example, was first only used when pointing to a real dog but then was used in pointing to pictures of dogs in various books. A new word that entered J. P.'s vocabulary in May was "uh-oh," which he would say after having an accident like spilling juice, or

---

[1] We would like to give special thanks to John Peregrine Munro for providing us with such rich data and for being such a delight in every possible way. Also, thanks are in order to Drs. Pamela and Allen Munro, J. P.'s parents, for their painstaking efforts in recording these data.

when he deliberately poured his yogurt over the side of his high chair. His use of this word shows his growing use of language for social purposes. At this time he also added two new words meaning "no," [do:] and [no]. He used these frequently when anyone attempted to take something from him that he wanted, or tried to make him do something he didn't want to do. He used this negative either imperatively (for example, "Don't do that!") or assertively (for example, "I don't want to do that."). One can see that, as early as this holophrastic stage, words are being used to communicate a variety of ideas, feelings, and social awareness.

According to some child-language researchers, the words in the holophrastic stage serve three major functions: they are either linked with a child's own action or desire for action (as when J. P. would say "up" to express his wish to be picked up), or are used to convey emotion (J. P.'s "no"), or serve a naming function (J. P.'s "Cheerios," "shoes," "dog," and so on).

At this stage the child uses only one word to express concepts or predications that will later be expressed by complex phrases and sentences.

Phonologically, J. P.'s first words are, like the words of most children at this stage of learning English and other languages, generally monosyllabic with a CV (consonant-vowel) form; the vowel part may be diphthongal, depending on the language being acquired. His phonemic or phonetic inventory (at this stage they are equivalent) is much smaller than is found in the adult language. It has been suggested by the linguist Roman Jakobson that children will acquire the sounds found in all languages of the world first, no matter what language they are exposed to, and in later stages will acquire the "more difficult" sounds.[2]

J. P.'s phonological inventory at that early stage included the consonants [b, m, d, k], which are frequently occurring sounds in the world's languages.

Many studies have shown that children in the holophrastic stage can perceive or comprehend many more phonological contrasts than they can produce themselves. Thus, even at this stage, it is not possible to determine the extent of the grammar of the child simply by observing or noting speech production.

THE TWO-WORD STAGE

Around the time of their second birthday (but remember, this can be earlier or later, since there is great variability among children), children begin to produce two-word utterances. At first these appear to be strings of two of the child's earlier holophrastic utterances, each word with its own single-pitch contour. Soon after this juxtaposition, children begin to form actual two-word sentences, with the relation between the two words showing definite syntactic and semantic relations and the intonation contour of the two words extending over the whole utterance rather than being separated by a pause between the two words. The following "sentences" illustrate the kinds of patterns that are found in children's utterances at this stage.[3]

[2] Jakobson, R. 1941. *Kindersprache, Aphasie, und allgemeine Lautgesetz* (Almqvist and Wiksell. Uppsala, Sweden); English translation by A. Keiler, *Child Language, Aphasia, and Phonological Universals* (Mouton. The Hague. 1968).

[3] All the examples given in this chapter are taken from utterances produced by children actually observed by the authors or reported in the literature. The various sources are listed in the reference section at the end of the chapter.

allgone sock
hi Mommy
byebye boat
allgone sticky
more wet
beepbeep bang
it ball
Katherine sock
dirty sock
here pretty

During the two-word utterance stage there are no syntactic or morphological markers; that is, no inflections for number, or person, or tense, and so on. Pronouns are rare, although many children do use "me" to refer to themselves, and some children use other pronouns as well. Bloom has noted that in noun + noun sentences, such as *Mommy sock,* the two words can express a number of different grammatical relations which will later be expressed by other syntactic devices.[4] Bloom's conclusions were reached by observing the situations in which the two-word sentence was uttered. Thus, for example, *Mommy sock* can be used to show a subject + object relation in the situation when the mother is putting the sock on the child, or a possessive relation when the child is pointing to Mommy's sock. Two nouns can also be used to show a subject-locative relation, as in *sweater chair* to mean "the sweater is on the chair," or to show conjunction, to mean "sweater and chair."

TELEGRAPH TO INFINITY

There doesn't seem to be any "three-word" sentence stage. When a child starts stringing more than two words together, the utterances may be two, three, four, or five words or longer. Many linguists working on child language do, however, study the increasing lengths of the utterances that children use. They believe that a comparison across children as to stage of language acquisition can best be made by the **mean length of utterances** (MLU) rather than by chronological age. That is, children who are producing utterances which on the average are 2.3 to 3.5 morphemes seem to have acquired other, similar aspects of the grammar.

But these first utterances of children that are longer than two words have a special characteristic. Usually the small "function" words such as *to, the, can, is,* and so on, are missing; only the words that carry the main message —the "content" words—occur. Children often sound as if they were reading a Western Union message, which is why such utterances are called **telegraphic speech:**

Cat stand up table
What that?
He play little tune
Andrew want that
Cathy build house
No sit there

[4] L. M. Bloom. 1970. *Language Development: Form and Function in Emerging Grammar* (M.I.T. Press. Cambridge, Mass.).

JP's early sentences are very similar.

AGE IN MONTHS

25 months	[dan ʔiʔ tˢɪʔ]	"Don eat chip"
	[bʷaʔ tat]	"block (is on) top"
26 months	[manis tu hæs]	"Mommy's two hands"
	[mo bʌs go]	"where's another bus?"
	[dædi go]	"where's daddy?"
27 months	[ʔay gat tu dʸus]	"I've got two (glasses of) juice"
	[dō bayʔ mi]	"don't bite (kiss) me"
	[kʌdər sʌni ber]	"Sonny colored (a) bear"
28 months	[ʔay gat pwe dɪs]	"I'm playing with this"
	[mamis tak mɛns]	"Mommy talk(ed to the) men"

When the child begins to produce utterances that are longer than two words, these utterances appear to be "sentence–like"; they have hierarchical, constituent structures similar to the syntactic structures found in the sentences produced by the adult grammar:

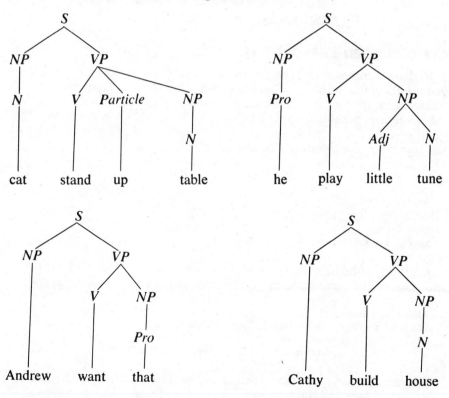

The child's utterances are not simply randomly strung together words but, from a very early stage, reveal his or her grasp of the principles of sentence formation.

When we refer to these simple sentences as telegraphic, this is merely a descriptive term because the child does not deliberately leave out the non-content words, as does an adult sending a telegram.

As children acquire more and more language, or more closely approximate the adult grammar, they not only begin to use syntactic or grammatical function words but also acquire the inflectional and derivational morphemes of the language. Brown and his associates at Harvard studied the spontaneous utterances of three children—Adam, Sarah, and Eve—over a long period of time, noting the appearance of grammatical morphemes, free and bound.[5] They found that the sequences of acquisition of the morphemes were pretty much the same, and this has been replicated by other researchers working with other children. It seems that -*ing*, the ending which represents the present progressive form of the verb, as in *Me going park*, is the earliest inflectional morpheme acquired. The prepositions *in* and *on* enter the children's speech next, and then the regular plural ending.

Eventually all the other inflections are added, along with the syntactic rules, and finally the child's utterances sound like those spoken by adults.

Theories of Child Language Acquisition

DO CHILDREN LEARN BY IMITATION?

Various theories have been proposed to explain how children manage to acquire the adult language. There are those who think that children merely imitate what they hear. Imitation is involved to some extent, of course, but the sentences produced by children show that children are *not* imitating adult speech. From whom would children hear *Cat stand up table* or any of the sentences like these they produce?

a my pencil.
other one pants.
two foot.
Mommy get it my ladder.
what the boy hit?
cowboy did fighting me.

Even when children are deliberately trying to imitate what they hear they are unable to produce sentences that cannot be generated by *their* grammar.

Adult: He's going out	*Child:* He go out
Adult: That's an old-time train	*Child:* Old-time train
Adult: Adam, say what I say:	
Where can I put them?	*Child:* Where I can put them?

Neither can the "imitation" theory account for another important phenomenon. There are children who are unable to speak for neurological or

[5] R. O. Brown. 1973. *A First Language: The Early Stages* (Harvard University Press. Cambridge, Mass.).

physiological reasons. Yet these children learn the language spoken to them and understand what is said. When they overcome their speech impairment they immediately use the language for speaking.

DO CHILDREN LEARN BY REINFORCEMENT?

Another theory of language acquisition suggests that children learn to produce "correct" sentences because they are positively reinforced when they say something right and negatively reinforced when they say something wrong. This view assumes that children are being constantly corrected for using "bad grammar" and patted on the head when they use "good grammar." Even if this happened (and it seldom does), how do children learn from such adult responses what it is they are doing right or wrong? This view does not tell us how children construct the correct rules. Whatever "correction" takes place is based more on the content of the message than on its *form*. That is, if a child says "Nobody don't like me," the mother may say "Everybody likes you."

Besides, all attempts to "correct" a child's language are doomed to failure. Children don't know what they are doing wrong and are even unable to make the corrections when they are pointed out to them, as is shown in the following examples:

(1) CHILD: Nobody don't like me.
MOTHER: No, say "Nobody likes me."
CHILD: Nobody don't like me.
    (dialogue repeated eight times)
MOTHER: Now, listen carefully, say *"Nobody likes me."*
CHILD: Oh, nobody don't likes me.

(2) CHILD: Want other one spoon, Daddy.
FATHER: You mean, you want *"the other spoon."*
CHILD: Yes, I want other one spoon, please, Daddy.
FATHER: Can you say "the other spoon"?
CHILD: Other . . . one . . . spoon.
FATHER: Say . . . "other."
CHILD: Other.
FATHER: Spoon.
CHILD: Spoon.
FATHER: Other . . . spoon.
CHILD: Other . . . spoon. Now give me other one spoon?

Such conversations between parents and children do not take place very often. Mothers and fathers are usually too busy to correct their children's speech. Besides, they are delighted that their young children are talking at all and consider every utterance to be a gem. The "mistakes" children make are "cute" and repeated endlessly to anyone who will listen.

CHILDREN FORM RULES AND CONSTRUCT A GRAMMAR

The "reinforcement" theory fails along with the "imitation" theory. Neither of these views accounts for the fact that children are constructing their own rules. Different rules govern the construction of sentences as the grammar is learned. Consider, for example, the increasing complexity of one child's negative sentences. At first the child simply added a *no* (or some negative morpheme) at the beginning or at the end of a sentence:

no heavy
no singing song
no want stand head
no Fraser drink all tea
no the sun shining.

He didn't hear such sentences. This is a simple way to *transform* a declarative into a negative. At some point he began to insert a *no* or *can't* or *don't* inside the sentence.

He no bite you
I no taste them
That no fish school
I can't catch you.

The child progressed from simple rules to more complex rules, as is shown below:

Declarative: I want some food.

Negative (i):   No want some food.   (*no* added to beginning of sentence)

Negative (ii):   I $\begin{Bmatrix} \text{no} \\ \text{don't} \end{Bmatrix}$ want some food.   (negative element inserted; no other change)

Negative (iii):   I don't want no food.   (negative element inserted; negation "spread"; that is, *some* becomes *no*)

Negative (iv):   I don't want any food.   (negative element correctly inserted, *some* changed to *any*)

All children do not show the same development as the child described above, but they all show similarly regular changes. One child studied by Carol Lord first differentiated affirmative from negative sentences by pitch; her negative sentences were all produced with a much higher pitch. When she began to use a negative morpheme, the pitch remained high but then the intonation became normal as the negative syntactic markers "took over."

The same increasing complexity is found in the learning of question constructions. Our examples are taken from the study of one child. Other children may show some differences, but all show the same regular kind of development. At first, the child forms a question by using a "question intonation" (a rise of pitch at the end of the sentence):

Fraser water?
I ride train?
Sit chair?

At the next stage the child merely "tacks on" a question word in front of the sentence; he doesn't change the word order or insert *do*.

What he wants?
What he can ride in?
Where I should put it?

Where Ann pencil?
Why you smiling?

Such sentences are perfectly regular. They are not "mistakes" in the child's language; they reflect his grammar at a certain stage of development.

The child seems to form the simplest and most general rule he can from the language input he receives, and is so "pleased" with his "theory" that he uses the rule wherever he can. The most obvious example of this "over-generalization" is shown when children treat irregular verbs and nouns as if they were regular. We have probably all heard children say *bringed, goed, doed, singed,* or *foots, mouses, sheeps, childs.*

These mistakes tell us more about how children learn language than the "correct" forms they use. The child couldn't be imitating; children use such forms in families where the parents would never utter such "bad English." In fact, children may say *brought* instead of *bringed,* or *broke* instead of *breaked,* before they begin to use these incorrect forms. At the earlier stage they never use any regular past-tense forms like *kissed, walked,* or *helped.* Thus, they probably don't know that *brought* is a "past" at all. When they begin to say *played* and *hugged* and *helped* as well as *play, hug,* and *help,* they have "figured out" how to form a past tense—**they have constructed the rule.** At that point they form **all** past tenses by this rule—they overgeneralize—and they no longer say *brought* but *bring* and *bringed.* Notice that the "correct forms" were already learned (reinforced?), but the acquisition of the rule is more important than any previous or "practice" reinforcement. At some time later, children will learn that there are "exceptions" to the rule. Only then will they once more say *brought.* Children seem to look for general patterns, for systematic occurrences.

Such overgeneralizations have also been observed in children's acquisition of the semantic system. They may learn a word such as *papa* or *daddy,* which they first use only for their own father. This word may then be extended to apply to all men. As they acquire new words, the "overgeneralized" meaning becomes narrowed down until once more it has a single referent. The linguist Eve Clark has found this to be true of many other words and semantic features. She has observed that children make overgeneralizations which are based on shape, size, sound, taste, and texture. One child's word for "moon" /mo: i/ became the name for cakes, round marks on windows, writing on a window, round shapes in books, tooling on leather book covers, round postmarks, and the letter *O.* Similarly, the word for "watch," *tick tock,* was used for all objects shaped like a watch: clocks, gas meters, a fire hose wound on a spool, a bath scale. The word for *fly* /flai/ was used for other small-sized objects like specks of dirt, dust, all small insects, his own toes, crumbs; and /dani/ was first used for the sound of a bell, and then for a clock, a telephone, a door bell. As more words are added, and semantic features become more specified, the meaning of these words becomes narrowed. But again the child's ability to find general systematic patterns is observed.

The child's ability to generalize patterns and construct rules is also shown in phonological development. In early language children may not distinguish between voiced and voiceless consonants, for example. But when they first begin to contrast one set—that is, when they learn that /p/ and /b/ are distinct phonemes—they also begin to distinguish between /t/ and /d/, /s/ and /z/, and so on.

The child's phonological and morphological rules emerge quite early. In 1958, Berko-Gleason[6] conducted a study that has now become a classic in our understanding of child language acquisition. She worked with preschool children and with children in the first, second, and third grades. She showed each child a drawing of a nonsense animal like the funny creature below, and gave the "animal" a nonsense name. She would then say to the child, pointing to the picture, "This is a wug."

Then she would show the child a picture of two of the animals and she would say, "Now here is another one. There are two of them. There are two ———?" The child's "task" was to give the plural form, "wugs" [wʌgz]. Another little make-believe animal was called a "bik," and when the child was shown two biks, he or she again was to say the plural form [bɪks]. Berko-Gleason found that the children did apply the regular plural formation rule to words never heard before. Since the children had never seen a "wug" or a "bik" and had not heard these "words," their ability to add a [z] when the animal's name ended with a voiced sound and an [s] if there was a final voiceless consonant showed that the children were using rules and not simply imitating words they had previously heard.

Such regular stages and patterns support the notion that language acquisition is grammar construction. The Russian linguist Kornei Chukovsky writes: "It seems to me that, beginning with the age of two, every child becomes for a short period of time a linguistic genius. Later, beginning with the age of five or six, this talent begins to fade."[7]

Children have to construct all the phonological, syntactic, and semantic rules of the grammar. This is a difficult task indeed, especially since all they ever hear are the "surface structures" of sentences. The learning of negative and question rules shows they are forming transformational rules, and at some stage children, like adults, will know that *It is too hot to eat* has at least three meanings.

The Acquisition of Sign Language

People talking without speaking,
People hearing without listening. . . .
Paul Simon, "The Sounds of Silence"[8]

Obviously, deaf children who are unable to hear the sounds of spoken language do not acquire spoken languages as normal hear-

---

[6] Berko, J. "The child's learning of English morphology." *Word, 14,* 150–177, 1958.

[7] Kornei Chukovsky. 1968. *From Two to Five,* trans. and ed. by M. Morton (University of California Press. Berkeley.).

[8] Paul Simon, "The Sounds of Silence"; © 1964, 1965 by Paul Simon. Used by permission.

ing children do. However, deaf children of deaf parents who are exposed to sign language from birth parallel the stages and development of language acquisition by hearing children learning oral languages. These sign languages are human languages that do not utilize sounds to express meanings. Instead, hand and body gestures are the forms used to represent morphemes or words. Sign languages are fully developed languages, and those who know sign language are capable of creating unlimited numbers of new sentences just as speakers of spoken languages.

About one in a thousand babies is born deaf, or with a severe hearing deficiency. One major effect of such a tragedy is the difficulty the deaf have in learning a spoken language. It is extremely difficult for those unable to hear language to learn to speak naturally. Normal speech depends to a great extent on constant auditory feedback. Hence a deaf child will not learn to speak without extensive training in special schools or programs designed especially for the deaf.

Although deaf persons can be taught to speak a language intelligibly, they can never understand speech as well as a hearing person. Seventy-five percent of the words spoken cannot be read on the lips with any degree of accuracy.

If, however, human language is universal in the sense that all members of the human species have the ability to learn a language, it is not surprising that nonspoken languages developed as a substitute for spoken languages among the nonhearing part of humanity.

The major language used by the deaf in the United States is **American Sign Language** (or **AMESLAN** or **ASL**). ASL is an independent, fully developed language that historically is an outgrowth of the sign language used in France and brought to the United States by the great deaf educator Gallaudet, after whom Gallaudet College for the Deaf in Washington, D.C., is named. ASL has its own morphology, syntax, and semantics, and its formal units, corresponding to the phonological elements of spoken language, were originally called **cheremes** by the linguist William Stokoe[9] (to correspond to the term *phoneme*) and are now more often referred to as **primes.** The signs of the language that correspond to morphemes or words of spoken language can be specified by primes of three different sets including hand **configuration,** the **motion** of the hand(s) toward or away from the body, and the **place of articulation** or the locus of the sign's movement.

Figure 10-1 illustrates the hand configuration primes.

There are minimal pairs in sign languages just as there are in spoken languages. Figure 10-2[10] shows minimal contrasts involving hand configuration, place of articulation, and movement.

The sign meaning "arm" can be described as a flat hand, moving to touch the upper arm. Thus it has three prime features: flat hand, motion toward, upper arm.

Just as spoken language has sequences of sounds that are not permitted in the language, so sign languages have forbidden combinations of features. These differ from one sign language to another, just as the constraints on

[9] W. C. Stokoe, Jr., D. Casterline, and C. Croneberg. 1965. *A Dictionary of American Sign Language on Linguistic Principles.* (Gallaudet College Press. Washington, D.C.)
[10] Figures 10-1 and 10-2 are from E. S. Klima and U. Bellugi. 1979. *The Signs of Language.* (Harvard University Press. Cambridge, Mass.) Pp. 46 and 42.

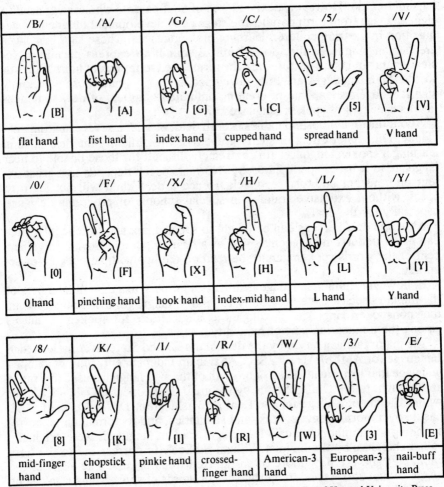

Figure 10-1 Hand configuration primes arranged in order of frequency (with descriptive phrases used to refer to them).

sounds and sound sequences differ from one spoken language to another. A permissible sign in a Chinese sign language may not be a permissible sign in ASL, and vice versa.

The linguistic study of ASL also reveals a complex system of morphology[11] and syntactic rules that parallel those found in spoken languages.

The other sign language used in the United States is called **Signed English** (or **Siglish**). Essentially, it consists in the replacement of each spoken English word (and morpheme) by a sign. The syntax and semantics of Signed English are thus approximately the same as that of ordinary English. It is thus a rather unnatural language similar to speaking English but translating

[11] T. Supalla and E. Newport. "How Many Seats in a Chair? The Derivation of Nouns and Verbs in American Sign Language." in P. Siple, ed., *Understanding Language through Sign Language Research*. Academic Press. New York. Pp. 91–132.

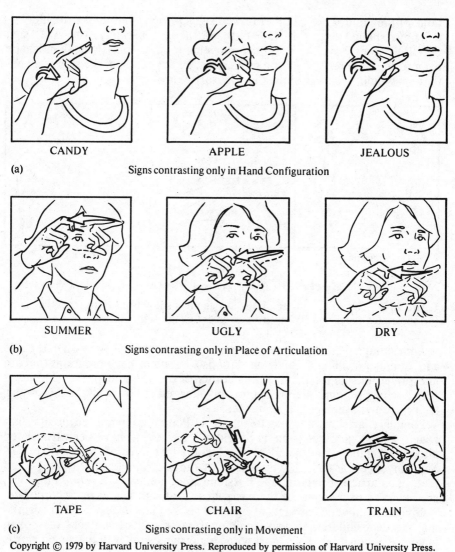

CANDY   APPLE   JEALOUS

(a)   Signs contrasting only in Hand Configuration

SUMMER   UGLY   DRY

(b)   Signs contrasting only in Place of Articulation

TAPE   CHAIR   TRAIN

(c)   Signs contrasting only in Movement

Figure 10-2   Minimal contrasts illustrating major formational parameters.

every English word or morpheme into its French counterpart. Of course, there is not always a parallel morpheme, and that would create problems just as it does in signing English. If there is no sign in ASL, signers utilize another mechanism, the system of **finger spelling.** This is also used to add new proper nouns or technical vocabulary. Sign interpreters of spoken English often finger spell such words. A manual alphabet consisting of various finger configurations, hand positions, and movements gives visible symbols for the alphabet and ampersand. Signs, however, are produced differently than are finger-spelled words. As pointed out by Klima and Bellugi[12] "The sign DECIDE cannot be analyzed as a sequence of distinct, separable configura-

---

[12] Klima and Bellugi, p. 38.

tions of the hand. Like all other lexical signs in ASL, but unlike the individual fingerspelled letters in D-E-C-I-D-E taken separately, the ASL sign DECIDE does have an essential movement . . . [but] [t]he handshape occurs simultaneously with the movement. In appearance, the sign is a continuous whole." This is shown in Figure 10-3.[13]

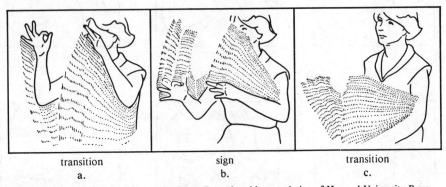

transition   sign   transition
a.   b.   c.

Figure 10-3   The ASL sign DECIDE. (a.) and (c.) show transitions from the sign; (b.) illustrates the single downward movement of the sign.

An accomplished signer can "speak" at a normal rate, even when there is a lot of finger spelling. Television stations sometimes have programs that are interpreted in sign for the deaf in a corner of the TV screen. If you've ever seen such a program, you were probably amazed at how well the interpreter kept pace with the spoken sentences.

Language arts are not lost to the deaf. Poetry is composed in sign language, and stage plays such as Sheridan's *The Critic* have been translated into sign language and acted by the National Theatre of the Deaf (NTD). Sign language was so highly thought of by the anthropologist Margaret Mead that, in an article discussing the possibilities of a universal *second* language, she suggests using some of the basic ideas that sign languages incorporate.

Given the universal aspects of sign and spoken languages, it is not surprising that deaf children of deaf signing parents parallel the stages of spoken language acquisition. They start with single signs similar to the single words in the holophrastic stage and then begin to combine signs. There is also a telegraphic stage in which the signed sentences omit the "grammatical" signs. Function signs appear at around the same age for deaf children as function words in spoken languages.

Bellugi and Klima[14] point out that deaf children's acquisition of the negative morphemes in American Sign Language (ASL) shows very much the same pattern as in spoken language described above. *No* and *neg* (a headshake) are frequently used signs in adult ASL, with different restrictions on their use. The children acquiring ASL used them interchangeably in initial position of a signed sentence, like hearing children starting negative sentences with *"no"* but unlike the ways in which negative signs are used in

---

[13] *Ibid.* p. 62.
[14] U. Bellugi and E. S. Klima. 1972. "The roots of language in the sign talk of the deaf." *Psychology Today* 6:60, 60–64, 1976.

adult ASL. We see that the acquisition of ASL cannot be simple imitation any more than spoken language is acquired simply by imitation.

Hearing children of deaf parents acquire both sign language and spoken language when exposed to both, although studies have shown that the child's first signs emerge a few months before the first spoken words. It is interesting that deaf children appear to begin producing signs earlier than hearing children produce spoken words. Hoffmeister and Wilbur[15] suggest that this may be because control of hand muscles develops earlier than the control of oral and laryngeal muscles.

Deaf children of hearing parents who are not exposed to manual sign language from birth suffer from a great handicap in acquiring language. Yet language learning ability seems so strong in humans that even they begin to develop their own manual gestures to express their thoughts and desires. A study of six such children[16] revealed that they not only developed individual signs but joined pairs and formed sentences (up to 13 "words") with definite syntactic order and systematic constraints.

This, of course, should not be surprising; sign languages are as "grammatical" and systematic as are spoken languages. We saw in Chapter 1 that the signs are conventional or arbitrary and not imitative. We see that sign languages resemble spoken languages in all major aspects, showing that there truly are universals of language despite differences in the modality in which the language is performed.

The Biological Foundations of Language Acquisition

The ability of children at such a young age to form complex rules, to construct the grammars of spoken and sign languages, and to do so in such a relatively short time is indeed phenomenal. The fact that the stages through which a child learns a language are so similar across children and languages of different nations reveals interesting aspects of the acquisition process. Children seem to be equipped with special abilities to know just what generalizations to look for, to know what they can ignore, and to discover all the regularities in the language. Children seem to learn language the way they learn to walk. We do not enter the world being able to stand and walk but all normal children begin to do so at around the same age. No one teaches us to walk. Obviously "learning to walk" or "learning language" is different than "learning to read" or "learning to ride a bicycle." Many people never learn to read because they are not taught to do so. As we have noted, there are large groups of people in many parts of the world that do not have any written language. But they all have language. As George Henry Lewes wrote in 1879:[17] "Just as birds have wings, man has language."

---

[15] R. Hoffmeister and R. Wilbur, 1980. "Developmental Acquisition of Sign Language." In *Recent Perspectives on American Sign Language*. H. Lane and F. Grosjean, eds. Lawrence Erlbaum Associates. Hillsdale, N.J. Pp. 61–78.

[16] H. Feldman, S. Goldin-Meadow, and L. Gleitman. 1978. "Beyond Herodotus: The Creation of Language by Linguistically Deprived Deaf Children." In A. Lock, ed. *Action, Symbol, and Gesture: The Emergence of Language*. Academic Press. New York. Pp. 351–413.

[17] G. H. Lewes. 1879. *The Study of Psychology*. Riverside Press, Cambridge, Mass. P. 143.

Chomsky explains the ability to acquire language in the following way:

It seems plain that language acquisition is based on the child's discovery of what from a formal point of view is a deep and abstract theory—a generative grammar of his language. . . . A consideration of the character of the grammar that is acquired, the degenerate quality and narrowly limited extent of the available data, the striking uniformity of the resulting grammars, and their independence of intelligence, motivation, and emotional state, over wide ranges of variation, leave little hope that much of the structure of the language can be learned by an organism initially uninformed as to its general character . . . it may well be that the general features of language structure reflect, not so much the course of one's experience, but rather the general character of one's capacity to acquire knowledge. . . .[18]

It is this human capacity to acquire language that has led to "the innateness hypothesis" of child language acquisition. We are far from understanding the nature of our genetic "pre-wiring," or the specific details of the language-learning device with which the human animal appears to be born. The human brain does seem specially equipped for language acquisition, however. Chapter 12 will consider some aspects of the organization of the brain that appear to underlie our language abilities.

Learning a Second (or Third or . . .) Language

He that understands grammar in one language, understands it in another as far as the essential properties of Grammar are concerned. The fact that he can't speak, nor comprehend, another language is due to the diversity of words and their various forms, but these are the accidental properties of grammar.
Roger Bacon (1214–1294)

Anyone who has attempted to learn a second language in high school or college or when visiting a foreign country knows that the process is rather different from learning our first, native language. Even those among us who are "talented language learners" often require some instruction, or find that at least a dictionary and "grammar" help speed up the process. Some of us are total failures. We may be extremely fluent in our native language, may get all A's in composition, may even write poetry, and may still never learn to understand or speak another language.

What is so strange is that learning a language is easier the younger you are. Yet there are few if any other complex systems of knowledge that are more easily acquired at the age of two or three than at the age of thirteen or twenty.

Young children before the age of puberty who are exposed to more than one language seem to acquire all the languages equally well. There are many bilingual and multilingual speakers who have acquired their languages early in life. Sometimes one language is the first learned, but if the child is exposed to additional languages at an early age he or she will learn those languages.

[18] Noam Chomsky. 1965. *Aspects of the Theory of Syntax.* (M.I.T. Press. Cambridge, Mass.).

DENNIS THE MENACE   **Hank Ketcham**

"Gina is by lingal . . . that means she can say the same thing twice, but you can only understand **it** once."

DENNIS THE MENACE (R) used by permission of Hank Ketcham and © by Field Enterprises, Inc.

There appears to be a "critical age" for language acquisition, or at least for language acquisition without special teaching and without the need for special learning. We will review some neurological views of this special period in the chapter on Language and the Brain (Chapter 12). For now, we simply wish to point out that our discussion on language acquisition has been primarily concerned with first language learning, or with the ability of children to learn languages without even trying, whereas adults do not seem to have this "talent."

SUMMARY

When children learn a language, they learn the grammar of that language —the phonological, morphological, syntactic, and semantic rules—as well as the words or vocabulary. No one teaches them these rules; children just "pick them up."

Before infants begin to produce "words," they produce sounds, some of which will remain if they occur in the language being acquired, and others that will disappear. This **babbling** stage is thus a prelinguistic period.

A child does not learn the language "all at once. ' Children's first utterances are one-word "sentences" (**holophrastic** speech). After a few months, the **two-word stage** arises, in which the child puts two words together. These two-word sentences are not random combinations of words; the words have definite patterns and express grammatical and semantic relationships. Still later, in the **telegraphic** stage, longer sentences appear composed primarily of *content* words and lacking *function* or *grammatical* morphemes. The child's early grammar lacks many of the rules of the adult grammar, but eventually it mirrors the language used in the community.

A number of theories have been suggested to explain the acquisition process. Neither the **imitation theory,** which claims that children learn their language by imitating adult speech, nor the **reinforcement theory,** which hypothesizes that children are conditioned into speaking correctly by being negatively reinforced for "errors" and positively reinforced for "correct" usage, is supported by observational and experimental studies. Neither can explain how children form the *rules* that they then use to produce new sentences.

Deaf children exposed to sign language show the same stages of language acquisition as do hearing children exposed to spoken languages. Sign languages, including the major language of the deaf in America, called **American Sign Language** (or **AMESLAN** or **ASL**), are fully developed, complete languages with grammars paralleling those of spoken languages. The signs, representing the morphemes and words, are constructed from a finite set of **primes**—hand configurations, movements of the hands, places of articulations—that permit the generation of an infinite set of sentences. The grammars of sign languages include, in addition to their lexicons, rules of sign formation, morphology, semantics, and syntax.

The universality of the language-acquisition process, of the stages of development, of the relatively short period in which the child constructs such a complex grammatical system suggests that the human species is "innately" endowed with special language-acquisition abilities, that language is biologically and genetically part of the human neurological system. This may also account for the differences in learning a first language as a child and a "foreign" language as a teenager or an adult.

All normal children everywhere learn language. This ability is not dependent on race, social class, geography, or even intelligence (within a normal range). This ability is uniquely human.

EXERCISES

1. *Baby talk* is a term used to label the word-forms that many adults use when speaking to children. Examples in English are words like *choo-choo* for "train" and *bow-wow* for "dog." Baby talk seems to exist in every language and culture. At least two things seem to be universal about baby talk: The words that have baby-talk forms fall into certain semantic categories (for example, food), and the words are "phonetically simpler" than the adult forms (for example, *tummy* for "stomach"). List all the baby-talk words you can think of in your native language, then (1) separate them into semantic categories, and (2) try to state general rules for the kinds of phonological "reductions" or "simplifications" that occur.

2. In this chapter the way a child learns "negation" of sentences and "question formation" was discussed. Can these be considered examples of a process of overgeneralization in syntax acquisition? If so, for each stage indicate *what* is being overgeneralized.

3. Suppose a friend of yours has a son, Tommy, who is three years old. Your friend has been explaining to you that Tommy has a problem in his speech in that he does not form "past tenses" of verbs. That is, Tommy says "Yesterday I go to park" and "Last week I swim in pool." But your friend has a plan: He is going to spend one hour each day with Tommy, having the child imitate the past-tense forms of the verbs, and he will give Tommy a piece of candy for each correct imitation. Explain to your friend (and to us) why his plan won't work.

4. Find a two-year-old child and play with her/him for about thirty minutes. Keep a list of all words that are used inappropriately. Can you describe what the child's meanings for these words probably are?

REFERENCES

Bloom, L. M. 1972. *Language Development: Form and Function in Emerging Grammar*. M.I.T. Press. Cambridge, Mass.

Bowerman, M. 1973. *Early Syntactic Development*. M.I.T. Press. Cambridge, Mass.

Brown, R. O. 1973. *A First Language: The Early Stages*. Harvard University Press. Cambridge, Mass.

Clark, H. H., and E. V. Clark. 1977. *Psychology and Language*. Harcourt Brace Jovanovich. New York.

Gleitman, H., and L. R. Gleitman. 1981. *Psychology*. W. W. Norton. New York. Chapter 10.

Klima, E., and U. Bellugi. 1979. *The Signs of Language*. Harvard University Press. Cambridge, Mass.

Macaulay, R. 1980. *Generally Speaking: How Children Learn Language*. Newbury House. Rowley, Mass.

Menyuk, P. 1969. *Sentences Children Use*. M.I.T. Press. Cambridge, Mass.

Slobin, Dan I. 1971. *Psycholinguistics*. Scott, Foresman and Company. Glenview, Ill.

de Villiers, Peter A., and Jill G. de Villiers. 1978. *Language Acquisition*. Harvard University Press. Cambridge, Mass.

Chapter 11

Animal "Languages"

No matter how eloquently a dog may bark, he cannot tell you that his parents were poor but honest.

Bertrand Russell

The articulated signs of human language are not like the expression of emotions of children or animals. Animal noises cannot be combined to form syllables.

Aristotle

If animals could talk, what wonderful stories they would tell. The eagle could already see that the earth was round when men were still afraid of falling off its edge. The whale could have warned Columbus about a barrier between Europe and India and saved that explorer a lot of anxiety. Justice would be more properly served if animals could give testimony. There would probably be a reduction in crime and quite possibly an increase in the divorce rate. All of us would have to alter our behavior in some way or another, for our environment would be considerably changed.

The idea of talking animals is as old and as widespread among human societies as language itself. No culture lacks a legend in which some animal plays a speaking role. All over West Africa, children listen to folk tales in which a "spider-man" is the hero. "Coyote" is a favorite figure in many American Indian tales. And there is hardly an animal who does not figure in Aesop's famous fables. Many authors have exploited the idea successfully, among them Hugh Lofting, the creator of the famous Doctor Dolittle. The good doctor's forte was animal communication, and he is no doubt fiction's most prodigious language learner. Still, Doctor Dolittle and his adventures are fantasies for children, and the idea of communicating with our fellow animal tenants of this globe as we communicate with our fellow human tenants is absurd. Or is it?

Whether language is the exclusive property of the human species is an interesting question. The answer depends on what properties of human language are considered. If language is viewed only as a system of communication, then obviously many species communicate. Humans also use systems other than their language to relate to each other and to send "messages." To understand human language one needs to see what, if anything, is special

346

and unique to language. If we find that there are no such special properties, then we will have to conclude that language, as we have been discussing it, is not, as claimed, uniquely human.

Most humans who acquire language utilize speech sounds to express meanings, but such sounds are not a necessary aspect of language, as was shown in the discussion of sign languages. The use of speech sounds is therefore not a basic property of human language and it is possible that the chirping of birds, the squeaking of dolphins, the dancing of bees, and the manipulation of plastic chips by chimpanzees represent systems similar to human language. If animal communication systems are *not* similar to human languages, it will not be because they fail to have speech sounds.

Conversely, if animals vocally imitate human utterances, this does not mean they possess language. We have already seen that language is a system which relates sounds and meanings (or gestures and meanings). "Talking" birds such as parrots and mynah birds are capable of faithfully reproducing words and phrases of human language. The birds imitate what they have heard. But when a parrot says "Polly wants a cracker" she may really want a ham sandwich or a drink of water or nothing at all. A bird that has learned to say "hello" or "goodbye" is as likely to use one as the other, regardless of whether people are arriving or departing. The bird's "utterances" carry no meaning. They are speaking neither English nor their own language when they sound like us.

Talking birds do not "dissect" the sounds of their imitations into discrete units. *Polly* and *Molly* do not "rhyme" for a parrot. They are as different as *hello* and *goodbye* (or as similar). One property of all human languages is the "discreteness" of the speech or gestural units, which are ordered and reordered, combined and split apart. A parrot says what it is taught, or what it hears, and no more. If Polly learns "Polly wants a cracker" and "Polly wants a doughnut" and also learns to imitate the single words *whiskey* and *bagel*, she will not spontaneously produce, as children do, "Polly wants whiskey" or "Polly wants a bagel." If she learns *cat* and *cats* and *dog* and *dogs* and then learns *parrot*, she will be unable to "form the plural" *parrots* (as in *cats*).

A parrot does not "take speech to pieces," nor can it form an unlimited set of utterances from a finite set of units. Thus, the ability to produce sounds similar to those used in human language cannot be equated with the ability to learn a human language.

In the seventeenth century, the philosopher and mathematician René Descartes pointed out what we have been discussing here: that the ability to use language is not based on the physiological abilities to produce speech or speechlike sounds. He concluded:

> It is not the want of organs that [prevents animals from making] . . . known their thoughts . . . for it is evident that magpies and parrots are able to utter words just like ourselves, and yet they cannot speak as we do, that is, so as to give evidence that they think of what they say. On the other hand, men who, being born deaf and dumb, are in the same degree, or even more than the brutes, destitute of the organs which serve the others for talking, are in the habit of themselves inventing certain signs by which they make themselves understood.[1]

[1] René Descartes, "Discourse on Method," part v. In *The Philosophical Works of Descartes*, trans. by E. S. Haldane and G. R. T. Ross, Vol. I, p. 116.

We shall examine various animal communication systems to see whether other creatures share with humans the ability to learn and use languages creatively.

The Birds

The birds and animals are all friendly to each other, and there are no disputes about anything. They all talk, and they all talk to me, but it must be a foreign language, for I cannot make out a word they say.

Mark Twain, *Eve's Diary*

Most animals possess some kind of "signaling" communication system. Among the spiders there is a complex system for courtship. The male spider, before he approaches his lady love, goes through an elaborate series of gestures to inform her that he is indeed a spider and not a crumb or a fly to be eaten. These gestures are invariant. One never finds a "creative" spider changing or adding to the particular courtship ritual of his species.

A similar kind of "gesture" language is found among the fiddler crabs. There are forty different varieties, and each species uses its own particular "claw-waving" movement to signal to another member of its "clan." The timing, movement, and posture of the body never change from one time to another or from one crab to another within the particular variety. Whatever the signal means, it is fixed. Only one meaning can be conveyed. There is not an infinite set of fiddler crab "sentences." Nor can the signal be "broken down" into smaller elements, as is possible in any utterance of human language.

The imitative sounds of talking birds have little in common with human language, but the calls and songs of many species of birds do have a communicative function, and they resemble human languages in that there may be "dialects" within the same species, and insofar as the songs of some species are acquired in stages.

Bird **calls** consist of one or more short notes that are innately determined "messages" associated with such features of the immediate environment as danger, feeding, nesting, flocking, and so on. Bird calls have meaning, so they are actually a more advanced form of communication than bird "talk," but the meanings comprise a small finite set and are responses to certain types of stimuli in the bird's "here and now." Species of animals other than birds have similar systems of calls with a similar, fixed range of meanings. None of these displays the creativity we associate with human language.

Bird **songs** are longer, more complex patterns of notes than bird calls, which are used to "stake out" territory and to attract mates. In some species the same song is used for both purposes; other species use different songs. Despite the complexity of bird songs there is no evidence of any internal structure. Songs cannot be segmented into independently meaningful parts as words of human language can often be segmented into morphemes. Often the "complications" of a bird's song have little to do with the actual message. In a study of the territorial song of the European robin,[2] it was discovered that the rival robins paid attention only to the alternation between high-pitched and low-pitched notes, and which came first didn't matter at all. The message varies only to the extent of expressing how strongly the robin feels about his possession and to what extent he is prepared to defend it and start a family in that territory. The different alternations therefore express "intensity" and nothing more. The robin is creative in his ability to sing the same thing in many different ways, but not creative in his ability to use the same "units" of the system to express many different "utterances" all of which have different meanings.

In Chapter 8 human languages were shown to consist of various dialects. The same sentence in English uttered by an Australian and an American will sound different—that is, will have a different form. The same phenomenon has been observed among birds. For example one of the calls of the chaffinch varies depending on the geographical area that the bird inhabits. The message is the same, but the "pronunciation" or form is different. Similar variation occurs in certain songs of the chaffinch and of other species as well. Usually a young bird will exhibit a basic version of the song shortly after hatching, and then later on undergo further learning in acquiring its final, dialectal version of the song. Since birds from the same brood will acquire different dialects depending on the area in which they finally settle, we may conclude that at least part of the song is learned, though some elements of it may be innate.

To what degree human language is innate and to what degree it is learned is one of the fundamental questions of linguistics. Some species of bird *calls* appear to be generally innate. These birds do not even need to hear the call of their species to produce one. The same is true for the songs of some bird species such as the cuckoo, which will sing a fully developed song even if it never hears another cuckoo sing. For other species, for example the bullfinch, songs are apparently completely learned and this bird will learn any song it is exposed to even if it is "unbullfinchlike." Other species such as the chaffinch will sing the song of its species in a simple, degraded form, even if it has never heard it sung, but will only produce the full form of its dialect area after hearing it. The chaffinch acquires its fully developed song in several stages, just as human children appear to acquire language in several stages, as discussed in Chapter 10. If a chaffinch is isolated from other birds at any stage, its song will not develop further.

From the point of view of human language research the relationship between the innate and learned aspects of the chaffinch song is very interesting. Apparently the basic nature of the song is biologically determined, but the details are learned. Many linguists, such as Chomsky, think that the basic nature of human language is biologically determined in the human species, whereas those details of languages that make them different from each other are learned. Those properties of language that are biologically based are, of course, among the linguistic universals.

Despite certain superficial similarities to human language, bird calls and

[2] R. G. Busnel and J. C. Bremond. 1962. "Recherche du Support de l'Information dans le Signal Acoustique de Défense Territoriale du Rougegorge." *C. R. Acad. Sci. Paris* 254: 2236–2238.

songs are fundamentally different kinds of communicative systems. They are "fixed" in terms of the messages that can be conveyed, and thus lack the creative element of human language.

And the Bees

Bees are very busy souls
They have no time for birth controls
And that is why in times like these
There are so many sons of bees

Honeybees have a system of communication that permits a forager to return to the hive and tell other bees where a source of food is located. It does so by performing a dance on a wall of the hive that reveals the location and quality of the food source.

The dancing behavior may assume one of three possible patterns: *round, sickle,* and *tail-wagging.*[3] The determining factor in the choice of dance pattern is the distance of the food source from the hive. The round dance indicates locations near the hive, within twenty feet or so. The sickle dance indicates locations at an intermediate distance from the hive, approximately twenty to sixty feet. The tail-wagging dance is for distances that exceed sixty feet.

In all the dances the bee alights on a wall of the hive and literally dances on its feet through the appropriate pattern. For the round dance, the bee describes a circle. The only other semantic information imparted by the round dance, besides approximate distance, is the quality of the food source. This is indicated by the number of repetitions of the basic pattern that the bee executes and the vivacity with which it performs the dance. This feature is true of all three patterns.

To perform the sickle dance the bee traces out a sickle-shaped figure-eight on the wall. The angle made by the direction of the open end of the sickle with the vertical is the same angle as the food source is from the sun. Thus the sickle dance imparts the information: approximate distance, direction, and quality (see Figure 11-1).

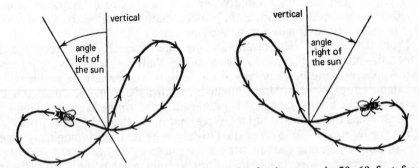

Figure 11-1 The sickle dance. In this case the food source is 20–60 feet from the hive.

---

[3] A species of Italian honeybee is described here. Details differ from species to species. We might say that different species have different "dialects" of honeybee "language."

The tail-wagging dance imparts all the information of the sickle dance with one important addition. The number of repetitions per minute of the basic pattern of the dance indicates the precise distance: the slower the repetition rate, the longer the distance (see Figure 11-2).

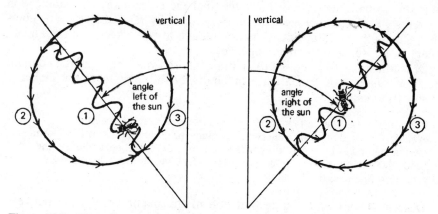

Figure 11-2 The tail-wagging dance. The number of times per minute the bee dances a complete pattern (1–2–1–3) indicates the distance from the food source.

The bees' dance is an effective system of communication, capable, in principle, of infinitely many different messages, and in this sense the bees' dance is infinitely variable, like human language. But unlike human language, the communication system of the bees is confined to a single subject or thought. It is frozen and inflexible. For example, an experimenter forced a bee to walk to the food source. When the bee returned to the hive, it indicated a distance twenty-five times farther away than the food source actually was. The bee had no way of communicating the special circumstances in its message. This absence of *creativity* makes the bees' dance qualitatively different from human language.

The bee's dance is also different from human language, and more like some bird calls and songs, in that it is completely innate, genetically determined behavior. Experiments have shown that experienced bees will communicate a more accurate message than novices, so certain refinements of the language may be learned, but a forager bee out for the first time will return to the hive and dance the appropriate dance of its species.

In previous chapters we have discussed the property of the **arbitrariness of the linguistic sign.** In all human languages the relationship between the **form** (usually the sounds) and the **meaning** of a word or phrase is arbitrary. What about the bees' dance? What are the forms of the sign, and to what meanings do they correspond? Are the relationships arbitrary or nonarbitrary? Consider the tail-wagging dance. One linguistic form is the vivacity of the dance, with a corresponding meaning "quality of food source." The relationship is clearly arbitrary, for there is nothing inherent about vivaciousness that indicates good or bad quality. In fact, we have been careful not to say whether more vivacity indicates a greater or lesser quality source of food. Because the relationship is arbitrary, there is no a priori way of telling.

The question about distance is more complicated. The slower the repetition rate, the greater the distance. On the surface this relationship may seem arbitrary, but let's use a little physics to reword the relationship: The longer it takes to complete the basic pattern, the longer it will take a bee to fly to the source. Thus we see that this sign is in some sense nonarbitrary. Similarly, the direction-determining aspect of the dance is perfectly nonarbitrary.

It should be remembered, however, that there are many communication systems which contain signs which are arbitrarily related to the meanings they stand for. "Arbitrariness" is not enough to make such a system a language in the sense of human language.

Descartes pointed out more than three hundred years ago that the communication systems of animals are qualitatively different from the language used by humans:

> It is a very remarkable fact that there are none so depraved and stupid, without even excepting idiots, that they cannot arrange different words together, forming of them a statement by which they make known their thoughts; while, on the other hand, there is no other animal, however perfect and fortunately circumstanced it may be, which can do the same.[4]

Descartes goes on to state that one of the major differences between humans and animals is that human use of language is not just a response to external, or even internal, emotional stimuli, as are the sounds and gestures of animals. He warns against confusing human use of language with "natural movements which betray passions and may be . . . manifested by animals."

All the studies of animal communication systems provide evidence for Descartes' distinction between the fixed stimulus-bound messages of animals and the linguistic creative ability possessed by the human animal.

Dolphins

I kind of like the playful porpoise
A healthy mind in a healthy corpus
He and his cousin, the playful dolphin,
Why they like swimmin like I like golphin.
Ogden Nash, "The Porpoise"[5]

Researchers are still trying to prove Descartes wrong. For a while the dolphin, the "monkey of the sea," appeared to be a good candidate for refuting the claim that language is unique to humans. The dolphin has a brain comparable in size to the human brain. Its surface, the cerebral cortex, is very wrinkled, like the surface of the human brain. However, the wrinkling is due to the thinness of the cerebral cortex; the dolphin's brain is even less complex than that of a rabbit, having fewer nerve cells.

But the dolphin does indeed use sounds to communicate. Dolphins produce clicking sounds. However, these are not produced to communicate with other dolphins. They are sonar detection sounds; that is, dolphins produce them to help locate objects which may get in their way, just as bats do.

---

[4] René Descartes, op. cit.
[5] "The Porpoise," copyright 1942 by Ogden Nash. From *Verses from 1929 On* by Ogden Nash, published by Little, Brown and Co. Reprinted by permission of Curtis Brown Ltd., London, on behalf of the Estate of Ogden Nash.

Dolphins also produce squawky sounds and whistles. The analysis of these "sound units" shows that, like other animal signals, they are closely related to emotional situations. Thus a falling-pitch whistle represents the dolphin's call of distress, and also at times the mating call of the male.

Whales, too, produce whistling or singing sounds at very low pitches and the signals they produce travel great distances under water. The "songs" are very long and display complex internal variations but no one as yet has figured out what they mean, if anything. They do not seem to produce predictable responses in other whales.

A number of experiments have been conducted with whales and dolphins to test their communicative ability. In one such experiment[6] a male and female dolphin were kept in a special tank. The female was shown either a continuous light or a flashing light. The male could see neither the lights nor the female. The task was as follows: If the continuous light was shown, the female had to press a right-hand paddle and "inform" the male by her calls to press his right-hand paddle too. If a flashing light appeared, the female had to press the left-hand paddle and again call out to the male to press his left-hand paddle. Only if both responded correctly would they be rewarded with fish. Remember that the male could not see either the light or the female. His response had to result solely from the signals he received from the female. It first appeared that the dolphins were indeed signaling each other. But later it became clear that they had learned their tasks as "conditioned responses," and had behaved more like Pavlov's dogs than communicating humans.

The great Russian physiologist Pavlov trained dogs to salivate when they heard a bell by giving them food whenever a bell rang, repeating this action over a long period of time. They became "conditioned" to salivate whenever they heard bells ringing, whether or not food followed the bells. Similarly, the female dolphin kept on pushing her paddles and producing her calls even when the male could see the lights for himself, and in fact even when the male was taken out of the tank. Her calls therefore had little to do with her desire to communicate with the male. She performed because she had been conditioned into believing the paddle-pressing and signal-giving would reward *her* with fish. She didn't really seem to care whether the male was fed or not. The male was no smarter. He had become conditioned to associate a certain paddle with a certain call, having learned that that would fill his stomach.

Such studies of animal communication systems provide evidence for Descartes' distinction between the fixed stimulus-bound messages of animals, and the creative linguistic ability possessed by the human animal.

The Chimpanzees

Children, behold the Chimpanzee:
  He sits on the ancestral tree
  From which we sprang in ages gone.
I'm glad we sprang: had we held on,
We might, for aught that I can say,
Be horrid Chimpanzees to-day.
Oliver Herford, "A Child's Primer of Natural History"

[6] See Claire Russell and W. M. S. Russell. 1971. "Language and Animal Signals." In Noel Muhnis, ed., *Linguistics at Large*. (Viking Press. New York.) Pp. 159–194.

The more nonprimate animal communication systems we examine, the more sure we become that language is uniquely human. Those systems seem to be either a nonproductive limited set of fixed messages, or emotionally conditioned cries.

Because the nonhuman primates (chimpanzees, monkeys, gorillas and so on) are closest in evolutionary terms to human beings, their systems of communication have been closely studied for similarities to human language. In their natural habitat, primates communicate with each other in systems that include visual, auditory, olfactory, and tactile signals. Many of these seem to have meaning associated with the animal's immediate environment or emotional state. They can signal "danger" to each other, and can communicate aggressiveness and subordination. Females of some species emit a specific call, indicating that they are anestrous (sexually quiescent), that inhibits attempts by males to copulate. But the natural sounds and gestures produced by all nonhuman primates show that their signals are highly stereotyped and limited in terms of the messages they convey. Most importantly, studies of such animal communication systems reveal that the basic "vocabularies" occur primarily as emotional responses to particular situations. They have no way of expressing the anger they felt yesterday or the anticipation for tomorrow.

Despite the primitive qualities of nonhuman primate *natural* systems of communication, there has been an interest in whether these animals may have a capacity for acquiring more complex linguistic systems than have developed in the wild state. If a chimpanzee was raised in a human environment and received language instruction, could it learn a human language? An early attempt to answer this question occurred in the 1930s, when Winthrop and Luella Kellogg raised their infant son together with an infant chimpanzee named Gua. Gua understood about 100 words at sixteen months, more words than their son at that age. But she never went beyond that. And as we have already seen, comprehension of language involves more than understanding the meanings of isolated words. When their son could understand the difference between *I say what I mean* and *I mean what I say*, Gua could not understand what either sentence meant.

A chimpanzee named Viki was raised by Keith and Cathy Hayes, and she too learned a number of individual words. She even learned to "articulate" with great difficulty the words *mama, papa, cup,* and *up*. But that was the extent of her language production.

Psychologists Allen and Beatrice Gardner recognized that one disadvantage suffered by the primates was their physical inability to pronounce many different sounds. Without a sufficient number of phonemic contrasts spoken human language is impossible. Many species of primates are manually dextrous, however, and this inspired the Gardeners to attempt to teach American Sign Language to a chimpanzee whom they named Washoe, after the Nevada county in which they lived and raised the chimpanzee. Washoe was brought up in much the same way as a human child might be, except that she was constantly in the presence of people who used ASL, and she was deliberately taught to sign.

By the time Washoe was four years old (June 1969) she had acquired 85 signs with such meanings as "more," "eat," "listen," "gimme," "key," "dog," "you," "me," "Washoe," and "hurry." According to the

Gardners, Washoe was also able to produce sign combinations such as "baby mine," "you drink," "hug hurry," "gimme flower," "more fruit." These results are remarkable and raised the question of whether Washoe's accomplishments are comparable to a deaf child's learning sign language. There is much debate concerning this question, which we will return to later in this chapter.

At about the same time that Washoe was growing up under the Gardners' tutelage, psychologist David Premack undertook to teach a chimpanzee named Sarah an artificial language designed to resemble human languages in some aspects.

The units of Sarah's "language" consisted of differently shaped and colored plastic symbols that were metal-backed. Sarah and her trainers "talked" to each other by arranging these symbols on a magnetic board. Sarah was taught to associate particular symbols with particular meanings. These symbols were the "words" or "morphemes" of Sarah's language. Thus, a small red square meant "banana" and a small blue rectangle meant "apricot." These and others revealed that Sarah learned words corresponding to English nouns, adjectives, and verbs. She even acquired symbols for abstract concepts like "same as" and "different from," "negation," and a symbol to represent "question."

The forms of these symbols are *arbitrarily* related to their meanings. For example, the color red is represented by a gray chip, and the color yellow by a black chip. Sarah learned the concepts "name of" and "color of." Premack was able to ask Sarah for "the color of name of blue" (that is, the color of the plastic chip that means "blue"). Sarah selected the gray plastic chip that means "red," since red is the color of the chip that means "blue." Sarah was apparently capable of using language as a metalanguage to describe her language. She also showed sensitivity to word order, which is part of syntax and semantics. For example, given the sentence

If Sarah put red on green, Mary give Sarah chocolate

Sarah would dutifully place a red card on top of a green card and collect her reward. The sentence

If Sarah put green on red, Mary give Sarah chocolate

evoked the response of placing a green card on a red one.

Sarah was capable of understanding some fairly complex sentences. She was first taught to respond correctly to sentences in the "chip" language such as

Sarah insert apple pail
Sarah insert banana dish

These are commands or "imperative" sentences instructing Sarah to "put the apple in the pail" or "put the banana in the dish." Later Sarah was given the "compound" sentence

Sarah insert apple pail Sarah insert banana dish

which she understood, and she carried out both tasks correctly. Finally she was given the sentence

Sarah insert apple pail banana dish

in which the second occurrence of the two "words" *Sarah* and *insert* is "deleted." Sarah understood this sentence to mean "put the apple in the pail and the banana in the dish," rather than "put the apple, pail, and banana in the dish"; she correctly grouped together *apple* with *pail* and *banana* with *dish* rather than incorrectly grouping *pail* with *banana,* and she did not put the apple, pail, and banana in the dish, as the word order would suggest. Based on this experiment Premack and others have suggested that when Sarah processes a sentence she does more than link words in simple linear order. She imposes subgroupings on the words, just as humans do (cf. Chapter 7).

There were drawbacks to the Sarah experiment. She was not allowed to "talk" spontaneously, but only in response to her trainers. And there was the possibility that her trainers unwittingly provided cues, which Sarah responded to rather than the plastic chips. To avoid these and other problems, in 1973 Duane Rumbaugh and his associates began to work with Lana, who was a 2½-year-old chimpanzee.

Instead of being taught to arrange plastic chips, Lana was taught to push buttons on a computer console located in her room. On each button is drawn a symbol (called a *lexigram*) that represents a meaning similar to Sarah's plastic chips. The buttons have to be pushed in just the right order to produce a grammatical sentence in "Yerkish." A computer monitors the console twenty-four hours a day and records all "conversations" between Lana and her trainers. The computer is also programmed to respond to Lana's requests for food, water, ventilation, entertainment, and so on. An example of a sentence addressed to the machine is:

please machine give Lana piece of apple

Like Sarah, Lana learned that objects have names and that the name and the object are arbitrarily related. (The symbol for apple doesn't resemble an apple. Each lexigram is a composite of one or more basic geometric shapes placed on a background that can be one of three different colors.) She also learned to regard word order as significant in producing composite meanings.

The experiment with Lana has one advantage over all previous linguistic experiments with primates. All of Lana's linguistic input and output was recorded by the computer. Such record keeping would be extremely tedious in the case of Sarah, and virtually impossible for a signing chimp such as Washoe. Still, because ASL *is* a human language, and the chip and lexigram languages are not, many researchers believe the use of ASL has advantages in the effort to explore primate intellectual and linguistic capacity and how it compares with human language and other cognitive abilities.

In the mid-seventies new experiments were begun to teach sign language to primates. One of these involved a gorilla named Koko. Koko was taught several hundred signs by her trainer at Stanford University, Francine

"Penny" Patterson. Patterson claims that Koko is able to put signs together to make "sentences" and that she is capable of making linguistic jokes and puns, composing rhymes such as *bear hair, squash wash,* and inventing metaphors such as *finger bracelet* for ring.

In a project specifically designed to test the linguistic claims that emerged from these chimpanzee experiments, another chimpanzee, named Nim Chimpsky, was taught ASL by his trainer, the psychologist H. S. Terrace, under careful experimental conditions that included thorough record keeping and many hours of video taping. Nim's teachers hoped to show beyond a reasonable doubt that chimpanzees had a humanlike linguistic capacity, in contradiction to statements by Noam Chomsky that human language is species-specific. The play on Chomsky's name was intended to be ironic.

In nearly four years of the project Nim learned about 125 signs, and during the last two years Nim's teachers recorded more than 20,000 "utterances" consisting of two or more signs. About half of these contained exactly two signs and about 1300 of these two-sign combinations were different from one another. As possible evidence that Nim had a sense of word order, his teachers observed that the sign for "more" occurred in the first position in 85 percent of those two sign combinations containing "more," such as "more banana," "more hug." In his use of transitive verbs, Nim placed the verb in first position more than 75 percent of the time.

Nim used sign language to express his emotional state when he was upset. He would often sign "angry" or "bite" and at the same time show his teeth in a clear display of aggressive behavior. But once having expressed his anger by signing, Nim often cooled down, suggesting that he could express an emotion symbolically through language rather than physically, as humans often do.

The outstanding feature of the Nim experiment was the attempt at careful record keeping, so that any claims about Nim's linguistic ability could be verified. During "Project Nim" the researchers were fairly enthused about his linguistic progress, and tentatively concluded that his two-word signs represented primitive sentences. At a later time the research team reexamined the data, which caused them to question their earlier claim, and moreover to doubt many of the claims of linguistic competence put forth for Washoe, Sarah, Lana, Koko, and other primates.

After analyzing the video tapes of Nim's conversations, the Project Nim researchers concluded that the way Nim signed with his teachers was significantly different than the way a child converses or signs with adults. Only 12 percent of Nim's utterances were spontaneous, and of the 88 percent where the teacher initiated signing, half of Nim's responses were full or partial imitations of the teacher's utterance. Children initiate conversations more and more frequently as they grow older, and their utterances repeat less and less of the adult's prior utterance. Some children hardly ever imitate in conversation. Children become increasingly more *creative* in their language use but Nim showed almost no tendency toward such creativity.

The lack of spontaneity and the excessive imitation in Nim's signing led to the conclusion that Nim's acquisition and use of language is qualitatively different from a child's.

Once it was discovered how frequently Nim was prompted by his teacher's signing, researchers began to examine films of Washoe, Koko, and others, and were led to similar conclusions. Much of what appeared to be creative signing was in fact prompted by occurrences of the same signs in the immediately preceding discourse.

Signing chimpanzees are also unlike humans in that when several of them are together they do not sign to each other as freely as humans would under similar circumstances, and the signing that does take place is generally confined to such subjects as eating and playing. There is also no evidence to date that a signing chimp will teach a nonsigning chimp to sign, or teach its offspring to sign, though it is too early to draw any conclusions on this. Left to themselves, signing chimps do not sign to each other very much, which raises doubts as to whether baby chimps would acquire sign language from their adult community, as human children do.

Sarah also took prompts from her trainers and her environment to produce plastic chip sentences. This may better reflect a chimpanzee's ability to recognize and act on subtle cues than a true linguistic ability. In responding to

Sarah insert apple pail banana dish

all Sarah had to figure out was to place certain fruits in certain containers, and she could do this by merely seeing that the apple symbol was next to the pail symbol, and the banana symbol was next to the dish symbol. There is no conclusive evidence that Sarah actually grouped strings of words into constituents. There is also no indication that Sarah would understand a *new* compound sentence of this type: again the creative ability of the chimpanzee, so much a part of human language, has not been demonstrated.

Similar problems exist in Lana's use of the lexigram language. There is no evidence that Lana's "linguistic" performance was anything other than a collection of complicated "tricks" that Lana used to receive rewards. Lana may have simply learned that under the appropriate circumstances, if she pressed certain keys on a computer console in a certain order, she would receive a reward. The fact that her trainers associated certain combinations of keys with certain semantic concepts does not necessarily mean that Lana was also doing so. Lana's behavior can be interpreted as conditioned responses, and such behavior can be taught to pigeons or rats.

There are also major differences between the way Sarah and Lana learned their languages and the way children learn theirs. In the case of the chimpanzees, each new "rule" or sentence form was introduced in a deliberate, highly constrained way. When parents speak to children they do not confine themselves to a few words in a particular order for months, rewarding the child with a chocolate bar or a banana each time the child correctly responds to a command. Nor do they wait until the child has "mastered" one rule of grammar before going on to a different structure.

Young children require no special training. Children brought up with little adult "reinforcement" or encouragement will acquire all the complexities of their language. This is demonstrated by children brought up in orphan homes or institutions. Of course, exposure to language is required. Feral children such as those raised by animals do not learn language, as pointed out in Chapter 1. Normal children, although they require exposure to language, are not taught language the way Sarah and Lana were taught.

The question of whether any nonhuman primates have a humanlike linguistic potential is still not fully answered, and many experiments are underway at the time of this writing. As often happens in science, though, the search for the answers to one kind of question leads to answers to other questions not originally asked. The linguistic experiments with primates have led to many advances in our understanding of primate cognitive ability. Premack, Sarah's original trainer, is now carrying out experiments to test chimpanzees' knowledge of causality: can a chimpanzee associate a picture of an apple cut in half with a picture of a knife? Lana's trainers are presently carrying out experiments designed to test the abilities of chimpanzees to communicate with one another by use of symbols, and some early results indicate that they can. And the experience in teaching language to primates has suggested more effective methods of enhancing the communicative abilities of severely retarded or autistic humans.

There is still doubt as to whether the ability to learn language is simply the result of greater general cognitive ability or whether it is due to a specific "language-learning" ability. The human animal appears to possess a brain capable of far greater analytic and synthetic abilities than does the chimpanzee, or any other animal. "Stupid" humans are far "smarter" than "smart" chimpanzees. And no animal language or communicative system has developed that is remotely as complex as human language, even with the intervention of human teachers. If other species have the ability equivalent to the human language-ability, one wonders why it has never been put to use. It thus seems that the kind of language learned and used by humans remains unique to the species.

Darwin expressed this view in *The Descent of Man:*

As the voice was used more and more, the vocal organs would have been strengthened and perfected through the principle of the inherited effects of use; and this would have reacted on the power of speech. But the relation between the continued use of language and the development of the brain has no doubt been far more important. The mental powers in some early progenitor of man must have been more highly developed than in any existing ape, before even the most imperfect form of speech could have come into use. . . .

SUMMARY

If language is defined merely as a system of communication, then language is not unique to humans. There are, however, certain characteristics of human language that are not found in the communication systems of any other species. A basic property of human language is its creative aspect—a speaker's ability to string together *discrete units* to form an *infinite* set of "well-formed" novel sentences. Also, children need not be taught language in any controlled way; they require only linguistic input to enable them to form their own grammar.

The fact that deaf children learn language shows that the ability to hear or produce sounds is not a necessary prerequisite for language learning. And the ability to "imitate" the sounds of human language is not a sufficient basis for the learning of language, since "talking" birds imitate sounds but can neither segment these sounds into smaller units nor understand what they are imitating.

Birds, bees, crabs, wolves, dolphins, and most other animals communicate in some way. Limited information is imparted, and emotions such as fear, and warnings, are emitted. But the communication systems are fixed and limited. They are *stimulus-bound*. This is not so of human language. Experiments to teach animals more complicated language systems have a history of failure.

Recently, however, attempts have been made to teach nonhuman primates systems of communication that purportedly resemble human language in certain aspects. Chimpanzees like Sarah and Lana have been able to manipulate symbols to gain rewards, but there is no conclusive evidence that their behavior is a reflection of underlying humanlike linguistic competence. Efforts to teach primates American Sign Language, while significant in understanding animal psychology, have also failed to provide indisputable similarities to human language. To date language still seems to be unique to the human species.

EXERCISES

1. What do the barking of dogs, the meowing of cats, and the singing of birds have in common with human language? What are some of the basic differences?

2. What is meant by the "arbitrary nature of the linguistic sign"? Describe at least one animal system of communication that includes arbitrary signs. Describe any communication system in which all the signs arc nonarbitrary. State the reasons for your choices in all cases.

3. Suppose you heard someone say: "My parrot speaks excellent English. He even says such complicated sentences as *I want jam with my cracker.*" Give reasons for or against this assertion.

4. A wolf is able to express very subtle gradations of expression by different positions of the ears, the lips, and the tail. There are eleven postures of the tail that express such emotions as self-confidence, confident threat, lack of tension, uncertain threat, depression, defensiveness, active submission, complete submission. This seems to be a complex system. Suppose there were a thousand different emotions which could be expressed in this way. Would you then say a wolf had language similar to a human? If not, why not?

5. Suppose you taught a dog to *heel, sit up, beg, roll over, play dead, stay, jump,* and *bark* on command, using the italicized words as cues. Would you be teaching it language? Why or why not?

6. What are the properties of Sarah's language that make it more like human language than like other animal languages?

7. Why have primates, principally chimpanzees, been chosen for attempts to discover whether human language is unique to the human species?

8. In what ways does the use of ASL by the signing chimpanzees resemble human language? In what ways is it different?

9. Why is a normal, human-child-like social environment important for a chimpanzee learning sign language? Or why is it not?

10. Suppose that Nim and a female chimpanzee learn sign language, and later, bear offspring. Is the question of whether they teach their offspring sign language a crucial one?

11. Chomsky has been quoted as saying:

It's about as likely that an ape will prove to have a language ability as that there is an island somewhere with a species of flightless birds waiting for human beings to teach them to fly.

In the light of evidence presented in this chapter, comment on Chomsky's remark. Do you agree or disagree, or do you think the evidence is inconclusive?

REFERENCES

Gardner, R. A., and B. T. Gardner. 1969. "Teaching Sign Language to a Chimpanzee." *Science* 165 (August).

Linden, Eugene. 1974. *Apes, Men, and Language*. Penguin. New York.

Premack, Ann J., and D. Premack. 1972. "Teaching Language to an Ape." *Scientific American* (October). Pp. 92–99.

Rumbaugh, D. M. 1977. *Acquisition of Linguistic Skills by a Chimpanzee*. Academic Press. New York.

Sebeok, T. A.; and Jean Umiker-Sebeok. 1980. *Speaking of Apes: A Critical Anthology of Two-Way Communication with Man*. Plenum Press. New York.

Terrace, Herbert S. 1979. *Nim: A Chimpanzee Who Learned Sign Language*. Knopf. New York.

Thorpe, W. H. 1967. "Animal Vocalization and Communication." In C. H. Millikan and F. L. Darley, eds. *Brain Mechanisms Underlying Speech and Language*. Grune and Stratton. New York.

Von Frisch, K. 1967. *The Dance Language and Orientation of Bees*, trans. by L. E. Chadwick. Belknap Press of Harvard University Press. Cambridge, Mass.

Chapter 12

Language and the Brain

*The nervous systems of all animals have a number of basic
functions in common, most notably the control of movement
and the analysis of sensation. What distinguishes the human
brain is the variety of more specialized activities it is capable of
learning. The preeminent example is language . . .*

Norman Geschwind[1]

Even if we completely understood the language-acquisition process and the production and perception of speech (and we are just
at the beginning of such knowledge), this would not tell us how the human
animal is able to accomplish these feats. Why are we the only species that
learns and uses language without being taught? What aspects of the human
neurological makeup explain this ability? How did these brain mechanisms
develop?

The attempts to understand the complexities of human cognitive abilities
are as old and as continuous as the attempts to understand language. One
way of investigating mental abilities and processes is by investigating language. As Fournier pointed out one hundred years ago, "Speech is the only
window through which the physiologist can observe the workings of the
cerebral life."

On the other hand, an investigation of the brain in humans and nonhuman
primates, anatomically, psychologically, and behaviorally, may help us to
answer the questions posed above. The study concerned with the biological
foundations of language and the brain mechanisms underlying its acquisition
and use is called **neurolinguistics.**

Although neurolinguistics is still in its infancy, our understanding has progressed a great deal since a day in September 1848, when a foreman of a road
construction gang named Phineas Gage became a famous figure in medical
history. He achieved his "immortality" when a four-foot-long iron rod was
blown through his head. Despite the gaping tunnel in his brain, Gage lived

---

[1] N. Geschwind. 1979. "Specializations of the Human Brain." *Scientific American*, September, 206:180–199.

for twelve more years and, except for some personality changes (he became "cranky" and "inconsiderate"), Gage seemed to be little affected by this terrible accident. This seemed miraculous. How could so much damage to the brain have so little effect? Both Gage and science benefited from this explosion. Phineas gained monetarily by becoming a one-man touring circus; he traveled all over the country charging money to those curious enough to see him and the iron rod. Science benefited because brain researchers were stimulated to learn why his intelligence seemed to be intact.

Since that time we have learned a great deal about the brain—the most complicated organ of the body. It lies under the skull and consists of approximately 10 billion nerve cells (neurons) and the billions of fibers that connect these cells. The nerve cells, or **gray matter,** form the surface of the brain, which is called the **cortex.** Under the cortex is the **white matter,** which consists primarily of the connecting fibers. The cerebral cortex is the decision-making organ of the body. It receives messages from all the sensory organs, and it initiates all voluntary actions. It is "the seat of all which is exclusively human in the mind." It is the storehouse of "memory" as well. Obviously, somewhere in this gray matter the grammar that represents our knowledge of language must reside.

The brain is divided into two parts (called **cerebral hemispheres**), one on the right and one on the left. These hemispheres are connected like Siamese twins right down the middle by the **corpus callosum,** which is a pathway leading from one side to the other, permitting the "two brains" to communicate with each other.

An interesting fact about these two hemispheres is that the left hemisphere controls the movements of the right side of the body and the right hemisphere the movements of the left side. That is, if you scratch your nose with your right hand, it is the left hemisphere which has "directed" your actions. If someone whispers into your left ear, the sound signal will go to the right hemisphere before crossing over the pathway to get to the left.

The **cerebellum,** also divided into two halves, is located underneath the cerebral hemispheres and is responsible for controlling equilibrium. At the bottom of the brain is found the **brain stem,** which connects the brain to the spinal cord.

The Two Sides of the Brain

It only takes one hemisphere to have a mind.
A. W. Wigan, 1844

Interest and research in the many functions of the human brain go back well over a century. There has been a basic assumption since the middle of the nineteenth century that it is possible to find a direct relation between language and the brain. There has been a continuous effort to discover direct centers where language capacities (competence and performance) may be **localized.**

In the early part of the nineteenth century F. Gall and G. Spurzheim put forth theories of *localization,* that is, that different human abilities and behaviors were traceable to specific parts of the brain. The bases for some of their theories are ludicrous when looked at from our present state of knowledge. Gall, for example, suggested that the frontal lobes of the brain were the locations of language because when he was young he had noticed that the most articulate and intelligent of his fellow students had protruding eyes, which he decided reflected overdeveloped brain material. This notion actually served as a stimulus to the scientists interested in brain function in the mid-nineteenth century. This period also saw the birth of "phrenology," a "theory" put forth by Spurzheim which was based on the idea that one's personality traits and intellectual abilities could be determined by an examination of the "bumps" on the skull.

Although phrenology—except for a few remaining adherents—has long been discarded as a scientific theory, Gall's view that the brain is not a uniform mass and that some linguistic capacities are functions of localized brain areas has been upheld.

It was not until April 1861 that language was specifically related to *the left side of the brain.* At a scientific meeting in Paris, Dr. Paul Broca stated unequivocally that we speak with the left hemisphere.[2] Broca had discovered that lesions or injuries of the front part of the left side of the brain (that is, the frontal or *anterior* part of the left hemisphere) resulted in poor articulation, "telegraphic" speech like that of children when they omit "function" words or grammatical morphemes, and other difficulties in speaking. Yet when they spoke, their utterances did convey the meanings they wished to communicate. Today, patients with such injuries are said to have **Broca's aphasia. Aphasia** of any kind refers to language disorders following strokes, cancer or tumors, gunshot wounds, or other brain injuries.

In 1873, Karl Wernicke presented a paper that also described language disorders resulting from brain damage. His patients, however, had lesions in the back or *posterior* portion of the left temporal lobe. These patients, unlike Broca's, spoke fluently with good intonation and pronunciation, but often with little semantic meaning. They also had great difficulty in comprehending speech, a problem that Broca's patients did not seem to have. The area of the brain that when damaged seemed to lead to these symptoms is now, not surprisingly, known as *Wernicke's area,* and the patients are said to suffer from *Wernicke's aphasia.* For similar reasons we refer to *Broca's area* and *Broca's aphasia.*

In 1870, experiments on dogs were conducted by two German doctors, who stimulated the cortex with electrodes. In the 1930s the surgeon Wilder Penfield and his collegues at the Montreal Neurological Institute stimulated different parts of the cortex of patients who required brain surgery. They found that if a particular point in the cortex is electrically stimulated the little finger will twitch, if other neurons are stimulated the foot will move, and so on.

In these ways, the human cortex was "mapped," showing the areas responsible for motor activities of different parts of the body, sensations of touch, visual perception, and so on. Figure 12-1 shows some of these areas of the brain.

Other kinds of language disorders following lesions to the left side of the brain have led to further classifications of aphasia types. Yet there continues to be a controversy among *localists*—those who believe that brain functions can be highly localized to specific parts of the brain—and *holists*—those

---

[2] In 1836, in a paper unknown to Broca, Dr. Mark Dax had made a similar claim, but little attention had been paid to it.

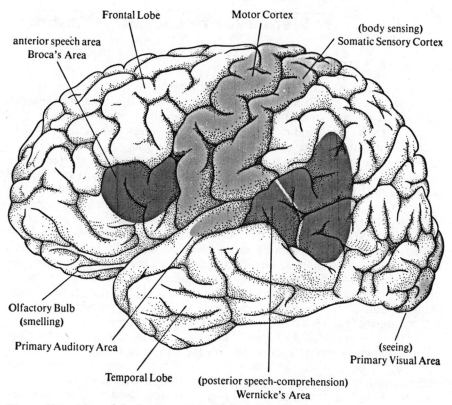

Frontal Lobe

Motor Cortex

(body sensing)
Somatic Sensory Cortex

anterior speech area
Broca's Area

Olfactory Bulb
(smelling)

Primary Auditory Area

(seeing)
Primary Visual Area

Temporal Lobe

(posterior speech-comprehension)
Wernicke's Area

Figure 12-1 Map of the human cortex of the left hemisphere.

who consider the brain to be a "more general processor," functioning as a unit. Others profess a position somewhat between these two extremes. There is, however, a consensus that there is some **lateralization** of function. Research, some of which will be discussed below, shows that though the nervous system is generally symmetrical—what exists on the left exists on the right and vice versa—the two sides of the brain form an exception. As a child develops, the two sides of the brain become specialized for different functions; *lateralization* (one-sidedness) takes place. Until recently it was believed that this brain asymmetry was found only in humans. New evidence however shows that both anatomically and functionally canaries and zebra finches display lateralization.

Aphasia studies provide good evidence that language is a left-hemisphere function.[3] In the great majority of cases, injuries to the left hemisphere result in aphasia but injuries to the right hemisphere do not (although such injuries often result in spatial perception difficulties, problems in pattern recognition, and other cognitive deficits). If both hemispheres were equally involved with language this should not be the case.

---

[3] For some people—about a third of all left-handers—there is still lateralization, but it is the right side that is specialized for language. In other words, the special functions are switched, but asymmetry still exists.

Evidence for Brain Lateralization

APHASIA STUDIES

The language impairments suffered by aphasics are not due to any impairments in general intelligence. Nor are they due to loss of motor or sensory controls of the nerves and muscles of the speech organs or hearing apparatus. Aphasics can produce sounds and hear sounds. Whatever loss they suffer has to do with the sounds of speech, or language.

Nor, as we saw with the different symptoms of Broca's and Wernicke's aphasias, is there total language loss. Rather, different aspects of language are impaired. Broca's aphasics reveal speech production breakdown and *phonological* deficits; Wernicke's aphasics reveal comprehension problems and a separation between syntax and semantics. That is, their sentences are well formed syntactically but devoid of meaning. Another aphasic type is called **anomia,** which occurs when a patient has difficulty in finding words although speech is relatively fluent and intact. This particular language problem is often associated with damage toward the center part of the left hemisphere. The errors in the naming of pictures and objects may reveal something about the grammatical categories, semantic features, and the organization of the lexicon of our mentally stored grammar.

We therefore see that the different kinds of language impairments found in aphasia patients provide information on the nature of the grammar. Those aphasic patients that produce long strings of "jargon" (sometimes called **jargon aphasia**), which sound like language but which are uninterpretable, show that the phonological and phonetic systems of language are indeed separate components of language. Some aphasics will substitute words in the same semantic class for the words they are asked to read (for example, they will read "liberty" for *democracy,* "chair" for *table*). This reveals the reality of semantic features. It is almost as if the patient in reading went to the stored written word and "looked up" its meaning and then immediately went to another word which shared these semantic features and read that word instead.

Others substitute phonologically similar words ("pool" for *tool* or "crucial" for *crucible*), which again shows that the patient goes to a related word in the mental dictionary. It is as if some access lines got crossed.

The difference between different syntactic classes of words is revealed in aphasia cases. Some patients can read nouns but not verbs, and others, when presented with a verb, will apply morphological derivational rules to read the word as a noun (for example *read* will be turned into "reading" and *decide* will be read as "decision"). The distinction between function or grammatical morphemes and lexical or content words is very evident from the errors made by some groups of aphasia patients. Some aphasics will simply delete or leave out all of the "little" function words like *the, a, was, it* in both speech and reading aloud. Two cases reported by Dr. Freda Newcombe of Oxford, England, are of particular interest. Pairs of homonyms in which one word was a function word and the other a content word were printed on cards and presented in random order to these patients. For example, the words *witch* and *which, hymn* and *him, inn* and *in*, were on the lists. One patient, when asked to define the word or use it in a sentence, would always read both words of the pair as if they were the content word; that is, when this patient was shown the word *which* he would say something like "Oh, you know, it's an old hag." The other patient would do just the opposite. What is of interest is that such differential language impairments show us a great deal about the nature of our mental grammars. The more we learn about the different aspects of language the more we can help these patients relearn or restore their language processing or representation.

Most of us have experienced some "aphasic symptoms," as did Alice when she said:

> "And now, who am I? I *will* remember, if I can. I'm determined to do it!" But being determined didn't help her much, and all she could say, after a great deal of puzzling, was "L, I *know* it begins with L."

This "tip-of-the-tongue" phenomenon is not uncommon. But if you *never* could find the word you wanted, you can imagine how serious a problem you would have.

There is much evidence from aphasia studies to support the distinction that has been made between linguistic knowledge or competence and linguistic performance. If one can speak and not comprehend or vice versa—as is the case with different groups of aphasics—it is clear that the grammar must be somewhere in the brain but only accessed in performance in either speaking or listening. This is also shown by patients who can write but not speak. One aphasia patient appeared able to speak and understand but could not answer a direct question such as "What is your wife's name?" After tremendous effort, he grabbed a piece of paper and a pencil and wrote the answer to the question but was unable to read what he had written.

The interest in aphasia goes back to long before Broca. In the New Testament, St. Luke reports that Zacharias could not speak but could write. And in 30 A.D. the Roman writer Valerius Maximus describes an Athenian who was unable to remember his "letters" (sounds) after being hit in the head with a stone.

It is, however, primarily in the last few decades that controlled scientific studies of aphasia have been conducted. They are revealing a great deal both about language and about the brain.

SPLIT BRAINS

As already pointed out, aphasia studies provide good evidence that language is primarily processed in the left hemisphere. Other evidence is provided by patients who have one of the hemispheres removed. If the right hemisphere is cut out, language remains intact, although other cognitive losses may result. Because language is such an important aspect of our daily life, surgical removal of the left hemisphere is performed only in dire cases.

"Split-brain" patients provide important evidence for language lateralization and for understanding brain functions. In recent years it was found that persons suffering from serious epilepsy could be treated by cutting the pathway connecting the two sides of the brain, with little effect on their lives. We mentioned above that the two cerebral hemispheres are connected by a body called the corpus callosum. This "freeway" between the two brain halves consists of tens of millions of nerve fibers connecting the cells of the left and

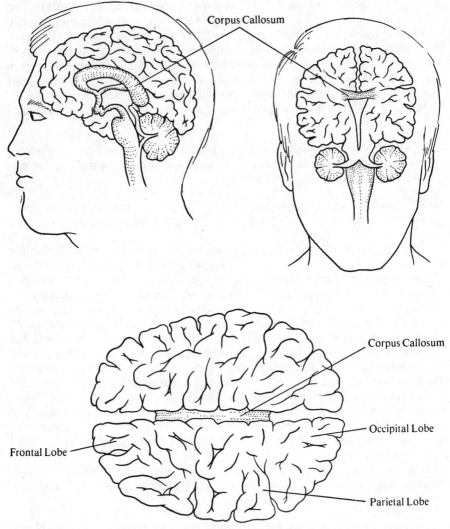

Figure 12-2 Three views of the cerebral hemispheres and the corpus callosum.

right hemispheres. The corpus callosum is shown in the two pictures in Figure 12-2. If this pathway is split there is no "communication" between the "two brains." The psychologist Michael Gazzaniga states:[4]

> With [the corpus callosum] intact, the two halves of the body have no secrets from one another. With it sectioned, the two halves become two different conscious mental spheres, each with its own experienced base and control system for behavioral operations. . . . Unbelievable as this may seem, this is the flavor of a long series of experimental studies first carried out in the cat and monkey.

When the brain is split surgically, certain information from the left side of the body is received *only* by the right side of the brain and vice versa (be-

[4] Michael Gazzaniga. 1970. *The Bisected Brain* (Appleton-Century-Crofts. New York).

cause of the "criss-cross" phenomenon discussed above). For example, suppose a monkey is trained to respond with its hands to a certain visual stimulus such as a flashing light. If the brain is split after the training period, and the stimulus is shown only to the left visual field (the right brain), the monkey will perform only with the left hand, and vice versa. Many such experiments have been done on animals. These all show the distinctness of the two sides of the brain, as well as the fact that each side of the animal's brain is capable of performing the same tasks.

Persons with split brains have been tested by psychologists. Unlike the results of experiments conducted with cats and monkeys, tests with these human subjects showed that messages sent to the two sides of the brain resulted in different responses. If an apple is put in the left hand of a split-brain human and his vision is cut off, he cannot describe the object. The right brain senses the apple, and is able to distinguish the apple from other objects, but the information cannot be relayed to the left brain for linguistic description. But if the same experiment is repeated and in addition a banana is placed in the right hand, the subject is able to describe the banana verbally, though he is still unable to describe the apple (see Figure 12-3).

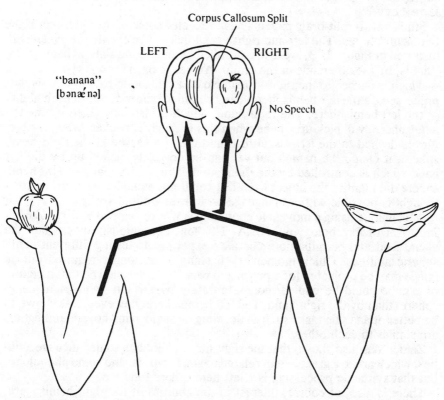

Figure 12-3 Sensory information is received in the *contralateral* (opposite) side of the brain from the side of the body in which it is sent. In a split brain patient the information in the right hemisphere cannot get across to the left hemisphere, and so the right brain cannot produce the word "apple."

Various tests of this sort have been performed, all providing information on the different capabilities of the "two brains." The right brain does much better than the left in "pattern-matching" tasks, or in recognizing faces, or in other kinds of spatial-perceptual tasks. The left hemisphere is superior for language, for rhythmic perception, for temporal-order judgments, for mathematical thinking. According to Gazzaniga, ". . . the right hemisphere as well as the left hemisphere can emote and while the left can tell you why, the right cannot."[5]

The importance of these experiments with split brains and the research they have generated is most clearly shown by the fact that in 1981 Dr. Roger W. Sperry was awarded the Nobel Prize for Physiology and Medicine for his work on the human brain, based on such studies. Dr. Sperry, Professor of Psychobiology at the California Institute of Technology, had conducted experiments with animals by severing the connections between the hemispheres. In 1961, Dr. Joseph E. Bogen, a neurosurgeon who was aware of these animal studies, proposed the split-brain surgery for a war veteran to ease the serious epileptic seizures of this man, which could not be controlled by drugs. Bogen's method proved to be highly successful and also made possible the exciting work with split-brain subjects conducted by a number of colleagues of Sperry, including Bogen, Michael Gazzaniga, Eran Zaidel, and Jerre Levy.

Studies with split-brain patients have revealed some of the functions of the two hemispheres. The left and right visual fields, like the tactile systems illustrated in Figure 12-3, are also controlled by their contralateral hemisphere (that is, by the other side of the brain). An image or picture—say, of a cube —which is flashed to the right visual field of a split-brain patient (and is thus processed by the *left* hemisphere) can be named, showing the speech ability of the left hemisphere. The right hand, which is also controlled by the left hemisphere, will pick up a cube when this is done. However, when the picture is flashed to the *left* visual field and thus processed in the *right* hemisphere, it cannot be named but yet can be correctly picked up by the *left* hand which is controlled by the *right* brain. This shows that the right hemisphere did identify the object even if it could not name it, which shows that thought is possible without language or at least without speech.

A technique using a moveable contact lens was developed by Eran Zaidel, Professor of Psychology at UCLA. This lens continuously blocks half the visual field and permits more complex experiments testing different hemispheric abilities. Quick momentary flashing is no longer required but an image may be projected for a prolonged period. Zaidel showed that a picture of a cube could be copied more accurately by the left hand (right hemisphere) than by the right hand. The left hemisphere, however, was shown to be better at analytic tasks such as deciding or analogizing how paired figures are similar to each other.

Zaidel[6] has also shown that the right hemisphere has some language abilities, which are to a great extent related to single words, and some phonology, but that syntactic processing is a left-hemisphere function.

There is also, of course, interest in the abilities of the right hemisphere,

[5] Ibid.

[6] E. Zaidel. 1975. "A Technique for Presenting Lateralized Visual Input with Prolonged Exposure." *Vision Research* 15: 283–289.

which at one time was thought to have no cognitive abilities at all. Bogen has taken a leading role in the investigation of right-hemisphere functions,[7] which appear to include the ability to recognize entire patterns ("gestalt" perception), face recognition, and spatial perception, among perceptual tasks.

MORE LATERALIZATION EVIDENCE

The evidence seems to be overwhelming; the human brain is asymmetrical. The left brain is the language or language-processing brain. We still do not know the ways in which the two hemispheres interact in linguistic performance. Nor can we tell in all aphasia cases whether parts of the grammar are totally destroyed or wiped out of memory or simply inaccessible. That is, we do not know whether competence or performance is defective.

Since aphasia studies and split-brain research all involve "nonnormal" human subjects (in one way or the other), other experimental techniques that can be used with all human subjects have been developed to explore the specialized capabilities of the two hemispheres.

One such method, called **dichotic listening,** uses auditory signals. Subjects hear two different sound signals simultaneously through earphones. For example, a subject may hear "boy" in one ear and "girl" in the other, or "crocodile" in one ear and "alligator" in the other. Or the subject may hear a horn tooting in one ear and a toilet flushing in the other. When asked to state what was heard in each ear, the responses to the right-ear (left-brain) stimuli are more correct when the stimuli are linguistic in nature (words, nonsense syllables, and so on), but the left ear (right brain) does better with certain nonverbal sounds (musical chords, environmental sounds, and so on). That is, if the subject hears "boy" in the right ear and "girl" in the left ear, she is more likely to report the sound heard in the right ear correctly. But if she hears coughing in the right ear and laughing in the left, she is more apt to report the laughing stimulus correctly.

Notice that if the left hemisphere is "processing" the incoming verbal stimuli, any sounds going to the right hemisphere have to cross over the pathway (the corpus callosum) to get to the left side of the brain.

One hypothesis as to why we make more errors for the words we hear through the left ear assumes that these signals have longer to travel (since they first go to the right side and then cross over) and are thereby weakened. The theory is that if the right hemisphere was equally capable of processing (as well as receiving) the signal from the left ear would be reported equally well as the signals from the right ear.

Figure 12-4 illustrates in a highly simplified fashion what may be going on. (The situation is actually much more complex. The signals entering the right and left ears do have a path that goes to the right and left brains, respectively, but these may be suppressed when there is another sound coming in from the crossed pathway.) In drawing A of Figure 12-4, "boy" coming in through the *right* ear goes directly to the *left* hemisphere, where it can be processed, since this is the language-processing side of the brain; "girl" coming in through the *left* ear goes directly to the *right* hemisphere and then

---

[7] J. E. Bogen. 1969. "The Other Side of the Brain: An Appositional Mind." *Bulletin of the Los Angeles Neurological Societies* 34: 135–162.

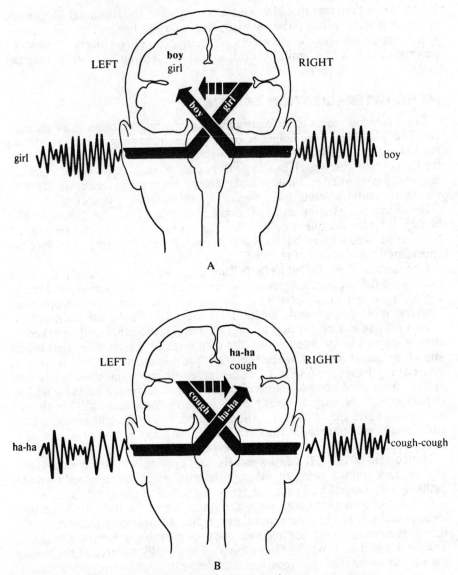

Figure 12-4 Illustration of dichotic listening experiments.

has to cross over to the left in order to be "understood." By the time it gets to the "language processor" it has been weakened, and so the subject makes more errors in reporting what is heard through this ear. In drawing B the reverse is true for nonlinguistic sounds—the laughing coming in through the *left* ear is heard more strongly.

The superior performance of the right ear for linguistic stimuli in such dichotic-listening tasks further reflects the left-hemispheric specialization for language.

These experiments were very important in that they showed that the left hemisphere is not superior for processing *all* sounds, but only for those which are linguistic in nature. That is, the left side of the brain is specialized for *language*, not sounds.

Other experimental techniques are also being used to map the brain and to investigate the independence of different aspects of language and also the extent of the independence of language from other cognitive systems.

Some researchers tape electrodes to different areas of the skull and investigate the electrical activity of the brain, comparing the signals emitted from these differentially placed electrodes. In such experiments the electrical signals emitted from the brain in response to different kinds of stimuli (called evoked potentials or event-related potentials or erps) are measured. For example, electrical differences may result when the subject hears speech sounds and nonspeech sounds. These experiments show that neuronal activity in different locations varies with different stimuli and different tasks, thus providing support for the views on lateralization presented above. The experiments are now being refined and should provide even more detailed information in the near future. In addition, blood-flow studies of the brain reveal different patterns of brain activity dependent on stimuli and mental processes.

These studies, using different techniques and different subject groups, are converging to provide the information we seek on the relationship between the brain and various language and nonlanguage cognitive systems.

The Critical Age Hypothesis

In Chapter 10 we mentioned that there appears to be a period during which language learning can proceed easily, swiftly, and without external intervention or teaching. The lateralization of the brain appears to be connected with the language-learning abilities of children. It may be that this "critical age" for first language acquisition coincides with the period when lateralization is taking place and ends when it is complete. This was the hypothesis put forth by Lenneberg,[8] but he placed the end at puberty, which appeared to be a crucial limit for ease of acquisition. Krashen,[9] however, has shown that lateralization may be complete by the age of five. Perhaps this is why so much of the grammar has already been acquired by the child at that age.

It was assumed that at birth the two sides of the brain are nonspecialized and **equipotential,** so that if damage occurs in the left hemisphere of an infant the right hemisphere can equally well acquire and use language. Even this may be too strong a view, since children with left hemispheres removed because of tumors or other problems do develop language, but their language may differ syntactically from normal language development.[10]

Language learning and lateralization may go hand in hand, but the relationship between the two is not clearly understood. We are not certain

[8] Eric H. Lenneberg. 1967. *Biological Foundations of Language* (Wiley. New York).

[9] S. Krashen. 1973. "Lateralization, Language Learning, and the Critical Period: Some New Evidence." *Language Learning* 23: 63–74.

[10] M. Dennis and H. A. Whitaker. 1976. "Language Acquisition Following Hemidecortication: Linguistic Superiority of the Left Over the Right Hemisphere." *Brain and Language* 3: 404–433.

"It's finally happening, Helen. The hemispheres of my brain are drifting apart."

Drawing by Lorenz; © 1980 The New Yorker Magazine, Inc.

whether language is a prerequisite for the development of lateralization or whether lateralization precedes language acquisition.

It is not surprising that we still have unanswered questions about such intricate and complex phenomena as the brain and language and the relationship between them. What is surprising is that we have learned so much about both. We have a long way to go and part of the path to understanding may be reached when we understand more about how human language arose in the course of evolution. Study of the human brain in comparison with the brains of other species allows us to see similarities and differences. There appears to have been both neural reorganization and a great expansion of brain size in humans, both of which may account in part for our linguistic ability. If one views language simply as one of many systems of communication, then one might be led to the "continuity" view of evolution. But when we examine the complexities of language, which is just one of the systems humans use to communicate with each other, a stronger case can be made for the "discontinuity" hypothesis. What seems to be quite clear no matter which view one holds is that the changes that occurred in the speech-producing and speech-receiving mechanisms of the species were accompanied or preceded by changes in the brain, showing that evolutionary restructuring of the brain played a significant role in the origin and development of human language.

SUMMARY

The attempt to understand what makes language acquisition and use possible has led to research on brain mechanisms and the relationship between the brain and language. The study of this relationship is called **neurolinguistics.**

The brain is the most complicated organ of the body, controlling motor and sensory activities and thought processes. Research conducted for over a century reveals that different parts of the brain control different body functions. The nerve cells that form the surface of the brain are called the **cortex,** which serves as the intellectual decision-maker, and as the organ that receives messages from the sensory organs and that initiates all voluntary actions. The brain of all higher animals is divided into two parts called the **cerebral hemispheres,** which are connected by the **corpus callosum,** a pathway that permits the left and right hemispheres to communicate with each other.

Although each hemisphere appears to be a mirror image of the other, the control of movements and sensation is accomplished **contralaterally,** or in a crossed fashion. That is, the left hemisphere controls the right hand, leg, visual field, and so on, and the right brain controls the left side of the body. Yet despite this seeming symmetry, there is much evidence that the left and right hemispheres may be specialized for different functions. Evidence from **aphasias**—language disfunctions as a result of brain injuries—surgical removal of parts of the brain, electrical stimulation studies, dichotic listening, and experiments measuring brain electrical activity, show a lack of symmetry of function of the two hemispheres. These results are further supported by studies of **split-brain** patients, who, for medical reasons, have had the corpus callosum severed. For normal right-handers and many left-handers, the left side of the brain appears to be specialized for language. This **lateralization** of functions develops from birth and, according to some neurologists, neuropsychologists, and neurolinguists, is closely related to the **critical period,** during which language acquisition occurs naturally.

Aphasia studies, and the other experiments mentioned, also show differential language impairment. Different parts of the grammar can be lost or become inaccessible. Thus, patients with **Broca's aphasia** seem to have an impaired phonological system and intact syntactic and semantic systems, whereas **Wernicke's aphasia** patients are fluent speakers but have difficulty in comprehension and produce semantically empty utterances. **Anomia** is a form of aphasia in which the patient has word-finding difficulties. These and related studies provide evidence regarding the organization of the grammar and the various components of language in the brain.

EXERCISES

1. The Nobel Prize laureate Roger Sperry[11] has argued that split-brain research shows that these patients have two minds:

   > Everything we have seen so far indicates that the surgery has left these people with two separate minds, that is, two separate spheres of consciousness. What is experienced in the right hemisphere seems to lie entirely outside the realm of experience of the left hemisphere.

   Another Nobel Prize winner in physiology, Sir John Eccles,[12] disagrees. He does not think the right hemisphere can think since he distinguishes between "mere consciousness," which animals possess as well as humans, and language, thought, and other purely human cognitive abilities. In fact, according to him, the human aspect of human nature is all in the left hemisphere.

   Write a short essay discussing these two opposing points of view, stating your own opinion on how one should define "the mind."

[11] R. W. Sperry. 1966. "Brain Bisection and Consciousness." In *Brain and Conscious Experience,* J. Eccles, ed. Springer-Verlag. New York.

[12] J. Eccles. 1965. *The Brain and Unity of Conscious Experience: The Nineteenth Arthur Stanley Eddington Memorial Lecture.* Cambridge University Press. Cambridge, England.

2. A. Some aphasic patients, when asked to read a list of words, substitute other words for those printed. In many cases there are similarities between the printed words and the substituted words that are read. The data given below are from actual aphasic patients. In each case state what the two words have in common and how they differ:

PRINTED WORD	WORD SPOKEN BY APHASIC
a. liberty	freedom
canary	parrot
abroad	overseas
large	long
short	small
tall	long
b. decide	decision
conceal	concealment
portray	portrait
bathe	bath
speak	discussion
remember	memory

B. What do the words in groups a and b reveal about how words are likely to be stored in the brain?

3. The following are some sentences spoken by aphasic patients collected and analyzed by Dr. Harry Whitaker of the University of Maryland. In each case state how the sentence deviates from normal nonaphasic language.

   a. There is under a horse a new sidesaddle.
   b. In girls we see many happy days.
   c. I'll challenge a new bike.
   d. I surprise no new glamour.
   e. Is there three chairs in this room?
   f. Mike and Peter is happy.
   g. Bill and John likes hot dogs.
   h. Proliferate is a complete time about a word that is correct.
   i. Went came in better than it did before.

4. A young patient of Drs. Freda Newcombe and John Marshall of the Division of Neuropsychology of the Radcliffe Infirmary, Oxford, England, following a head injury, appears to have lost the spelling representation of words. Below is his reading pronunciation of a number of words (the hyphens represent slight pauses between syllables):

"time"	[tɪmi]	or	[taymi]
"make"	[maki]		
"side"	[sɪdi]	or	[saydi]
"note"	[noti]		
"said"	[sa-ɪd]	or	[se-ɪd]
"alone"	[e-lon-i]		
"praise"	[pra-ays-i]		

It seems clear that his reading errors are not random, but are rule-governed. See if you can figure out the rules he uses which relate his (spelling) orthography to his pronunciation.

5. It has been shown that the left hemisphere of the brain is specialized (or lateralized) for the following: mathematical problem solving, judgments of the temporal order of events, analysis of a complex pattern into its component parts, determination of the sequencing of events, and, of course, language processing. Discuss what common factors may be said to "unite" these different tasks.

REFERENCES

Blumstein, S. 1973. *A Phonological Investigation of Aphasic Speech.* Janua Linguarum Series, 153. Mouton. The Hague.

Bogen, J. E. 1969. "The Other Side of the Brain: An Appositional Mind." *Bulletin of the Los Angeles Neurological Societies* 34: 135–162.

Caplan, D. (ed.). 1980. *Biological Studies of Mental Processes.* M.I.T. Press. Cambridge, Mass.

Gardner, H. 1978. "What We Know (and Don't Know) about the Two Halves of the Brain." *Harvard Magazine* 80: 24–27.

Gazzaniga, M. S. 1970. *The Bisected Brain.* Appleton-Century-Crofts. New York.

Lenneberg, Eric. H. 1967. *Biological Foundations of Language.* Wiley. New York.

Lesser, R. 1978. *Linguistic Investigation of Aphasia.* Elsevier. New York.

Newcombe, F., and J. C. Marshall. 1972. "Word Retrieval in Aphasia." *International Journal of Mental Health* 1: 38–45.

Penfield, W., and L. Roberts. 1959. *Speech and Brain Mechanisms.* Princeton University Press. Princeton.

Springer, S. P., and G. Deutsch. 1981. *Left Brain, Right Brain.* W. H. Freeman. San Francisco.

Index